## Praise for
## *Poverty and Power*

"*Poverty and Power* persuasively demonstrates the force of social structures in generating and perpetuating poverty. Challenging conventional arguments about the poor being poor as a result of their own choices, Royce clearly details how the exercise of power by actors in structurally advantaged positions—such as corporate lobbyists, employers, and the media—necessitates the existence of poverty. This important work should be required reading for students, scholars, and policy makers."

**—Monica McDermott, University of Illinois, Urbana-Champaign**

"In the area of economic inequality, there is no book I would adopt before *Poverty and Power*. Royce analyzes and synthesizes an astonishing amount of material. I challenge anyone to find a scholar more steeped in the literature on poverty than this author. *Poverty and Power* will broaden and deepen the knowledge base of any professor (let alone student) but without excessive disciplinary jargon. The result of Royce's painstakingly thorough research and elegant writing is a highly informative yet engaging and readable text. The first edition proved a hit with students in my senior seminar; we eagerly await this second edition!"

**—Lisa M. Tillmann, Rollins College**

"Edward Royce's *Poverty and Power* provides a comprehensive look at the reasons why poverty persists in the United States and why it is so often taken for granted by many Americans. Royce's compelling argument identifies the cause of poverty as rooted in inequalities in power and politics and shows the inadequacies of individualistic, cultural, and human capital theories of poverty."

**—Ellen Reese, University of California, Riverside**

# Poverty and Power

## The Problem of Structural Inequality

### Second Edition

Edward Royce

ROWMAN & LITTLEFIELD
Lanham • Boulder • New York • London

Published by Rowman & Littlefield
A wholly owned subsidary of
The Rowman & Littlefield Publishing Group, Inc.
4501 Forbes Boulevard, Suite 200, Lanham, Maryland 20706
www.rowman.com

Unit A, Whitacre Mews, 26-34 Stannary Street, London SE11 4AB,
United Kingdom

British Library Cataloguing in Publication Information Available

**Library of Congress Cataloging-in-Publication Data**
Royce, Edward Cary.
Poverty and power : the problem of structural inequality / Edward Royce. — Second
edition.
pages cm
Includes bibliographical references and index.
ISBN 978-1-4422-3807-7 (cloth : alk. paper) — ISBN 978-1-4422-3808-4 (pbk. : alk.
paper) — ISBN 978-1-4422-3809-1 (electronic)
1. Poverty—United States. 2. Equality—United States. I. Title.
HC110.P6R696 2015
339.4'60973—dc23
2014046656

Printed in the United States of America

*To my parents, Dick Royce and Phyllis Royce*

# Brief Contents

# Detailed Contents

# Acknowledgments

I could not have completed this book without the help I received from Doug Amy, Fran Deutsch, Eric Schutz, and Larry Van Sickle. These four friends kept me going, reading chapters as I wrote them and providing invaluable feedback and encouragement all along the way. I am extremely grateful for all the time and effort they devoted to this project. Several other people commented on parts of the manuscript, either the first edition, the second edition, or both. For their generosity, support, and criticism, I would like to thank Wendy Brandon, Dan Czitrom, Denise Cummings, Rick Eckstein, Michele Ethier, Meryl Fingrudt, Susan Libby, Shannon Mariotti, Julia Maskivker, Matt Nichter, Ellen Pader, Lisa Tillmann, Dave Walsh, and Tom Wartenberg. Several anonymous reviewers provided thoughtful and constructive recommendations for the second edition of the book. I am also very grateful to the late Alan McClare for all of his help and encouragement for the first edition, to Sarah Stanton for being so able and supportive in shepherding the second edition through the review and publication process, and to all the other fine people involved in the editorial and production work at Rowman & Littlefield.

*Chapter One*

# Poverty as a Social Problem

The most telling fact about poverty in the United States is how thoroughly it is ignored. The problem of poverty is rarely depicted on television shows or in the movies, receives only passing coverage from the news media, and is largely absent from the political agenda. The nation's leaders don't talk much about poverty either. Looking at the past fifty State of the Union addresses, Jeff Sheslo finds that "presidents of both parties have shown a rare, bipartisan resolve to avoid the subject."[1] With neither politicians nor the media defining poverty as an urgent social problem, there is little chance that the larger public will take notice or that any new government initiative will soon be launched to improve the lives of poorer Americans.

Poverty has not always been so invisible. In the early 1960s, in the wake of the civil rights movement, politicians and the press discovered the poor, and in 1964, President Lyndon Johnson declared an "unconditional war on poverty."[2] Martin Luther King Jr., along with other political and civil rights activists, kept the issue of poverty alive throughout most of the 1960s. Frustrated by the timidity and inadequate funding of Johnson's anti-poverty program, King put forward a more radical vision. He called upon the country to live up to its democratic ideals and moral principles: "The time has come for us to civilize ourselves by the total, direct and immediate abolition of poverty."[3]

More than five decades later, not only have we failed to eradicate poverty, but the very idea of such an undertaking is barely contemplated in the mainstream public discourse. At best, poverty is considered a low-priority problem or, even worse, it is perceived as an issue that does not merit the expenditure of public resources. After all, so it is imagined, the poverty of the poor is due primarily to their own personal failings and self-destructive behaviors; and, in any case, poor people in the United States, especially as compared to their counterparts in the Third World, do not really have it so bad. Many even own their own refrigerators and microwave ovens, as the right-wing Heritage Foundation likes to remind us.[4] This inclination to downplay the problem of poverty—what Michelle Goldberg calls "poverty denialism"—is not uncommon.[5] Indeed, conservative politicians and pundits are often heard complaining that the poor, thanks to a multitude of overly generous government programs, live a life of ease, so comfortable in their poverty in fact that they no longer have any incentive to "get off their couches" and go to work.[6]

In 2005, challenging this complacency, Hurricane Katrina brought into public view the harsh realities of class and racial inequality in the United States. The media's coverage of Katrina's aftermath revealed a long-standing pattern of racial segregation and concentrated poverty—by no means unique to New Orleans—and glaring disparities in neighborhood conditions, public services, and housing. It also exposed the shameful political neglect of the city's most vulnerable residents—both before and after what was a social disaster as much as a natural disaster.[7] Though initially fueling speculation that a renewed war on poverty might be on the horizon, the shocking images from New Orleans quickly faded, and the subsequent promise of "bold action" from the government went unfulfilled.[8] After a rare and fleeting appearance center stage, poverty once again slipped away behind the curtains.[9]

Two years later, toward the end of 2007, the equivalent of an economic hurricane hit the United States, and much of the rest of the world as well, thrusting the country into the deepest economic crisis since the depression of the 1930s. This Great Recession—so called because of its unusual length and severity—resulted simultaneously in the collapse of the financial sector, the collapse of the housing industry, and the collapse of the stock market. It also gave rise to a devastating "jobs disaster"—the loss of at least 8.5 million jobs, not counting those that would have been added in normal economic times; an extraordinarily high rate of unemployment, at one point climbing to over 10 percent; and a dramatic increase in long-term joblessness, with many frustrated job seekers permanently driven out of the labor force.[10] Remarkably, as Alan Blinder points out, for the seven-year period from 2005 to 2012, net job growth was *zero*.[11] Even now, more than five years into the recovery, the jobs disaster is far from over. Millions of Americans still can't find work, what job growth has occurred is mainly in the low-wage sector of the economy, the earnings of most workers continue to stagnate, the rate of poverty remains stubbornly high, and there is little prospect of any imminent turnaround.

As in the case of Hurricane Katrina, the Great Recession of 2007–2009 opened the door to a renewed public discussion of poverty and inequality. The election of Barack Obama in 2008 also raised expectations, holding out the promise of a more progressive economic agenda. In February 2009, less than a month after the inauguration, the Obama administration, despite the nearly unanimous opposition of both House and Senate Republicans, managed to get a much-needed economic stimulus package through Congress— the American Recovery and Reinvestment Act (ARRA). By increasing aggregate demand, this infusion of government spending bolstered a perilously weak labor market, at the very least containing the hemorrhaging of jobs. But even at more than $800 billion, the stimulus was nowhere near large enough to offset the jobs disaster caused by the Great Recession, much less overcome the persistent shortage of good jobs that has afflicted the American economy since the 1970s.[12]

The rise of the Tea Party in early 2009 and the increasing intransigence of congressional Republicans, fixated on the evils of government activism and deficit spending, dashed any hopes that the Obama administration might follow up with a more far-reaching program to spur job growth and reduce poverty.[13] The strength of the Tea Party—its ability to gain public attention and exert political influence—derives from the combination of ideological support from Fox News, financial support from wealthy free-market advocates, including the billionaire Koch brothers, and legislative support from the most extreme right wing of the Republican Party. With this backing, Tea Party activists have propagated a zealously anti-liberal, anti-Obama, and anti-government message. Though they have not yet been able to achieve many of their specific goals (e.g., the repeal of the Affordable Care Act), Tea Party Republicans, adamantly opposed to compromise, have managed to obstruct the enactment of even the most moderate legislative measures. They have had some success on the ideological front as well, promoting an image of a divided society, "us" versus "them"—on the one side, hardworking, taxpaying, white Americans, and on the other side a growing population of "moochers" ("takers" rather than "makers"), mostly non-white, living off the largesse of big government.[14] The policies of the Tea Party—the call for massive cuts in government spending, for example—have not won widespread popular support. The rhetoric of the Tea Party, however, has aggravated a situation where it was already difficult for the poor to be seen in a sympathetic light or gain visibility as deserving recipients of government assistance.

In September 2011, beginning with an encampment in Lower Manhattan's Zuccotti Park, another social movement appeared on the scene—the Occupy Wall Street movement. Occupy, as it came to be known, was not a poor people's movement, either in its composition or in its agenda. With its slogan—"we are the 99 percent"—it drew attention to the depredations of the rich more than the deprivations of the poor. But it did introduce a positive change in the economic policy discussion. While the Tea Party protested excessive taxation and out-of-control government spending, Occupy brought the issue of political and economic inequality into the public debate. And while the Tea Party blamed continued economic woes on a welfare state that catered to an undeserving population of freeloaders, the Occupy movement took aim at Wall Street tycoons, the corporate elite, and high-flying lobbyists.[15]

The Tea Party is still a potent force in American politics. And though Occupy, at least for the time being, has ceased operations, it did succeed in reclaiming the strategy of public protest and drawing attention to the growing economic gap between the super rich and everyone else. In a December 2013 speech, President Obama, seemingly embodying the spirit of Occupy, declared that the combination of increasing inequality and decreasing mobility was a "fundamental threat to the American Dream" and the "defining challenge of our time." But with Republicans making accusations of class warfare and Democrats worried about alienating middle-class voters, Obama quickly backed off from the unusually strong message of this speech, shifting the emphasis from the contentious issue of inequality to the more palatable issue of opportunity.[16]

In the American political context, politicians who dare treat economic inequality as a genuine social problem face considerable resistance. Poverty is fair game—but even then, only if portrayed as an individual problem, not as a failure of the American political economy. Most of what we hear about poverty in the mainstream news media, consequently, comes from centrist or conservative commentators. We are told about the work-averse culture of the poor, or their lack of personal responsibility, or the harmfulness of government dependency, or how the receipt of unemployment benefits undermines the work ethic, or the disgrace of able-bodied men and women collecting food stamps. We are told little, however, about the massive shortage of decent-paying jobs or about government policy that consistently favors the rich over the poor. Former vice-presidential candidate Paul Ryan's recent anti-poverty plan perfectly exemplifies this skewed understanding of the problem. Ryan proposes an arrangement in which case managers would work one-on-one with poor clients to help them make better life decisions; assist them in planning for the future; and, through careful monitoring and the application of rewards and penalties, set them on a path toward steady employment. Not a word, however, about the elephant in the room: how to create the millions of new jobs that would be necessary to achieve the goal of "expanding opportunity in America."[17]

Why does it take a Category 4 hurricane to draw attention to problems of poverty and inequality? Why, even with a massive recession and a persistently weak recovery, has the plight of poorer Americans not become a matter of more serious and sustained public discussion and more effective government policy? Why have we not heeded Martin Luther King's appeal to rid our society of poverty once and for all? One reason is this: for many Americans and policy makers, the real problem is not *poverty* at all; the real problem is the *poor*.[18] They have bad genes, poor work habits, and inadequate skills. Poverty is just a symptom, a regrettable by-product of individual failings. The hardships experienced by the poor stem from their own shortcomings, not from any dysfunctions of the system; thus grand schemes to alleviate poverty are inherently misguided. It might be appropriate, according to this view, for government to lend a modest helping hand, aiding the poor in overcoming their defects, but in the end, self-improvement, not social reform, is the only credible remedy.

This book argues that we need to abandon the simplistic idea that poverty results from the moral weaknesses, bad behaviors, and inferior abilities of the poor. This way of thinking about poverty misrepresents the nature of the problem, obscuring its root causes and tragic consequences, and it constitutes a powerful barrier to a workable solution. What we need instead is an alternative *structural* perspective, what Alice O'Connor calls a "new poverty knowledge."[19] We need to recognize that the problems of poverty and inequality are inextricably bound to power-laden economic and political structures. These determine the allocation of resources and opportunities, who gets what and how much. Theories attributing poverty to the failings of the poor neglect the big picture: the severity of the poverty problem ultimately depends on the availability of decent-paying jobs and the responsiveness of government to the needs of less-advantaged citizens.

## THE PROBLEM OF POVERTY

The problem of poverty in the United States is far more serious than is commonly imagined. Millions of Americans are denied equitable access to opportunities for a quality education, a good job, a healthy living environment, and a decent life. Poverty is hard on the poor. It is also inconsistent with the principles of equality and fairness to which most Americans subscribe. Can we be the kind of society we want to be while millions of Americans suffer an inadequate standard of living? Indeed, one important reason for investigating poverty is precisely to determine what kind of a society we really are. To study American poverty is simultaneously to study American society.

In the first section of this chapter, I set the stage by briefly examining several key aspects of the poverty problem in the United States.[20] My objective in this discussion is to provide readers with an overview of certain disturbing facts about poverty and inequality and to show that poverty in the United States is a social problem deserving far more serious public attention and political commitment than it currently receives. I then begin making the case for a structural perspective on poverty by comparing this approach to the more conventional individualistic perspective. I conclude this chapter by explaining how this book is organized and by describing the framework I use to communicate a structural understanding of American poverty.

### The Official Rate of Poverty in the United States Is Very High

The amount of poverty in the United States is substantial by any measure. In 2012, according to the calculations of the U.S. Census Bureau, 46.5 million Americans were poor, 15.0 percent of the population. The rate of poverty is even higher for selected subgroups: 21.8 percent for children, 27.2 percent for African Americans, 37.9 percent for black children, 25.6 percent for Hispanics, 33.8 percent for Hispanic children, and 30.9 percent for female-headed households.[21] Millions of other individuals and families live on the edge of poverty, barely scraping by, the American Dream well out of reach. Approximately 61 million people reside in households with incomes below 125 percent of the poverty line, and more than 106 million, a third of the country, have incomes below twice the poverty line, less than $48,000 a year for a family of four.[22] Many millions of Americans, these figures reveal, are doing poorly in today's economy, struggling just to eke out a living.

## The Real Rate of Poverty in the United States Is Even Higher

The Census Bureau in 2012 counted a four-person family with two children as poor if its yearly pre-tax income totaled less than $23,283.[23] Opinion polls show that the majority of Americans believe this is not nearly enough money to make ends meet. When asked what the poverty line should be for a family of four, the average response in a 2013 survey was $30,000.[24] The current poverty threshold, in the judgment of the U.S. public, is too low by several thousand dollars. To most Americans, the *real* poverty population is substantially larger than the *official* poverty population.[25]

Many experts agree.[26] As one alternative to the existing poverty measure, Elise Gould and her colleagues estimate "basic family budgets." Adjusted for family size, family type, and geographical location, these budgets are designed to "measure the income families need in order to attain a secure yet modest living standard."[27] In all areas of the country, the size of the poverty population according to this family budget measure is more than twice the official count. The United States has a serious poverty problem even according to the official measure, but in the assessment of the American public and many policy specialists as well, the level of real poverty and economic insecurity in the United States is much greater than the official numbers indicate.

## Poverty in the United States Is Worse than in Other Developed Countries

The rate of poverty in the United States is very high, and it looks even higher, extraordinarily so, in fact, when contrasted with the rate of poverty in other industrialized countries. The United States may be falling behind on some counts, but when it comes to producing poor people, we outperform our chief competitors by a wide margin. In a study of eight developed nations from circa 2000, using a "relative poverty line" set at 50 percent of median income, the United States comes out on top with a poverty rate of 17 percent, easily beating out our closest rivals, the United Kingdom with 12.3 percent and Canada with 11.9 percent.[28] More recent data on twenty-three developed nations from the late 2000s show that the United States still leads the pack with a relative poverty rate nearly twice the average of our peer countries.[29] The real purchasing power of poor families in the United States is also lower than in other advanced economies, and the income gap between the rich and the poor is greater.[30] The poor in the United States are worse off in absolute terms than are the poor in most other industrialized nations, and they are

worse off relative to their fellow citizens as well.[31] Based on a careful examination of the cross-national data, Alberto Alesina and Edward Glaeser conclude that, compared to the poor in European countries, the "American poor
are really poor."[32]

The rate of poverty among children in the United States is particularly
high by international standards. In 2009, the United States ranked number
one in child poverty among twenty-six developed nations, with a rate more
than twice that of other wealthy countries. Not only are there more poor
children in the United States than in our peer countries, but they are more
deeply poor as well, living further below the poverty line than elsewhere in
the industrialized world.[33] A 2013 UNICEF report reveals a similarly negative picture. Out of twenty-nine developed countries, the average rank of the
United States is twenty-sixth on five measures of child well-being—material
well-being, health and safety, education, behaviors and risks, and housing
and environment.[34] The sorry fact is this: children in the United States are
more likely to be poor than in just about any other developed country, far
more likely than in most; they are more likely to be deeply poor; and, beyond
simply lacking money, they are also more likely to suffer from a variety of
other material hardships. Poverty is a common occurrence for American
children, much more so than for children in other wealthy countries, and
child poverty in the United States is an uncommonly harsh experience as
well, with lasting social and economic consequences.

## Poverty in the United States Is a Persistent Problem

Not only is there a lot of poverty in the United States today, but the rate of
poverty has remained persistently high over the past four decades. The official poverty rate declined substantially during the 1960s, from 22.4 percent
in 1959 to a historic low of 11.1 percent in 1973. The level of poverty
remained relatively stable during the 1970s, increased during the 1980s, and
stayed at a high level throughout most of the next decade. As the employment picture improved in the late 1990s, poverty too began to decline, falling
to a near record low of 11.3 percent in 2000. Since then, however, and
significantly so since the recession of 2007–2009, the rate of poverty has
once again crept upward, rising to 15.0 percent in 2012.[35] While the size of
the poverty population fluctuates from year to year, the longer-term trend
line is sobering: even during periods of economic growth there has been no
large or lasting reduction in the rate of poverty since the 1960s.[36] And over
the past decade or so, things have only gotten worse. Since the beginning of

the new millennium, more than 15 million people have been added to the poverty population. It is remarkable to consider, moreover, that at no point since the government began collecting data on poverty have fewer than one in ten Americans been poor.

## More of Today's Poor Are Severely Poor

The poor in the 2000s are also more deeply poor than in previous decades.[37] One way to calculate the depth of poverty is to measure the "poverty gap": how far the average poor person or poor family falls below its respective poverty threshold. Between 1959 and 1973, the average poverty gap for families declined from $7,126 to $6,373. The extremity of poverty has increased significantly since the early 1970s, however, growing even during the boom years of the late 1990s. In 2000, the income of the average poor family fell $7,732 short of the poverty line, and by 2012, the poverty gap or "income deficit" of families in poverty had risen to $9,785.[38] Today's poor are more severely poor than in the past, with a longer climb to get out of poverty.

Another way to assess the severity of poverty is to calculate the percentage of the poverty population that is very poor: those persons whose income puts them below 50 percent of the poverty threshold. Poverty by this measure—what is typically called "deep poverty"—has become more extreme over time as well, rising to record highs in the wake of the Great Recession. The size of the very poor population, as a percentage of the total poverty population, increased from less than 30 percent in the mid-1970s to almost 44 percent in 2012. In that year, 20.4 million people, 6.6 percent of the total population, had incomes less than half the poverty line.[39]

A third measure of severe poverty reveals a similar pattern. H. Luke Shaefer and Kathryn Edin calculate the number of households in the U.S. between 1996 and 2011 that suffer from "extreme poverty." Households are considered extremely poor, according to Shaefer and Edin's definition, if they report two dollars or less per person per day in total cash income in a given month. The number of such households, they find, more than doubled between 1996 and 2011, increasing from 636,000 to 1.65 million, including 3.55 million children.[40] This striking growth in extreme poverty, Shaefer and Edin suggest, may be due to the 1996 reform of the welfare system which resulted in a sharp decline in the availability of cash assistance for needy families. Whatever the causes, however, daily life for households experiencing extreme poverty, as Gabriel Thompson observes, "can be a long string of emergencies."[41]

## The Relative Deprivation and Social Exclusion of the Poor

The official poverty measure in the United States, devised in the early 1960s, is based on an "absolute" standard. The poverty line is set at a fixed level of income, just enough to meet basic subsistence needs, and it is adjusted only for family size, number of children, and the rate of inflation. It is not revised to take into account changes in patterns of consumption or in customary notions about what people need to live a minimally decent life. The definition of poverty stays constant over time; the criterion for counting someone as poor is the same today as it was in the 1960s.[42]

Though the poverty threshold remains unchanged, the standard of living for average Americans has improved modestly over the past several decades, while at the same time the poor have become more deeply poor. The gap between the income of those officially regarded as poor and the income of households at the median has thus widened, and so has the distance between how they live their lives and the opportunities available to them. The poor in the 2000s, compared to the poor in the early 1960s, can less afford the life of the typical American where, for example, cable television, cell phones, computers, and Internet access are the norm. Even less can they afford those commodities whose prices have risen faster than the rate of inflation, including middle-class essentials like child care, health care, and college tuition.[43] The poor today, either as consumers or citizens, are less financially able than in the past to participate as equal and full-fledged members of society. The bar has been raised for entry into the social and economic mainstream, leaving poorer Americans more vulnerable to "social exclusion."[44] The deprivation endured by poor families is greater nowadays because they are worse off relative to middle-class American households than the poor of earlier decades and because they are much worse off relative to the rich.

## More of Today's Poor Are Stuck in Poverty

Poverty has become more of a trap in recent decades, both for adults and for their children. It is more difficult today for a poor family to get out of poverty and stay out of poverty. And children born into poverty are more likely in the current era to inherit their parents' economic status. Along with slower economic growth, the United States since the 1970s has experienced both rising inequality and, at least for those in the bottom quintile, declining social mobility. This combination, signifying the emergence of a more polarized and rigid class structure, threatens the principle of equality of opportunity and the ideal of the American Dream.

Many people who experience a year or two of poverty never entirely escape it; they tend to fall back into poverty periodically throughout the course of their lives.[45] Since the 1980s, poverty has become even more of an enduring condition. Low-income families today are more likely to remain low-income families and are less likely to escape poverty permanently.[46] As Annette Bernhardt and her colleagues show, this is due especially to the proliferation of low-wage jobs and the conversion of low-wage work into a lifetime career. They compare two cohorts of male workers, the first tracked from 1966 to 1981 and the second from 1979 to 1994. Over these two periods, they find, "wage growth has both stagnated and grown more un-equal," "there has been a marked deterioration in upward mobility," the percentage of workers who are stuck in low-wage jobs has more than dou-bled, and workers at the bottom of the wage distribution are especially liable to fall into the "bad-job trap."[47] Economic mobility is harder to attain in today's economy. A job is not enough, hard work does not necessarily pay, and few individuals are able to pull themselves up by their own bootstraps.[48] In the current era, as Lawrence Mishel and his collaborators reveal, "opportu-nities for families to move up are not as plentiful as the American dream would suggest."[49]

There is also much less intergenerational social mobility than implied by the American Dream ideology, and some studies show declining mobility since 1980.[50] Contrary to the Horatio Alger tale, it is quite rare for a poor child to become a rich adult or for a rich child to become a poor adult. The economic status of the family into which a child is born exerts a powerful influence on later life outcomes, especially at the extreme ends of the class structure. In one revealing study, Tom Hertz finds that a child born into the bottom income decile has a 31.5 percent chance of remaining in that decile as an adult and a meager 1.3 percent chance of reaching the top decile. A child born into the top decile has a 29.6 percent chance of staying in that decile and only a 1.5 percent chance of falling into the poorest decile.[51] The rich and the poor have at least one thing in common: they both tend to pass along their economic standing to their children. And this is true in the United States more so than in neighboring Canada.[52] It is also true in the United States more than just about anywhere else in the developed world.[53] We do indeed stand out from other countries: not because we have *more* opportunity and mobility, but because we have *less*.[54]

The United States is unique especially in the tendency for poverty to be passed along from generation to generation. But as a recent study shows, there is considerable geographical variation in the likelihood of children rising out of poverty. They more commonly experience upward mobility if they reside in communities where there is: (1) less residential segregation, (2) less income inequality, (3) higher-quality schools, (4) stronger social networks, and (5) greater family stability.[55] In general, however, because these favorable conditions are relatively scarce, a child born into a poor family in the United States is more likely than in most other industrialized nations to end up poor as an adult.[56] The persistence of poverty across generations is particularly strong for African Americans. Hertz's research shows more than 40 percent of black children born into the bottom income decile between 1942 and 1972 were still stuck in that decile as adults, and more than 60 percent of those born into the bottom income quartile remained in that quartile as adults.[57] The image of the United States as an exception among modern societies, a unique land of opportunity where, regardless of race or ethnicity, the children of the poor can rise to the top is far from true.

## The Shredding of the Safety Net

In 1996, Congress overhauled the welfare system, creating the new Temporary Assistance for Needy Families (TANF) program. Since then, and despite the massive joblessness resulting from the Great Recession and the steady increase in the rate and severity of poverty, the proportion of poor families receiving cash welfare benefits has dropped substantially, from 68 percent in 1996 to 27 percent in 2011.[58] Though applauded by the Republican leadership as a victory over dependency, the reform of the welfare system, as Peter Edelman observes, has "blown a huge hole in our national safety net," leaving thousands of families in desperate circumstances.[59] Although they may still benefit from a variety of social programs, including tax credits for low-wage workers, many of the poor have fallen through the cracks. The reformed welfare system provides cash assistance to a shrinking number of families, even as the size of the needy population continues to expand. Government policy, thanks primarily to the efforts of Republicans in Congress and Republican-dominated state legislatures, has made life harder for low-income households in other respects as well: the refusal to extend unemployment insurance payments despite the growth of long-term joblessness, the opposition to an increase in the minimum wage, reductions in food stamp benefits, and the continued unwillingness in twenty-plus states to permit the expansion of Medicaid benefits to the near poor. In the 1960s we had a war on poverty; in the 2000s we have a war on the poor.[60] Poverty is an especially serious problem in the United States today because the poor have less recourse than in the past to government assistance and a reliable safety net.

## Poverty Touches the Lives of Most Americans

In any particular year since the 1970s, somewhere between approximately 11 and 15 percent of the population has been poor. This is a lot of poverty, especially for a country with such great wealth. But on the brighter side, these numbers might leave the impression that only a relatively small minority of Americans are economically vulnerable. The reality is quite the opposite, however, as the research of Mark Rank and his collaborators demonstrates.[61] Calculating the likelihood that people during their adult years will undergo a period of economic hardship, they discover that poverty is a widespread phenomenon. In fact, the majority of Americans, and the majority of white Americans as well, experience at least a year of poverty during their adult lives, and about a third experience four years or more.[62] The likelihood that an adult will spend at least a year in poverty, moreover, is much greater today than it was in the 1960s and 1970s—one indicator of deteriorating economic prospects for working Americans.[63] Poverty, as Rank and his associates reveal, has "become a more common life course event over the past four decades."[64] Of course, poverty hits racial minorities harder and more frequently. Relatively few African Americans manage to stay above the poverty line over the entire course of their lives: over 90 percent endure at least one year of adult poverty. But even for non-Hispanic whites, poverty is an ordinary occurrence. Poverty in the United States is not a paradox or an anomaly, and it is not something that happens only to inner-city minorities, teenage mothers, or other "marginalized groups." American poverty, Rank emphasizes, is "endemic to our economic structure"; it is "as American as apple pie."[65]

## Living without an Economic Cushion

In the 1990s, a number of studies, including Michael Sherraden's *Assets and the Poor*, Melvin Oliver and Thomas Shapiro's *Black Wealth/White Wealth*, and Dalton Conley's *Being Black, Living in the Red*, drew attention to a critical limitation of most indicators of economic well-being: they consider income only, to the neglect of wealth.[66] Income consists of a periodic stream or flow of revenue, including wage earnings, private pension benefits, and government transfers—welfare, unemployment, and Social Security payments, for example. Wealth consists of an accumulated stock or reserve of resources, including savings, home equity, business assets, stocks, bonds, and real estate.

The distribution of wealth is far more unequal than the distribution of income, and like income inequality, wealth inequality is significantly greater in the United States than in most other developed countries.[67] In 2010, the richest 1 percent of American households received 17.2 percent of the nation's total income but owned 35.4 percent of the nation's total wealth. The bottom 90 percent, on the other hand, received 55.5 percent of total income but possessed only 23.3 percent of total wealth. In 2010, 22.5 percent of households had zero or negative net worth, and 35.1 percent had a total net worth of less than $10,000. As these figures reveal, more than one-third of American households have so little wealth that they are "extremely vulnerable to financial distress and insecurity."[68]

Families possessing a sizable asset cushion have something to fall back on during hard times. They also have access to capital and credit that can be invested in housing, education, retirement, and a secure economic future for themselves and their children. Assets help families to both avoid downward mobility and achieve upward mobility. Households are usually considered "asset poor" if their wealth holdings are insufficient to cover the cost of basic needs for a period of three months.[69] Such households do not have a reserve of funds they can use to pay the bills and put food on the table should they experience a job loss or some other interruption in their flow of income. To get through costly emergencies and even to cover ordinary day-to-day expenses, they are often forced to borrow money or max out their credit cards, and are then left weighed down by exorbitant interest payments.

The level of asset poverty in the United States is substantially greater than the level of income poverty. In 2013, the rate of asset poverty reached 26.0 percent based on a measure of net worth and 43.9 percent based on a measure of liquid assets, meaning savings that can be drawn upon to cover expenses. This latter measure shows that nearly half of American households do not have enough cash or near-cash resources to survive above the poverty line for three months without a paycheck. Families who are "liquid asset poor" are financially insecure. They have no personal safety net to help them get through a difficult period. [70] For African American and Hispanic households, the rate of asset poverty is much higher, over 40 percent measured by net worth and over 60 percent measured by liquid wealth. [71] The problem of asset poverty has worsened over time as well, with younger cohorts experiencing greater vulnerability to financial insecurity. [72]

Millions of American families do not make enough money to enjoy a minimally decent standard of living. An even greater number are asset poor, a problem that has worsened over the past two decades. Between 1983 and 2010, the bottom 60 percent of households in the United States saw a *decline* in their net worth. [73] More families today live on the edge, from paycheck to paycheck, often deep in debt, and "persistently vulnerable to adversities." [74] Even if their income puts them above the poverty line, they have little or nothing in reserve to smooth out the ups and downs that have become commonplace for working families in today's economy. And they do not have a nest egg they can draw upon to build a better future for themselves and their children.

## Economic Growth Is Not the Cure for Today's Poverty

The level of economic inequality remained stable for the first quarter century after World War II, but it has increased dramatically since the 1970s. Nowadays the rich are taking a much bigger slice of the economic pie, at the expense of everyone else, especially those toward the bottom of the income distribution. [75] The real earnings of low-end workers declined throughout the 1980s and into the 1990s, increasing only with the tightening of the labor market during the final years of that decade. In 2013, the hourly wages of workers in the bottom two deciles were lower than they were in 1979. In today's economy, with slumping wage growth for the majority of workers, the benefits of increasing productivity and wealth creation, rather than trickling down to the poor, gush up to the rich instead. [76] The economy expands, corporate profits grow, the rich get richer, and the poor get poorer.

The past three decades teach a clear lesson: a growing economy by itself is no solution to the problem of poverty. In a context of high and rising inequality, an expanding economy will do little to improve the well-being of the poor. A war on poverty cannot be won simply by unleashing the forces of the free market or by a policy promising to stimulate job creation through tax cuts for the rich. In the absence of more far-reaching political measures, millions of Americans will continue to be poor. A policy of laissez-faire is doomed to failure. Poverty is not going to disappear naturally with the passage of time. An effective anti-poverty program will have to address the problem directly, through a strategy combining economic growth with better jobs, a living wage, a stronger safety net, and a more equitable distribution of the national income. This will require a fundamental change in political policy. Poverty demands serious attention because it is a problem that will not be resolved simply by staying the economic course.[77]

## The Conditions That Cause Poverty Harm Nearly Everyone

Median household income has grown over the past four decades, from approximately $48,500 in 1973 to $51,000 in 2012, down from a high of $56,100 in 1999. This modest increase from 1973 to the present is explained almost entirely by the rise in the labor force participation of women, as men's earnings have stagnated since the early 1970s.[78] Households around the median are holding their own, maybe gaining a little ground, but only because family members are working more hours, and even then the distance between them and the rich continues to grow. Middle-income Americans are trapped on a treadmill, running harder and harder just to stay in place. The cost of what Fred Block calls the big "four H's"—housing, high-quality child care, higher education, and health insurance—has increased dramatically since the early 1970s, far outstripping the growth of earnings and the overall rate of inflation. As a result, millions of families, and not just those officially counted as poor, are finding it difficult to realize the American Dream.[79]

The middle class in the United States is not as well off as it used to be, and in recent years it has lost its status as the most affluent middle class in the world.[80] Many middle-income families occupy the same leaky boat as the poor, buffeted by the same economic and political forces responsible for the persistence of poverty. The adversities experienced by the poor, though less extreme in their effects, are shared by millions of Americans above the poverty line: job instability, stagnant or volatile earnings, rising personal debt, burdensome mortgage payments, stressful family lives, inadequate health coverage, retirement insecurity, expensive child care, and soaring tuition costs.[81] The interests of the middle class and the poor do not perfectly correspond, of course, especially given divisions of race and residence, and the existence of poverty may even provide benefits for the non-poor—cheap labor and low prices, for example.[82] Still, middle-class Americans ignore the poor at their peril, for the conditions that give rise to poverty cause hardships that touch the lives of nearly everyone other than the privileged few at the top. The problem of poverty is not just an issue for the poor; it is a problem of American society.

## Persistent Poverty Undermines Social Justice

The presence of a large poverty population, especially in such a wealthy country, and the massive and still growing gap between the rich and the poor, inhabitants of two vastly different worlds, run contrary to any sensible vision of social justice. Consider some of the signs of the times. Approximately 46.5 million Americans languish in poverty, nearly half of them severely poor and millions more nearly poor. These people live hard lives, and many suffer genuine deprivation. In 2012, 17.6 million households, approximately 49.0 million people, had insufficient money to ensure a dependable supply of food throughout the year for all family members. Of these households, 7 million had "very low food security," meaning they experienced disruptions in their eating patterns and reduced food intake.[83] One consequence is that an increasing number of children, many for the first time, have come to rely on subsidized school lunches, 21 million in 2011, up from the pre-recession level of 18 million.[84] Low-income households experience other hardships as well: substandard housing, crowded living conditions, and trouble paying utility bills.[85] They lack adequate access to reliable transportation, quality education, affordable child care, and regular medical attention. And their jobs, if they are lucky enough to find regular employment, not only fail to pay a living wage and offer reasonable benefits but are also often alienating and exploitive, demeaning, and unhealthy. For low-income racial and ethnic minorities, matters are even worse. Several million impoverished African Americans and Latinos live in segregated, high-poverty neighborhoods and send their kids to segregated, high-poverty schools, all but guaranteeing that the disadvantages of one generation are passed along to the next.

The story is quite different on the other side of the economic ledger. Between 1970 and 2010, the income share of the top 10 percent increased from less than 30 percent to almost 50 percent, and the income share of the top 1 percent more than doubled during this period, increasing from approximately 8 to 17 percent.[86] In 2012, with most Americans still reeling from the aftereffects of the recession, the compensation received by executives heading companies in the S&P 500 was 354 times that of rank-and-file employees, and for the first time ever the top ten highest-paid CEOs each received paychecks of more than $100 million.[87] In the following year, 2013, the twenty-five highest-earning hedge fund managers raked in a total of $21.15

billion in compensation, with David Tepper, the top earner, receiving $3.5 billion (up from a measly $2.2 billion in 2012).[88] And while the ranks of the poor have become poorer and more numerous, the numbers of millionaires (9.63 million) and billionaires (492) in the United States have reached record highs.[89] Though working Americans are struggling, the rich are getting richer, and the super rich are getting conspicuously richer than the "merely rich." According to Steven Rattner, the top 1 percent of taxpayers in 2010 received 93 percent of the additional income created that year, with the top 0.01 percent (just fifteen thousand households) getting fully 37 percent of that additional income.[90] It is difficult to imagine how any conception of economic justice can accommodate the astounding inequalities revealed by these numbers.

A society with such inequality, with so much wealth and power at the one extreme and so much poverty and hardship at the other, is neither healthy nor just. Not surprisingly, according to a social justice index developed by the Bertelsmann Foundation, the United States ranks near the bottom of the industrialized world. This index, intended to compare countries in the extent to which they provide opportunities for self-determination and self-realization, consists of six dimensions: poverty prevention, access to education, labor market inclusion, social cohesion and non-discrimination, health, and intergenerational justice. The United States does not make it into the top ten, or even the top fifteen, on any of these six dimensions, and its overall social justice rank is a pitiful twenty-seventh out of thirty-one countries.[91]

The widening economic divide in the United States is an affront to commonsense notions of fairness, erodes feelings of social solidarity, undermines the principle of equality of opportunity, reinforces huge and dangerous disparities in power, and subverts the democratic ideal of political equality. Widespread poverty amid great wealth: what does this say about the kind of society we are and aspire to be? Poverty is a serious problem in the United States, not just because it raises troubling economic questions, but because it raises troubling moral questions as well.

## THE INDIVIDUALISTIC PERSPECTIVE AND
## THE STRUCTURAL PERSPECTIVE

To acknowledge that American poverty is a serious problem would be a significant step forward. But a contentious issue remains: what are the causes of poverty? It is useful to address this question by examining two opposing perspectives: the individualistic and the structural.[92] The conflict between these captures a familiar ideological divide in the United States, one that goes to the heart of many current controversies. Is poverty caused by "lack of effort" on the part of the poor or by "circumstances beyond their control"?[93] Are people poor because of their own weaknesses or because of the weaknesses of the American political economy? Do poor people bear the burden of responsibility for overcoming their hardships, or should the government do more to alleviate problems of poverty and inequality? Is poverty best combated by reforming the poor or by reforming society?

The distinction between the individualistic perspective and the structural perspective is evident in the public consciousness and the political policy arena, as well as in social science scholarship. Bradley Schiller, for example, compares the "flawed character" theory, which attributes poverty to the defects of the poor, and the "restricted opportunities" theory, which underlines poor people's lack of access to good schools and good jobs.[94] Mark Rank rejects the "old paradigm" ascribing poverty to the deficiencies of the poor in favor of a "new paradigm" emphasizing lack of opportunities and an inadequate safety net.[95] Within the discipline of economics, the dispute between the mainstream, "neoclassical" approach and the "political economy" approach also parallels the conflict between the individualistic perspective and the structural perspective.[96] For mainstream economists, poverty is a function of supply and demand, and people are poor because they lack marketable skills. For proponents of the political economy view, poverty is a function of power, and people are poor because of inequities in government policy and labor market institutions.

The opposition between the individualistic perspective and the structural perspective is a recognizable feature of the public discourse on poverty. But for this distinction to be truly useful—whether the purpose is conducting research, raising public awareness, entering into political debate, or teaching and learning in the classroom—it needs to be formulated more explicitly and brought more fully into play in the analysis of poverty. My approach in this introductory chapter, and in the rest of the book as well, is to sharpen the contrast and underscore the differences between these two perspectives. This strategy is intended to draw close attention to the divergence in the underlying assumptions, arguments, and implications of these opposing views. And, as I hope to show, the added benefit of placing these two ways of thinking about poverty alongside one another and explicitly reiterating their differences is that it brings to the surface the inherent deficiencies of the individualistic perspective and the comparative strengths of the structural perspective.

These two perspectives propose radically dissimilar theories of poverty. For the individualistic perspective, poverty results from individual weaknesses, failings, and inadequacies. People are poor for some combination of the following reasons: they are deficient in intelligence, competence, and ability; they are insufficiently experienced, skilled, and educated; they lack ambition, determination, and perseverance; they have poor attitudes, motivations, and values; they make bad choices and engage in self-destructive behaviors; and they are unable or unwilling to exert the necessary effort or take advantage of the opportunities available to them. Poverty is an individual problem, according to this perspective; it is a by-product of the characteristics and behaviors of the poor.

The structural perspective, on the other hand, attributes poverty to an assortment of economic, political, cultural, and social forces outside the immediate control of the individual: a shortage of jobs that pay a living wage; a corporate profit-making strategy focused on the reduction of labor costs; a governing system that caters to the concerns of the wealthy while ignoring the interests of low-income families; a political and media rhetoric that variously disparages the poor, treats them as objects of charity, and renders them invisible; and the persistence of discrimination, residential segregation, and social isolation. Poverty is a social problem, according to this perspective; it is a by-product of the distribution of power and the organization of society.

The individualistic perspective explains poverty mainly by reference to the choices and actions of the poor. They drop out of high school; they reject marriage and sexual monogamy; they have children out of wedlock; they join gangs, do drugs, and commit crimes; and they refuse to stick with a job. From the individualistic perspective, poor people are victims of their own bad decisions and lifestyle preferences. The structural perspective, on the other hand, explains poverty mainly by reference to the choices and actions of the people who occupy positions of political and economic power. They downsize the workforce, relocate factories overseas, and impose wage and benefit reductions. They legislate cutbacks in social welfare programs, enact tax cuts for the rich, craft trade agreements that profit multinational corporations at the expense of workers, and pass laws hindering the ability of employees to form labor unions. They also spend millions of dollars to disseminate the message that the "free market" is fair and efficient, government programs are doomed to failure, and poverty is the fault of the poor. From the structural perspective, poor people are victims of the decisions and behaviors of political and economic elites.

Theories of poverty imply theories of society. And these two perspectives convey sharply conflicting images of the United States, particularly concerning issues of inequality. From the individualistic perspective, American society is a meritocracy. Hard work and determination pay off. Through the magic of the market, the rewards people receive correspond to their economic contribution. From the structural perspective, the distribution of earnings, income, and wealth is not so much a reflection of differences in individual ability and effort as it is an outcome of economic and political struggles, past and present, and enduring disparities in power. The individualistic perspective and the structural perspective disagree about a variety of related issues as well: are current inequalities fair or unfair, is social mobility extensive or limited, are opportunities for getting ahead plentiful or scarce, do individuals compete on a level or tilted playing field, does discrimination continue to play a significant role in explaining race and gender inequalities, and is the American Dream a reality or a myth? The table appended to this chapter provides a summary overview of the key differences between the individualistic perspective and the structural perspective.

## ORGANIZATION OF THE BOOK

This book, through a synthesis of the literature, develops a sustained critique of individualistic theories of poverty and makes a case for an alternative structural perspective. It is intended for classroom use and written in an accessible manner. The book is organized into three parts, plus this introductory chapter and a concluding chapter. In part I, consisting of chapters 2 through 4, I critique in turn each of the three main individualistic theories of poverty: the biogenetic theory, the cultural theory, and human capital theory. These theories, often found in some combination, attribute poverty to the failings of the poor, though they each underline a somewhat different set of failings. In the biogenetic theory, the poor are deficient in cognitive ability; in the cultural theory, they are deficient in achievement motivations; and in human capital theory, they are deficient in education and skills.

My plan in each of these chapters is to highlight the key empirical claims of the theory in question, describe as clearly as possible the logic of the argument, and flesh out the underlying assumptions and implications. I then identify the most serious omissions of each theory and discuss its empirical

and conceptual weaknesses. Along the way, I begin making the case that we
need to abandon individualistic theories in favor of a structural alternative.
These three chapters constitute only an opening salvo in my critique of the
individualistic perspective, as many of the criticisms presented in these early
chapters are expanded and new ones introduced in later chapters.

In parts II and III, I use two different organizational devices, each designed to single out specific structural causes and render them immediately
intelligible and visible. First, in what I refer to as the "systems" chapters
(chapters 5 through 8), I examine separately the economic, political, cultural,
and social forces affecting the rate and severity of poverty in society. This
familiar four-systems format expressly shifts the focus from individual-level
variables to larger social forces. Second, in what I refer to as the "obstacles"
chapters (chapters 9 and 10), I devote about five pages each to ten structural
obstacles or institutional problems that contribute to the adversity of the poor
and hinder their ability to survive and overcome their poverty. This framework of four systems and ten obstacles is intended to portray poverty as both
a social condition and a lived experience. In the systems chapters, I concep-
tualize the determinants of poverty more from the top down, while in the
obstacles chapters, I take a more bottom-up approach, examining the day-to-
day problems regularly encountered by low-income households as they endeavor to make ends meet.

The four chapters in part II focus in turn on the economic, political,
cultural, and social systems. Each of these systems consists of a *structure of
power*—a hierarchical distribution of access, influence, and decision-making
authority. The unequal distribution of power within these systems enables
some individuals and groups more than others to shape the course of the
economy (the economic system); to dictate the direction of government policy (the political system); to influence the opinions, preferences, and beliefs
of the public (the cultural system); and to control avenues of social and
economic mobility (the social system). Power is always contested, however,
so each of these four systems also constitutes a *site of conflict*—an arena
within which contending groups struggle to achieve favorable outcomes and
vie for access to scarce opportunities and resources. My objective in these
chapters, in direct opposition to the individualistic perspective, is to demonstrate the significance of a wide range of system variables—economic, political, cultural, and social forces beyond the immediate control of the individual. These variables exert a decisive effect on the rate and severity of poverty,

and they help to explain why some people are more vulnerable to economic hardship than others.

I examine five structural obstacles in each of the two chapters in part III. In chapter 9, I address problems of racial discrimination, residential segregation, housing, education, and transportation. In chapter 10, I address problems of sex discrimination, child care, health care, retirement insecurity, and legal deprivation. I refer to these obstacles as *structural* because they originate from the combined workings of the economic, political, cultural, and social systems; because they are caused by social forces, arrangements, and practices outside the control of any particular individual; because they are experienced by the poor and the near poor as elements of the external social landscape, circumscribing their lives and limiting their options; and because they reflect the allocation of political and economic power and the distribution of resources and opportunities. Poverty is a *structural* problem insofar as the hardships of the poor and the persistence of their poverty can be traced back to these obstacles rather than to the failings and deficiencies of poor people themselves.

The main argument of this book is that the key to the persistence of poverty in the United States is not the intractable deviance of the poor, but the increasingly unequal distribution of power. The current problem of American poverty is the consequence of an economic, political, and cultural transformation ongoing since the 1970s, accompanied by a growing imbalance of power between business and labor, the haves and the have-nots. Employers have gained the upper hand in the labor market and workplace, putting a downward pressure on wages. Corporate interests have achieved a dominant position in the political arena, reinforcing the conservative tilt of government policy. And the ideology of the right has come to prevail in the public discourse, thanks especially to a compliant news media and the ascendancy of conservative think tanks. On the other side of the class divide, working Americans and the poor have been shunted to the margins. They are trapped at the low end of the economy, competing for dead-end jobs that pay less than a living wage. They are deprived of political influence, disenfranchised in some cases, and otherwise denied equitable access to a system where money and connections count more than ever. And their voices are largely excluded from the mainstream political debate. Only from the standpoint of a structural perspective, I argue—bringing power, politics, conflict, and inequality into the story—can we begin to understand and address effectively the problem of poverty in the United States.

# APPENDIX

## The Individualistic Perspective and the Structural Perspective

| *Individualistic Perspective* | *Structural Perspective* |
| --- | --- |
| Poverty is an individual problem, the result of the failings of the poor. | Poverty is a social problem, the result of the failings of society. |
| The source of poverty and the causes of its persistence are located in the values, attitudes, and behaviors of poor people themselves. | The source of poverty and the causes of its persistence are located in the economic, political, cultural, and social institutions of society. |
| Poverty derives from the inadequacies, weaknesses, and deficiencies of the poor. | Poverty derives from inequalities in the distribution of power, opportunities, and resources. |
| Poverty is due to the inability or unwillingness of the poor to take advantage of the opportunities available to them. | Poverty is due to the inability of the economic and political systems to provide sufficient opportunities. |
| Poor people suffer from bad life decisions. | Poor people suffer from limited options. |
| The primary obstacles to economic achievement are internal, located within individuals themselves. | The primary obstacles to economic achievement are external, located within the larger societal environment. |
| The problem of poverty is one of lazy, low-skilled, poorly educated workers. | The problem of poverty is one of lousy, low-paying, dead-end jobs. |
| Poverty is a cultural and moral problem, resulting from the weakening of family values and the decline of the work ethic. | Poverty is an economic and political problem, resulting from the economic exploitation and marginalization of the poor. |
| The poor and the middle class are similar in the opportunities available to them, but differ fundamentally in their values and aspirations. | The poor and the middle class are similar in their values and aspirations, but differ fundamentally in the opportunities available to them. |
| Equality of opportunity is the predominant reality in the United States: individuals compete on a roughly equal playing field, with everyone having a reasonable chance to achieve economic success. | Inequality of opportunity is the predominant reality in the United States: individuals compete on an unequal playing field, and many people are denied a reasonable chance to achieve economic success. |
| Prejudice and discrimination on the basis of race/ethnicity and gender no longer constitute significant barriers to economic achievement. | Prejudice and discrimination on the basis of race/ethnicity and gender continue to constitute significant barriers to economic achievement. |
| Individual choice matters more than environmental constraints in explaining people's economic outcomes. | Environmental constraints matter more than individual choice in explaining people's economic outcomes. |

| | |
|---|---|
| Poverty is an outcome of the decisions and choices made by poor people themselves. | Poverty is an outcome of the decisions and choices made by economic and political elites. |
| Market outcomes are efficient and fair, and government intervention to alleviate poverty is generally unnecessary and undesirable. | Market outcomes are inefficient and unfair, and government intervention to alleviate poverty is necessary and desirable. |
| Poverty can best be combated by reforming and resocializing the poor to provide them with the skills, attitudes, and motivations necessary to compete successfully in the labor market. | Poverty can best be combated by reforming and restructuring the labor market to create better job opportunities and boost the earnings of low-wage workers. |
| The allocation of valued resources in society is a by-product of individual striving and the distribution of ability. | The allocation of valued resources in society is a by-product of social conflict and the distribution of power. |
| The best strategy for the poor to overcome poverty is to improve their skills and exert greater individual effort. | The best strategy for the poor to overcome poverty is to participate in collective political action to achieve a more equitable distribution of social resources. |

*Part I*

# Individualistic Theories of Poverty and Inequality

*Chapter Two*

# The Biogenetic Theory of Poverty and Inequality

## OUR FATE IS IN OUR GENES

People differ. Some are high school dropouts; others have PhDs. Some have jobs pushing paper; others flip hamburgers. Some give orders; others take orders. Some are law abiding; others spend years in prison. Some have a lot of money, power, and prestige; others have little. The future is bright for some, bleak for others. When sociologists are called upon to explain such differences, they usually commence by invoking the triumvirate of gender, race, and class: the kind of life we live depends on whether we are born male or female, white or black, blueblood or redneck.

In sharp contrast to the sociological tradition, in the biogenetic theory the characteristic with the most profound influence on people's life prospects is not their social status, but their native intelligence.[1] Nature, not society, dictates our place in the world. Inequalities in educational achievement, occupational attainment, and other social outcomes are due to inherited differences in cognitive ability. People endowed with a high level of intelligence are destined to be rich, the moderately intelligent are slated for the middle class, and those born with low intelligence are doomed to poverty. Regardless of the circumstances of their birth, smart people rise to the top and dumb people fall to the bottom.

In this chapter, I focus on Richard J. Herrnstein and Charles Murray's controversial book *The Bell Curve: Intelligence and Class Structure in American Life*.[2] This is the most important and widely cited recent statement of the biogenetic theory of poverty and inequality. It received extraordinary attention in the popular media when it was published in 1994, and it has since generated a small library of reviews, commentaries, replications, and critiques.[3]

According to the authors of *The Bell Curve*, modern American society is becoming increasingly segregated into unequal social classes. The "decisive dividing force" in this new class system is not family background, but inherited "cognitive ability."[4] The distinction between the upper class and the lower class is more and more a distinction between bright people and dull people. Intelligence is also unevenly distributed by race and ethnicity, they argue, with black people being generally less intelligent than white people. This intelligence gap, they propose, not discrimination, is what explains the persistence of racial inequality.[5]

Two developments, according to Herrnstein and Murray, have transformed the system of social stratification in the United States such that cognitive ability has now become the key to economic success. First, equality of opportunity has come to prevail, diminishing the influence of race, gender, and class background on individual achievement and social mobility. People now compete for access to schools and jobs on a level playing field. Who wins and who loses in this competition is due primarily to merit, merit is primarily a matter of intelligence, and intelligence is primarily a matter of genes. Second, the technological upgrading of the economy has engendered a growing demand for workers with sophisticated cognitive skills. Today's high-tech economy places a premium on intellect. The result is increasing inequality between the high-IQ people who possess the requisite brainpower and the low-IQ people who do not. Modern "technological society" has thereby given rise to a new upper class, a "cognitive elite" occupying the top echelons by virtue of its superior intelligence.[6]

For Herrnstein and Murray, the class divide in the United States has become a cognitive divide, with rich bright people on one far end of the class spectrum and poor dull people on the other. Nowadays, IQ rather than family status, inherited wealth, or social connections is what gets people into the good schools and the good jobs. With the "democratization of higher education," admittance into elite colleges is open to anyone with the necessary intellectual qualifications. The same "cognitive partitioning" occurs within the occupational system, as workers are sorted into jobs on the basis of their IQs.[7] In the modern meritocracy, how far individuals advance within the educational and occupational arenas is dictated by their inborn mental ability.

High intelligence yields success and low intelligence yields failure. Not much can be done to alter this equation either, at least not without undermining economic efficiency and social justice. Innate cognitive ability, in sum, because it governs access to educational institutions and occupational positions, is the principal determinant of who gets ahead. "Putting it all together," Herrnstein and Murray conclude, "success and failure in the American economy, and all that goes with it, are increasingly a matter of the genes that people inherit."[8]

Just as rich people are rich because they are smart, so too poor people are poor because they are not so smart. In the biogenetic theory, poverty results from individual deficiencies in cognitive ability. People with low IQs are vulnerable to poverty because their intellectual inferiority makes them less able to learn, attain a quality education, acquire advanced skills, and perform competently in high-status jobs. The intellectually dull are also prone to bad decisions and self-destructive behaviors that lead them into poverty, keep them there, and prevent them from getting ahead. They are likely to have irregular job histories, experience bouts of unemployment, indulge in excessive drug and alcohol consumption, have unplanned pregnancies and out-of-wedlock births, drop out of high school, and participate in criminal activities and other forms of deviance. Since low cognitive ability is generally associated with "socially undesirable" behaviors, according to Herrnstein and Murray, the less intelligent are not only impeded in their economic mobility, but they also tend to create problems for everyone else.[9] People with low IQs, *The Bell Curve* alleges, are the source of most of society's troubles: a "large proportion of the people who exhibit the behaviors and problems that dominate the nation's social policy agenda have limited cognitive ability."[10]

My critique of *The Bell Curve* is divided into three sections. In the first, I discuss Herrnstein and Murray's view of intelligence; in the second I examine their analysis of the relation between IQ and life outcomes; and in the third section I focus specifically on their theory of poverty.

## GENES, IQ, AND INTELLIGENCE

The argument of *The Bell Curve* rests on a conception of human intelligence consisting of four disputable propositions: (1) Intelligence is a single, unitary phenomenon consisting of a "core human mental ability." This "general intelligence" underlies all forms of "complex mental work."[11] (2) Standardized intelligence tests provide a precise measure of general intelligence, making it possible to rank individuals on a linear scale according to their intelligence quotient. (3) Intelligence is "substantially inherited," with genes accounting for at least 40 percent and as much as 80 percent of the variation among individuals in cognitive ability.[12] (4) People at birth are either blessed or doomed with a level of intelligence that is largely unalterable. Social and educational interventions cannot appreciably raise the cognitive ability of persons born with low IQs. I will briefly discuss each of these issues in turn.

First, many critics of *The Bell Curve* argue that intelligence is a multidimensional rather than a unidimensional phenomenon. It is not one thing but many different things, and these are not all strongly correlated with one another or equally derivative of "general intelligence."[13] People may be smart in some respects, in some contexts, and at some tasks, but not in others. Some may have a facility for numbers, others for words; some may have good business sense, others artistic talent; some may have classroom smarts, others street smarts. The kind of intelligence facilitating high performance in one arena does not necessarily have the same payoff in another. Individuals cannot be classified as uniformly bright or dull, therefore, and their ranking on a single intelligence continuum cannot explain much about their social and economic outcomes. The multidimensional view implies that success and failure, to the extent these have anything to do with intelligence, are not predicated on the one single property, "general intelligence," that conventional IQ tests presume to measure. There are many kinds of cognitive abilities and many kinds of social endeavors as well, each favoring a somewhat different set of skills and talents. IQ scores, therefore, tell us little about people's overall practical competence, nor do they dictate social and economic destinies.

Second, standardized intelligence tests are direct measures of *performance* only, not ability, and how well test takers perform may be affected by anything from mood to comfort level to test-taking experience.[14] Such tests measure ability only indirectly, and even then they measure a "developed" ability, a quality formed over time and within a specific social context, not an "innate" ability.[15] As measures of intelligence, standardized tests are also limited because they assess only a specific set of test-taking competencies, skills associated with achievement on time-restricted paper-and-pencil examinations. They do less well at measuring diverse forms of practical intelligence, abilities exhibited in everyday problem solving, or the broader, more context-dependent kinds of "intellectual functioning" individuals employ in navigating classrooms and workplaces.[16] A single numerical score—an intelligence quotient—does not adequately measure the full range of people's intellectual potential or their ability to function effectively in the day-to-day worlds of school, work, and family life. [17]

Third, *The Bell Curve*, according to many critics, overestimates the genetic basis and heritability of IQ and underestimates the influence of the social environment. Herrnstein and Murray's method for calculating heritability and the implications they draw from this exaggerate the extent to which cognitive ability is an inborn and unchanging trait genetically transmitted from one generation to the next. [18] While they claim the heritability of IQ may be as much as 80 percent, other research, drawing on a wider range of studies, suggests a much lower figure, somewhere between 30 and 50 percent. [19] The reality is even more complex, however, because how much genes matter depends on the social context. For children raised in poverty, for example, where material deprivation suppresses the full realization of intellectual potential, the heritability of IQ approaches zero. [20] To many experts, indeed, genetic and environmental factors are so closely intertwined that it is impossible to parcel out to each a fixed percentage of influence. [21]

Fourth, according to Herrnstein and Murray, intelligence, because it is substantially genetic, cannot be easily raised, and efforts to do so have yielded "disappointing results." "For the foreseeable future," they state, "the problems of low cognitive ability are not going to be solved by outside interventions to make children smarter." [22] Though it is not impossible to boost IQ, they admit, it is impractical because of insufficient knowledge and limitations in "the available repertoire of social interventions." The problem is not that nothing can be done, but that an "*inexpensive*, reliable method of raising IQ is not available." [23] This is a political, not a scientific, judgment, however; and as James Heckman observes, Herrnstein and Murray fail to carry out the cost-benefit analysis required to justify their do-nothing standpoint. [24]

The deeper problem with their argument is that Herrnstein and Murray misleadingly equate heritability with immutability. They falsely assume that if there is a large genetic component to IQ, then social reforms cannot significantly raise intelligence. But as the title of one critique puts it, "the malleability of intelligence is not constrained by heritability." [25] The empirical evidence, moreover, does not support *The Bell Curve*'s pessimism about the prospects for improving cognitive ability. Herrnstein and Murray tend to overlook or dismiss studies documenting how social and educational interventions, especially in early life, can increase children's intelligence, enhance their ability to benefit from school, and aid them in the acquisition of marketable skills.[26] One review of the literature concludes that "intelligence can be increased substantially without the need for heroic [or prohibitively expensive] intervention."[27] Simply improving children's prenatal or maternal environment, for example, can produce significant gains in IQ.[28] Intensive early childhood education, the earlier the better, and schools with high-quality teachers can also improve the cognitive skills of poor children.[29] Other research shows that schooling improves people's economic outcomes regardless of IQ, and that educational policies "have the potential to decrease existing, and growing, inequalities in income."[30] Contrary to the biogenetic theory, neither people's level of cognitive ability nor their socioeconomic fate is sealed at conception.

## IS IT BETTER TO BE BORN SMART OR BORN RICH?

In part 2 of *The Bell Curve*, the core of their book, Herrnstein and Murray purport to demonstrate that inherited cognitive ability exerts a powerful influence on people's life outcomes. They make their case not by showing that IQ matters greatly, but by showing that IQ matters more than family background, as measured by parental socioeconomic status (SES). They proceed by comparing how much IQ and SES affect various "social behaviors." Included among these are poverty, unemployment, welfare usage, and crime. Are people with low IQ scores more or less likely, for example, to drop out of high school than people with low SES? Their purpose in weighing IQ and SES in this manner is to determine which is more important: nature or nurture, genes or environment. The data they report generally reveal IQ to have a larger influence than SES on social behaviors. The problems people experience in their lives, poverty and unemployment, for example, appear to be due more to lack of cognitive ability than adverse upbringing. The implication is that genes count more than the social environment in shaping economic outcomes. People fare poorly in their lives, Herrnstein and Murray insist, not because they are socially disadvantaged, but because they are intellectually inferior.[31]

Among the many problems with Herrnstein and Murray's analysis of the relative importance of IQ and SES, three stand out: they employ a questionable measure of intelligence, they treat IQ as though it were entirely the product of genes, and their index of SES fails to capture the full range of relevant social variables. *The Bell Curve*, as a result, overestimates the influence of innate cognitive ability on life outcomes, including poverty, and underestimates the influence of the social environment.

Herrnstein and Murray measure IQ using the Armed Forces Qualification Test (AFQT). This test, administered to respondents when they were between the ages of fifteen and twenty-three, after years of accumulated experiences and schooling, measures achievement more than aptitude; it measures what people have learned more than their inborn capacity for learning.[32] In their reanalysis of the data, Janet Currie and Duncan Thomas find that AFQT scores reflect the influence of socioeconomic status rather than genetics, and that such scores are less indicators of innate intelligence than of family background.[33] Perhaps it is possible to construct and administer an IQ test that actually measures native intelligence, assuming such a thing exists, but the AFQT is not such a test, and it cannot justifiably serve to estimate the influence of genes on social outcomes.

Herrnstein and Murray recognize, in principle, that intelligence is not *entirely* a product of genetic inheritance. As much as 60 percent and at least 20 percent of the variation in IQ, they acknowledge, is due to nurture rather than nature, or at least to a nurture-nature interaction. They typically neglect this qualification in their interpretation of the data, however, and implicitly treat IQ (as measured by the AFQT) as though it were a purely genetic product.[34] By their own account, however, far from simply attesting to the potency of genes, any correlation between IQ and life outcomes reflects in part—and probably in large part— the influence of social conditions on cognitive ability. Weighing the effect of SES and IQ on life outcomes is not an appropriate test of the power of social background versus the power of genes, because IQ, by their own admission, is itself partly an expression of the social environment.

Herrnstein and Murray's conception of SES, in addition, to cite the strong words of one critic, is "unspeakably crude."[35] They measure respondents' social environment by constructing an index of parental socioeconomic status consisting of four variables: mother's education, father's education, family income, and parents' occupational status. This index is limited even as a measure of family background; as an instrument for estimating the cumulative effects of "social and economic disadvantage," it is exceedingly narrow.[36] It excludes an assortment of important social variables pertaining both to respondents' parental background and to their own current social and economic circumstances, including family size and composition, quality of education, local employment opportunities, community and neighborhood characteristics, and quality of social contacts.[37] Several replications of Herrnstein and Murray's analysis using more refined measures of socioeconomic background find that *The Bell Curve* consistently underestimates the influence of the social environment relative to IQ on life outcomes.[38]

Perhaps the most serious problem with Herrnstein and Murray's argument is that their own data, buried in one of the appendixes to their book, reveal only very weak correlations between IQ scores and social outcomes.[39] According to the statistics they report, IQ has at best a modest effect on how individuals live their lives; contrary to their central argument, it is not "a major predictor of income."[40] One team of economists, reanalyzing the data used in *The Bell Curve*, found that cognitive ability, *even in combination with education and experience*, explains "at most one third of the total variance in wages." Herrnstein and Murray, they report, "dramatically overstate the degree to which differences in wages among individuals can be attributed to differences in cognitive ability."[41] This conclusion would not be so damaging if the objective of *The Bell Curve* were only to prove that IQ, along with many other variables, has *some* influence on life outcomes. But Herrnstein and Murray maintain that intelligence is the *predominant* force in people's lives, and this claim is refuted by their "small to middling" correlations.[42] Though not entirely irrelevant to economic achievement, cognitive ability, inherited or not, does not play anything like the powerful role Herrnstein and Murray attribute to it.

## GENES, IQ, AND POVERTY

*The Bell Curve* proposes a simple theory of poverty: people are poor because they are deficient in inherited cognitive ability. The poor are victims of their own bad genes, and social and educational interventions can do little to remedy the problem. In what follows, I identify five key weaknesses of Herrnstein and Murray's theory: their individualistic premise blinds them to the structural causes of poverty, their argument rests on the erroneous assumption of equality of opportunity, they misrepresent the relationship between IQ and poverty, they present an unrealistic analysis of how people are matched to jobs, and they fail to address the problem of poverty in the aggregate.

## Individualistic Bias

The very language of *The Bell Curve* reveals an "individualistic bias."[43] Herrnstein and Murray describe poverty, unemployment, and the like as "social behaviors," implying these are purely personal problems, unrelated to the structure and functioning of society. They regard poverty as a predicament low-IQ people get themselves into because they are unable to perform adequately in school and on the job and because they are prone to bad choices and self-destructive behaviors. Their terminology conveys the message that poverty is not so much a condition of society as it is an instance of individual inferiority and deviance.

More importantly, Herrnstein and Murray's individualistic bias is reflected in their assumption that poverty can be explained solely in terms of personal attributes. Indeed, they propose a *single-factor* individualistic theory, pinpointing just one variable, an allegedly biological variable at that, as the key to explaining the complex phenomenon of poverty. And while they emphasize the limits set by genes from the inside, Herrnstein and Murray acknowledge no outside obstacles to achievement. They consider parental socioeconomic status, only to dismiss it, but they otherwise disregard the numerous external social forces affecting life outcomes. They not only deny the influence of family circumstances on people's economic outcomes, but they also ask us to believe that the incidence of poverty is unrelated to the state of the economy or to government social welfare and labor market policies.

## Inequality of Opportunity

In modern American society, Herrnstein and Murray insist, individuals compete for access to schools and jobs under conditions of equality of opportunity.[44] Cognitive ability, not family background or social status, is the key to success or failure. In reality, however, neither the educational nor the occupational systems are meritocracies.[45] Children encounter vast and cumulative educational inequalities from the very first moment they begin learning all the way through their college years and beyond. Poor children are less likely to receive high-quality child care, attend high-quality preschool programs, or benefit from a cognitively stimulating home environment. By the time they are old enough for kindergarten, they are already well behind their more affluent peers.[46] Once they enter the highly segregated school system, packed into the country's worst classrooms, they encounter a new round of disadvantages. Jonathan Kozol's books *Savage Inequalities* and *The Shame of the Nation* vividly document massive inequities in education for children, and recent quantitative studies also reveal the persistence of significant disparities in school quality by class and race/ethnicity. [47] And while Herrnstein and Murray proclaim the "democratization of higher education," an outpouring of recent research demonstrates increasing class disparities in access to college. The combination of budgetary constraints, rising tuition costs, declining scholarship money, and stagnant family incomes has made higher education unaffordable for many qualified students. Money has increased in importance relative to brains as a determinant of who gets a college degree. Thus Peter Sacks concludes that "a wealthy low-achiever in America has a significantly greater chance of attending a four-year university than a highly accomplished student from a lower-income family." [48]

Herrnstein and Murray fail to acknowledge inequalities of opportunity in the labor market as well. In particular, they downplay racial and gender discrimination and the persistent disadvantages associated with social class. A study conducted by a team of economists, drawing on the same data used in *The Bell Curve*, shows that wage levels for women and racial minorities are lower compared to white males at the same level of cognitive ability. A white man might earn a decent living even with a relatively low IQ, while a woman or an African American might struggle even with a relatively high IQ. The data on earnings, the authors conclude, are "inconsistent with Herrnstein and Murray's claim that the labor market is meritocratic." [49] The rates of poverty for African Americans and women are also significantly higher than what would be expected if equal opportunity prevailed and if cognitive ability were the primary determinant of economic outcomes. [50] The evidence reveals, contrary to the meritocracy ideal, that women and racial minorities are unable to cash in on their cognitive ability to the same extent as their white male counterparts.

More generally, Herrnstein and Murray refuse to recognize how life chances are structured by "durable inequalities," and how such inequalities are transmitted through the family, along with genes. [51] As one important critique of *The Bell Curve* concludes, "parents' advantages—property, learning, personal contacts, practical crafts, social skills, cultural tools, and so on—are passed on to their children and are also passed from older members of a community to younger ones. Disadvantages are passed on, too." [52] Contrary to Herrnstein and Murray's assumption, neither the educational system nor the occupational system deserves to be called a meritocracy.

Significant and enduring disparities in access to education and employment persist. Poor people are poor not because they have limited intelligence, but because they have limited opportunities for gaining a quality education and a decent job.

## The Correlation between IQ and Poverty

People with low IQs are more likely to be poor than people with high IQs. Herrnstein and Murray infer from this correlation that inherited cognitive ability exerts a causal influence on economic status—low intelligence leads to poverty.[53] They jump to this conclusion for two reasons. First, they treat intelligence as a cause, never as an effect; they refuse to see intelligence as "responsive to social conditions."[54] Second, they treat poverty as an effect, never as a cause; they refuse to see poverty as something that shapes behavior and life outcomes.[55] Poor children are raised in poor families, and they often live in poor housing, reside in poor neighborhoods, and attend poor schools; they suffer disproportionately from nutritionally inadequate diets and from poor mental and physical health; and if they are African American or Latino, they experience prejudice and discrimination, residential segregation, and social isolation. Children born into poverty face multiple and cumulative disadvantages. If their IQ scores were not lower than average, it would be nothing short of miraculous.

By downplaying the influence of the social environment on cognitive ability, Herrnstein and Murray overlook a highly plausible alternative to their interpretation of the modest correlation between IQ and poverty: "*It is not that low intelligence leads to inferior status; it is that inferior status leads to low intelligence test scores.*"[56] Poverty hinders the full development of cognitive functioning. Low-income families often lack the financial means, social supports, and institutional resources necessary to nurture fully the abilities and aptitudes of their children.[57] Perhaps the issue is as simple as this: rich kids score higher on intelligence tests mainly because they are raised in rich environments with an abundance of resources and opportunities, and poor kids score lower on such tests mainly because they are raised in poor environments with a paucity of resources and opportunities. The fundamental problem for the poor is their poverty, not their IQs.

## Getting a Job

Herrnstein and Murray claim that individuals, through the operation of an "invisible hand," are sorted into the occupational system according to their cognitive ability.[58] Differences in intelligence are thereby translated into differences in earnings. High-IQ workers are slotted into the good jobs and low-IQ workers, if they are not entirely superfluous, are slotted into the bad jobs. This occupational sorting process, for Herrnstein and Murray, is uniform, objective, rational, inevitable, and meritocratic: *uniform*, because all employers rely on essentially the same criteria for evaluating workers; *objective*, because the screening process is relatively free of subjective judgment, prejudice, and false impressions; *rational*, because it maximizes efficiency; *inevitable*, because it is bound to the imperatives of a technological society; and *meritocratic*, because it guarantees that ability is the primary determinant of who gets ahead.

Herrnstein and Murray's theory of occupational sorting rests on an implausible assumption: the only handicap people suffer in the labor market is a low IQ. Independent of cognitive ability, however, as a vast social science literature shows, individuals may be disadvantaged by, among other things, their race, ethnicity, gender, age, and sexual preference. They may be bumped from the inside track because they lack the requisite references. They may be perfect for a job, but unaware that an opening exists. Employers might overlook cognitively qualified candidates because they have the wrong social or cultural background, have the wrong credentials, come from the wrong neighborhoods, know the wrong people, have the wrong physical appearance, or speak with the wrong accent. Applicants might be rejected because they are perceived to be lacking in proper work attitudes, loyalty, discipline, compatibility, people skills, or willingness to obey authority. The occupational sorting process is way too messy to imagine that workers are matched to jobs primarily on the basis of their "general intelligence." A good theory of poverty needs to be able to explain, among other things, why particular individuals lose out in the labor market. But it is absurd to think this is simply a matter of some people having low IQs.

## The Problem of Poverty in the Aggregate

The individualistic bias of *The Bell Curve* is evident also in how Herrnstein and Murray frame the poverty problem. They implicitly conceive the central empirical issue as one of identifying the characteristics of individuals that make them more or less vulnerable to poverty. This is an important topic, but because of this narrow focus, they fail to address adequately the problem of poverty in the aggregate.[59] Their theory purports to explain why some people are poor, but it cannot explain why *anyone* is poor, or why there is as much (or as little) poverty as there is.[60] And it cannot explain why the gap between the rich and the poor is so large, why those at the low end of the occupational system are rewarded so much less for their labor than those on the high end, or why day-care workers, say, earn eight dollars an hour rather than sixteen dollars an hour. It is not a requirement of genetics that millions of workers in the U.S. economy are paid less than a living wage.

The flaw in Herrnstein and Murray's theory derives from the fact that individual deficiencies, in themselves, do not cause people to be poor. During an economic boom, for example, a person with few skills may have no trouble earning a decent living. But during an economic bust, as jobs become scarce, that same person might end up unemployed and in the ranks of the poor. Whether or not a low IQ, or any other individual-level characteristic, leads to poverty depends on the availability of decent-paying jobs. The biogenetic theory can predict (though, as it turns out, not with a great deal of accuracy) who is likely to fall into poverty when the economy goes sour. But it cannot explain the fluctuations in the rate of poverty or the causes of the economic booms and busts underlying those fluctuations. Was the decline in the rate of poverty in the United States from 12.8 percent in 1989 to 11.3 percent in 2000 due to an upsurge in the average IQ of Americans during that period, and why has the rate of poverty increased since 2000? Does the United States have the highest rate of poverty in the industrialized world because Americans on average are so much less intelligent than people in other countries? Some individuals are bound to be less able and less skilled than others, of course, but whether this leaves them above or below the poverty line depends largely on government policy and the state of the economy.

The statistical relationship Herrnstein and Murray find between IQ and poverty in the United States is not a fact of nature. It is a contingent product of the existing economic and political rules of the game. Change the rules, and the relationship between IQ and poverty likewise changes. Under a different regime, with different economic and political structures, different cultural norms and ideals, different conceptions of fairness, different regulations governing the operation of the labor market, and different social policies, cognitive ability might play less (or more) of a role in the allocation of income and wealth. Herrnstein and Murray argue that intelligence cannot be raised; but even accepting this dubious assertion, it does not follow that people with low cognitive ability are destined to be poor. As the authors of *Inequality by Design* emphasize, the fate of low-IQ people is not set by their genes, but by social structures and public policy. And these can be altered.

## CONCLUSION

Herrnstein and Murray propose that people are poor for the simple reason that they are born with a deficiency in cognitive ability and that not much can be done about this. This view of poverty, and the more general biogenetic theory of inequality that underlies it, is flawed in many respects. I will not attempt to summarize here the numerous weaknesses of *The Bell Curve*, but I do want to conclude by restating four key problems. First, Herrnstein and Murray's own statistical findings, confirmed by subsequent studies, show that differences in IQ account for only a very small portion of the variation among individuals in wages and income, approximately 10 percent.[61] Individuals differ in their economic standing and in their vulnerability to poverty for many reasons. Cognitive ability, whether inherited or not, far from being a predominant factor, plays a relatively small role in determining people's life outcomes. Second, the modest relationship between cognitive ability and poverty testifies more than anything to the influence of social and economic deprivation on children's test performance. The biogenetic theory overstates the influence of IQ on poverty and understates the influence of poverty on IQ. Third, contrary to the supposition of *The Bell Curve*, research shows that social, political, and educational policies can raise children's cognitive ability and can improve their later-life economic outcomes. People's life chances are not fixed at birth. Fourth, the biogenetic theory completely ignores the myriad economic, political, cultural, and social forces that influence the distribution of resources and opportunities, the rate of poverty, and the severity of the hardships experienced by the poor.

Herrnstein and Murray's analysis serves less to illuminate the problem than to divert attention away from the real causes of poverty and inequality in the United States. Their theory, with its potent mixture of individualism and racism, plays naturally into the prevailing blame-the-victim mentality. While Herrnstein and Murray do not quite hold poor people themselves responsible for their own poverty (after all, the problem is in their genes), at the same time their theory does not attribute poverty to any sort of inequity or injustice. The conclusion that people are poor because they are deficient in inherited cognitive ability, at the very least, adds fuel to an already fashionable cynicism, one that dovetails with a prevailing skepticism about the ability of government to remedy social problems. Herrnstein and Murray, indeed, go out of their way to cast doubt on the practicality of policies intended to achieve greater equality or improve the economic prospects of the poor. Their book contributes to an atmosphere where poverty is perceived as a quasi-natural phenomenon, where problems of poverty and inequality are absent from the political agenda, and where the larger structural forces that underlie increasing inequality and persistent poverty are ignored.

## Chapter Three

# The Cultural Theory of Poverty and Inequality

## POVERTY AS DEVIANCE

The underlying logic of the cultural theory resembles that of the biogenetic theory. Both attribute poverty to the inadequacies of the poor: low IQs for the one and bad values for the other. In the biogenetic theory, the poor lack cognitive ability; in the cultural theory, they lack the motivation to achieve. In either case, poverty is blamed not on the failings of the American political economy, but on the deficiencies of the poor.

In calculating the size of the poverty population, the Bureau of the Census employs a monetary definition: individuals and families are counted as poor if their income falls below a certain threshold. From the standpoint of the cultural theory, however, poverty—insofar as it is deemed a social problem—is not primarily a matter of economic resources. The poor become visible from a policy standpoint not because of the hardships they endure, but because of the troubles they cause. They come into public view only when they are unmarried with children, when they abuse alcohol and drugs, when they commit crime, and when they receive food stamps. In this theory, conventional anti-poverty remedies, including welfare, training, and job creation, are bound to be ineffective. Such programs, based on the assumption that poverty is essentially an economic condition, fail to address the root problem: the deviant way of life of the poor. A war on poverty can be won, the cultural theory submits, only by changing poor people themselves, by

compelling them to embrace the values of family, work, and personal responsibility.

## THE ORIGINS AND DEVELOPMENT OF
## THE CULTURAL THEORY

Why do some countries develop more quickly than others, and why do some
ethnic groups forge ahead while others lag behind? One popular answer is
that the cultural characteristics of nations and groups differ, with some promoting and others impeding economic prosperity.[1] In the United States, for
example, the economic mobility of Jews and Asian Americans, especially as
compared to African Americans, has often been ascribed to their allegedly
superior cultural ideals.[2] Differences in cultural traits are presumed to explain differences in economic outcomes; some cultures are more conducive
to economic attainment than others. This same logic, applied to individuals
as well as groups, characterizes the cultural theory of poverty. For this theory, people are poor because they lack the psychological attributes, intellectual
dispositions, and moral commitments that foster economic achievement.

The modern cultural theory of poverty—more commonly called the "culture of poverty" theory—came on the scene in the United States in the early
1960s and has been the subject of intense controversy ever since.[3] While it
subsequently became the centerpiece of conservative analysis, the culture of
poverty concept, ironically, was introduced to American audiences through
the work of two men on the left, Michael Harrington[4] and Oscar Lewis.[5]
Unlike many later advocates of the cultural theory, neither Harrington nor
Lewis held poor people solely responsible for their poverty, and both regarded the culture of the poor as a symptom of poverty, not its cause. They
both employed the culture of poverty concept to underline the multifaceted,
persistent, deep-rooted, and tenacious nature of the problem. By drawing
attention to its cultural dimension, moreover, neither Harrington nor Lewis
intended to downplay the economic and political causes of poverty. Indeed,
they both understood poverty to be an outgrowth of capitalism, and they both
regarded the culture of the poor as something resulting from problems of
economic deprivation, social segregation, and political exclusion.

By the end of the 1960s, the culture of poverty theory had become a
staple of conservative social criticism in the United States. In their adaptation
of this theory, conservatives shifted the onus of responsibility for poverty
from society to the individual, prompting liberals to charge them with "blam-

ing the victim."[6] Unlike Harrington and Lewis, conservatives regarded the culture of the poor as the cause of their poverty, not its consequence. This version of the cultural theory has gained intellectual and political prominence since the 1970s, contributing to a shift in the public discourse on poverty away from concerns about inequality, discrimination, and job scarcity and toward issues of welfare dependency, the "underclass," and the decline of "family values."[7]

## THE CULTURE OF THE POOR

The cultural theory maintains that poor people have a distinct set of values, aspirations, beliefs, attitudes, dispositions, and psychological characteristics. These putative cultural traits and the style of life corresponding to them constitute a unique culture of poverty, one often conceived as the antithesis of mainstream culture. In an influential early statement of this theory, Edward Banfield posits a "class-cultural scale," with "lower-class" culture at one end of the continuum and its opposite, "upper-class" culture, at the other.[8] The culture of the lower class, he states, is characterized by "the existence of an outlook and style of life which is radically present-oriented and which therefore attaches no value to work, sacrifice, self-improvement, or service to family, friends or community."[9] People from the lower class, Banfield asserts, have little awareness of the future, they are incapable of self-discipline, and their behavior is governed by impulse and "bodily needs (especially for sex)." The poor, he declares, are also inclined toward "violent crime and civil disorder," they are "not troubled by dirt and dilapidation," and they prefer "the 'action' of the street to any steady job." Their presence turns neighborhoods into "slums" and schools into "blackboard jungles."[10] The poverty of this lower class, furthermore, Banfield alleges, is "'inwardly' caused," the outcome of a psychological inability to plan for the future. The habitual "ways of thinking and behaving" that characterize the poor are deeply rooted as well, such that "improvements in external circumstances" are likely to have little effect.[11] For Banfield, lower-class "attitudes, habits, and modes of behavior," as with cognitive ability for Herrnstein and Murray, cannot be easily changed. His call for action, accordingly, consists mostly of measures that would subject the lower-class poor to more stringent mechanisms of social control—intensified policing and quicker imprisonment, for example.[12]

For other proponents of the cultural theory, the problem is not so much the deep attachment of the poor to a deviant subculture as it is their superficial allegiance to mainstream norms. The poor give "lip service" to middle-class values, William Kelso contends, but they rarely abide by these and "feel no sense of obligation to harmonize their beliefs with their actions."[13] They might talk the talk, but they don't walk the walk. For Lawrence Mead, similarly, the poor affirm cultural ideals "in principle but not in practice."[14] They profess adherence to values of work and marriage, but they do not have regular jobs or stable family lives. The inability of the poor to live up to conventional norms, he insists, is not due to any external obstacles, but to their own negative outlook on life. They are victims of a "defeatist culture," and this mentality is the "chief cause" of their poverty.[15] The poor remain poor because they are resigned to failure, easily discouraged, and do not try very hard to get or keep a job. They are deficient in the "self-discipline" necessary "to get through school, obey the law, work steadily, and avoid trouble." The persistence of poverty, according to Mead, is due primarily to poor people's misguided defeatism and their lack of "personal organization."[16]

Employment opportunities are plentiful, according to the cultural theory, and anyone willing to put in the necessary effort can work their way out of poverty. Joblessness among the poor, Mead argues, is not caused by discrimination, disability, or low wages, nor is it due to unaffordable child care or unreliable transportation.[17] The real problem is psychological: the long-term poor are simply incapable of mobilizing the inner resources necessary to secure a job. Charles Murray offers an even harsher judgment. The "underclass" is chronically unemployed, he asserts, not because they lack opportunities or skills, but because they are unwilling and unable "to get up every morning and go to work."[18] For Myron Magnet, likewise, the poor are held back not because they are unfairly denied the chance to succeed, but because of their own inferior psyches: they are "equipped with different, and sparser, mental and emotional furniture, unhelpful for taking advantage of the economic opportunities that American life offers." The poor, he concludes, are victims of their own bad behavior and "the worldview from which that behavior springs."[19]

Whether the poor have succumbed to a deviant subculture or a defeatist psychology, the implication is the same: poverty is the result of poor people's own impaired values. They have only themselves and their families to blame. They lack ambition and initiative, perseverance and diligence; they have weak moral convictions and are easily lured into delinquency and crime; they are lazy and unmotivated, preferring government handouts or criminal activity to hard work; they lack strength of character and are too quick to give up in the face of adversity; and they reject the values of personal responsibility, sexual restraint, and monogamous marriage. As a result of their inner defects, the poor are likely to drop out of high school, become unmarried mothers and fathers, experience chronic joblessness, and succumb to welfare dependency. The negative psychological and behavioral traits of the poor persist from generation to generation as well. Through the process of socialization and the bad example set by their parents, poor children learn to emulate the errant behaviors of their elders. Poverty and its culture endure, this theory proposes, because the poor "pass on to their children a self-defeating set of values and attitudes, along with an impoverished intellectual and emotional development, that generally imprisons them in failure as well."[20]

The cultural theory of poverty tells a simple story, an "us" and "them" morality tale essentially. The well-to-do are rewarded with success because they have good values and behave responsibly. The poor are stuck in poverty because they have bad values and behave irresponsibly.

## THE SOURCES OF THE CULTURAL DEVIANCE OF THE POOR

If, as the cultural theory contends, people are poor because they are deficient in the values and motivations that lead to economic achievement, then what is the source of this deficiency? The challenge for this theory is to come up with an explanation for the distinct psychological and cultural traits of the poor without conceiving these as consequences of their poverty. For some proponents of this theory, the cultural characteristics imputed to the poor are simply taken as given. For others, the culture of poverty is a product of some combination of (1) the legacy of slavery, (2) the political and cultural revolutions of the 1960s, and (3) the liberal welfare state.

According to one version of the cultural theory, addressing specifically the case of black poverty, the cultural and behavioral deviance of the poor derives from the legacy of slavery. Daniel Patrick Moynihan, in a controversial government report made public in 1965, proposed that slavery and Jim Crow, along with urbanization and unemployment, undermined the ability of males to assume the breadwinner role in the black family. This resulted in the emergence of a matriarchal family structure that was "out of line with the rest of American society."[21] The weakness of the black family, according to

Moynihan, engendered "aberrant, inadequate, or anti-social behavior" among the younger generation, thus causing an ongoing "cycle of poverty and deprivation."[22] This "tangle of pathology," he argues, highlighting the point that discrimination is no longer the key problem, "is capable of perpetuating itself without assistance from the white world."[23] The legacy of slavery, in Moynihan's view, gave rise to a now autonomous matriarchal subculture, and this is the central causal factor in the continuation of black poverty.

The slave experience had lasting effects, according to another formulation of this thesis, not just through its influence on black family formation, but also through its broader impact on African American culture. Mead surmises, for example, that the worldview of African Americans, formed by "group memories of slavery and Jim Crow," promotes a powerful hopelessness that inhibits effort.[24] Dinesh D'Souza proposes a more elaborate theory. Black people, he claims, devised certain strategies of resistance under slavery. They refused to work hard, they stole from their masters, and they acted in a defiant manner. Over time, D'Souza imagines, these congealed into a "distinctive ethnic identity" that persists today in the form of "destructive and pathological patterns of behavior."[25] Included among these, he alleges, are "excessive reliance on government, conspiratorial paranoia about racism, a resistance to academic achievement as 'acting white,' a celebration of the criminal and outlaw as authentically black, and the normalization of illegitimacy and dependency." These behaviors originated as a "response to past oppression," but now they "are dysfunctional and must be modified."[26] By underscoring the cultural and distant historical roots of black poverty, D'Souza and others want to suggest that the impoverished circumstances of today's poor have nothing to do with racial discrimination or with current economic conditions. Poverty, they conclude, is the fault of the black poor themselves: they have been too slow to shed the values and attitudes that grew out of the slave experience and that have since turned pathological.[27]

A second version of the cultural theory attributes the presumably aberrant values and behavior of the poor to the social, political, and cultural changes of the 1960s. According to Magnet, Kelso, and others, the ascendancy of liberalism, the sexual revolution, and the hippie counterculture combined to create a new and pernicious set of values, norms, and beliefs.[28] Liberal social programs, from the war on poverty to affirmative action, fostered ideologies of victimization and entitlement, undermining traditional ideals of individual initiative, hard work, and merit. The sexual revolution, along with feminism, sparked a transformation of values that "reshaped family life, increasing divorce, illegitimacy, and female-headed families."[29] And the sixties counterculture inspired a do-your-own-thing hedonism that demeaned precisely those moral principles—the work ethic, sexual responsibility, and deferred gratification—most conducive to individual achievement.[30] The cultural upheaval of the 1960s, Magnet and Kelso believe, had an especially adverse effect on the poor. As the "Victorian principles" of self-control and hard work gave way to a "more laissez-faire morality," poor people, only weakly committed to conventional norms to begin with, "abandoned the values of self-restraint even more quickly than the rest of society." This cultural devolution left "many indigents without a moral compass" and caused the "economically poor" to mutate into a destructive "underclass."[31] While in the past the poor just lacked money, today they lack values.

A third version of the cultural theory holds the welfare state responsible for the deviant values and behaviors of the poor.[32] According to this thesis, the welfare system rewards the poor for not working, for not marrying, and for having babies out of wedlock. By offering money for nothing, welfare encourages the laziness of the poor, sunders "the psychological link between effort and reward," and destroys the motivational foundation of "long-run upward mobility."[33] It undermines personal responsibility, saps individual initiative, and fosters an ethos of dependency. The welfare system, according to its conservative critics, perpetuates a dysfunctional culture of poverty, inhibiting the poor from achieving economic independence.

These arguments assume the existence of what they set out to explain: a deviant black identity, the decline of moral standards, and a destructive welfare culture. They posit a connection between today's poverty and past developments but establish this more through supposition than careful investigation. And they rest on the dubious assumption of a bifurcated poverty population, one divided into the "bad" and the "good": the black poor versus the white poor, the post-1960s poor versus the pre-1960s poor, the welfare poor versus the working poor. These arguments lack empirical credibility, but they enable conservative critics to ignore issues of economics, inequality, and discrimination, while at the same time giving them a platform to extol traditional values, vent their hostility toward the decade of the 1960s, and denounce the welfare state.

## THE CULTURAL SOLUTION TO THE PROBLEM OF POVERTY

To conquer the problem of poverty, according to the cultural theory, the poor must be induced or compelled to renounce their self-destructive lifestyles and adopt the values of hard work, self-restraint, and individual responsibility. "The opportunity is there," Lawrence Harrison avows. What the poor need is a new message: "Go for it!"[34] According to Republican congressman Paul Ryan, the poor can replace their "vicious cycle of despair" with a "virtuous cycle of hope" only by "embracing the attributes of friendship, accountability, and love."[35] George Gilder also exhorts the poor to change their ways. The "only dependable route from poverty," he declares, "is always work, family, and faith."[36] Explicitly urging "moral reform," Joel Schwartz proposes that the poor can best escape their poverty by adhering faithfully to traditional virtues of diligence, thrift, sobriety, and family responsibility.[37] Kelso, likewise, calls for a "strenuous effort . . . to resocialize the poor into playing by the 'rules of the game.'"[38] For these proponents of the cultural theory, conventional solutions, which throw money at the problem or seek only to expand opportunities, are doomed to failure. Such remedies ignore the deeper cultural roots of poverty. An intervention into the lives of the poor is required, something invasive enough to undo their counterproductive values, attitudes, and behaviors.

For many conservative adherents of the cultural theory, the necessary first step toward rehabilitating the poor is to dismantle a welfare state that creates incentives for people to behave badly. According to Dick Armey, former congressional representative and now Tea Party front man, the key to ending poverty is to "scrap today's failed welfare system and replace dependency with work, marriage, and personal responsibility." He favors the "'Tough Love' option": kick the poor off welfare and trust they can make it on their own. And for those who do fall through the cracks, the solution is not "Big Government," but "the natural safety net" of "family, friends, churches, and charities."[39]

Armey's solution builds on the thinking of Marvin Olasky, the architect of "compassionate conservatism."[40] As with other adherents of the cultural theory, Olasky believes poverty is less a problem of economics than of attitudes. The poor do not need a government handout, he contends; they need a strong dose of spiritual reform and moral instruction. The poor are "caught within a dysfunctional culture," Newt Gingrich explains, summarizing Olasky's theory, and the only way for them to change their behavior and escape poverty is to "transfer their loyalties, beliefs, and practices to another culture." Government bureaucrats lack the competence to effect such a transformation. Faith-based organizations are the only institutions capable of mounting such a momentous undertaking. The poor can be moved out of "the culture of violence and poverty and into a better culture" only through the moral influence of religiously inspired "missionaries."[41]

Mead also believes the poor need to change their outlook on life and their patterns of behavior. But unlike right-wing critics of the welfare state, he thinks government can play a positive role in helping poor people to "reorganize their lives." Calling for a "new paternalism," Mead proposes that public authorities, to address the "lifestyle causes of poverty," place recipients of government assistance under close supervision.[42] By carefully monitoring the poor and enforcing mandatory compliance with conventional values and behavioral rules—work requirements, for instance—government agencies might be able to steer poor people into the cultural mainstream.

Proponents of the cultural theory achieved a tremendous victory with the 1996 enactment of the Personal Responsibility and Work Opportunity Reconciliation Act (PRWORA). This legislation replaced a long-standing program, Aid to Families with Dependent Children, with a new welfare program, Temporary Assistance for Needy Families (TANF).[43] This radical overhaul of the welfare system bears the undeniable imprint of the cultural theory's policy agenda. Under TANF, poor women are allowed to receive welfare benefits for a total of no more than sixty months during their adult lives. And to further guard against dependency, TANF requires recipients to fulfill strict work obligations, in accordance with a "work first" philosophy.[44] The premise is that what poor women need—more than money, more than training and education, and more than child-care assistance—is a psychological and attitudinal makeover. They need to acquire a sense of individual responsibility and self-respect. These qualities, it is supposed, will follow naturally from the experience of having a regular job, showing up for work on time, and following the orders of employers. For advocates of this philosophy, work is a powerful socializing experience, furnishing an education in virtue. Poor women, thrust into the labor force, even if their jobs pay very low wages, will learn the value of work and will undergo the psychological refurbishment needed to lift themselves out of poverty.

The cultural theory, in sum, makes five key claims: (1) The psychology and worldview of the poor differ markedly from those of the middle class, with poor people being deficient in the attitudes, beliefs, and commitments that promote stable families and economic achievement. The poor have, at best, a weak commitment to the values of work, marriage, and personal responsibility. (2) Because of their aberrant cultural and psychological traits, the poor are predisposed toward a self-destructive lifestyle, leaving them trapped in welfare dependency, single parenthood, and chronic joblessness. (3) The cultural and behavioral deviance of the poor—not economic conditions, lack of opportunities, or discrimination—is the primary cause of their poverty. (4) The psychological and motivational deficiencies of the poor are transmitted through the process of socialization from one generation to the next. Because of their deep cultural roots, these deficiencies have the status of relatively fixed personality traits and cannot be remedied simply by changing the social environment of the poor. (5) Only by uprooting the culture of poverty itself, only by compelling poor people to undergo a regimen of resocialization and moral reform, can the problem of poverty be alleviated.[45]

## IS THE CULTURE THEORY PLAUSIBLE?

The cultural theory is appealing, in part, because it plays on popular stereotypes about the poor and affirms the American Dream ideology, the notion that opportunities are abundant and that anyone can make it if they try. But even at first glance, there are many reasons to doubt the validity of this theory. And, as we will see, it is not consistent with what we know about the characteristics of the poverty population or with current research on the values and behaviors of the poor.

One good reason to be suspicious about the cultural theory is it purports to explain poverty by reference to one chief cause: the psychology of the poor. Any single-factor theory such as this lacks surface plausibility, especially when applied to an extraordinarily complex and multifaceted phenomenon such as poverty. This theory would have us believe that values and attitudes are the only things that matter, and that larger economic and political forces exert little influence on life outcomes. Even in the wake of the Great Recession, proponents of the cultural theory dismiss or give short shrift to a host of potentially relevant structural forces: the loss of jobs in the manufacturing sector, the growth of low-wage service industries, the accelerated pace of globalization and outsourcing, the decline of trade unions, the erosion in the real value of the minimum wage, and the surge of inequality. The cultural theory's interpretation of recent American history and its analysis of poverty largely ignore these developments, offering up instead a simpleminded story of family breakdown and declining values.

We should be skeptical about this theory for other reasons as well. The proposition that poor people share a monolithic culture that diverges from the mainstream and is passed on from generation to generation is inconsistent with certain basic facts about the poverty population. First, as Jens Ludwig and Susan Mayer show, most of today's poor grew up in precisely the sort of families celebrated by conservative critics—mainstream families where parents were married, had regular jobs, and attended religious services.[46] The large majority of today's poor adults were not reared in some aberrant cultural environment, and they did not inherit bad values from their parents. Contrary to the thesis of the cultural theory, there is no massive family-values upbringing gap that explains why some children become poor adults and others do not.

Second, while the poor are alike in that they do not have much money, they are otherwise a diverse group, contrary to popular impressions and common stereotypes.[47] Some are old and some young, some male and some female. Many of the poor are African American and Latino, a smaller number are Asian American and Native American, but most are non-Hispanic white. Some poor people live in single-parent households, some in two-parent households, and others live alone. The poor vary also in their residential location: they reside in inner cities, in the rural countryside, and even in the suburbs.[48] Some poor people are unemployed or out of the labor force, but many have jobs in the growing low-wage service sector. Some are poor for only short periods of time, others for many years. It is difficult to imagine this heterogeneous group sharing a common deviant culture.

Third, the poor are not only a diverse population; they are a constantly changing population as well. The number of people below the official poverty line increases in some years and decreases in others. The poverty population also undergoes regular turnover, with thousands of people moving into poverty and thousands of others moving out of poverty all the time.[49] As Mark Rank shows, it is not just marginal groups that experience poverty; indeed, a majority of the population is poor at least one year during their adult lives.[50] Poverty is a "'mainstream event," Rank argues; it is not something unique to a deviant "other" or to those who are somehow culturally disfigured.[51]

Fourth, contrary to the cultural theory's "us" versus "them" imagery, the poor on the whole are not all that different from the non-poor. In its determination to represent the poor as some deviant underclass, the cultural theory exaggerates the divide separating the poverty population and the working population.[52] The cultural theory maintains credibility by suppressing the similarities between the poor and the non-poor and by depicting the poor as falling entirely outside the American mainstream. Only through this strategy can it sustain the argument that the problems of the poor are of their own making and have little to do with the social and economic forces that sometimes cause hardship for the more respectable members of society.

The poor, in sum, comprise a diverse population, and one that, as Bradley Schiller emphasizes, is "not markedly different from . . . the rest of society."[53] It is implausible to think that this varied and changing group possesses a common outlook on life, much less one antithetical to mainstream values. The very heterogeneity of the poverty population casts doubt on the cultural theory's simple single-factor psychological explanation.

## HOW WELL DOES THE CULTURAL THEORY KNOW THE POOR?

The vast majority of Americans who experience a spell of poverty do not fit the cultural theory's stereotypical portrait of the poor. They are not lazy and irresponsible, they are not enmeshed in a deviant subculture, and they are not engaged in criminal or immoral activities. Though proponents of the cultural theory say little about such people, they usually admit that many, if not most, of the poor do not conform to the theory's psychological and demographic profile. They sidestep this inconvenient fact by specifying the theory so that it pertains not to the *entirety* of the poverty population, but to a restricted *segment*—an "underclass" that is typically said to include long-term welfare recipients, the chronically unemployed, teen mothers, and assorted troublemakers.[54] By targeting this ill-defined "underclass," and by conceding that most poverty falls outside its purview, the cultural theory strains for empirical credibility, but it also sacrifices any standing it might claim as a general theory of poverty, and it acknowledges, if only implicitly, that the larger problem of poverty is not foremost a cultural phenomenon. But even in this narrowed-down version, the cultural theory lacks plausibility. Its sweeping and highly stereotypical allegations about the deviant values, negative attitudes, and pernicious motivations of the poor (or some segment of the poor) presume intimate knowledge of the daily lives and state of mind of millions of people. It is difficult enough to gain insight into the psychology of any single individual. On what basis can one claim to understand the "inner life" of the poor as a whole—to know this large population's "values and aspirations" and "the particulars of their daily decisions"?[55]

The cultural theory's conclusions about the worldview and lifestyle of the poor would be more credible if they were derived from hours of in-depth interviews or years of close-up observation in low-income communities. In fact, however, they are mainly the results of armchair psychological speculation and dubious inference. Advocates of this theory often extrapolate from small and unrepresentative samples or they summon a handful of cases tailored to fit their negative profile. Consider Myron Magnet's statement that the 5 million or so people who make up the "underclass" are poor because of their sparse "mental and emotional furniture" and because they suffer from an "inner defect." The evidence marshaled in support of this contention is not impressive. Magnet cites a smattering of newspaper articles and a couple of sensationalistic anecdotes.[56]

In fact, proponents of the cultural theory rarely provide any direct evidence about poor people's values, attitudes, and beliefs at all; they rely on indirect evidence instead. Rather than studying the world of the poor first-hand, an admittedly laborious task, their typical approach is to infer the psychological dispositions of the poor from more easily accessible data on the observable circumstances of their lives.[57] If the employment and family status of the poor diverge from the mainstream, it follows they must be in the grips of a deviant culture. If black people comprise a disproportionate share of the long-term poor, they must be "uniquely prone to the attitudes contrary to work."[58] If the poor live in slums, they must prefer a life of "squalor and misery."[59] If they fail to climb out of poverty, they must be lacking in perseverance.[60] If they are unemployed, they just don't want to work. If they receive government assistance, they must have surrendered to an ethic of dependency. The difficulty with such inferences, of course, is that individuals do not always have the means to conform to their cultural preferences, live up to their ideals, or realize their desires. People's circumstances inevitably impose constraints on their choices, causing them to do one thing even while they believe in another—to be a single mother, even though they dream about marriage; to be unemployed, even though they desperately want a job; to be on welfare, even though they prefer economic self-sufficiency. The lives people lead are shaped not just by their psychological and cultural dispositions, but by their access to resources and opportunities as well.

## DO THE POOR DIFFER FROM THE NON-POOR,
## AND IF SO HOW AND WHY?

Since the cultural theory appeared on the scene in the 1960s, social scientists—through a combination of survey research, in-depth interviews, and ethnographic studies—have sought a more empirically grounded understanding of the values, beliefs, and way of life of the poor. Many of these studies have focused on precisely those people presumed to be most susceptible to the culture of poverty, including single mothers, welfare recipients, and the residents of urban ghettos. This research reveals a complicated picture, but one that clearly contradicts the cultural theory's image of poverty and the poor. No brief summary can do justice to the numerous studies that have been conducted in recent decades. Nevertheless, two key conclusions deserve to be singled out from this body of research. (1) The fundamental values and aspirations of the poor do not differ significantly from those of the middle class. (2) Many of the poor lead lives that diverge from the mainstream—they are chronically unemployed, they live in single-parent households, and they sometimes receive a welfare check—but these outcomes are due largely to inadequate opportunities, not deviant values.

The vast majority of the poor, for better or worse, adhere to traditional cultural ideals. They believe in the importance of individual effort, education, family, and personal responsibility.[61] Despite experiences that might be expected to teach a contrary lesson, most poor people remain wedded to the ideology of individualism. They think opportunities are available and education and hard work are the keys to success. Even residents in the poorest Chicago neighborhoods, according to William Julius Wilson, "agreed that America is the land of opportunity where anybody can get ahead, and that individuals get pretty much what they deserve."[62] Though they tell complicated stories, Jennifer Hochschild and Andrew Young both cite a surprisingly strong belief in the American Dream among poor African Americans.[63] In a study of impoverished households in Chicago, Sandra Barnes reveals a widespread endorsement of a conventional "achievement ideology" emphasizing the importance of work, education, and merit.[64] Naomi Farber shows that poor teen mothers, just like their middle- and working-class counterparts, "hold aspirations that reflect mainstream values about educational and vocational achievement."[65] Poor people, it seems, are not so different, certainly not the alien "other" envisioned by the cultural theory. They want what most Americans want: a decent education, a good job, a stable family, a happy marriage, and a nice home. Based on data from a large national sample, Rachel Jones and Ye Luo conclude that on issues of work, family, and welfare, there is little empirical support for "traditional culture of poverty arguments."[66]

There is no vast cultural divide that separates the poor from the non-poor. But in several respects rarely mentioned by proponents of the cultural theory, the poor are certainly different. They lack money, prestige, power, and all the advantages that go along with these, including safe neighborhoods, good schools, social connections, and political influence. The aspirations of the poor resemble those of the affluent, but the poor are limited in their access to the means required to realize those aspirations. As Joel Devine and James Wright observe, "the truly meaningful distinction between the underclass and the rest of society lies in the *differential capacity to translate and actualize one's values into a socially desirable repertoire of behaviors.*"[67] I will briefly illustrate this point for the two key areas of work and family. The essential message is this: while poor people are mainstream in their ambitions, they often lack the opportunities and resources necessary to secure full-time jobs and to establish stable marriages. The poor do in fact sometimes live unconventional lives, but this does not mean they adhere to unconventional values, much less that their values are the cause of their unconventional lives.

## Work

"I just want to become able, stable, with a life, you know, a good life," one black man explained. "I just want to work, man. I just want to work."[68] Contrary to the diagnosis proposed by 2012 vice-presidential candidate Paul Ryan, this man, and millions of others like him, does not suffer from a cultural aversion to work.[69] Indeed, most poor people, even the jobless, are work oriented, and few seem resigned to their fate or think they deserve a free ride.[70] Roberta Iversen and Naomi Farber show that young black women, many already employed, place a high value on work, are encouraged by their parents to become self-supporting, and hold largely negative attitudes about welfare.[71] In a study of labor force activity among poor parents in Chicago, Marta Tienda and Haya Stier found that only a small minority do not want to work. Most are either working or looking for work. According to their evidence, "willingness to work" is the prevailing norm, and joblessness is largely involuntary, not a sign of "shiftlessness."[72] Barrio residents, like those of the ghetto, Daniel Dohan reports, also demonstrate a strong commitment to the work ethic. Despite often being treated shabbily in the low-wage labor market, poor Mexican Americans share a common belief that work is "a worthwhile and important activity."[73] Interview data reveal that welfare recipients also have conventional attitudes toward work. They dislike being on welfare, they want jobs that will allow them to support their families, and they often struggle to survive in the low-wage labor market.[74] "I hate being on welfare," one young black woman explained. "I want to be independent; I want to be on my own. I want to have a good job."[75]

These expressions of support for the work ethic are not just a case of respondents giving lip service to socially sanctioned ideals. Attesting to their willingness to work, Stephen Petterson finds that African American men regularly settle for jobs that pay less than their "reservation wage," that is, less than what they regard as a fair wage.[76] We should also keep in mind that millions of Americans—approximately 25 percent of all employees, significantly more than in other developed countries—show up to work every day at grueling low-wage jobs.[77] And if they are complaining about anything, it is not working *too much*, but working *too little*. More than 7 million men and women in 2014 were involuntarily stuck with part-time jobs; they preferred *more* hours of work per week, not *fewer*.[78] This is hardly evidence of an anti-work, freeloader mentality. Many poor people are understandably worried and frustrated about their economic prospects, but the problem they suffer from is not a cultural disinclination to work but a lack of good jobs.[79]

The work effort of the poor varies in tandem with the ups and downs of the economy, and this also suggests that joblessness is more a function of employment opportunities than bad values. Several studies show that when labor markets are tight, the unemployed poor, including less-educated minority youths, are drawn into the labor force. When jobs are available, the poor go to work.[80] For example, the rates of poverty for African Americans and Latinos in particular fell significantly between 1995 and 2000, as poor minorities took advantage of the unusual upsurge in the availability of jobs.[81] The big problem poor people face is that periods of sustained job growth and low unemployment are rare and short-lived, and even when labor markets are at their tightest, there are still never nearly enough job vacancies to absorb the pool of willing workers.[82]

Most able-bodied, working-age poor people participate in the paid labor market. Some have steady jobs, some cycle in and out of the labor force, and some work in the underground economy. But many of the poor, especially young, less-educated black males, do have extended bouts of unemployment or experience chronic joblessness.[83] This problem cannot be reduced to one of insufficient motivation and bad values. To be sure, some of the long-term unemployed are not adequately prepared for vocational success. They lack skills, work habits, employment experience, and knowledge of the ins and outs of the labor market and the workplace. They are not very confident, sometimes unrealistic in their expectations, and uncertain how to translate their occupational aspirations into a regular job.[84] They often have physical health, mental health, and other personal difficulties that inhibit work effort. An increasing number of young black men are also burdened with the "mark of a criminal record," making it nearly impossible for them to find work no matter how hard they might try.[85] They also encounter a variety of other structural problems limiting their ability to work their way out of poverty, including racial discrimination, residential segregation, a scarcity of employment opportunities, and the low quality of available jobs. Single mothers, including welfare recipients, face additional hurdles, including assorted child-care, health-care, transportation, and housing problems.[86] Poor people who are disconnected from or only weakly attached to the labor market need help as individuals, certainly. But no amount of resocialization, moral reform, or faith-based inspiration will fix the multifaceted problems that keep the jobless poor out of work and trapped in poverty.

## Family

Contrary to the assumption underlying marriage-promotion initiatives, poor women "do not have to be convinced about the value of marriage."[87] Most of them, single mothers included, affirm conventional family values and extol the virtues of two-parent child rearing. Kathryn Edin and Maria Kefalas, having spent five years doing research in inner-city communities, report "astonishingly little evidence of the much-touted rejection of the institution of marriage among the poor."[88] Regardless of class or race, low-income teen mothers, according to Naomi Farber, uphold "ideal visions" about marriage and childbearing that "are congruent with traditional values."[89] Robin Jarrett discovered nearly unanimous support for the concept of marriage among the eighty-two never-married African American women she interviewed. "I would like to be married," one woman declared, expressing the general sentiment. "I want to be married. I'm not gonna lie. I really do."[90]

Though professing adherence to the ideal of the two-parent family, many poor women have children as teens and experience years as single mothers. This outcome does not reflect a weak commitment to traditional values, however. The relationship between poverty and single motherhood is due primarily to the circumstances under which poor women make decisions about marriage and childbearing. As in the case of work, the behavior of the poor with respect to family formation is largely a product of the limited options available to them.[91] Many poor mothers are reluctant to marry because the fathers of their children are themselves poor, often jobless or incarcerated, or otherwise "unmarriageable."[92] As one teen mother explained, "If I can't find [a man] that got a job or that can help me in some way, I don't want him."[93] According to another woman, "I don't want to marry nobody that don't have nothing going for themselves. . . . I could do bad by myself."[94] An environment of poverty contributes to single motherhood also because it heightens women's mistrust of the men in their lives; it makes them more cautious about marriage and more determined to preserve their independence. Poor single women face difficult lives, and they are wary of making a bad situation worse by entering into a potentially troublesome long-term relationship.[95] For some poor women, in addition, motherhood, even in the absence of marriage, is a desirable route to social standing, maturity, and respect, particularly when other paths to adulthood and a meaningful life are closed off.[96]

In a direct challenge to the cultural theory, Edin and Kefalas show that poor women are prone to single motherhood not because they repudiate family values but, ironically, because they value marriage and children so highly, even more so perhaps than their middle-class counterparts. Poor women, they report, fully embrace the ideal of a lifelong marriage, so much so in fact that they are reluctant to tie the knot even when they become mothers, for fear they may face the disappointment and stigma of a divorce down the road. It is worse to be an ex-wife than an unwed mother, they believe, and pregnancy is no excuse for foolishly rushing into a marriage. Their first priority is to get financially established, get settled in their lives, and get to know their prospective husbands to make sure their relationships will last.[97] They want to be married, certainly, but they do not want to be trapped in a bad marriage or face the humiliating prospect of abandonment or divorce. Poor women are also eager to be mothers and cannot imagine a life without children. But because "good, decent, trustworthy men are in short supply," they cannot wait for a husband to appear on the scene before taking up motherhood.[98] Given the options available to them, poor women are led to elevate the institution of motherhood over marriage. Their choices may not be entirely conventional, but they are an understandable response to difficult circumstances—an adaptation to poverty, not its cause—and they certainly do not constitute evidence of cultural pathology.[99]

The poor and the middle class are similar in their aspirations and ideals, but they differ in their life circumstances. Despite the value they place on work, education, individual responsibility, and the two-parent family, the poor are more likely to be chronically unemployed, drop out of high school, be on welfare, and raise their children in single-parent homes. These are not lifestyle choices, however, and they are not indications of character flaws or a deviant culture. The unconventional lives of the poor are predictable consequences of residential segregation, racial discrimination, social isolation, poor schools, lousy jobs, and an inadequate system of public support. Poor people do not lack mainstream values; they lack the means to get a quality education, secure a good job, and create a stable marriage. The problem for the poor is their poverty, not their culture.

## CONCLUSION

Poor people are not saints, and in this respect they are like everyone else. In all fairness, though, we should acknowledge that the circumstances of the poor are less conducive to saintliness than are those of the affluent. As Michael Zweig observes, it is far more difficult to manage "mainstream" behavior when one lives under "non-mainstream conditions."[100] This is not to imply, of course, that poor people bear no responsibility for their actions or that economic deprivation excuses bad behavior. Nor is there anything wrong with wishing that some of the poor would conduct themselves in a more virtuous manner, though this end might be more effectively achieved by changing their "non-mainstream conditions" than by public condemnation and punitive reforms. We should also be aware, however, that most poor people already live respectable lives: working hard at thankless jobs, raising their children as best they can, and tending to their communities. They do not need resocialization, government supervision, or an education in the rules of the game.

Conservative proponents of the cultural theory have brought issues of values and morality into the poverty debate. In one important example, Joel Schwartz proposes "fighting poverty with virtue." He maintains that "mundane moral virtues such as diligence, sobriety, and thrift . . . make it easier to escape from poverty."[101] This seems sensible enough as far as it goes, but he does leave some important empirical questions unanswered. How widespread is the lack of virtue among the poor? Is it a serious problem, more so than a lack of jobs, education, and child care? How much of a difference would adherence to traditional values make in the lives of the poor, and how much would it increase their probability of escaping poverty? Virtuous behavior might conceivably give someone an edge over more profligate rivals in the labor market, but given the relative scarcity of jobs that pay a living wage, how far can good behavior go toward reducing the level of poverty in the aggregate?

Schwartz rightly criticizes theorists who represent the poor as nothing other than passive victims. But his conception of moral agency is exceedingly narrow. He emphasizes diligence and thrift but ignores other virtues, including compassion and cooperation. He insists that poor people take responsibility for their own lives, but he focuses only on their conduct as individuals, overlooking how they might pursue worthy goals by rallying together as a group, a community, or a social movement. When Schwartz calls upon the poor to take moral action to overcome their poverty, he is not thinking of *collective* action; he is not suggesting that poor people organize among themselves to press for social reform. When he admonishes the poor to "act in ways that are self-advancing rather than self-defeating," he means they should exercise self-control, not that they should mobilize for political purposes.[102] Schwartz may be correct in his assumption that self-help is the only reliable means through which poor people can improve their circumstances. But what form of self-help is likely to be most helpful: diligence or militance, sobriety or solidarity, thrift or protest?

Schwartz believes that moral reform must have a prominent place in the anti-poverty arsenal. But his conception of what this entails is astonishingly one-sided. He urges the poor to embrace virtue, in the expectation that this will ease their path out of poverty. Arguably, however, if not obviously, the persistence of poverty in the United States is due less to the misbehavior of the poor than to the "higher immorality" of the men and women who occupy positions of political and economic power.[103] It is not just unfair to demand that poor people carry the burden of moral reform; it is also not an effective anti-poverty strategy. If we are really serious about fighting poverty with virtue, then we need to talk about employers who cheat their employees out of overtime pay, who illegally fire workers with pro-union sentiments, and who transform full-time jobs into part-time jobs. We need to talk about corporate executives who negotiate exorbitant salaries for themselves while imposing pay and benefit reductions on the workers they have not yet downsized, who travel around the globe in search of the cheapest possible labor, and who devise clever accounting schemes to enrich themselves at the expense of employees, shareholders, and the larger public. We also need to talk about politicians who refuse to raise the minimum wage, who cut back social programs targeted to the poor while enacting huge tax cuts for the rich, who solicit campaign contributions from special interest lobbyists, and who provide generous subsidies to corporations while turning a blind eye to deteriorating inner cities.

Moral and cultural reform has a legitimate place on the poverty agenda. But why target only the culture of the poor? The corporate culture and the political culture seem every bit as dysfunctional, and with a far greater impact on the larger society. Why not expand our moral vision beyond the values of diligence, sobriety, and thrift to incorporate also the principles of equity, fairness, and equality of opportunity? More virtuous behavior on the part of the poor might prove beneficial, but we are likely to achieve substantial progress in the war against poverty only if we are prepared to conduct a moral crusade on a much larger scale. As a strategy for fighting poverty, moral reform requires the creation of a "moral economy"—one in which self-interest and the bottom line are not the only standards of behavior.[104] In their call for a renewed emphasis on values, proponents of the culture theory set their sights too low. The demand for moral reform cannot be separated from the larger movement for economic justice.

*Chapter Four*

# The Human Capital Theory of Poverty and Inequality

## EDUCATION IS THE KEY TO SUCCESS

When asked the best way to alleviate poverty, Americans commonly reply that government should see to it that everyone is furnished with a good education.[1] Education is the key to success, and lack of education is the primary cause of poverty. Human capital theory, an important strand of mainstream or "neoclassical" economics, offers a technically sophisticated version of this popular adage. The central idea of this theory, as it pertains to the problem of poverty, is that people are poor because they are deficient in education, skills, and work experience.[2]

In human capital theory, differences in earnings correspond to differences in productivity. The most capable and proficient workers get the best jobs, while less-competent workers, if they are able to find employment at all, are channeled into the low-wage sector of the economy. Workers are more or less productive, in turn, because they possess more or less *human capital*—education, training, and skills. Those rich in human capital contribute more to economic output, growth, and profitability, and they rightfully command a higher wage. The American economic system, in this theory, is a well-functioning meritocracy with workers getting what they deserve and deserving what they get.

Individuals vary in their level of human capital, this theory claims, because of differences in the choices they and their families have made about how much time, energy, and money to put into their education and training.

These choices are thought of as investment decisions, and they come into play as individuals consider how to live their lives and as they select between immediate and future rewards, leisure and work. How much people choose to invest in education and training depends primarily on their personal tastes and preferences. From the standpoint of human capital theory, these are exogenous variables. This means that the theory does not presume to explain people's desires (assigning this task to other disciplines, like psychology and sociology), but rather takes these as given. In mainstream economics, there is no accounting for taste. For whatever reasons, people vary in their aspirations and in how they wish to spend their time, and thus they are led to make different decisions regarding education and work. For example, human capital theory argues that women, preferring the role of mother, are generally less dedicated to a career than men, so they voluntarily work fewer hours and accumulate less job training and experience, and this, not discrimination, explains the bulk of the gender pay gap.[3]

With respect to poverty specifically, human capital theory, like the biogenetic and cultural theories, maintains that people are poor because they are lacking in qualities associated with job performance. In the biogenetic theory the poor have low IQs, and in the cultural theory they have negative attitudes. In human capital theory, similarly, people are poor because a history of unwise investment decisions has left them deficient in education, skills, training, and job experience. Poverty can best be reduced, accordingly, by inducing the poor to invest more in themselves (the conservative human capital solution) or by implementing government policies to assist the poor in overcoming their human capital weaknesses (the liberal human capital solution). In either case, proponents of this theory recommend as an antidote to poverty that individuals, for example, stay in school, earn a degree, build a record of stable employment, and take advantage of training opportunities. From the human capital perspective, the most effective way to combat poverty is to build up the skills of the poor. Whether through individual initiative or government programs, efforts to enhance the education and training of the poor will improve their prospects in the labor market, enabling them to work their way out of poverty.

In the following sections, I discuss two broad problems with human capital theory. First, this theory, with its emphasis on individual investment decisions, fails to deal adequately with the structural constraints hindering disadvantaged individuals from acquiring productive skills. How much training and education people receive is not primarily a matter of personal choice. It is dependent on family resources, access to opportunities, and business strategies and government policies beyond the control of the individual. Second, this theory also presents a misleading conception of the labor market. The process through which individuals convert their human capital into employment and earnings is not nearly as smooth and equitable as human capital theory implies. People vary in how much they are compensated for their skills, a good job does not necessarily follow from a good education, and economic success is dependent on a number of factors other than human capital, not least the availability of employment opportunities. At best, this theory offers a partial explanation for earnings differences, and the education and training proposals it recommends for fighting poverty are likewise bound to have only limited effectiveness.

## ACQUIRING HUMAN CAPITAL

People are poor, according to human capital theory, because they are deficient in education and skills, and this deficiency is the consequence of their own personal investment decisions. For this theory, as with the cultural theory, poverty results ultimately from the deviant preferences and misguided choices of the poor.[4] Their earnings are low because they have elected to live their lives in a manner that has left them inadequately prepared for the world of work. This excessively individualistic view of economic behavior fails to acknowledge how people's desires and decisions are influenced by the larger social and cultural context. Preferences are not purely personal qualities. They are the products of "social experiences and circumstances." They are shaped by "such factors as advertising, community standards, job expectations, the judgments of friends and relatives, and ideologies such as consumerism and religion."[5] The goals people pursue and the choices they make are also affected by the means at their disposal. As Jon Elster observes, preferences are "adaptive"; they reflect our social and economic status. We adjust our desires according to the possibilities allowed by our place in society.[6] Children from affluent families aspire to attend elite colleges and secure high-paying professional jobs in part because they are made aware from an early age that the resources to make this dream come true are readily available. Children from poor and working-class families, on the other hand, tend to scale down their ambitions to conform to their less favorable circumstances. And if they do not envision themselves going off to an Ivy League college in preparation for some high-status career, the fundamental cause may not be a lack of ambition, but a lifetime of inadequate resources.

Human capital theory's conception of investment behavior gives priority to preferences over constraints, choice over opportunity. It emphasizes the decisions people make concerning their education and training, but says little about the opportunities available to them and says even less about the social, economic, and political forces shaping those opportunities.[7] People succeed or fail not only because they make good or bad decisions, but also because of the circumstances under which they decide and the menu of alternatives placed before them. Individuals make choices, but they always do so within a given social context. The residents of poor communities, for example, confront a severely restricted range of educational possibilities. "What if all your [educational] choices are bad ones?" This is the dilemma faced by many parents in impoverished urban neighborhoods.[8] However determined they might be to ensure their kids get the best possible education, and however rational they might be in selecting a course of action, the schooling their children receive is still likely to be inferior. The extent and quality of the human capital people acquire, and their economic outcomes more generally, are not simply a product of their investment *decisions*; they are a product of their investment *options* as well.

People's decisions about education and training are conditioned not only by the opportunities at hand but also by their financial resources. People are "free to choose," certainly.[9] But they typically make the choices they can afford to make. Money matters. Poor parents do not have sufficient income to enroll their children in high-quality preschool programs, send them to private schools, hire tutors, purchase homes in neighborhoods with superior public schools, or ensure their children are afforded an abundant variety of educationally enriching experiences. And with tuition costs skyrocketing and scholarships in short supply, an increasing number of high school graduates from poor and working-class families have been priced out of a college education.[10] Even many solidly middle-class parents are "going broke" investing in their children's schooling.[11] Resource constraints may also limit access to forms of human capital other than formal education. Unemployed workers, for example, may not have the funds needed to enroll in a job-retraining program or finance a move across the country in search of new employment opportunities. People's level of investment in human capital is not just a product of their preferences and choices; it is also dependent on their economic resources and on the financial wherewithal of their families.

Individuals and families make human capital investments, but so do businesses and governments. Business firms invest in their employees by introducing new technologies and implementing training programs to upgrade workers' skills. Federal, state, and local governments invest in citizens, spending billions of tax dollars on education. How much human capital an individual accumulates therefore is not simply a function of personal choice; it is contingent also on the practices of business firms and the policies of government agencies. Employers decide whether or not to offer job-training opportunities in the workplace and which employees are eligible to receive them. This is not something that is normally at the discretion of the individual worker. Parents, likewise, do not in any simple manner choose how much public money is apportioned to the education of their children. This is decided in the political arena, as voters contend over tax issues and as communities and neighborhoods compete to maximize their share of scarce educational resources. The allocation of public funds for education is a matter of political power, not individual choice.[12]

Poor people are disadvantaged because they lack the opportunities and resources to invest fully in human capital. In addition, they often work in jobs with limited prospects for training and advancement, and they often reside in neighborhoods lacking the political clout to make sure their children's schools receive adequate funding. Bringing opportunities and resources more fully into the picture, and recognizing the role played by business and government investors as well, makes it clear that the amount of education and training people acquire cannot be attributed primarily to individual choices and personal preferences. People's access to human capital is conditioned by a multitude of factors beyond their control. Human capital differences, indeed, are much more the *consequence* of inequality than its *cause*.

An anti-poverty strategy predicated on enhancing the human capital of the poor would seem to have the cart before the horse. It is precisely their poverty—their economic marginalization, their lack of political power, their social and residential segregation—that limits poor people's access to education and training. In the absence of reforms addressing the more fundamental economic and political inequalities underlying persistent poverty, it is difficult to envision how the deep class and race disparities in access to education might be eradicated.[13] In any case, acknowledging the influence of poverty on the accumulation of human capital turns the basic thesis of this theory on its head. *People are not poor because they are deficient in human capital; they are deficient in human capital because they are poor.*

## CONVERTING HUMAN CAPITAL

It is one thing to acquire human capital, but it is quite another to cash in on the human capital one acquires. And just as people may encounter barriers in their efforts to accumulate productive skills, they may also face problems converting their education and training into earnings, employment, and social mobility. A diploma, after all, cannot be turned in at the bank for a weekly paycheck. Education is the key to success only if it unlocks the door to a good job, and there is nothing automatic about this, as many of today's college graduates are discovering.[14] Despite human capital theory's belief in the abundance of opportunities and the efficacy of the free market, there is no assurance that investments in human capital will be rewarded or rewarded equally.

In the ideal human capital theory world, productivity and earnings would perfectly correspond. Workers' wages would reflect their contribution to economic output. In the real world, however, human capital variables account for only a modest portion of the wage differences among individuals. Howard Wachtel estimates that even sophisticated measures of human capital explain only "about 20 percent of the variation in individual incomes."[15] Large earnings differences exist among workers with equivalent productive skills, and much of the rise in inequality in recent years is among individuals with similar levels of human capital.[16] Since the early 1970s, furthermore, the schooling and skill level of American workers have increased, yet wages have stagnated; while educational inequalities have decreased, earnings have grown more unequal.[17] The idea that education is the key to getting ahead is also difficult to reconcile with the fact that even before the Great Recession many highly skilled and professional workers were struggling to maintain their middle-class lives.[18] And since 2007, as Heidi Shierholz shows, the rate of long-term unemployment has increased for all educational groups, including those with a college degree.[19]

Human capital theory tells only a small part of a complicated story. People's employment and earnings outcomes are substantially influenced by variables unrelated to education, training, and job experience. Success or failure, as I will explain in the following four sections, is not just a product of what you know, as human capital theory implies. It is also dependent on (1) who you are, (2) who you know, (3) where you work, and (4) the availability of jobs.

## WHAT YOU KNOW OR WHO YOU ARE?

What counts most in the labor market according to human capital theory is what you know. But who you are also makes a big difference, and one aspect of who you are is how you look. For women especially, as Dalton Conley shows, physical attractiveness, weight in particular, has a significant effect on life chances. Women who are overweight suffer a wage penalty, while women who are conventionally good looking "can get a boost in their economic status." The "bottom line," Conley concludes, is that success for women "is less related to talent and hard work, since beauty muscles into the equation too."[20] In the following pages I will discuss three other aspects of who you are that also matter in the labor market: race/ethnicity and gender, cultural capital, and psychological capital.

### Gender and Race/Ethnicity

Women and racial/ethnic minorities encounter numerous disadvantages and obstacles in the labor market and are far more vulnerable to poverty than white males.[21] Even when comparing workers with equivalent levels of human capital, significant employment and wage inequalities by gender and race remain. Men have higher earnings than equally qualified women, and white workers have higher earnings that equally qualified minorities.[22] A college education, for example, is worth less on average for a woman than for a man, and less for a Latino or black man than for a non-Hispanic white man. Merit is not the only factor at play in the labor market. Race and gender influence which candidates get what jobs, who is promoted and who is not, who is fired and who is retained, and how much money workers make.[23] Individuals are not equal in their capacity to convert accumulated human capital into employment, nor are they equal in the rate of return they receive on their investments in education, training, and experience. The monetary value people derive from their human capital (and the quantity and quality of human capital they acquire) depends on a variety of ascribed traits, including whether they are male or female, black or white, Asian or Latino.

## Cultural Capital

The French sociologist Pierre Bourdieu is usually credited with bringing the concept of cultural capital into the study of inequality.[24] Cultural capital refers to certain dispositions, competencies, and preferences acquired through the process of socialization that influence social and economic outcomes.[25] As a result of their upbringing, people differ not only in their education, but also in their cultural background, experiences, and resources; in their "style, bearing, manner, and self-presentation skills"; in their "tastes in music, leisure, food, fashion"; and in their ability to "fit in" comfortably in diverse settings.[26]

Workers have a competitive edge in the labor market if their cultural capital puts them on the same page as employers, supervisors, and managers—the gatekeepers responsible for evaluating job performance and making decisions about hiring and promotion. Individuals who are attuned to the ways of the dominant culture are more at ease and perform better in the pre-job interview; they feel comfortable seeking advice and mentoring from co-workers; they are less likely to fall victim to misunderstandings in the workplace or experience prejudice and discrimination; and they are more likely to be perceived in a positive light by employers. Some retail and service firms, in fact, only hire individuals with the right look and the right sound, workers who can represent and embody the company's "brand."[27] The problem faced by many poor and working-class individuals, and by racial and ethnic minorities in particular, is that they do not project the right image. Their cultural repertoire may be dissimilar from, sometimes even at odds with, those of people in positions of power and authority. Because of differences in demeanor, dress, linguistic style, and the like, some workers may inadvertently foster negative impressions, leave themselves open to misjudgment, or evoke antipathy and hostility on the part of employers, co-workers, or customers. While human capital theory gives primacy to what you know, the concept of cultural capital draws attention to how lower-status workers may also be disadvantaged in the labor market by who they are.

## Psychological Capital

Another body of research highlights the importance of a different aspect of who you are: "noncognitive traits" and behavioral and personality attributes.[28] Employers hire and promote not just on the basis of workers' training and skills, but also on the basis of their "attitudes" and "character."[29] They desire *good* workers, not just skilled workers. They seek workers who are diligent, responsible, and conscientious, of course. But from the management standpoint, a good worker is also someone who is psychologically predisposed to obey the rules, comply with authority, perform in a habitually dependable manner, and identify with the firm.[30] In addition to "purely technical skills," employers value personality and behavioral traits that facilitate the accommodation of employees to the workplace "system of power."[31] In the blunt words of Roger Waldinger and Michael Lichter, "bosses want *willing* subordinates."[32] Employers are likely to be wary of job applicants who display a strong independent streak, who are prone to questioning orders, or who appear to have issues with authority. The workplace, particularly in the low-wage sector of the economy, as Barbara Ehrenreich observes, is more a dictatorship than a democracy.[33] Employers want subjects not citizens. The most desirable workers are those who follow rules rather than assert rights, who are dutiful rather than demanding, who are inclined to go along rather than speak out, and who exhibit loyalty to the employer rather than solidarity with co-workers.

Some of the characteristics employers might desire in their employees—subservience and conformism, for example—are not qualities normally valued in individuals outside the workplace. A "cheerful robot" might make a good worker, but not so much a good family member, friend, or citizen.[34] In the short run, workers gain by submitting to the regimen of the work setting—they receive a paycheck. In the long run, however, compliance to "workplace authoritarianism" takes a "psychological toll." "If you're made to feel unworthy enough," Ehrenreich suggests, "you may come to think that what you're paid is what you are actually worth."[35] In addition, by reinforcing the attributes often demanded of the working poor, low-status jobs, rather than serving as stepping stones to upward mobility, might leave workers unprepared and unqualified for higher-status jobs, where different psychological and behavioral traits are deemed desirable. A worker in the fast food industry who is taught to perform strictly according to the workplace manual may end up lacking in the qualities of self-determination and initiative that better jobs sometimes require.

The challenge posed by this research goes even deeper, however. The premise of human capital theory is that schools influence earnings by imparting productivity-enhancing skills. Among the key pieces of evidence in support of this contention is the correlation, albeit modest, between education and income. But as Samuel Bowles and Herbert Gintis argue, education raises earnings not only because students acquire productive skills in the classroom, but also because the school experience promotes attitudes and patterns of behavior that "assist in the exercise of the employer's authority."[36] Schools transmit knowledge, but they also function as agents of socialization, preparing students psychologically and behaviorally for the world of work.[37] Employers want educated workers not just because schooling makes students more skilled, but also because it habituates them to a regimented environment and renders them more easily subject to discipline and control. The statistical relationship between education and earnings does not unequivocally support the thesis of human capital theory. Schools increase what you know, making graduates more educated and skilled, but they also affect who you are, molding students into the kinds of workers valued by employers.

The quality of employers' information about the attitudes and character of job candidates is highly imperfect, with the result that hiring decisions, especially in the low-wage service sector, are based on inherently subjective judgments. Women and racial/ethnic minorities are particularly disadvantaged in this environment because there is so much room for stereotypes, prejudices, and cultural misconceptions to influence employers' assessments of who is an acceptable worker and what particular job he or she is best suited for. Employers' preference for *good* workers, not just skilled workers, in combination with racial and gender stereotypes, means that many poor people cannot necessarily expect to lift themselves out of poverty simply by increasing their education, training, and job experience.

## WHAT YOU KNOW OR WHO YOU KNOW?

Two individuals with equivalent levels of human capital may experience very different labor market outcomes due to differences in the characteristics of their social networks. One person is not well connected. She has few acquaintances outside a close circle of family members and neighbors, she has limited personal contacts in the work world, and she has no friends in high places. She is only aware of job vacancies when they are advertised in the newspaper; she lacks influential contacts who might advocate on her behalf when she does submit an application; and even when she lands a job, she cannot count on anyone to acquaint her with the ins and outs at her new place of employment. A second person knows people who know people. He regularly hears about job openings through the grapevine, he gets unsolicited calls from employers requesting he send in a resume, he can depend on a small army of acquaintances to certify he is the right man for the job, and friends of friends at his new workplace are eager to show him the ropes. While the first person may have her nose to the grindstone, the second has his foot in the door.

Human capital theory maintains that what you know is the key to success. As we have seen, who you are matters too. People's fortunes in the labor market are also conditioned by their social capital: the extent and quality of their social networks, social connections, and social ties. *Who* you know is often as important in getting ahead as *what* you know. The earnings and employment differences among individuals do not simply reflect inequalities in human capital; they reflect inequalities in social capital as well.[38]

Social networks are important because they are potential conduits of information and influence. They vary, however, in their value, in the extent to which individuals can exploit them to improve their life chances. Some social networks are "resource rich," while others are "resource poor."[39] Some individuals are embedded in networks yielding extensive and high-quality information and comprising people far enough up in the social hierarchy to influence the hiring decisions of prospective employers. Other people are embedded in networks conveying little useful information and made up of people—like themselves—who do not have much leverage in the labor market. Social capital is a valuable resource because it facilitates the conversion of human capital into employment and earnings; it lubricates the process through which workers are matched to jobs. High school graduates, for example, can more easily make the transition into the labor market, turning their degree into a job, if they have numerous friends who are already working, who keep them informed of employment vacancies, and who are willing to put in a good word for them. How well people are connected is one of the main determinants of who wins and who loses in the competition for jobs.

People differ in the extent and quality of their ties to others and in the resources available through such ties, and these differences influence their economic prospects. If someone is mired in poverty, the chief cause might not be so much a human capital, skills deficiency as a social capital, connections deficiency. The problem of resource-poor social networks is especially common among racial minorities isolated in segregated neighborhoods.[40] In a study of the working poor in the Harlem fast food industry, Katherine Newman found that residents had strong connections, but mainly to other workers in the low-wage labor market. These "lateral" networks made it relatively easy for workers to move from one low-wage job to another, but they rarely had friends, acquaintances, or personal contacts who could help them move up into higher-status jobs. While they gained skills and experience, and learned proper work attitudes as well, they nevertheless lacked the social network resources necessary to convert their accumulated human capital into a viable career.[41]

Racial minorities also encounter blocked opportunities because they are excluded from white social networks that tend to be more resource rich. In a remarkable study, Deirdre Royster compared the employment experiences of black and white working-class males, all graduates from the same trade school. The black males in her sample were equal, if not superior, to their white counterparts in human capital and in the personal qualities typically valued by employers. But black students did not receive the invaluable "networking support" from teachers and older workers that enabled white students, though often less qualified, to succeed in the labor market.[42] Particularly in an environment where most employers are white, black job seekers, despite having the requisite education and training, are significantly disadvantaged by their lack of well-placed connections. They do not have relatives, friends, and neighbors who can vouch for them, put them in contact with employers, or trade on past relationships to land them a job. Royster's study provides strong evidence that who you know can be more important than what you know, especially when race enters into the picture.

## WHAT YOU KNOW OR WHERE YOU WORK?

People differ, and so do their jobs. Some are located in the manufacturing sector, others in the service sector; some in the private sector, others in the public sector; some in large corporations, others in small businesses; some in growing and highly profitable industries, others in declining industries. The relationship between employers and employees is cooperative in some jobs, antagonistic in others; some are typically occupied by men, others by women; some are full time and secure, others part time and insecure; some are unionized, others not; and some offer opportunities for advancement, while others are dead end. Jobs differ in many, many other respects as well, but the bottom line is that some are better than others.

Individuals succeed or fail not just because they are good or bad workers, but also because they have good or bad jobs. What you know certainly influences where you work, but the process through which people are matched to jobs is contingent on many other factors as well, including who you are and who you know. It is not simply the case that good workers are inevitably slotted into good jobs and bad workers into bad jobs. Indeed, a good job might turn an otherwise bad worker into a good worker; and a bad job might turn an otherwise good worker into a bad worker. The recognition that some jobs are better than others underlines a key problem with human capital theory: by focusing exclusively on the qualities of workers, it downplays the independent influence of job characteristics on people's ability to accumulate valuable human capital and cash in on their skills and education. Success or failure, contrary to the premise of human capital theory, depends on where you work, not just what you know.

Human capital theory posits a causal relationship between productivity and earnings, suggesting that low-income workers can increase their wages by investing in productivity-enhancing human capital. An alternative perspective, drawn from "efficiency wage" theory, implies a reverse relationship.[43] According to this theory, higher wages—because they have a positive effect on motivation, effort, morale, and loyalty—can stimulate an increase in the productivity of the workforce. Well-paid employees are less likely to quit, shirk, or complain; they have an incentive to work hard because they have more to lose if they are fired; they are less likely to require costly supervision; and with higher wages they also have the financial resources to invest further in their own human capital. If the working poor are not very productive, perhaps this is due to their being stuck in low-wage jobs where effort reaps few rewards and where prospects for advancement are limited. Low-income workers have low productivity (and low earnings) not just because they are deficient in human capital, but also because they are trapped in bad jobs. How productive workers are and how much money they make depends on where they work, not just what they know.

Most work skills, economists argue, are learned on the job, and this is especially true in the case of workers just entering the labor force.[44] Jobs differ, however, in the extent to which they enable otherwise equal workers to acquire valuable skills. Workers accumulate human capital not just from the choices they *make*, but also from the jobs they are *given*. Human capital, this suggests, may be less a ticket to a good job than something one attains from having a good job.[45] The key to getting ahead, accordingly, is not just what you know, but where you work; where you work, furthermore, influences what you eventually come to know. Human capital theory assumes that poorly skilled workers end up in bad jobs. But the opposite is also true: bad jobs cause workers to be poorly skilled. People are poor not just because their choices have left them deficient in human capital, but also because they lack access to jobs that would allow them to increase their skills, acquire additional training, and enhance their productivity.

## SKILLS DEFICIT OR JOBS DEFICIT?

Human capital theory's account of employment and earnings outcomes downplays the effect of job characteristics, but it also falsely assumes that suitable employment opportunities are sufficiently available for qualified individuals.[46] If workers are doing poorly in the labor market, according to this theory, the only possible explanation is that they are poorly skilled. Human capital theory implies that jobs are essentially unlimited, such that all workers, at least over the long run, will find employment that corresponds to their level of education and training. It is not necessary, therefore, to change the economic system to remedy the problem of poverty. In this "field of dreams" image, as Teixeira and Mishel describe it, all that is needed is for poor people to acquire more education: "If we build the workers, jobs will come."[47]

From the human capital perspective, the problem of poverty is one of deficient workers, not deficient jobs, and the solution is to make workers less deficient. For many critics, however, poverty results more from a shortage of good jobs than a shortage of skilled workers. D. W. Livingstone, in a sustained analysis of the problem of "underemployment," documents a persistent and growing "education–jobs" gap.[48] More and more workers, he shows, are overqualified for their jobs, as in the case of the proverbial college graduate employed at Starbucks. Millions of people possess credentials, knowledge, skills, and talents that are underutilized in their work. Frederic Pryor and David Schaffer find that over the quarter century going into the 1990s, "jobs requiring relatively little education have increased faster than the number of less-educated prime-age workers," while "jobs requiring more education have increased more slowly than the number of more-educated prime-age workers."[49] Stephen Vaisey also documents widespread underemployment. He estimates that between 20 and 55 percent of full-time workers were overqualified for their jobs in 2002, almost double the rate for 1972.[50] This trend, exacerbated by the Great Recession, has become even more pronounced since 2000. According to Richard Vedder and his collaborators, more than 20 million college graduates were underemployed in 2010, with this number projected to rise to nearly 30 million by 2020. Over the next decade, millions of college graduates will be stuck working in jobs requiring only a high school degree.[51] Education does not guarantee success because the economic system cannot absorb all the skilled workers that the educational system can produce. The problem is not a shortage of good workers; it is a shortage of good jobs.

What is bad news for college graduates is disastrous news for the less educated. When many well-educated people are unable to find employment appropriate to their credentials, they search for jobs lower down in the labor market. The effect, however, is to crowd out less-educated workers who would otherwise get those jobs. These workers, then, are bumped down to an even lower tier or driven out of the labor force altogether.[52] The less educated are caught between a rock and a hard place. They are impeded from moving up into better jobs because of growing competition from more educated workers moving down. And if not forced into joblessness, they are confined to the low end of the labor market where employment opportunities have deteriorated over the past quarter century.[53]

With a surplus of educated workers, employers can afford to be choosy. They now hire college graduates for jobs that used to be filled by high school graduates. They may even insist that applicants have a college degree, even though less-educated workers are sufficiently skilled to perform competently on the job.[54] Such credential inflation—raising the level of education required of workers to be considered for a job—creates the illusion that occupational skill demands are increasing. The larger reality, however, contrary to the skill-deficit thesis, is that the American economy is simply not generating enough decent-paying jobs to accommodate the supply of able workers. This is the primary reason many people find it difficult to convert their human capital into a meaningful career: even in the best of times, there are not enough good jobs to go around. This jobs shortage, which is at the heart of the problem of poverty in the United States, hits the least educated hardest of all, limiting them to a low-wage career or shutting them out of the labor market entirely. Less-educated workers are forced to choose between a bad job and no job. The problem for many of the poor is not where you work, but if you work.

## CONCLUSION

Human capital theory maintains that people are poor because a history of unwise investment decisions has left them deficient in education, training, and job skills. This theory misdiagnoses the causes of poverty and prescribes remedies that will not solve the problem.

First, in human capital theory, people are poor because they lack education. The more valid conclusion, however, is that people lack education because they are poor. Low-income families do not have the resources and opportunities to make sufficient investments in education and training, either for themselves or their children. Nor, typically, are such families the chief beneficiaries when governments and businesses make collective human capital investments. Some poor people do indeed suffer from a deficiency in human capital, but this arises from the constraints of poverty and powerlessness, not the preferences of the poor.

Second, in human capital theory, the more skilled workers are, the more productive they are, and the more productive they are, the more they are paid. In contrast to this theory's highly idealized image of the labor market, in the real world, human capital is not so easily converted into employment and earnings, and it is not the key determinant of economic outcomes. Race and gender matter, and so do other forms of capital, including cultural, psychological, and social capital. Success or failure is not just due to what you know; it is also contingent on who you are, who you know, and where you work.

Third, in human capital theory, poverty is best alleviated by increasing the education, training, and job experience of the poor. This remedy ignores many other barriers commonly encountered by poorer Americans, including discrimination. More fundamentally, however, the human capital solution to poverty addresses only the problem of skills deficit and ignores entirely the problem of jobs deficit. The human capital remedy, making poor people into more productive workers, will not solve the problem because there are not enough good jobs to absorb the supply of good workers.

*Part II*

# A Structural Perspective on Poverty — Four Systems

*Chapter Five*

# The Economic System and Poverty

## THE ECONOMICS OF POVERTY

Patricia Reed, a fifty-seven-year-old college-educated woman, lost her job at Boeing four years ago and has been fruitlessly hunting for another one ever since. She worries she may never work again. "I have had nightmares about becoming a bag lady," she says. Struggling to support his family, Eduardo Shoy works more than seventy hours a week combining two low-wage jobs, one as a deliveryman in the fast food industry and the other as a forklift operator. "Tired," he asks? "I'm too busy to be tired." He was recently persuaded to join the union movement. "The restaurants are making all the money," Shoy remarks. "The worker isn't getting anything." Norman Echeverri works at LaGuardia Airport making $6.15 an hour, less than the minimum wage because it is presumed he sometimes receives tips for his services. "My life is not easy," he explains, "but they tell me there are a thousand out there who would take my job." Chardé Nabors, a Chicago mother of two, is employed as a cashier at Sears making nine dollars an hour. On Thanksgiving she worked from 7:30 p.m. to 6 a.m. "I'm here watching shoppers buy all these items, and I'm working to help these people, and I can't even buy my children the same products." Frank Sanders, a sixty-four-year-old Vietnam veteran, lost his factory job and has now run out of unemployment benefits. He and his disabled wife are living on a monthly Social Security check of $948. "I'm wondering where the next dollar is going to come from, or the next meal," he says. "When I'm not looking for work, my day is filled with a lot of pacing back and forth." Mary Carmen Acosta and her husband both lost their jobs three years ago. She helps put food on the table for her family by selling homemade *paletas* (ice pops). "We used to have a different kind of life, where we had nice things and did nice things." Now, she says, "we just worry."[1]

The ongoing transformation of the American economy has turned many lives upside down, as the experiences of these people and millions of others attest. Though certainly making the rich richer, four decades of economic restructuring, topped off by the most severe recession since the Great Depression, have brought significant hardship to working Americans: long-term unemployment for some, reduced wages for others, no health insurance for many, and increasing economic insecurity for most. Millions of families are falling behind, and millions more, in what some fear has become a permanently stagnant economy, have little chance of getting ahead.[2] Contrary to what the individualistic perspective would have us believe, the problem is not that Americans are deficient in cognitive ability, are lacking in skills, or have abandoned the work ethic. Indeed, no matter how diligently researchers might collect data on the demographics of low-income families and the characteristics of the poor, their findings will reveal little about the causes of today's poverty. The problem, rather, originates from a succession of fundamental and troubling changes that have occurred in the American political economy since the early 1970s.

Most of us need to find employment to earn a living and keep our heads above the poverty line. As individuals, however, we have little control over whether or not jobs are available and how much they pay. We are subject to the vicissitudes of the labor market. This market dependence is precisely what makes poverty a structural problem. Our life chances are contingent on external circumstances, on the dynamics of distant and seemingly mysterious economic powers. Far from being masters of our own economic fate, we are at the mercy of larger social forces: the vagaries of supply and demand, the uncertain judgments of policy makers, the hiring practices of employers, and the management strategies of business firms.

Change in the structure of employment opportunities is the primary determinant of fluctuations in the rate of poverty.[3] As a result of impersonal economic developments and the policy decisions of elites, it is sometimes easier to find a decent job and, as many millions of Americans are discovering today, sometimes downright impossible. When jobs are plentiful and wages high, the income of Americans goes up and the rate of poverty goes down, as happened, for example, during the short-lived boom of the late

1990s. When jobs are scarce and wages low, the income of Americans goes down and the rate of poverty goes up, as has been the case since the onset of the recession in 2007. The story is more complicated than this, of course. But still, if the objective is to understand the causes of poverty, the most sensible strategy is to begin by investigating the economic and political forces determining the quantity and quality of available jobs.

The economic well-being of the American population depends on the state of the economy. Nothing could be more obvious. Most people, even if they do not always read the financial tea leaves correctly, know that economic indicators convey good news or bad news: interest rates rise or fall, the stock market turns bullish or bearish, productivity growth speeds up or slows down, the trade deficit expands or contracts. Most people are also familiar with the vocabulary of economic turmoil: plant closings, outsourcing, offshoring, downsizing, layoffs, deindustrialization, and globalization. Americans realize, certainly, that external economic forces affect people's chances for a good life. They see abandoned factories, jobs moving overseas, and many of their communities decimated by mass unemployment; they experience wage reductions, benefit cuts, and downward mobility; and they recognize that some people enjoy tremendous advantages in life while others suffer great disadvantages. And yet, despite all the evidence to the contrary, many Americans persist in believing that individual effort is sufficient for success and that people are poor because they are lazy. Even in the midst of economic hard times, the individualistic perspective exerts a powerful hold on Americans' understanding of poverty and inequality.

## POVERTY AND ECONOMIC GROWTH

Looking back at American history since the end of World War II, we can discern two distinct eras: the period from 1945 to 1973 and the period from 1973 to the present. During the first period, sometimes referred to as the "golden age" of American capitalism, the standard of living in the United States, fueled by strong economic growth and rising productivity, more than doubled.[4] Real wages for workers rose steadily, and the rate of poverty declined sharply, from over 20 percent in the early 1960s to a historic low of 11.1 percent in 1973. This was an era of unprecedented economic prosperity. The future looked bright. The American Dream had become a reality, even if considerably less so for racial and ethnic minorities. During this golden age, the rising tide of economic growth did indeed lift most boats. As the economy grew, nearly everyone benefited: the rich got richer, the middle class thrived, and the poor became less poor and fewer in number. Beginning in the early 1970s, however, the American economy came unglued. Increasing prosperity turned into persistent stagnation. The economic boom of the postwar period gave way to what Harold Meyerson calls a "forty-year slump."[5] The pace of productivity growth and economic expansion slowed; corporate profits fell; earnings declined for much of the workforce; and unemployment and inflation increased simultaneously, yielding the new phenomenon of stagflation.[6] The early 1970s heralded the onset of a profound economic transformation, one that would alter the nature of work, the relationship between business and labor, and the economic future of American families. These years ushered in a new era of rising inequality and increasing economic insecurity.[7]

In the 1950s and 1960s, a growing economy fostered job creation and wage increases, enabling many low-income families to work their way out of poverty. Since the 1970s, however, the anti-poverty effectiveness of economic growth has greatly diminished: there has been "a reduced 'bang' for the economic growth 'buck.'"[8] An expanding economy today, as compared to the 1960s, generates fewer new jobs and has less of a positive effect on wage levels. In today's world, even in the midst of an economic upsurge, it is harder to get a good job than it was in the past and much harder to earn enough with a job to enjoy a decent standard of living. Economic growth is both more difficult to sustain in the present climate and less effective as a means for reducing poverty.[9]

The breakdown in the relationship between economic growth and the rate of poverty, first apparent in the 1980s, is a product of increasing earnings inequality. The economic pie continues to expand, though more slowly than in the past, but the wealthiest Americans are taking a bigger slice, leaving less for everyone else. As Thomas Piketty observes, income inequality in the United States has "exploded." The share of national income going to the top 10 percent increased from 30 to 35 percent in the 1970s to 45 to 50 percent in the 2000s, and the share going to the top 1 percent increased from 9 percent in the 1970s to 20 percent in the 2000s. Even more remarkably, the top 10 percent claimed 75 percent of the country's growth from 1977 to 2007, just prior to the financial collapse, and the top 1 percent alone, Piketty reports, "absorbed nearly 60 percent of the total increase of US national income in this period."[10] Since the end of the recession, the distribution of income has become even more skewed, with the wealthiest 1 percent gaining "93 percent of the additional income created in the country in 2010, as compared with 2009."[11] Because the gains from wealth creation and productivity growth have become increasingly monopolized by the rich, people in the bottom half of the income distribution are less able than in the 1960s to achieve self-sufficiency through work.[12] Increasing earnings inequality has thus severed the relationship between economic growth and poverty reduction. This circumstance is one of the key causes of continued poverty in the United States.[13]

## SKILL-BIASED TECHNOLOGICAL CHANGE

Increasing inequality causes the rate of poverty to remain high even during periods of economic growth. This is a significant discovery, but, as Isabel Sawhill observes, it merely substitutes "one puzzle for another."[14] Why has earnings inequality increased? One popular explanation attributes growing inequality to "skill-biased technological change" or skills mismatch. Technological advances, according to this theory, have altered the demand for labor. On the one hand, technology has increased productivity in the manufacturing sector. Labor-saving machinery makes it possible for fewer employees to produce more manufactured goods, thus decreasing the demand for blue-collar workers. On the other hand, technological innovations, particularly the introduction of computers into the workplace, have raised the demand for workers with sophisticated cognitive skills, making higher education more than ever a requirement for getting a good job. Technological change, this theory argues, has induced a shift in the demand for labor—to the advantage of those with more education, increasing their employment prospects and earnings, and to the disadvantage of those with less education, decreasing their employment prospects and earnings. The result is growing inequality and, for less-educated workers, a greater risk of poverty.[15]

According to the thesis of skill-biased technological change—a first cousin to human capital theory—less-educated workers do poorly in the current labor market and are unable to benefit from a growing economy because they are deficient in the abilities needed in today's increasingly computerized work world. If workers receive low wages, this is because they are lacking in skills or there is a mismatch between whatever skills they possess and the skills demanded by employers. The solution to problems of unemployment and low earnings, this line of thinking suggests, is the old standby: education and training.[16]

Though the technology theory enjoys widespread support, it cannot be easily reconciled with the data on income inequality. The big earnings gains since the 1970s have not gone to the wide swath of college graduates or technically trained workers, but to the top 1 percent or even the top 0.1 percent.[17] Is it conceivable that such a small minority so monopolizes the cognitive skills needed in today's economy? Workers in high-tech, computer-related fields, moreover, have not experienced notably rising wage levels in recent years.[18] Today's chief winners, making vast sums of money, consist of a small elite of corporate executives, investment bankers, and hedge fund managers.[19] And it is not just high school dropouts who are struggling in the current economy; more than a third of low-wage workers have at least some college education, and almost 10 percent are college graduates.[20] The problem with the technology theory is this: way too few people are gaining ground in today's economy and way too many are losing ground to believe that the distribution of earnings mirrors the distribution of technical skills.

The earnings gap between college-educated workers and those with a high school degree or less narrowed during the 1970s but widened significantly in the two subsequent decades, particularly during the 1980s.[21] This finding is often cited as evidence in support of the theory of skill-biased technological change. Economists, observing this pattern, often speak of a growing "college premium" or a rising "return to skills." College graduates, this language implies, are outpacing their less-educated counterparts because, with information technology invading the workplace, they possess increasingly valuable knowledge and abilities. This is misleading, however. In fact, the growing wage gap between college- and non–college-educated workers is due more to the declining earnings of the latter than to the rising earnings of the former. Between 1979 and 1994, according to Peter Gottschalk, the earnings of high school graduates declined by 20 percent, while the earnings of college graduates increased by only 5 percent.[22] Less-educated workers since 2002 have seen a further decline in their wages, but contrary to the skills shortage thesis, the earnings of college graduates in the 2000s have declined as well.[23] The major story—and the phenomenon most requiring explanation—is not that college-educated workers have gained so much ground in recent decades, but that most workers since 2000, college graduates included, have not fared well at all.

If technological change does play a role in causing earnings inequality, this is less because it rewards educated workers than because it punishes less-educated workers. But even in this modified formulation, the technology theory remains unconvincing. College graduates and high school graduates differ, of course, in their level of education, and college graduates, presumably (though with less certainty), are also more skilled than high school graduates. But because they differ in many other respects as well, the earnings gap between the more and less educated may be due to factors other than skill differences. For example, non–college-educated workers are more likely to be found in industries and occupations affected by the minimum wage, international trade, and unionization. Earnings for high school graduates have taken a nose dive over the past three or four decades not necessarily because technology has rendered less-educated workers obsolete, but because they have been hit especially hard by the fall in the real value of the minimum wage, heightened competition with cheaper foreign workers, and a decline in the size and strength of labor unions.[24] These developments have increased the exposure of high school graduates to competitive market forces, driving their wages down. On the other hand, for the time being anyway, at least some college graduates occupy protected professions. Their income is "safeguarded by elaborate systems of immigration control, licensing, educational credentials, and legal mandates." The salaries of professionals, Gordon Lafer argues, have been "propped up not by the rarity of their skills but by their ability to erect institutional barriers to competition."[25] The disadvantage faced by less-educated workers may not be so much a deficit of skills as a deficit of institutional support and bargaining power. As compared to college-educated workers, high school graduates are less able to shield themselves from the ravages of the market or to protect themselves from management cost-cutting strategies.

There are other reasons to be skeptical about the technology thesis. Technological change could have caused the sharp growth in earnings inequality, especially severe in the 1980s, only if an unusual acceleration of technological development kicked in sometime in the late 1970s. But there is no credible evidence of an extraordinarily rapid upsurge since 1980 in the normal pattern of skill upgrading in the occupational system. Neither the demand for skilled labor nor job requirements have risen faster since 1980 than in prior decades.[26] And since 2000, the demand for highly skilled labor has declined, while at the same time—shedding further doubt on the presumption of a skills shortage—the rate of unemployment for educated workers has increased.[27] Nor does it appear that the jobs of the future will be open only to those with high-tech skills. Fifteen of the thirty occupations projected to add the most jobs to the U.S. economy through 2022 require only "short-term on-the-job training," and another four of the thirty require only "moderate-term on-the-job training."[28] The implication that less-educated workers have been stranded at the station by some "roaring technological locomotive" is not supported by the available data.[29]

The increasing use of computers since the 1980s is commonly cited as the prime example of skill-biased technological change.[30] A computerized workplace necessitates a more skilled workforce, boosting the demand for the more educated and depressing the demand for the less educated. But, as James Galbraith observes, it does not require a college degree to work a computer, as the example of millions of American children attests.[31] Basic computer skills of the sort required in many work settings are not extraordinarily difficult to learn. Depending on the occupation, furthermore, computerization does not necessarily increase skill requirements at all and may even lead to deskilling: cashiers using scanners at the checkout counter, for example.[32] In addition, as many critics have pointed out, the pattern and timing of computerization does not correspond very well to the pattern and timing of changes in earnings inequality.[33] For example, much of the decline in the income of less-educated workers occurred early in the 1980s, before computer use became widespread.[34] And since the information technology revolution transformed the workplace, particularly in the period since the middle 1990s, the growth of the earnings gap between high school and college graduates has slowed.

The theory of skill-biased technological change is also inconsistent with the international data. Because developed nations are subject to the same technological imperatives, the pattern of increasing wage inequality observed in the United States should be evident in other advanced countries as well. As several studies show, however, only in the United States and the United Kingdom was there a substantial increase in wage inequality during the 1980s.[35] If technological change is such a potent cause of growing inequality, why are its effects not felt more deeply and uniformly throughout the industrialized world? Something other than technology must be responsible for the collapse in wages for low-end workers in the United States, since less-educated workers in European countries, where computerization is equally pervasive, have not experienced the same pattern of wage decline over the past quarter century.[36]

Technological development is not irrelevant to the fate of American workers, of course. But the consequences of technological change—whether it causes wages to go up or down, the rate of poverty to rise or fall, and the

distribution of earnings to become more or less equal—depend on the response of policy makers and the surrounding "institutional framework," the
rules of the game, and these in turn reflect the existing constellation of
political and economic power.[37]

## A SHIFT IN THE BALANCE OF ECONOMIC POWER

The "power shift" theory is the chief rival to the thesis of skill-biased technological change.[38] This theory recognizes a fundamental division of interest
between business owners, impelled to maximize profits and shareholder value, and workers, pursuing higher wages and better working conditions. The
conflict between these two classes—played out in the labor market and the
workplace, the political arena and the news media—is a primary determinant
of wage levels and profit rates. While the technology theory underscores the
presumably neutral market forces of supply and demand, the power shift
theory emphasizes how employers over the past thirty years or so have become firmly ensconced "in the driver's seat," and how this shift in the balance of power between business and labor has affected the distribution of
income and wealth.[39] From this perspective, millions of Americans suffer
from low earnings and inadequate employment not because they lack useful
skills, but because they lack economic and political power.

American corporations in the 1970s, at the close of the post-war golden
age, embarked on a program to restructure the American economy.[40] By
altering investment strategies, transforming employment relations, and reor-
ganizing the workplace, corporate leaders sought to boost profits, primarily
on the backs of the working class.[41] To remain competitive, business firms
might have pursued a "high road," "carrot" strategy. They might have tried to
enhance efficiency by enlisting the cooperation of the labor force, by investing in the human capital of their workers, and by winning the commitment of
employees through an equitable sharing of the fruits of increased productivity.

Despite the success of this "high road" strategy in other countries, most
American corporations, increasingly wedded to the short-term goal of max-
imizing shareholder value, adopted a "low road," "stick" strategy instead.[42]
With a single-minded devotion to the bottom line, they disinvested in basic
industry; they relocated manufacturing plants to low-wage countries; they
initiated an aggressive and exceedingly successful campaign against labor
unions; they assumed a highly adversarial stance in labor negotiations,

threatening layoffs and plant closings to force employees to accept wage concessions and benefit reductions; and they downsized the labor force, eliminating many standard jobs and replacing permanent employees with a disposable workforce of temporary workers, part-timers, and contract laborers. American corporations since the 1970s—placing their interests and the interests of shareholders above those of workers, customers, communities, and the country itself—have followed the "low road" to profitability. This explicit management strategy, which both emanated from and added to the growing imbalance of power between business and labor, has resulted in a decline in the rewards of work. Four growing disparities provide evidence on this point.

*The profits–wages disparity.* Corporate profits have increased as a share of national income growth, while wages and salaries have decreased. This trend, evident in the late 1970s, has escalated dramatically since 2001. After-tax corporate profits in 2013 reached a post–World War II record high, and employee compensation fell to a record low.[43] This pattern, as Tali Kristal shows, is due primarily to the decline of unionization and the consequent erosion of workers' bargaining power.[44] During the "golden age" of the immediate post-war years, it was not implausible to imagine that what was good for American corporations was good for American workers and that rising profits would rebound to the benefit of all. In the current era, however, the supposition that "we are all in the same boat," that when business prospers everyone gains, is no longer credible.

*The productivity–pay disparity.* In the 1960s, workers' earnings rose proportionately to productivity. Beginning in the 1970s, however, with business leaders determined to cut labor costs, a sizable pay–productivity gap emerged. Worker compensation fell behind productivity growth. Between 1973 and 2011, labor productivity increased by more than 80 percent, while hourly wages grew by only 10.7 percent.[45] Indeed, according to one study, over the entire period from 1966 to 2001, only the top 10 percent of Americans received real earnings gains equal to or greater than the rate of productivity growth.[46] In the new economy of the twenty-first century, workers produce more and are paid less.

*The supervisory work–production work disparity.* Wage and salary employees can be categorized as either production workers or supervisory workers. As David Gordon shows, a "massive income shift" has occurred since the 1970s from the first group, those who actually do the work, to the second group, those who watch over those who do the work. The rewards from productive labor have declined relative to the rewards from supervisory labor.[47]

*The corporate executive–worker disparity.* A comparison of the compensation of corporate executives and workers reveals the same increasingly skewed distribution of income. From 1978 to 2013, CEO earnings increased by nearly 1,000 percent, while the typical worker during this period enjoyed an increase in earnings of barely 10 percent. In 2013, the typical CEO of a large firm received in compensation 296 times that of the typical worker. This was down from a peak compensation ratio of 383 to 1 in 2000, but far greater than the quaint 1965 ratio of 20 to 1.[48]

According to the technology theory, wages are regulated by neutral market mechanisms, ensuring a fair distribution of earnings. Increasing inequality, from this perspective, is the result of inexorable technological changes and the impersonal laws of supply and demand. According to the power shift theory, on the other hand, wages are set by antagonistic power relations, with *might* more than *merit* determining the allocation of rewards. Increasing inequality, from this alternative perspective, is the result of contingent economic and political decisions. In the technological theory, poverty is primarily a problem of lousy workers; in the power shift theory, lousy jobs. In the technology theory, the least powerful people in society bear responsibility for the persistence of poverty. Low-income workers have failed to make the necessary investments in human capital and are thus unable to take advantage of the opportunities afforded by today's high-tech economy. In the power shift theory, the most powerful people in society bear responsibility for the persistence of poverty. Corporate executives have used their economic leverage to drive down employee compensation and boost profits, and they have used their political leverage to pressure government officials to pursue an agenda favoring business over labor.

The structural perspective, building on the power shift theory, draws attention to how the transformation of the American economic system since the early 1970s has produced a deterioration in the quality of jobs, especially for less-educated workers. The key to the declining prospects of low-end workers over the past three decades is not a technology-induced shift in the demand for labor, but rather a business-induced shift in the balance of economic and political power. This chapter focuses specifically on how certain broad economic changes—including deindustrialization, globalization, and corporate restructuring—have undermined the American dream for millions of working Americans, increasing their vulnerability to poverty. From this structural perspective, the poor and the near poor suffer from low earnings and joblessness not because they are deficient in cognitive skills, work motivation, or human capital, but because they are deficient in economic and political power.

## DEINDUSTRIALIZATION

In June 2003, the Hoover vacuum cleaner factory located in Canton, Ohio, laid off much of its workforce, including fifty-five-year-old Jim Greathouse. He had worked for Hoover for nearly three decades, sometimes earning as much as $50,000 a year. Because of mass job losses in the manufacturing sector in the Midwest, Greathouse was unable to find work in another tool-and-die plant. As of September 2003, he was contemplating personal bankruptcy and awaiting career advice from a vocational counselor. Many laid-off blue-collar workers like Greathouse will never find another factory job, and if they remain in the labor force they will be drawn into the burgeoning service sector instead. "A lot of people are going to work at Wal-Mart," explained one longtime veteran of Republic Steel. "But how do you live on the $7.50 an hour Wal-Mart pays?"[49]

Jim Greathouse, along with tens of thousands of other workers like him, is a victim of "one of the major transformations of the twentieth century."[50] In a landmark study from the early 1980s, Barry Bluestone and Bennett Harrison refer to this transformation as the "deindustrialization of America."[51] Beginning in the 1970s, they argue, corporate America, in response to declining profits and increased international competition, undertook "a widespread, systematic disinvestment in the nation's basic productive capacity." Instead of using investment funds to upgrade and expand essential manufacturing industries, corporate executives diverted the nation's financial resources from "productive investment" into "unproductive speculation, mergers and acquisitions, and foreign investment." This management strategy, though it improved the bottom line for many businesses, left in its wake "shuttered factories, displaced workers, and a newly emerging group of ghost towns."[52]

In one case study, economists Charles Craypo and David Cormier examine the effects of deindustrialization on the lives of workers and their families in South Bend, Indiana.[53] In the 1950s and 1960s, South Bend was predominantly a manufacturing city, but over the next two decades, much of its basic industry disappeared. Employment in manufacturing decreased from 63 percent to 20 percent between 1951 and 1994, while employment in services, including retail trade, increased from less than 30 percent to 70 percent.[54] In combination with union decline, deindustrialization depressed wages and precipitated a rise in the number of working-poor households. The low earnings of workers in South Bend today, Craypo and Cormier insist, explicitly challenging individualistic theories, are not due to lack of human capital, but to a dearth of good jobs. The problem of poverty in South Bend, as elsewhere, is a structural one: it derives from the poor quality of employment opportunities, not the poor quality of the workforce.[55]

The phenomenon of deindustrialization has occurred, with regional variations, throughout the country.[56] Between 1959 and 1969, the number of U.S. workers in manufacturing increased from 15.3 to 18.6 million.[57] Three decades later, in 1999, with a labor force almost twice the size, the number of factory jobs was down to 17.3 million. The decline of manufacturing employment has escalated in the 2000s, hitting a historic low of 11.5 million in 2010, rising modestly to 12.1 million in 2014. The number of workers currently employed in retail trade alone, one of the lowest-paying job classifications, exceeds the number in manufacturing.[58]

The scale of this economic transformation is even more apparent by looking at changes in the share of employment by industry. The broad trend shows a marked decline in the percentage of workers in the "goods-producing" sector, consisting mostly of manufacturing jobs, and a significant increase in the percentage of workers in the "service-providing" sector.[59] Between 1970 and 2014, the share of private-sector non-agricultural employment in manufacturing declined from 38 percent to less than 11 percent. Almost 85 percent of non-agricultural private-sector jobs today are in the service-providing industries. This pattern is anticipated to continue into the future. Though jobs in mining and construction are expected to increase, the number of manufacturing jobs is predicted to decline through the next decade. The thirty occupations projected to add the most jobs to the U.S. economy through 2022, mostly low-paying jobs, are almost all located in the service sector.[60]

The deindustrialization of America has reshaped the labor market and transformed the structure of employment opportunities. The decline of the manufacturing sector and the rise of the service sector have significantly altered the characteristics of the jobs available today, the kinds of careers people might pursue, and the possibilities for them to achieve a secure future. Service jobs, on average, pay less than manufacturing jobs, and wage levels in the service sector, as compared to those in the manufacturing sector, are also much more unequal. At one end are high-paid lawyers, doctors, and investment bankers, while at the other end are low-paid child-care workers, waitresses, and home health-care aides.[61] A shift in the composition of employment from manufacturing, where there is less inequality and fewer low-paying jobs, to services, where there is greater inequality and more low-paying jobs, yields an overall rise in earnings inequality and an increase in the number of workers stuck in the low-wage job market.[62]

The service-providing industries include an assortment of jobs "encompassing many of the 'best' jobs in the economy and a substantial share of the 'worst.'"[63] It is incorrect, certainly, to characterize service employment as necessarily bad. It is equally incorrect to think of manufacturing employment as necessarily good. As Ruth Milkman reminds us, many of the bygone factory jobs were brutal. The workers in the General Motors automobile plant she studied often used the "metaphor of imprisonment" to describe their term of employment.[64] But while working conditions were awful, the pay and benefits, thanks to strong labor unions, enabled many blue-collar workers with limited formal education to enjoy a middle-class standard of living.[65]

In the immediate post-war years, young men just out of high school could reasonably hope to get a union job in a factory and build a successful career in manufacturing. Deindustrialization, by closing off the traditional blue-collar route to the American Dream, has hit non–college-educated workers especially hard. Relatively few entrants into the U.S. labor force in the twenty-first century will work in what remains of the automobile or steel industries; and those who do will discover that manufacturing jobs today do not pay nearly as well as they did during the heyday of American industry.[66] Most new job seekers, in any case, will end up working as waiters and waitresses, food preparation workers, nursing aides, retail salespersons, janitors, receptionists, and security guards. As compared to manufacturing jobs of the past, the service jobs most of today's non-college-educated workers will get are likely to be significantly inferior in pay, benefits, hours, advancement prospects, and job security.[67] In general, the contrast between the manufacturing sector and the service sector is not one of good jobs versus bad jobs. But from the standpoint of less-educated workers specifically, this is the essential reality. Deindustrialization, along with the proliferation of low-paying service-sector jobs, has eroded opportunities for workers without a college degree to earn a decent living and avoid poverty through employment.

There is nothing necessarily regrettable about deindustrialization. Nor is it inevitable that the replacement of manufacturing jobs by service jobs be accompanied by a decline in the standard of living of American workers. In many European countries, where institutional protections are in place, workers have not been hit so hard by the shrinking of the manufacturing sector.[68] Service workers in the United States fare poorly not because of any iron law of economics but because they lack the leverage to bargain for better pay and improved working conditions, they are poorly protected by existing labor laws, they are rarely unionized, and the minimum wage remains too low. Without a general improvement in the quality of low-end service jobs—turning these bad jobs into good jobs—millions of employees, however hard they might work, will continue to earn less than a living wage.

## GLOBALIZATION

The term "globalization" is commonly used to refer to the growing integration of national economies, an outcome of increased international trade. As compared to the 1950s and 1960s, countries today are more heavily dependent on exports, imports, foreign investment, and immigrant labor. What most characterizes the current era of globalization is the increasing permeability of national borders and the heightened velocity of capital mobility, evidenced by the incessant and worldwide movement of production facilities and investment funds. Technological advances, including the development of giant shipping containers, have facilitated globalization by lowering the costs of air and sea transportation.[69] Because shipping is cheaper, business firms are less tied to a single location. They can readily manufacture goods in one country and sell them in another; they can fabricate a final product by assembling components produced in plants at multiple and distant sites; and, with new telecommunication technologies, a corporation headquartered in one country—with the aid of instant messaging and e-mail, cellular phones and conference calls—can monitor and coordinate business activities in far-flung places around the globe.[70] Globalization is not only an economic and technological phenomenon, however; it is a political phenomenon as well. Policies legislated by national governments, inscribed in trade agreements, and presided over by international organizations have played a pivotal role in facilitating capital mobility. Policy-making institutions and agreements, including the World Trade Organization and the North Atlantic Free Trade Agreement, have set forth "rules of the new global economy" promoting free trade and free capital flows.[71] Talks are currently under way to create a new Trans-Pacific Partnership. But as is typically the case in such negotiations, public interest groups are relegated to the sidelines while "big corporations are playing an active role in shaping the American position."[72] In the politics setting forth the rules of the new global economy, the "rights of workers" are subordinate to the "rights of capital."[73]

During the quarter century following World War II, imports composed only a small portion of domestic purchases, and American corporations in the U.S. market were relatively insulated from foreign competition. Consumers did not have to be urged to "buy American"—they had little alternative. By the 1970s, however, Japan and Western Europe, rebuilt from wartime destruction, emerged as powerful economic rivals to the United States. Foreign businesses came into competition with American corporations not only in markets abroad, but for the dollars of American consumers as well. Between 1969 and 1979, the value of imports to the United States, as a percentage of gross national product, nearly doubled.[74] In the 1980s and 1990s, international competition only intensified, as developing countries in Asia and Latin America, vying to export their own manufactured goods, entered the fray. In more recent years, China, India, and the former Soviet Union—benefiting from rapid technological development, the expansion of higher education, and a seemingly endless supply of low-wage labor—have become big players in the global market economy. Fierce competition from China, abetted by giant retailers like Walmart, has driven numerous U.S.-based manufacturing firms overseas or out of business, with millions of American workers losing their jobs. Meanwhile, the ratio of imported goods to exported goods has risen substantially since the mid-1980s, enlarging the trade deficit, with most of this due to increasing imports from low-wage, developing countries.[75]

In a global economy, where trade and investment flow freely, workers in relatively high-wage countries like the United States, particularly those with no more than a high school degree, find themselves in competition with millions of workers in less-developed countries. While they sometimes lack the education, skills, and experience of the labor force in developed nations, foreign workers are attractive to employers because they can be hired at a fraction of the cost. This circumstance places U.S. workers in a precarious position, especially those in the trade-sensitive manufacturing sector. By enlarging the "global labor pool," doubling its size according to Richard Freeman, the internationalization of the economy renders American workers more replaceable—increasing their economic insecurity, diminishing their bargaining power, and putting a downward pressure on wages.[76] Some people are bound to benefit from international trade, but in the United States it has exacerbated the imbalance of power between business and labor, and the gains so far have been distributed in a highly unequal manner, with multinational corporations winning big and less-educated workers losing big.[77]

The phenomenon of globalization attests to the profound influence of larger structural forces on people's life chances and economic outcomes. Globalization has reshaped the labor market, reducing the quality of jobs available to many Americans. It has shifted the balance between corporations and governments, limiting the scope for democratic decision making. And it has altered the relationship between business and labor, weakening the ability of workers to negotiate a fair share of the nation's growing wealth. The following list identifies some of the pathways, both direct and indirect, through which globalization adversely affects the employment opportunities and economic prospects of American workers.[78]

First, many American businesses, in an effort to reduce labor costs, have turned to outsourcing or offshoring. The goods sold by an increasing number of U.S.-based firms are assembled from imported components that used to be manufactured by American workers.[79] In other cases, U.S. manufacturers have relocated their entire production facilities to low-wage countries where workers are plentiful and easy to mobilize and manage. Levi Strauss, for example, along with other jeans manufacturers, ended all production in North America in the early 2000s, laying off thousands of workers and moving its operations to the Caribbean, Latin America, and Asia where labor is cheaper. "What happens to our American dream?" asks one twenty-four-year veteran of the jeans industry, now facing an uncertain future in the service sector.[80] Apple is another example. Almost all the millions of iPhones and iPads sold each year, along with most other consumer electronics, are manufactured outside the United States. The Foxconn City facility in China has 230,000 employees, more than a quarter of whom live in company barracks. Many of the workers who assemble iPhones at this facility, some working more than sixty hours a week, make less than seventeen dollars a day. These jobs, which translate into big profits for American corporations, will not be coming back to the United States.[81] Manufacturing workers have been hit hardest by globalization, but with employers seeking to benefit from the surplus of

educated labor in China, India, and elsewhere, the movement of jobs overseas is a growing concern for skilled service-sector workers as well.[82]

Second, global competition, by putting pressure on American firms to
lower labor costs, also affects job quality in the United States. International
trade, Adrian Wood argues, prompts "defensive innovation." To "fight off"
imports and remain competitive, domestic businesses introduce new "methods of production" that reduce the need for or the price of unskilled labor.[83]
Such "defensive innovation" has occurred, for example, in the agricultural
industry. U.S. farm workers barely average six dollars an hour. But while
agricultural labor in this country is cheap, as one California raisin grower
states, it "isn't cheap enough." To remain competitive with foreign industry
where labor costs are much lower, American agribusiness has turned to labor-saving technologies, replacing hand harvesting of crops with mechanical
harvesting.[84] In a competitive international environment, U.S.-based firms
have become exceedingly cost conscious, determined to reduce the price of
labor, whether by displacing workers with machines or by forcing workers to
accept lower wages.

Third, workers dislocated by plant closings and layoffs due to globalization, if they remain in the labor force, typically have to settle for service-
sector jobs with lower wages and fewer health and retirement benefits. With
the decline of manufacturing employment, formerly blue-collar workers, as
well as many new entrants into the labor market who might have pursued a
factory job, are thrown into an already crowded low-wage service sector,
creating a "glut of job candidates."[85] In this manner, globalization not only
threatens manufacturing employment; it also keeps a lid on the wages of
service workers, even though many service jobs are not directly exposed to
foreign competition.[86]

Fourth, globalization has negative wage and employment effects because
it provides employers with a powerful weapon in their battle to discourage
the formation of labor unions. As plant closings and outsourcing have become everyday realities, business firms can credibly threaten to shut down or
relocate operations if workers attempt to unionize. In a systematic study of a
large sample of union organizing drives in 1998 and 1999, Kate Bronfenbrenner found that plant closing threats, in combination with other tactics
both legal and illegal, were a "pervasive and effective component of employer anti-union strategies." "In the current climate of corporate restructuring,
burgeoning trade deficits, constantly shifting production, and the fear of job
loss they have engendered," Bronfenbrenner argues, "most workers take

even the most veiled employer plant closing threats very seriously."[87] Globalization creates an economic environment enabling employers to more effectively resist unionization.

Fifth, global competition and plant closings have engendered an atmosphere of "heightened job insecurity." According to former Federal Reserve Chairman Alan Greenspan, this explains why wages remained unexpectedly low during the 1990s, and why "profits and rates of return on capital have risen to high levels."[88] Even when unionization is not an issue, employers—invoking the specter of international competition—effectively exploit worries about job security to force workers into accepting wage cuts and benefit reductions.[89] In the new global context, employers have the upper hand, and they are not reluctant to use it. According to a *New York Times* report, "even many employers with solid profits are demanding concessions."[90] By fueling fears of job loss, globalization has altered the balance of power between business and labor, enabling employers to insist that workers take a smaller piece of the economic pie.[91]

Sixth, globalization undermines democracy. The increased mobility of capital adds to the leverage corporations have over local, state, and national governments and augments the "privileged position" of business in the American political system.[92] Because firms nowadays are freer to relocate, governments are even more constrained than normally to do the bidding of business. "When business can produce and invest abroad as easily as at home," James Crotty observes, "any government policy not perceived to be business friendly may induce the export of jobs and productive capital."[93] For fear of provoking capital flight, governments have less leeway to pursue policies that might increase workers' incomes: raising the minimum wage, easing requirements for organizing labor unions, or increasing taxes to strengthen the safety net. Capital mobility impedes the ability of governments to introduce redistributive tax and spending policies, including programs that might compensate the losers in international trade.[94] By imposing constraints on government policy, globalization adds to the economic hardship experienced by many workers, and not just those in industries directly susceptible to foreign competition.[95]

The deterioration of the earnings and employment prospects of American workers is due to a variety of economic and political forces. Globalization is only one cause among many, and it does not inevitably generate job losses or wage reductions. The culprit, indeed, is not globalization as such, but its existing form, what some call "neoliberal" globalization.[96] Three characteristics of the neoliberal regime stand out: (1) a philosophy preaching the dangers of intervention by national governments (e.g., regulatory policies and tariff barriers) and heralding the superiority of free-market and free-trade practices; (2) a system of rules governing trade established by international agencies, such as the World Trade Organization, whose operation is unconstrained by any democratic accountability; and (3) the premise that good trade policies are those that best serve the goals of multinational corporations. Neoliberal globalization, with little regard for the interests of labor, promotes free-market capitalism on an international scale, and in this incarnation, globalization does indeed play a significant role in the perpetuation of poverty and inequality. But even under these conditions, national political institutions and policies mediate the effects of international trade on employment and earnings.[97] The impact of globalization is more or less harsh depending, for example, on the strength of a country's welfare state and on whether or not social programs exist to compensate victims of economic dislocation. Many of the negative consequences of globalization in the United States arise not from international economic imperatives, but from domestic political choices. The problem in this country is that we have a "more cutthroat form of capitalism" where individuals, more so than in other developed countries, are left on their own in managing the destructive consequences of an increasingly global economy.[98]

## CORPORATE RESTRUCTURING

Globalization has diminished employment opportunities, depressed wages, and increased the likelihood of poverty for many Americans. But workers employed in industries subject to foreign competition and capital mobility are not the only ones to encounter hardship in today's economy. Globalization is only part of the problem. Deindustrialization is another factor. Workers typically receive lower wages and fewer benefits as they are pushed out of manufacturing jobs and pulled into service jobs. But deindustrialization too is only part of the problem. Much of the increase in earnings inequality since the 1970s has been within industry sectors, and both service workers and manufacturing workers have experienced declining economic fortunes over the past three decades. Changes in hiring and wage-setting practices and in the relationship between business and labor are a third important factor. Sometimes referred to as corporate restructuring, this shift in employment relations has caused adversity for workers across the board—those in occupations exposed to global competition as well as those relatively insulated from international trade, those in the shrinking manufacturing sector as well as those in the expanding service sector.

As part of their restructuring efforts, U.S. corporations have replaced many of their regular, full-time employees with workers who occupy a "contingent" or "nonstandard" status.[99] Robert Kuttner describes this "move to insecure, irregular jobs" as the "most profound economic change of the past four decades."[100] This strategy permits employers to fulfill their need for labor without making any costly long-term commitment to the workers who supply it. In 1993, *Time* magazine drew attention to the changing nature of employment in a featured story entitled "The Temping of America." Lance Morrow, in an introductory piece, announced the advent of a new epoch: "America has entered the age of the contingent or temporary worker, of the consultant and subcontractor, of the just-in-time work force—fluid, flexible, disposable. This is the future. Its message is this: You are on your own." In this new regime, he reports, companies have become "strangely conscienceless," jobs are "vanishing into thin air," full-time workers are reduced to part-timers, and employees are "throwaway." The "human costs" of this "merciless and profound" transformation, Morrow declares, are "enormous."[101] In an accompanying article, Janice Castro describes the rise of the "disposable" workforce as "the most important trend in business today."[102]

With business firms relying more heavily on a flexible and low-cost contingent labor force, opportunities for workers to secure permanent employment have diminished. Of course, some people prefer something other than a nine-to-five job with a single employer. But most non-standard workers—including those employed as day laborers, temporary workers, and part-timers—are forced into these precarious labor arrangements because they cannot get regular jobs. The people who compose this involuntarily disposable workforce (1) consist disproportionately of women and racial and ethnic minorities; (2) are typically paid less than regular employees with comparable skills and experience; (3) are less likely to receive fringe benefits; (4) tend to be employed in the secondary or low-end sector of the economy; (5) are rarely represented by labor unions; and (6) face highly uncertain employment, career, and retirement prospects.[103]

## Day Labor

On any single day, according to the National Day Labor Study, nearly 120,000 workers seek jobs as day laborers, trying to eke out a living on a day-to-day basis.[104] They search for work at informal street markets, at curb-side labor pools outside places like Home Depot, or through temporary employment agencies and "hiring halls."[105] Most day laborers are men, and most are undocumented immigrants.[106] They are typically employed in construction, landscaping, and gardening, as movers and haulers, painters and roofers, housecleaners, farmworkers, and dishwashers.[107] Their median hourly wage is ten dollars, but they sometimes wait around for long periods of time without getting a job, and because of the instability of their work, their monthly and yearly wages place them squarely "among the working poor."[108] On Long Island, in the midst of the recession, and with fierce competition for jobs, day laborers were lucky to find work two days a week. One man, hoping to make enough money to return to Mexico, reported that he is sometimes unable to sleep because he is "thinking about work and nothing else."[109] With jobs scarce and no money for housing, many day laborers since the recession have been forced into homelessness.[110] Besides being low paying and unstable, the jobs they manage to obtain rarely provide "benefits or workplace protections."[111] Vulnerable also due to their race and immigrant status, day workers are routinely denied their legal rights.[112] They are regularly cheated out of their wages, abused and insulted by employers, denied food and water breaks, and harassed by the police and local residents. Their jobs are unusually hazardous as well, with the majority of day laborers losing some work time due to employment-related injuries.[113]

## Temporary Workers

The "explosive growth" in the use of temporary workers, now "an integral feature of firms' personnel strategy" in blue-collar as well as white-collar industries, is one of the most notable signs of the changing nature of employment in the United States.[114] The share of private-sector workers employed by temp agencies increased from 1.3 percent in 1990 to 2.3 percent in 2006; and throughout much of 2003 and into 2004, temps were "the fastest-growing segment of the work force."[115] Though many were laid off during the recession, since the beginning of 2010, more than a quarter of added private-sector jobs have been filled by temporary workers. And with employers reluctant to commit themselves to permanent hires, the ranks of the temporary labor force are bound to grow.[116] For most job seekers, temping is a last resort, with numerous drawbacks. Temporary workers receive lower wages, they have less job security, they have little prospect for advancement, they are typically ineligible for retirement benefits or employment-based health insurance, and they are vulnerable to poverty.[117] Most temps, of course, would rather have permanent jobs, but like Jeffrey Rodeo who applied for almost seven hundred full-time positions without getting an offer, they have little choice in the matter.[118] And with regular jobs in short supply, many temps have become permatemps, condemned to a perpetually insecure economic existence.

Companies derive numerous advantages from hiring temporary rather than permanent workers. They are cheaper. They are easy to replace, with new ones just a phone call away. They enable businesses to avoid "costly overstaffing."[119] Employers can increase or decrease the size of the workforce at will, and they can do so at a moment's notice without troublesome hiring and firing procedures or worries about wrongful termination and anti-discrimination lawsuits. Since temps are expected to bring the requisite skills with them, companies are free of costly job-training responsibilities. Because they are not attached to any particular firm, temporary workers also have less of an incentive to build alliances with co-workers or join union organizing drives. In many workplaces, in fact, a schism exists between temporary and permanent workers. Because of their second-class status, temps sometimes resent permanent workers; because they fear for the security of their own jobs, permanent workers sometimes feel threatened by the presence of temps. According to one account, some companies "use temps to undercut worker solidarity and to weaken a bargaining unit." By hiring temporary workers and playing on regular employees' fears of job loss, employers augment their leverage over the permanent workforce.[120]

## Regular Part-Time Workers

Part-time work, usually meaning less than thirty-five hours per week, is the most prevalent form of non-standard employment, with nearly 20 percent of the workforce in the United States consisting of part-timers.[121] Many employees prefer not to work full time. But since 1970 almost all of the growth in this form of non-standard employment has come from an increase in involuntary part-time work.[122] According to data from the Bureau of Labor Statistics, as of May 2014, approximately 7.3 million people worked part-times jobs "for economic reasons," meaning they lost hours because of the slack economy or they could not find full-time work. Another 19 million people were employed part time for "noneconomic reasons," including child-care problems and family obligations.[123] Involuntary part-time workers are part of the "invisible unemployed"; they turn to these jobs out of desperation only because they cannot find full-time work. These are not typically good jobs, and they do not typically enable workers to live a decent life. In many cases, their status as part-timers makes employees ineligible for benefits. They are also often stuck with irregular and unpredictable schedules, not knowing from week to week when or how many hours they will be working. And they are sometimes forced to rely on food stamps to supplement their low earnings and Medicaid to cover their health-care expenses.[124] This is a particularly serious problem because most of the job growth since the end of the recession in 2009 has been in the low-wage service sector, particularly the fast food industry.[125] Besides paying low hourly wages, these jobs— "McJobs," as they are sometimes called—are disproportionately part time, and they also offer limited opportunities for mobility.[126] The increasing prevalence of part-time jobs makes it all the more difficult for people to avoid or escape poverty through work. And while part-time employment, because it reduces labor costs, is a good deal for employers, it causes economic insecurity for employees, leaving many workers permanently trapped in the low-wage labor market.[127]

* * *

A ruthless bottom-line mentality prevails in today's economy, the culmination of years of economic restructuring. Embracing a "hard-nosed, cost-cutting philosophy," business firms in the United States, *Business Week* reports, "are tearing up pay systems and job structures, replacing them with new ones that slice wage rates, slash raises, and subcontract work to lower-paying suppliers."[128] Shedding permanent full-time positions, employers have turned to alternative, or non-standard, employment arrangements. They have also extracted concessions from their regular employees, downgrading the quality of standard work as well. In the post-war era, workers expected to see their circumstances improve in tandem with the performance of their companies, and only firms that were doing poorly laid off workers. Since the 1970s, however, downsizing and restructuring have become common even for healthy companies. Business firms today are quicker to fire and slower to hire, and fewer workers can look forward to stable careers.[129] Job tenure has declined, especially for men. The number of dislocated workers, those experiencing involuntary job loss, has grown. The time it takes to locate a new job has lengthened, and since the 2007 recession, many of the long-term unemployed have lost any hope of eventually restoring their previous standard of living.[130] If they are lucky enough to find employment, dislocated workers typically receive lower pay and are often forced into part-time positions. And a rising number of job seekers, discouraged by the lack of employment opportunities, have dropped out of the labor force entirely.[131]

## A SHORTAGE OF JOBS

Deindustrialization, globalization, and corporate restructuring aggravate a problem endemic to American capitalism: a shortage of jobs. While this is a crisis for workers, from the standpoint of business, the presence of a large pool of surplus labor is beneficial. It enhances the ability of employers to dictate the terms of employment and exercise control over the labor force. The constant reminder that they can be replaced weakens employees' bargaining power. Insecure workers are less willing to insist on higher wages, make demands for better working conditions, protest exploitation by employers, or participate in union organizing drives.

Widespread poverty persists in the United States largely because there are not enough jobs to go around, even during periods of strong economic growth, and because many existing jobs fail to pay a living wage.[132] The vast majority of able-bodied poor people do want to work, many already do, and many others are desperately looking for employment. The American economic system, however, at least under current conditions, simply cannot accommodate the supply of willing workers, and even less can it guarantee a good job to everyone who wants one. This is precisely what makes poverty a structural problem: it originates not from the deficiencies of the poor, but from political and economic forces limiting opportunities for decent employment. Instead of asking what is wrong with poor people that they do not want to work, the structural perspective poses a better question: what is wrong with the American political economy that millions of able people cannot find jobs that pay an adequate wage?

There are two aspects to the U.S. employment crisis: the job availability problem and the job quality problem.[133] The number of people who want to work or who could work far exceeds the number of jobs, of any quality. Timothy Bartik estimates that even in a booming economy, between 5 and 9 million additional jobs are needed to achieve real full employment.[134] Arne Kalleberg calculates an "underemployment" rate of 11.1 percent for 2005, which means 17.1 million people were unable to find jobs or were involuntarily employed as part-time workers.[135] L. Randall Wray and Marc-Andre

Pigeon also provide evidence of an enduring shortfall of jobs. By their measure, approximately 14 million "potentially employable" people were left jobless even during the economic upturn of the 1990s.[136] A "rising tide, alone—no matter how robust," they conclude, "is unlikely to generate a sufficient number of jobs for all who might wish to work."[137] Philip Harvey maintains, likewise, that the rate of unemployment, which hovers between 5 and 6 percent in normal times, would have to fall to an unprecedented 2 percent to eradicate involuntary joblessness. According to his calculations, in 1999, with a level of unemployment barely over 4 percent, at least 14.5 million potential workers did not have full-time jobs.[138] The fundamental problem, Harvey insists, is "there are not enough jobs to provide work for everyone who is actively seeking it, let alone for everyone who says they want to work or whom society believes should be working."[139]

The jobs shortage is even more severe if we shift the focus from the problem of job availability—how many additional jobs are needed so every aspiring worker can find employment—to the problem of job quality—how many additional good jobs are needed so every worker has the opportunity to earn a living wage. For millions of people, the problem is not their joblessness but their jobs. Despite "doing all they can to support themselves," Marlene Kim argues, many workers remain poor because they are trapped in "lousy jobs": "Their wages are too low and their jobs fail to provide fulltime and full-year employment."[140] An extraordinarily large percentage of American workers, 27.5 in 2013, receive wages that are insufficient to permit a family to live above the poverty line.[141]

The problem of "insufficient adequate jobs," according to Bob Sheak and Melissa Morris, "remains a permanent and significant feature of the [U.S.] economy."[142] By calculating the percentage of the labor supply that is subemployed, they provide a quantitative estimate of the shortfall of "adequate" jobs. The subemployed fall into one of four groups: (1) the "active unemployed," those who are officially counted as "unemployed"; (2) the "inactive unemployed," those who have given up looking for a job, but still want one ("discouraged" workers); (3) involuntary part-time workers; and (4) full-time, year-round workers who earn less than a poverty-level wage.[143] The economic expansion of the 1990s improved employment prospects, they acknowledge, but the rate of subemployment remained remarkably high at 22.9 percent. And this was during the best of times. Despite relatively strong growth, the U.S. economy in the late 1990s failed to provide adequate job opportunities for nearly 33 million workers. Using a more realistic earnings standard, set at 150 percent of the official poverty threshold, Sheak and Morris find that over 50 million people were subemployed, more than a third of the potential workforce.[144] Gordon Lafer also documents a massive jobs problem.[145] For 1996, he estimates that the number of Americans who needed a job exceeded the number of living wage jobs by almost 24 million.[146] The data are indisputable, Lafer concludes: "There simply are not enough decently paying jobs for the number of people who need them."[147]

Today's employment crisis, as the data from the 1990s suggest, originated long before the Great Recession, but the 2007–2009 economic meltdown has certainly exacerbated both the job availability deficit and the job quality deficit. What is most worrying about the current economic recovery, as was true also for the previous recovery following the 2001 recession, is the unusually slow pace of job creation.[148] As of May 2014, nearly 10 million people were officially unemployed, many for more than six months; several million more were underemployed, either working in jobs for which they were overqualified or working part time but wanting full-time work; and countless others—so called "marginal" workers—have dropped out of the labor force after months of fruitless job search.[149] The bulk of job creation since 2009, furthermore, is in the low-wage industry, and these jobs are not serving as stepping stones to high-wage work. The result is that even workers lucky enough to land a job are finding it difficult to make ends meet, much less envision a secure and prosperous future.[150] Profits are soaring, the stock market is at a near record high, and the wealthiest 1 percent are amassing ever greater wealth, but from the standpoint of the typical worker, the economic outlook remains grim. "For corporate America," as David Leonhardt reports, "the recession is over. For the American work force, it's not."[151]

Proponents of the individualistic perspective regularly admonish the poor to get an education, to develop better work habits, and to make more of an effort to get and keep a job. If poor people would only improve their skills and adopt a more positive attitude, these theorists argue, they could eventually find employment and work their way out of poverty. To be sure, education, training, and moral uplift might benefit particular individuals, but only by enhancing their competitive standing, giving them an edge over their rivals in the labor market. Person A now gets the job that would have otherwise gone to person B, but this reshuffling yields no improvement in the aggregate.[152] Reforming poor people might make sense in conjunction with job creation, but by itself it is no solution. The fundamental problem is a structural one: a shortage of decent-paying jobs. Only through policies that substantially increase the bargaining power of workers and the quantity and quality of employment opportunities can more people, and not just some people, escape poverty.

## CONCLUSION

The publication in recent years of numerous studies on the low-wage labor market and the working poor attests to a troubling and ongoing change in the American economy: over the past three or four decades, employment opportunities have worsened considerably, especially for people already disadvantaged by their race, gender, and class background. For most Americans, getting a decent job is the only way to escape or avoid poverty. Millions of Americans do not have jobs, however; millions more do not have good jobs; and in the 2000s, especially since the Great Recession, the supply of able workers continues to outrun the availability of jobs that pay a living wage. This is a structural problem, not an individual problem. It derives from the workings of the American economy, not from the deficiencies of American workers. Deindustrialization, globalization, corporate restructuring, and the growing imbalance of power between business and labor—these economic forces, forces beyond the immediate control of the individual, have contributed to the deterioration of employment opportunities. As a result, and despite their best efforts, millions of American households in the twenty-first century remain chronically vulnerable to poverty.

*Chapter Six*

# The Political System and Poverty

## THE POLITICS OF POVERTY

Government is a pervasive force in society. Public officials, elected and appointed, exercise authority on a wide range of matters—from campaign finance to criminal justice, from health care to housing, from education to retirement, and from the environment to national security. Executive mandates, court rulings, and legislative measures establish—to the detriment of some and the benefit of others—innumerable procedures, regulations, and laws that dictate, among other things, eligibility requirements for social programs and subsidies; the distribution of the tax burden and the disbursement of government revenues; the prerogatives and obligations of businesses and unions; the organization and operation of election systems and political parties; and the rights and responsibilities of employers and employees, producers and consumers, creditors and debtors.

Through these and countless other means, government sets forth the rules of the game. These inevitably favor some interests over others. The normal functioning of the political system unavoidably allocates costs and benefits, powers and privileges. Everything government does—whether at the federal, state, or local level—redistributes resources and opportunities. The share of the economic pie we each receive is not simply proportionate to some combination of cognitive ability, work effort, and human capital. It is instead very much a product of myriad social conflicts, political choices, legislative battles, and court cases, past and present. As we saw in the previous chapter, the state of the economy shapes our economic outcomes and, as this chapter shows, so too does government policy. [1]

Who wins and who loses in the political process reflects the balance of power between contending groups. Government is most responsive to those who speak loudest. If people have plenty of time and money, if they benefit from social status and insider connections, they can effectively turn up the volume for their side. They can publicize political causes, attract the attention of the news media, finance and manage advocacy groups, lobby legislators, and help candidates get elected to office. Poorer Americans cannot so easily make themselves heard. On top of their many other disadvantages, they suffer from a shortage of political assets. This is an important cause of poverty. Poor people lack money, but they also lack political power, and one reason they lack money is precisely *because* they lack political power.

Whether we have more or less poverty in the United States depends on a multitude of political factors. Both through what it does and what it refrains from doing, government causes the rate of poverty to rise and fall, and it makes the lives of the poor sometimes better and sometimes worse. Fluctuations in the amount and severity of poverty mirror changes in government policy, and the contours of government policy, in turn, reflect the alignment of political forces. Poverty is not simply an individual problem. It is an economic problem, and it is a political problem as well. To understand the dynamics of poverty, therefore, we need to examine the structure of our political institutions, the characteristics of the surrounding political environment, the exercise of political power, and the causes and consequences of government policy.

## WE'RE NUMBER ONE: THE UNITED STATES IN COMPARATIVE PERSPECTIVE

The United States has the highest level of economic inequality in the developed world, and the gap between the rich and the poor in this country has widened more since the late 1970s than in any other industrialized nation. [2] This increasingly skewed distribution of income and wealth helps to explain why the United States, despite its vast resources, has such an extraordinarily large poverty population. In 2000, the poverty rate dropped to a near record low, but even so, the United States at the turn of the century still had more poverty than just about any other rich country. [3] Since then, with the recession of 2001, followed by a jobless recovery, and the Great Recession of

2007, followed by yet another stubbornly anemic recovery, the rate of poverty has increased substantially and remains significantly higher than in our peer countries.[4] In the late 2000s, the overall rate of poverty in the United States was almost twice the average of twenty other affluent nations. The rate of poverty for children was *more* than twice the international average, with the United States at 23.1 percent compared to Iceland at 4.7 percent, Norway at 6.1 percent, Sweden at 7.3 percent, and Germany at 8.5 percent.[5]

The poverty level remains high in this country partly because so many jobs pay low wages. Compared to fourteen other industrialized nations, the United States has "the highest proportion of workers in relatively poorly paid full-time jobs."[6] The income of low-wage workers is also lower in the United States than in most other industrialized countries, and the rate of working poverty is higher.[7] This circumstance is not just the result of a poorly performing economy. Politics also contributes to the severity of the poverty problem. Relative to the size of the economy, government social expenditures in the United States are significantly lower than in many other advanced countries.[8] Spending in the United States on social programs specifically, including social security, is barely half the level of the European average, and spending on "labor market programs," including unemployment compensation, constitutes a minuscule 0.4 percent of GDP, compared to a European average of 2.7 percent.[9] Social expenditures for the non-elderly in the United States are particularly meager: 2.8 percent of GDP compared to 6.0 percent in Canada, 8.9 percent in Germany, and 12.6 percent in Sweden.[10] The rate of poverty is higher here than in other developed nations not only because earnings for low-wage workers have stagnated, if not declined, but also because the United States continues to devote far less money to social welfare programs, particularly those targeted to families and working-age adults.[11]

Citizens in Europe and elsewhere in the industrialized world are also less poor because they enjoy an assortment of government services and benefits typically unavailable in the United States, or less generous and inclusive when they are available. Most Europeans and Canadians receive comprehensive coverage for sickness and disability and are protected by universal health-care systems guaranteeing access to regular medical attention.[12] Americans are not so fortunate. Although the Affordable Care Act is likely to increase access to health care, as things stand, nearly 50 million people lack health insurance, and millions more have inadequate coverage. Despite Americans' devotion to "family values," moreover, government policy in the

United States is unique in the paltry level of assistance allotted to families with children.[13] Few parents in the United States, in contrast to those in Europe, receive publicly supported child care or early childhood education or are eligible for paid maternity or paternity leave.[14] Nor do Americans benefit from the sort of government-provided child and family allowances common in other developed nations, which help considerably to reduce non-elderly poverty.[15] Most European countries and Canada too have better coverage for the unemployed, a higher minimum wage, and other labor market regulations that do more to safeguard the living standard of ordinary workers.[16]

We can assess more precisely the efficacy of government social welfare programs by comparing the "post-transfer" rate of poverty and the "pre-transfer" rate of poverty. Pre-transfer poverty is calculated by counting the share of the population whose income falls below the poverty threshold before adding in the effects of government benefits and taxes. Post-transfer poverty is calculated by counting the share of the population whose income falls below the poverty threshold after adding in the effects of government benefits and taxes. The difference between the post-transfer rate and the pre-transfer rate measures the anti-poverty effectiveness of government policy. This before-and-after comparison tells us how much government contributes to the reduction of poverty.

The pre-transfer rate of poverty in the United States is actually somewhat lower than the average in the developed world. But because our government does so little to assist the poor, the post-transfer rate of poverty is not dramatically different from the pre-transfer rate. Indeed, by international standards, the anti-poverty effectiveness of government policy in the United States is astonishingly low.[17] In a study of eight industrialized countries, Timothy Smeeding reports that government spending and taxation on average lowered the rate of poverty from 26.1 percent to 9.8 percent, while government policy in the United States only reduced the rate of poverty from 23.7 percent to 17.0 percent. The United States does even worse for families with children, much worse in fact. For one- and two-parent households, respectively, the post-transfer rates of poverty were 41.4 percent and 13.1 percent, down only modestly from the pre-transfer rates of 48.6 percent and 13.9 percent. Government spending and taxation for the eight countries averaged had a much greater effect, lowering the rate of poverty from 52.3 percent to 25.2 percent for one-parent households and from 12.2 percent to 6.6 percent for two-parent households. In the United States, as these numbers show, families with children are far more vulnerable to poverty than are families in other industrialized countries. Platitudes about "big government" notwithstanding, social expenditures in the United States are among the lowest in the western world, and the American welfare state does less comparatively to reduce the overall rate of poverty and far less to reduce the level of child poverty. [18]

Conservative critics claim that government programs intended to help the poor have the perverse effect of causing more poverty. [19] The reality is quite the opposite. Cross-national data demonstrate that social welfare policies reduce poverty, and that generous policies reduce poverty a lot. [20] While government in the United States has not won as much ground in the war against poverty as other countries, this is more from lack of trying than anything else. The simple story is this: when government allocates more resources to fighting poverty, the result is fewer poor people and less economic hardship; when government allocates fewer resources to fighting poverty, the result is more poor people and greater economic hardship. Other industrialized nations have less poverty for the obvious reason: their governments do more to help the poor.

Poverty in the United States is not an intractable social problem; it is not a by-product of uncontrollable demographic forces; it is not the outcome of inviolable economic laws; and it is not the result of Americans being unusually deficient in intelligence, values, or skills. Poverty, fundamentally, is a political phenomenon; it is the reflection of political policy, the product of human design. Poverty remains high because the level of political commitment to assisting the poor remains low. Why is the United States so much less successful at combating poverty than other industrial nations? "It's simple," Timothy Smeeding says. "We choose to tolerate a lot more poverty than do other countries." [21] This of course begs the question of who precisely this "we" is and why "we" make the political choices we make. Nevertheless, cross-national studies of tax, spending, labor market, and social welfare policies demonstrate clearly that explicit political decisions decisively affect the extent of poverty in society and the severity of the hardships experienced by the poor. The problem of poverty cannot be explained by reference to individual deficiencies. To understand the persistence of poverty in the United States, we need to shift our focus from the values and behaviors of the poor to the forces that shape government policy.

# THE STRUCTURE OF THE AMERICAN POLITICAL SYSTEM

Though most countries in the industrialized world are nominally democratic, their governing systems differ. Some are more genuinely representative than others, more responsive to the needs of ordinary citizens, and more open to egalitarian social reforms. The American political system, contrary to the popular image, falls well short of conventional "democratic standards."[22] More so than those in Western Europe, political institutions in the United States favor the rich over the poor, business over labor. This helps to explain why the American welfare state is relatively underdeveloped; why policy makers, even in response to growing inequality, resist enacting compensatory tax and spending measures; and why the rate of poverty is the highest in the industrialized world. Government in the United States does little to fight poverty or promote equality partly because the very structure of American politics hinders redistributive reforms. The two-party, winner-take-all election system; the presence of multiple veto points and elaborate checks and balances in the policy-formation process; and a federal system that divides political power between the central government and the states—these and other features of the American political structure are designed more to protect the interests of the privileged than to serve the needs of the poor.[23]

## The American Election System

Elections in most European democracies operate according to one or another system of proportional representation.[24] Though the procedures vary from one country to the next, the basic principle underlying this type of system is straightforwardly democratic: political parties are allocated legislative seats according to their share of the vote. A party that wins 20 percent of the votes receives approximately 20 percent of the seats in the legislature. This election method encourages the formation of multiple political parties, and it enables minority parties, including labor and socialist parties, to participate effectively in the exercise of political power, usually in coalition with more centrist parties. Proportional representation offers voters more choices, opens up political debate to a wider range of views, and allows the working class and the poor to gain a real voice in the legislative process.[25] This voting system also engenders government policies more favorable to the interests of less-advantaged citizens. Social welfare expenditures, for example, are significantly higher in countries where legislators are elected through proportional representation.[26]

In the United States, by contrast, the principal method for selecting representatives to Congress and to state and local legislatures is the single-member-district, winner-take-all system.[27] In the House of Representatives, for example, candidates in 435 separate geographically defined districts compete for office every two years. The winning candidate in each district is the one receiving the most votes. This sounds very democratic, but it can produce perversely undemocratic outcomes. For example, if a single political party receives 51 percent of the votes in every district election in a state, that party would get 100 percent of the legislative seats, leaving almost half of the electorate without anyone to speak for their interests in government. This procedure for selecting legislative members violates the principle of fair representation. It "tends to overrepresent majority constituencies and underrepresent minority constituencies."[28] The winner-take-all system yields governing bodies that do not truly reflect voter preferences.

Political parties operating under the winner-take-all formula can become viable political forces only if they are consistently capable of attracting the support of a majority of the electorate. This voting system is usually coupled with a two-party political structure, as in the United States, for example, where the only real choice is between the Republicans and the Democrats. A vote for a third party is typically a wasted vote, and the supporters of such parties, even though they may constitute a sizable percentage of the populace, cannot normally expect to gain representation in the legislative arena. The winner-take-all election system thus inhibits the formation of parties on the left that can usually be counted on to support egalitarian causes, and it favors the appearance of more conservative political regimes. Cross-national studies disclose a clear pattern: multiparty proportional representation systems typically give rise to left-center governments that favor redistribution, while majoritarian two-party systems typically give rise to right-center governments that oppose redistribution.[29] American-style electoral institutions hinder social democratic and leftist political parties from gaining a presence in government, thus weakening the influence of constituencies likely to press for and benefit from more expansive and generous tax and spending policies. This explains, in part, why social welfare expenditures in the United States are relatively low and why levels of poverty and inequality are relatively high.[30] The essential reality is this: the American voting system, through its effect on the distribution of political power, causes poor people in the United States to be worse off than their counterparts in other modern democratic societies.

## Checks and Balances

The American political system consists of three independent branches of government—the executive, the legislative, and the judicial. It has two congressional chambers—the House and the Senate—and a legislative process that operates according to a byzantine set of rules and procedures. Legislative proposals are shuffled back and forth through numerous committees and subcommittees in both the House and the Senate, and they also require the approval of the president and sometimes the courts. This complex arrangement of separated powers, established less to promote than to restrain democracy, results in a law-making process that is prone to gridlock.[31] In the American political system, there are a million ways for a bill to die. The parliamentary systems that are common in Europe, where political authority is less fragmented and where policy initiatives only have to be approved by one elected body, offer fewer opportunities for powerful special interest groups to block redistributive reforms.[32]

The system of checks and balances that characterizes American government causes three kinds of distortions. First, it creates an unlevel legislative playing field. The multilayered policy-making process gives a decisive edge to wealthy campaign contributors, business interests, and other well-organized constituencies that benefit from political connections, insider knowledge, and personal ties to lawmakers. Powerful lobbyists and advocacy groups have numerous opportunities to quash, or at least declaw, threatening policy measures. Congressional initiatives promising to bring comprehensive reforms are progressively watered down as they wind their way through a labyrinthine legislative process.[33]

Second, the maze of checks and balances, along with other institutional and procedural obstacles to majoritarian rule, favors slow and incremental change, creating a powerful status quo bias.[34] In the American political system, it is easier to *stop* something from happening than to *make* something happen. The legislative process in the United States is designed for small ball rather than the home run. Fundamental reforms are difficult to achieve not only because organized interest groups possess veto power, but also because policy making is so much a product of compromise, concession, and accommodation. When lawmakers are not simply kowtowing to the interests of economic elites, legislative procedures funnel policy formation toward the moderate middle, weeding out strong measures that might really make a difference in the lives of the poor.

Third, the status quo bias in American politics is less of an obstruction when powerful business groups press for new legislation to promote free trade, deregulation, and tax cuts for the rich. But when a transformation in the economic environment threatens the well-being of millions of working Americans—precisely what has happened since the 1970s—political paralysis sets in with a vengeance. The result is what Jacob Hacker and Paul Pierson call "drift": the "systematic, prolonged failures of government to respond to the shifting realities of a dynamic economy." The problems of inequality and poverty have grown worse over the past three decades because the combination of institutional gridlock, abetted by the increasing use of the Senate filibuster, and the veto power possessed by corporate interests has prevented the updating of social policy to meet the new and pressing demands of a changing socioeconomic environment.[35]

The do-nothing tendency of American government advantages the big winners in the economic lottery, those who profit most from market conditions. Unlike the majority of ordinary Americans, the wealthy, as Charles Noble argues, have less need for "an active government on their side." They already reap huge rewards in the private sector. The political process further bolsters their dominant economic position by empowering them also to "stop other people from using government to claim their fair share."[36] The American political structure gives privileged groups a multitude of means and opportunities to thwart legislation that confers benefits on the less privileged. The system of checks and balances in the United States constrains government from implementing the sort of major initiatives that would be necessary to achieve a more equitable distribution of income and wealth.

## Federalism

Political power in the United States is distributed among many different geographically based governments. States and localities possess autonomous authority on a wide range of matters, including taxation and spending. This decentralized federal structure diminishes the power of the national government, limiting its potential to undertake large-scale redistributive reforms. With its fragmented lines of authority, the American version of federalism favors defenders of the status quo over advocates of social change; it dilutes the power of disadvantaged groups while augmenting the power of the privileged. The dispersed nature of political authority makes government slow to respond to social problems, creates many points of access for dominant groups to block legislation harmful to their interests, and lessens the ability of reform-minded movements to mobilize and target their typically limited resources.[37]

By distributing political power to economically vulnerable cities and states, federalism increases the pressure on local government officials to defer to business interests, typically at the expense of the working class and the poor. In a capitalist economy, private business firms control investment decisions, and these decisions can make or break a community. This circumstance compels politicians to be especially sensitive to the preferences of corporate elites and to avoid actions—including especially redistributive tax and spending measures—that might threaten "business confidence."[38] Federalism enhances what Charles Lindblom calls the "privileged position" that business normally occupies in the political system.[39] States and localities are reliant on business investment for job growth and tax revenues. This gives corporations a great deal of political leverage, particularly in the current environment of heightened capital mobility. In effect, they can extort city and state governments; they can threaten to locate or relocate elsewhere unless elected officials meet their demands. And by playing one locality off against another, corporations can elicit favorable tax treatment, generous subsidies, and business-friendly regulatory policies. Municipalities often end up big losers from these transactions. Taxpayers in Indiana, Illinois, Florida, Michigan, Texas, and elsewhere, desperate to attract jobs, have handed over millions of dollars to business firms only to see them take the money and run.[40]

\* \* \*

Poverty is a structural problem, due not only to the structure of the American economic system, but also to the structure of the American political system. The persistence of poverty in the United States is partly the by-product of long-standing political institutions that amplify the power of business, inhibit the formation of leftist political parties, and impede efforts to achieve redistributive reforms. The very organization of the political system marginalizes the interests of poorer Americans and prevents enactment of the sort of government policies that might move us down the path toward a more just society.

## THE POLITICAL MOBILIZATION OF BUSINESS

The American political system has a built-in conservative bias, with policy makers largely ignoring the problem of poverty. Disadvantaged groups are not typically able to attract much public attention through normal political channels.[41] Government tends to be receptive to their needs only when, through such means as protests, strikes, demonstrations, and boycotts, they cause enough social disruption to force themselves into the political spotlight, as was the case with the civil rights movement of the 1950s and 1960s, and as is the case today in battles around the country to increase the minimum wage.[42]

Since the 1970s, the naturally rightward slant of American politics has tilted even further to the right, and American government policy, marred by a long history of negligence toward the poor, has turned downright punitive. Just as the early 1970s marked an economic watershed, these years also marked a political watershed. At the same time employers were undoing the implicit social contract of the post-war years, a parallel power shift was under way in the political system. This growing imbalance of power gradually gave rise to a right turn in fiscal, monetary, and regulatory policy. Over the past four decades, as a changing economy has made life harder for low-income households and riskier for most Americans, government in the United States has exacerbated the problem by pursuing a political agenda that rewards the haves and penalizes the have-nots.[43]

Corporate America in the early 1970s found itself besieged from all sides: growing international competition; declining profits; resistance to U.S. presence abroad by Third World countries; and political setbacks at the hands of consumer, environmental, and labor groups.[44] Business leaders were alarmed by the direction in which the country seemed to be going. As one executive put it, "If we don't take action now we will see our own demise. We will evolve into another social democracy."[45] And take action they did. In response to what they perceived to be a heightened level of threat to their political and economic standing, business groups launched a well-financed and multifaceted counteroffensive.

Corporate leaders in the 1970s entered a period of sustained political activism.[46] They poured millions of dollars into "advocacy advertising" to sell the public on the virtues of big business and the evils of big government, on the merits of the free market and the malevolence of trade unions. To shore up the ideological case for the corporate agenda, they doled out truckloads of money to conservative think tanks, including the newly formed Heritage Foundation.[47] They formed powerful lobby organizations, most importantly the Business Roundtable. Initially established in 1973 to formulate a strategy for fending off labor unions, this elite organization of top executives subsequently became the "political arm of big business," dedicated to advancing the broad goals of corporate America.[48] Business leaders became more actively involved in electoral politics as well, increasing their financial commitment to corporate political action committees. Beginning in the late 1970s, they also adopted a more aggressive strategy for disbursing campaign contributions. Rather than playing it safe by giving money to both Democrats and Republicans, they reserved funds for candidates outspoken in their support for pro-business policies.[49] Through these means and others, corporate America sought to smash organized labor, roll back government regulations, lower the tax burden on the rich, and reduce spending on social welfare programs. This ongoing offensive has been very successful. Business has achieved much of what it fought for and has attained a politically dominant position vis-à-vis American labor.

## THE POLITICAL MARGINALIZATION OF THE WORKING CLASS AND THE POOR

The rightward power shift underway since the 1970s is due not only to the political mobilization of corporate America and its allies, but also to a concomitant decrease in the organized power of "workers, communities, consumers, and others."[50] While business has gotten stronger, countervailing forces have gotten weaker. The political playing field is stacked heavily in favor of the affluent. Consider, for example, the class-skewed pattern of political participation. Compared to wealthier Americans, those on the lower end of the income distribution are less likely to vote, belong to political organizations, donate time and money to political campaigns, or engage in other forms of political activity. The political participation gap between the rich and the poor is large, more so in the United States than in other democratic nations, and by some measures it is growing. These "disparities in political voice," Kay Schlozman and her colleagues state, are "substantial" and "persistent," so much so that they undermine the conditions required for political equality.[51]

In recent decades a considerable number of Americans, more so those in the lower half of the income distribution, have withdrawn from political life and community affairs, or have been shut out, leaving an open field for powerful business groups and special interest organizations.[52] What accounts for this rising level of political and civic disengagement? Robert Putnam proposes one answer. Americans born since the 1940s, he claims, unlike the public-spirited generation that came of age during World War II, have failed to acquire enduring habits of political involvement. Due especially to the isolating effect of television, post-war generations have come to live lives that are more private than public, more personal than political.[53] Robert Dahl cites a related factor. Americans today, he argues, prodded by advertisers to envy and emulate the rich and the famous, have abandoned a "culture of citizenship" in favor of a "culture of consumerism."[54] We talk about our possessions not our politics, what to buy not who to vote for; instead of attending political meetings, we visit the shopping mall. To other critics, the current practice of journalism is the culprit. Americans have become disaffected and depoliticized by news programming drawn toward sensationalism, scandals, celebrities, and feel-good human interest stories. Reporters do a poor job of keeping citizens interested and informed. And the media's often negative and disparaging coverage of government and politicians fuels a climate of political cynicism and apathy.[55] The media, however, are by no means solely to blame for the rising tide of political skepticism. Since the 1970s, political leaders, Democrats included, have retreated from the progressive policies of the New Deal and the war on poverty, turning a blind eye to the interests and concerns of the working class and the poor. The result has been an erosion in trust. Americans today are more politically disillusioned than in the past, more likely to see the system as rigged, and more negative in their assessment of politicians and government.[56] Finally, it is also worth noting that for many low-income adults, non-participation is a largely involuntary matter. Several million Americans are barred from voting by felony disenfranchisement laws, or they are denied the right to cast a ballot by duplicitous efforts to suppress voter turnout, or they are unable to manage the sometimes onerous registration requirements and long lines at voting booths, or they are prevented from voting because they cannot get time away from work.[57] These features of American politics, along with the limited choices available to voters in a two-party system, lessen the political involvement of citizens and jeopardize the health of American democracy. The combination of political disengagement and voter suppression weakens the voice of the least advantaged, diminishes the accountability of government, and makes elected officials more susceptible to the influence of economic elites.

The class bias in political representation and government policy is the product of a political environment that specifically disadvantages and disempowers the working class and the poor. In what follows, I discuss in somewhat greater length four changes in the political landscape since the 1970s that have contributed to the political marginalization of low-income Americans.

## The Decline of Organized Labor

In 2013, only 11.7 percent of wage and salary employees were represented by a labor union, and in the private sector only 6.7 percent of workers were union members, down from more than one-third in the mid-1950s.[58] This dramatic decline in the level of union density is a significant cause of wage stagnation, increasing income inequality, and the growth of working poverty.[59] The cross-national data confirm the connection between union strength and worker compensation. Compared to the United States, the rate of unionization is higher in most other nations in the industrialized world. European countries also have more centralized wage-setting institutions. This adds to the economic influence of organized labor as wage settlements negotiated by unions apply to much of the non-unionized labor force as well.[60] By contrast, only a relatively small percentage of American workers are protected by collective bargaining agreements. The weakness of labor unions in the United States, and the correspondingly immense imbalance of power between capital and labor, goes a long way toward explaining why poverty and inequality in this country are much greater than in other developed nations.[61]

The decline of unions is good for business, but bad for workers, and it is bad for American democracy as well. Though they have not always lived up to their promise in the United States, labor unions, especially when they are allied with civic associations and community groups, perform a variety of essential political functions. They help ensure that government operates according to the rule of law; that it is impartial, effective, and accountable; and that it serves the needs of the broad electorate.[62] At their best, in addition, unions offer members the opportunity to develop their abilities as citizens, mobilize low-income voters often neglected by the major political parties, provide support for left-liberal political candidates, and keep economic justice issues alive on the political agenda. Because labor unions also "serve as the only truly important political 'voice' of lower- and middle-status people," their presence helps preserve some degree of political equality.[63] Without the backing of organized labor, working Americans lack the institutional means to make their interests visible in the public sphere. In this respect, unions constitute an indispensable counterweight, blocking business from simply converting its massive economic power into political power. Indeed, in a capitalist society, where large corporations occupy a dominant economic position, a strong labor movement is vital to the functioning of democratic government.

The weakened condition of organized labor in the United States has not only eroded workers' bargaining power in the economic system; it has also altered the configuration of political power. Unions today lack the influence they possessed in the 1950s and 1960s when membership levels were much higher. They are less effective at turning out voters to support pro-worker candidates, they are less capable of exerting pressure through strikes or social protests, they carry less weight within the Democratic Party, and they are less able to represent the interests of wage-earning Americans in the political system. With the decline of union power, business groups and their political and ideological allies have gained a stranglehold over government policy on core economic issues. International trade, workplace health and safety, labor law, the minimum wage, and social welfare policy—on these and other issues critical to the economic well-being of ordinary people, the interests of corporate America have come to predominate over those of the working class and the poor.[64]

## The Transformation of American Liberalism

In the 1970s and after, the "class content of American liberalism underwent a profound shift," with middle-class professionals displacing blue-collar workers as the chief constituency of the Democratic Party.[65] This development was partly due to the decline of organized labor, but it resulted also from the emergence of a new constellation of liberal organizations embodying the growing concerns of the more educated public. These organizations, including environmental and consumer groups, raised awareness on vital matters, but their ascendancy also significantly altered the legislative priorities of the Democratic Party. According to Jeffrey Berry, the citizens' groups that have appeared on the scene since the 1970s, groups that nowadays define the liberal agenda, are "focused largely on issues unconnected to the problems of the poor, the disadvantaged, or even the working class."[66] This "new liberalism," fixated on "postmaterial" and quality-of-life issues, Berry argues, has diverted attention from problems of poverty and economic inequality.[67] The changing configuration of liberalism, along with the more recent drift of the

Democratic Party toward a more pro-business, free-market neoliberalism, has left the working class and the poor underrepresented in the political system and underserved by government policy.

## The Transformation of American Civic Life

American "civic democracy," according to Theda Skocpol, has also undergone a transformation, one paralleling the evolution of American liberalism.[68] Since the 1970s, she argues, "membership" organizations, which facilitated the civic engagement of less-privileged Americans, have given way to a proliferation of "advocacy" groups. Membership organizations, from veterans' groups to trade unions, derived their strength from the active involvement of their constituents. They mobilized voters, encouraged public deliberation, and educated people in the art of citizenship. While membership organizations promoted a sort of democracy from below, opening opportunities for popular participation, advocacy organizations, including diverse business, professional, and citizens groups, have a more elitist cast. They are organized in a "top-down" manner, typically run by a professional staff located in New York or Washington. They depend on fund-raising and the expertise supplied by full-time managers, consultants, and lawyers. They focus less on grassroots activism than on research, publicity, lobbying, and litigation. And they are "heavily tilted toward upper-middle-class constituencies."[69] Advocacy organizations have produced benefits for many Americans, but their preeminence reinforces the class bias of political participation and government policy. This "civic transformation," Skocpol believes, has diminished "America's capacity to use government for socioeconomically redistributive purposes," and it has, if only unwittingly, contributed to the exclusion of economic justice issues from the political agenda.[70]

## The Politics of Race

Animosities and conflicts arising from racial and ethnic differences also contribute to the political weakness of the working class and the poor. The enduring pattern of residential segregation, the persistence of racial stereotypes, the continued use of racially coded political rhetoric, and the emergence of new and subtler forms of racism in the post–civil rights era impede unity among less-advantaged Americans.[71] The political ramifications of this racial divide are especially severe because African Americans and Latinos make up a disproportionate share of the poor, and they loom even larger in the public perception of poverty. Indeed, as Martin Gilens shows, many white Americans view poverty mainly as a black problem due primarily to laziness.[72] It is difficult to rally popular support for an expanded welfare state when the white majority suspects undeserving minorities will be the primary beneficiaries.[73] The politics of race undercuts the politics of redistribution.[74] Alberto Alesina and Edward Glaeser provide striking cross-national evidence illustrating this point. The level of social welfare spending, they find, is significantly lower in racially diverse countries like the United States than in more racially homogeneous countries. Their data on state spending levels in the United States reveal a similar pattern. Welfare benefits are least generous in states with the largest black populations.[75] Divisions of race and ethnicity make poor people easy targets of scapegoating, lessen the ability of ordinary citizens to promote common economic interests, and undermine support for policies to combat poverty.

\* \* \*

The decline of unions, the changing face of liberalism, the transformation of civic life, and the politics of race—for these and many other reasons, the working class and the poor are unable to exert much sustained political influence, further tilting the political system in favor of business over labor. Working Americans are not totally without power, of course, and they have even managed to win some significant victories in recent years. At state and local levels, for example, campaigns to increase the minimum wage have achieved notable successes.[76] But the big story since the 1970s is how the upward redistribution of political power has intensified the class bias of government policy. This in turn has worsened the economic prospects for less-affluent Americans and has resulted in persistently high levels of inequality and poverty.

## THE SYNERGY OF MONEY AND POWER

The synergy of money and power has reinforced the rightward shift in the American political system. Politics in the United States has become a cash game. To be a serious player nowadays, even just to get a seat at the table, requires a huge stack of chips. Poorer Americans are relegated to the role of spectators, and even then they rarely get to observe the big-money games. These are conducted outside the public eye, in corporate boardrooms, the offices of lobby firms, and the proverbial smoked-filled corridors of government.

In American politics, "money talks," and since the 1970s, it talks louder than ever.[77] Making matters worse, money has become a more powerful political force at the same time inequality in the distribution of income and wealth has escalated. The result is a "vicious cycle."[78] Economic inequality causes political inequality, as the rich use their money to buy political access and shape the policy agenda. Political inequality causes economic inequality, as the rich use their political influence to amass even more money. And so on. This fusion of money and power threatens to make government more than ever the servant of the wealthy and threatens to make the wealthy more than ever a dominant political class. Gary Burtless and Christopher Jencks take note of this ominous synergy in their assessment of "American inequality." The most worrisome consequence of the growing concentration of income and wealth, they conclude, is its impact "on the distribution of political influence." What are the implications for American democracy, they ask, if the rich can convert their money into political power and so manipulate government policy to increase even further their share of the nation's resources?[79]

Money talks, but what really matters is what it says. If what the wealthy want from government is more or less the same as what the average American wants, then the influence of big money, though contrary to the democratic ideal, is less consequential. In fact, however, to no great surprise, the preferences and priorities of the richest Americans, the top 1 percent or the top 10 percent, differ significantly from those of the general public. On economic issues particularly, the affluent are much more conservative than the non-affluent. As compared to other Americans, the wealthy, for example, are more in favor of deficit reduction, tax cuts, and reduced spending on social welfare programs, and they are less in favor of a higher minimum wage, government job creation, and national health insurance. To the extent that money talks—and rich donors certainly think it does—then government policy, at least on certain key economic issues, will reflect the minority interests of economic elites rather than the majority interests of the general public.[80]

Money enters into the political arena through many pathways, but two stand out. First, it takes a lot of money to run a political campaign, giving wealthy donors inordinate influence in determining who competes for elected office. Second, it takes a lot of money to lobby public officials, giving wealthy donors inordinate influence in the day-to-day formulation of government policy. As the power of money in U.S. politics grows, opportunities shrink for meaningful participation by the poor. Money undermines the democratic ideal of political equality. It empowers the rich way beyond their numbers, and it precludes ordinary citizens from gaining a fair hearing in the political process.

Candidates for political office who are able to raise money are not guaranteed victory, of course, but if they cannot attract donors, they cannot effectively compete. At every level of government, politicians are reliant on private contributions to finance their political campaigns, increasingly so in recent decades. Campaign costs have skyrocketed as candidates have become dependent on expensive television advertising and the costly advice of polling experts, professional consultants, and public relations specialists. Over the past thirty years, consequently, money has appreciated in value more than time as a resource in political campaigns. This development exacerbates the class bias of the political process, since the wealthy—conservative business interests, in particular—contribute far more money to candidates than do less-affluent voters, including union members.[81] According to recent data from the Center for Responsive Politics, for example, political contributions from business outweigh those from labor by a ratio of fifteen to one.[82] Even more remarkably, in 2012 more than 40 percent of all campaign contributions in federal elections, up from less than 10 percent in 1982, came from just the top 0.01 percent of the voting-age population.[83]

Since 2010, court decisions, including the *Citizens United* ruling, have struck down limits on political contributions in the form of "outside money."[84] The predictable result is a dramatic increase in the ability of the wealthy to exploit their financial advantage in the political arena. Outside money includes advocacy and campaign spending by individuals or groups that is not directly coordinated with the organization of any particular candidate. Through super PACs, for example, wealthy political investors, acting independently, can spend an unlimited amount of money on behalf of (or against) candidates of their choice.[85] In the 2012 election cycle, super PACs accounted for nearly half of all outside spending, with 112 donors contributing at least a million dollars each, and Sheldon and Miriam Adelson by themselves donating nearly $92 million in support of Republican candidates.[86] The rise of super PACs and other such vehicles for channeling ever-larger sums of money into the electoral process exacerbates an already present threat: the transformation of American democracy into American "dollarocracy."[87]

Money has a corrosive effect on the electoral process. It narrows the range of viable candidates, it narrows the range of issues brought before the public, and it narrows the range of voters participating in elections. Jay Mandle argues that private financing of electoral contests results in political platforms and debates that poorly reflect the concerns of citizens who cannot afford to make large campaign contributions. This depresses voter turnout, particularly among the low-income population, those most likely to favor and benefit from redistributive social welfare policies. In the United States and other countries where campaigns are funded privately rather that publicly, the rate of voter turnout and the level of government spending on health, education, and pensions are substantially lower. The influence of private money in the electoral process, Mandle concludes, reduces "the scope of democratic choice," limits the parameters of political debate, and engenders government policy that is "biased toward the interests of the wealthy."[88]

Money matters after elections are over, too. In 2013, the total number of registered lobbyists, hardly any of whom speak for the poor, exceeded twelve thousand, with countless others serving in various unofficial lobbying capacities, and the total amount of money spent on lobbying exceeded $3.2 billion. During the period from 1998 to 2014, the U.S. Chamber of Commerce, contributing more than $1 billion, headed the list of top spenders, with most of the other big political investors consisting of trade organizations, business groups, and corporations.[89] Overall, as Kay Lehman Schlozman and her colleagues show, the class bias in organized political participation far exceeds the class bias in individual political participation. Organizations representing business interests, they report, account for 72 percent of expenditures on lobbying, with unions, social welfare groups, and public interest groups combined accounting for less than 5 percent of total lobbying expenditures. They also find, furthermore, that in "no domain of organized interest activity does activity by organizations that provide services to or political representation of the poor register more than a trace."[90] Why is there so much poverty and inequality in the United States? One reason is the distribution of organized political power. In the high-stakes world of lobbying, the rich dominate and the poor are voiceless.[91]

Corporations and the wealthy possess in abundance the resources that fuel the lobby system: organization, expertise, connections, and money. Business groups have an army of well-informed and well-financed professional lobbyists to watch over their interests on a daily basis. The poorest of Americans, those most in need of government assistance, partly because they lack an organized political presence, are severely disadvantaged in the high-powered world of pressure politics. They do not have anything like a meaningful chance to participate in the policy arena, and even less do they have an equal say in the formation of government policy. In the competition to gain the ear of legislators, ordinary citizens "speak in a whisper while the most advantaged roar."[92] The result is predictable: the U.S. political system, as one authoritative report concludes, "is a great deal more responsive to the preferences of the rich than to the preferences of the poor."[93]

Recent studies provide striking confirmation of this conclusion, while at the same time raising doubts about the reality of American democracy. In one analysis, Larry Bartels examines the voting behavior of senators in the late 1980s and early 1990s. He finds that senators' votes on a range of economic and social issues were somewhat responsive to the ideological views of middle-income constituents, very responsive to the views of high-income constituents, and entirely *unresponsive* to the views of low-income constituents. Bartels underlines a "profoundly troubling" fact for those who believe in the ideal of political equality: "senators consistently appear to pay no attention to the views of millions of constituents in the bottom third of the income distribution."[94] Martin Gilens, in a meticulous assessment of the correspondence between public preferences and policy outcomes, draws a similar conclusion. He finds that when there is a divergence between the political preferences of the affluent (the top 10 percent) and the political preferences of middle-income Americans, the affluent, despite their minority status, consistently emerge as victors in the policy arena. And when the preferences of the affluent and the poor diverge, government is completely unresponsive to the concerns of the poor, and this is true even when the poor have the middle class on their side. This pattern, Gilens acknowledges—with economic elites exerting unparalleled influence over government policy—is consistent with the cynical judgment that the American political system is more of a *plutocracy* than a *democracy*.[95]

## POLICY CONSEQUENCES OF THE POWER SHIFT: ROBIN HOOD IN REVERSE

Individualistic theories, by attributing poverty to the deficiencies of the poor, obscure the obvious: people's economic outcomes are dependent on government, and government policy since the 1970s has become increasingly skewed toward the interests of the rich. The poor are not victims of their own failings; they are victims of an unresponsive political system. In this era of rising inequality and widespread economic insecurity, rather than stepping in to assist the millions of Americans struggling to keep their heads above water, elected officials have enacted tax, spending, trade, and regulatory measures that only reinforce the growing gap between the haves and the have-nots. In the following pages, to further illuminate the political aspect of the poverty problem, I briefly examine four important policy arenas: the minimum wage, unemployment insurance, welfare reform, and labor law. My objective in each case is to illustrate how government leaders over the past three or four decades have turned their backs on the working class and the poor.

## The Minimum Wage: Lowering the Floor

The minimum wage law was created as part of the Fair Labor Standards Act of 1938, a legislative measure intended to curtail "labor conditions detrimental to the maintenance of the minimum standard of living necessary for health, efficiency and general well-being of workers."[96] The minimum wage establishes a floor on hourly earnings. It is not indexed to the rate of inflation, however, so its real value declines over time as the cost of living increases. This is where politics enters the picture. Whether or not the minimum wage is raised, how often, and by how much is a matter decided by Congress and state and local representatives. The level of the minimum wage is thus an outgrowth of political struggles, usually pitting low-wage workers and labor groups, with support from the liberal wing of the Democratic Party, against Republican legislators, free-market ideologues, and employers, particularly small-business owners. How much workers earn, therefore, and the likelihood of their escaping or avoiding poverty, is contingent on the balance of power between contending interests and the inevitably politicized decisions of elected officials. The magnitude of economic inequality in the United States and the severity of the poverty problem are partly the by-product of the politics of the minimum wage.

The real (inflation adjusted) value of the minimum wage trended upward throughout the 1950s and 1960s, peaking in 1968 at $9.40 per hour (in 2013 dollars) and declining somewhat in the 1970s. It fell more rapidly in the 1980s, in tandem with the rightward trajectory of American politics, dropping almost 30 percent during the Reagan era, as Congress legislated no increase from January 1981 to April 1990. Despite four modest raises in the 1990s, the last in 1997, the purchasing power of the minimum wage in the late 1990s remained well below its 1968 level. From September 1997 until July 2007, the federal minimum wage was stuck at $5.15 per hour, the longest period without an increase since its inception, longer even than the nine-year stretch of the 1980s. Congress finally raised the federal minimum by 70 cents in 2007, and it reached its current level of $7.25 per hour in 2009.[97] Tipped workers, however, including waitresses and waiters, have not had a raise since 1991—twenty-three years ago! The minimum wage for this large and growing category of workers, mostly women, stands at a mere $2.13 per hour.[98]

Full-time workers earning the federal minimum make approximately $15,000 a year before taxes—$3,500 less than in 1968—not enough even to lift a family of two above the poverty line. They are worse off today than in the past relative to the middle class as well. The hourly wages of workers at the minimum in 2013 were only 36 percent of average hourly wages, down from 53 percent in 1968.[99] Not surprisingly, they have also fallen further behind the rich. To cite just one particularly relevant example, the earnings of top CEOs in the restaurant industry, where many minimum wage workers are employed, were 721 times the minimum wage in 2013, up from 609 in 2006.[100]

Minimum wage workers today are paid substantially less than their counterparts in the 1960s and 1970s, and so are millions of other employees whose wages, though higher than the minimum, are affected by the federal standard. They are also paid substantially less than their minimum wage counterparts in most other developed counties.[101] The Fair Minimum Wage Act of 2013, which calls for an increase in the minimum to $10.10 by 2016, would improve the lives of low-wage workers greatly, by one estimate "either directly or indirectly" raising the earnings of 27.8 million workers.[102] But with strong opposition from congressional Republicans, this bill is apparently dead in the water.

According to a 2014 survey conducted by the Center for American Progress, 80 percent of respondents, including 67 percent of Republicans, expressed support (58 percent strong support) for an increase in the minimum wage.[103] The many successful campaigns to raise city- and state-level minimum wages, often through ballot initiatives, also attest to strong public support for a higher minimum.[104] In its continued refusal to raise the federal minimum wage, Congress is not responding to the wishes of the electorate.

The decline in the real value of the minimum wage since the 1960s testifies to the inordinate power of business interests in Congress and to the weakened state of American democracy.

## Unemployment Insurance: The Fraying of the Safety Net

The Unemployment Insurance (UI) program was enacted as part of the Social Security Act of 1935.[105] It is intended to provide temporary and partial "income support during a spell of involuntary unemployment."[106] Administered and financed jointly by the federal government and the states, this program, due primarily to underfunding, has been in a "state of disrepair" for some time, now exacerbated by the Great Recession.[107] The UI system suffers from another long-standing failing as well. Since state governments have considerable discretion over eligibility requirements and funding levels, there are substantial inequities across the country, with workers in some states being much better served by the system than workers in others.[108] Most state programs, however, share certain common problems. First, they are excessively complicated and—with persistently high levels of unemployment—increasingly overburdened, often leaving qualified workers deterred from applying. Second, even though their wages are subject to the payroll tax—the source of funding for unemployment insurance—many workers are denied benefits by unreasonable and outdated eligibility formulas. And third, payment levels, averaging around $300 per week, with significant variation from state to state, typically replace only about half of workers' wages, far less than in most European countries, leaving many families below the poverty line.[109]

The percentage of the unemployed who receive benefits has declined over the past several decades. After reaching a peak of 75 percent in 1975 and dropping to 50 percent in 1980, the recipiency rate through 2009 has averaged somewhere between one-third and one-half.[110] In 2008, in the midst of the financial collapse, Congress authorized the Emergency Unemployment Compensation (EUC) program. In combination with the Extended Benefits (EB) program, which provided an additional thirteen to twenty weeks of UI benefits, this enabled many of the long-term unemployed to avoid poverty or at least to keep their heads above water while looking for a job. At the end of 2013, however, the EUC program, facing strong Republican opposition, was not renewed, and the EB program is no longer operational as state rates of unemployment have fallen below the threshold for triggering extended benefits. The recipiency rate, as a result—that is, the percent of the officially unemployed population receiving UI benefits—has dropped to a record low, somewhere around 25 percent.[111] Here we see the essential shortcoming of the U.S. unemployment system: the majority of today's unemployed workers, even before the Great Recession and many more since, are falling through the unemployment insurance safety net. The current program, now more than seventy years old, was designed for a different world. In today's economy with today's labor force, it no longer adequately safeguards the living standard of jobless workers.

Among the many deficiencies of the unemployment insurance program, four stand out. First, in most states, non-standard workers, including part-timers and temps, who compose approximately 30 percent of today's labor force, are ineligible to receive unemployment benefits.[112] Second, female workers, who typically shoulder the burden of child-care and domestic labor duties, are poorly served by an unemployment system designed for male breadwinners. As a result of work–family conflicts, women are disproportionately job "leavers" rather than job "losers."[113] The demands of the care-taking role, tending a sick child, for example, compel many women to at times withdraw temporarily from the labor force. Because they are more likely to be out of work "voluntarily" and for "personal" reasons, women, particularly working mothers, face a greater likelihood of being disqualified for unemployment benefits.[114] Third, the unemployment program in most states unfairly penalizes workers with low hourly wages. To fulfill minimum earnings requirements, low-wage employees have to work more hours prior to losing a job than higher-wage employees; since 1990, some states have even raised earnings requirements, excluding more of the working poor from eligibility.[115] According to one report from the mid-1990s, only about 18 percent of jobless low-wage workers received unemployment benefits, compared to 40 percent of jobless high-wage workers.[116] Fourth, under normal conditions, workers may receive unemployment compensation for a maximum of twenty-six weeks. In the economy of the past couple of decades, however, as evidenced by higher rates of long-term unemployment, and especially since the 2007 recession, it takes more time for laid-off workers to find a new job. Between 2007 and 2009, of the 15 million newly jobless workers, only half received UI benefits, with one-fourth of recipients exhausting their benefits by early 2010, and an estimated 3 to 4 million more running out of benefits in 2010 and 2011.[117] The Unemployment Insurance system is failing the people it is supposed to help. To cite just one example, a North Carolina resident lost her job in June 2013. Twenty weeks later her benefits ran out, and she and her teenage son were "living on close to nothing." "I worked for 26 years," she says. "I lost my job through no fault of my own. This is what I get?"[118]

Unemployment policy has failed to keep pace with a changing economy and with the circumstances of a changing workforce. Wage earners, especially those most vulnerable to poverty, "are losing both coming and going—many are denied benefits while others see their benefits run out long before the job market rebounds."[119] In today's economy, with jobs in short supply, government leaders have allowed the unemployment safety net to unravel, and millions of working Americans are left to fend for themselves.

## Welfare Reform: The War on the Poor

One of the most significant expressions of the right turn in American politics was the enactment in 1996 of the Personal Responsibility and Work Opportunity Reconciliation Act. This legislation abolished Aid to Families with Dependent Children and replaced it with a new welfare program, funded by block grants to the states, entitled Temporary Assistance for Needy Families (TANF).[120] Initiated by congressional Republicans, and receiving the eventual acquiescence of the Clinton administration, this overhaul of the welfare system was advertised to combat "welfare dependency" and promote work, marriage, and two-parent families. TANF established time limits, permitting poor mothers to receive benefits for a lifetime total of no more than sixty months, with states allowed to set even shorter limits. To facilitate a rapid transition from "welfare dependency" to "economic self-sufficiency," TANF mandated work requirements as well, forcing poor mothers to get jobs in exchange for their benefits, even if this meant abandoning their education or leaving their children with unreliable care providers. And as a mechanism of enforcement, TANF also established a system of sanctions, including reduced-benefit penalties for non-compliance with work rules and other welfare regulations.[121]

The TANF program, in conjunction with the strong economy of the late 1990s, had one particularly notable effect: the welfare rolls fell dramatically. The number of families receiving cash welfare payments declined from over 5 million in 1993 and 1994 to less than 2 million in recent years, leaving a total of fewer than 5 million adult and child recipients in 2010, down from over 14 million in the mid-1990s. Disturbingly, however, the decline in the welfare caseload has continued even as the rate and severity of poverty have worsened. And while one might think that in the wake of the Great Recession the welfare rolls would have expanded significantly, in fact the number of families receiving TANF benefits in 2010 was no greater than it was in 2006, before the recession hit.[122] Consider also that between 2000 and 2012, the number of poor children increased by more than 4 million, the number of poor female-headed households increased by nearly 2.4 million, and the number of people in deep poverty (below half the poverty threshold) reached a near record high of more than 20 million.[123] And yet, despite the increasing severity of the poverty problem and the continued weakness of the economy, the number of people receiving TANF benefits, though rising modestly in 2009 and 2010, is still considerably lower than it was in 2000. Since most states do not adjust benefit levels to the rate of inflation, not only are fewer families receiving cash assistance today, but the amount they are receiving had declined by approximately 30 percent since the 1996 welfare reform act.[124]

What accounts for the seemingly paradoxical decline in the welfare case-load during a decade or so of increasing economic hardship? Certainly there has been no reduction in the number of needy families or in the number of poor families *eligible* for TANF. What has declined, rather, is the number of eligible families *enrolled* in TANF. In a statement to congress, Kay E. Brown, representing the Government Accountability Office, reported that almost 90 percent of the decrease in the cash assistance caseload in the decade following the enactment of TANF "resulted from fewer eligible families participating in the program."[125] This outcome, in turn, was largely the intended product of state agencies, now possessing almost complete discretion in the management of the program, to reduce welfare rolls, both by discouraging entry into the program and by hurrying exit from the program. With the enactment of welfare reform, cash assistance ceased being an entitlement. Unlike Social Security or food stamps, under the TANF program, eligibility does not confer a right to benefits. As a result, countless deserving families have been denied aid during difficult times.[126] This reveals the dark side of welfare reform: the government safety net for poor mothers and their children has been severely weakened, leaving more low-income families to make do on their own.

The passage of TANF has also had the effect of forcing more poor mothers into a crowded low-wage labor market, exerting additional downward pressure on already low wages.[127] The early results of this "work first" initiative, based mostly on data collected prior to the 2001 recession, have been mixed at best. The employment outlook and earnings of some former recipients have improved, but most are still laboring below or near the poverty line.[128] More recent studies, however, based on in-depth interviews with low-income women, including both current and former TANF recipients, point to serious defects in the reformed welfare system. Poor women have not received adequate help in their efforts to reconcile work–family conflicts, secure decent housing, find affordable and reliable child care, resolve periodic transportation problems, or deal with health-care issues. Nor has the reform of the welfare system helped poor women, if able to find jobs at all, escape the low-wage labor market, work their way out of poverty, and attain economic self-sufficiency.[129]

Leaders of both political parties have overwhelmingly judged welfare reform a success. But this tells us less about the workings of welfare than about the priorities of government policy makers. If the purpose is to reduce the welfare rolls and increase the labor force participation of poor mothers, then welfare reform has been reasonably effective. But if the purpose of a welfare system is to make sure needy families have an adequate income and the opportunity to improve their lives, then welfare reform has been an abysmal failure.

## Labor Law: The Assault on Unions and Workers' Rights

A survey by Peter Hart Research conducted in December 2006 found that 53 percent of workers said they would join a union if they could.[130] Clearly, the remarkably low level of unionization in the United States, less than 7 percent in the private sector, cannot be attributed to the preferences of employees. The issue is one of power.[131] Workers in the United States seeking to form unions face "an exceptionally hostile terrain," and this terrain has become even more hostile since the 1980s.[132] Employers are extraordinarily powerful in their own right, and they have devised, with the aid of union-busting consultants, an impressive array of legal and illegal union avoidance strategies.[133]

The National Labor Relations Act of 1935, intended to protect the rights of workers to unionize and engage in collective bargaining, and the National Labor Relations Board, created to oversee union elections and adjudicate claims of unfair labor practices, have become increasingly ineffective, unable to ensure an equitable balance of power between employers and employees. Labor laws repeatedly go unenforced, and when they are enforced, the penalties imposed on employers are insufficiently costly to deter violations.[134] The playing field is even more tilted against workers, however, because court cases over the past several decades have limited collective bargaining rights, denied class-action suits (as in the gender discrimination case *Wal-Mart v. Dukes*), and restricted the ability of organizers to communicate pro-union information to employees.[135] The combination of weak labor laws, lax enforcement, court rulings, and the anti-union animus of government—evident especially during the Reagan and Bush II administrations, and still very much alive in many state legislatures today—has given rise to a "culture of impunity" in which employers are effectively free to deny workers the right to unionize.[136]

If government officials do not support the right of workers to form unions, if they rarely enforce laws protecting workers' rights, and if employers suffer only minimal penalties for violating the law, then, to be sure, labor laws will be broken. And they have been broken, routinely and increasingly so over the past several decades. Employer opposition to unions has intensified in the 2000s, according to Kate Bronfenbrenner, with heavier reliance on coercive, retaliatory, and intimidation tactics, including plant closing threats, harassment, and firings.[137] According to a report by John Schmitt and Ben Zipperer, the number of illegal firings of pro-union workers during union organizing efforts rose toward the end of the 1970s, skyrocketed during the 1980s, declined somewhat in the 1990s, and then started climbing again in the 2000s.[138] For the period from 2001 to 2007, they estimate that "union organizers and activists faced a 15 to 20 percent chance of being illegally fired."[139] A unionization drive can be derailed by the illegal termination of union activists, of course, but beyond this immediate effect, the firing of union leaders sends a powerful message, deterring other workers from acting on their pro-union sentiments.

Workers seeking union representation face daunting hurdles. But the situation is even worse for many categories of workers who are explicitly excluded from labor law protection—including agricultural workers, domestic workers, independent contractors, low-level supervisors, and in some states, public employees.[140] In one ruling, for example, the NLRB, adopting an inordinately broad definition of supervisory work, "expanded the pool of workers exempted from union membership" to include registered nurses performing modest supervisory duties.[141] Many part-time and temporary workers, who constitute a large and growing share of the workforce, also do not have the right to unionize.[142] The same is true for an assortment of workers engaged in national security duties, including baggage screeners and employees in the Department of Homeland Security.[143] In addition, numerous states, particularly those in the South, have long-standing "right to work" laws that effectively create business-friendly union-free zones.[144] Even when workers, against all odds, manage to form a union, existing labor laws often prevent them from exercising any real power. For example, workers are prohibited from participating in secondary boycotts or sympathy strikes, and while they cannot be legally fired for going out on strike, in what amounts to practically the same thing, their jobs can be filled by "permanent replacements."[145]

It is not only when workers participate in union activity that business owners treat them unfairly and violate their rights. Gordon Lafer documents how employers in many states throughout the country, with the help of corporate-backed lobbyists and business-friendly legislators, have engaged in tenacious battles on the minimum wage front. Employers and their allies have fought, often successfully, to prevent cities and states from increasing the minimum wage, bar measures pegging the minimum wage to the rate of inflation, restrict the categories of workers subject to the minimum wage, establish subminimum wages for certain industries and types of workers, and otherwise create loopholes in the application of the minimum wage law.[146] Workers on the job are mistreated in other ways as well, sometimes legally, sometimes illegally: not being allowed to take sick days, denied meal breaks, retaliation for complaints about employer abuses, and restrictions on free speech. Perhaps the most egregious and frequent violation workers experience today is wage theft. This widespread and growing practice is made possible by the weak enforcement of labor standards. Employers steal from their employees because it is profitable to do so; because they can typically get away with it; and because if they get caught with their hands in the till, the penalties are minimal. Wage theft takes many forms: paying workers below the legal minimum, denying workers overtime pay, insisting that employees work off the clock, tip stealing by supervisors or managers, illegal deductions from workers' paychecks, and simply refusing to pay wages earned (a problem for undocumented workers in particular). The annual amount of money stolen from workers through wage theft is considerable too, according to Lafer, "far greater than the combined total stolen in all the bank robberies, gas station robberies, and convenience store robberies in the country."[147]

What is most troubling is not that employers habitually engage in anti-union activities that violate the spirit and letter of the law or that they are willing to resort to just about any means to reduce labor costs. This is to be expected of self-interested, profit-maximizing business firms. More troubling is that a putatively democratic government, if only by passively standing on the sidelines, has become an enabler of this employer malfeasance. In the ongoing and highly successful business offensive against organized labor and the rights of workers more generally, government has effectively lined up against working Americans. In the current political climate, a product of the rightward shift in American politics, the right of employers to resist unions and exploit workers is subject to far more legal protection than is the right of workers to form unions and be treated fairly.

* * *

Government policy since the 1970s has become increasingly skewed in favor of the interests of business over labor. This is reflected both in what policy makers have done and in what they have failed to do. The minimum wage, unemployment insurance, welfare reform, and labor law—in all these policy areas, government officials have pursued an agenda that in hard times makes life even harder for the working class and the poor. The same right-turn story could be told about monetary policy, tax policy, trade policy, and regulatory policy.[148] The conservative, pro-business bias in American politics is evident also in the refusal of government leaders to pass the sort of worker- and family-friendly legislation common in most other advanced industrialized countries, including universal health insurance, subsidized child care, and paid parental leave.

This is not to say the U.S. government does nothing to help low-income families. The Earned Income Tax Credit boosts the wages of low-income workers, food stamps and other nutrition programs help fight hunger, and Medicaid offers health care to the poor and the disabled.[149] Contrary to the claims of anti-government crusaders, moreover, these and other programs, all currently under attack by the right, show that government can make a positive difference in the lives of average Americans. In drawing attention to the class bias of political policy, therefore, we should not overlook the benefits many people still derive from government programs. And by the same token, we should not underestimate how much low-income families would be harmed if the ongoing assault on the welfare state continues and if existing programs, however limited, are subject to further reductions.

# CONCLUSION

The ongoing power shift in American politics underlies the continued refusal of government to contemplate policies that might reduce growing inequalities and alleviate economic hardships. The American political system, even more so since the 1970s, is strongly resistant to egalitarian social reforms. This is the case, as we have seen, for an assortment of reasons. Business is exceptionally powerful, organized labor is exceptionally weak, government leaders are unresponsive to the policy preferences of low-income Americans, the working class and the poor are politically marginalized, and the synergy of money and power gives economic elites an overwhelming political advantage. The combination of these factors, in a country whose political institutions lean naturally to the right, explains why redistributive policies are absent from the political agenda and why levels of inequality and poverty remain so persistently high. In the current political context, poorer Americans lack equitable access to one of the most important means for improving their economic prospects: government. The working class and the poor are not only denied a fair share of the gains from increasing productivity; they are also denied a fair share of the benefits from public policy.

*Chapter Seven*

# The Cultural System and Poverty

## HEARTS AND MINDS

An ideological battle is being waged in the United States. In this ongoing culture war, activists on the right and the left are locked in a struggle for the hearts and minds of the American public. On issues ranging from abortion to gay rights, from immigration to evolution, antagonists fight it out in diverse venues of public discourse: the news and entertainment media, court cases, legislative hearings, political campaigns, and meetings of church groups, school boards, and civic organizations. In the trenches of everyday life, too, skirmishes arise between family members, friends, neighbors, classmates, and co-workers. This war of ideas—the expression of conflicting values, interests, and visions of society—is a dynamic force, influencing the formation of public opinion, political culture, and social policy.

On one important front in this larger culture war, opposing versions of "poverty knowledge" are pitted against one another.[1] The clash of conflicting poverty theories and policy prescriptions resounds in the public sphere, though louder at some times than others. Think tanks, business groups, academic experts, political pundits, labor activists, and welfare rights advocates—each weighing in on the plight of the poor—all contend to gain a hearing in the arenas of public opinion and policy formation. The stakes in this battle are high. The winning side at any particular historical moment defines the problem of poverty, sets the terms of debate, and controls the political agenda.

145

When individuals ponder issues of poverty, inequality, and welfare, their thinking is shaped by the larger cultural context. Ann Swidler envisions the surrounding culture as a "tool kit" of symbolic resources that individuals dip into selectively to construct meanings and devise courses of action.[2] Included within this tool kit is the reigning vocabulary of poverty. Among the terms gaining prominence since the 1970s are "personal responsibility," "illegitimacy," "underclass," and "welfare dependency." These and other keywords dictate the prevailing definition of the poverty problem, the boundaries of respectable disagreement, and the policy responses deemed appropriate.

The cultural tool kit also consists of various "storylines," as Eduardo Bonilla-Silva calls them. These enable us to translate the immense complexity of the social world into commonsense principles and folk theories. In the United States, for example, the American Dream ideal, the narrative of triumph over adversity, and the Horatio Alger myth are among the story lines most commonly invoked when people are prompted to wonder why some are rich and others poor. Story lines such as these are widely available. They are deposited in our cultural heritage and circulate in movies, television shows, books, magazines, and fairy tales. These story lines equip us with ready-made formulas we "use to make sense of the world, to decide what is right and wrong, true or false, important or unimportant."[3]

As in the case of the economic and political systems, the cultural system is an arena of power and conflict. What transpires within this system, and which terminology and story lines win acceptance, determines whether average Americans are informed or uninformed about social issues, whether they perceive the poor as "deserving" or "undeserving," and whether they believe government should do more or less to help disadvantaged groups. The cultural system matters, as people's thinking about poverty and welfare shapes their political preferences and voting behavior. The attitudes and beliefs of the American public have economic and political significance.

This chapter turns the individualistic perspective on its head. In its preoccupation with the culture of the poor, the conventional view ignores the other side of the picture: how the mainstream culture, particularly through its influence on government policy, affects poor people's access to resources and opportunities. After all, a lot hinges on whether ordinary Americans respond to poverty with apathy or outrage, whether they regard the poor with hostility or generosity, and whether they view poverty as an inevitable condition or a resolvable problem. Whether we have more or less poverty and whether the hardships experienced by the poor are more or less severe depend on the temper of the middle-class culture.

Because of their narrow focus on the deficiencies of the poor, individualistic theories, as we have seen, fail to recognize adequately how the rate and depth of poverty in the United States depend on power struggles within the economic and political systems. The purpose of this chapter, revealing another weakness of the individualistic perspective, is to show how the lives of the poor and their prospects for escaping poverty are also constrained by ideological forces outside their immediate control. Poverty is not only an economic problem and a political problem; it is also a cultural problem. We have the poverty we have in this country in part because of the beliefs and attitudes prevalent among the larger population. The poor are held hostage not only to the decisions of economic and political elites, but to the beliefs and opinions of the middle class as well.

My objective in this chapter is to illustrate the importance of the cultural system for understanding the persistence of poverty in the United States. I pursue this by first looking at popular beliefs about poverty and welfare, focusing especially on how Americans' thinking about social problems is conditioned by the dominant individualistic ideology. I then discuss how the U.S. news media and the right-wing ideology machine reinforce this ideology, creating a cultural and political bias favoring individualistic explanations and remedies over structural ones. I conclude by considering the rightward turn of public discourse on issues of poverty and welfare over the past four decades. This cultural power shift has not only engendered a change in the language Americans use to talk about the poor; it has also made life harder for low-income families and has moved us further away from a real solution to problems of poverty and inequality.

## THE AMERICAN DREAM AND THE IDEOLOGY OF INDIVIDUALISM

In 2002, a Pew Center poll asked a sample of people from forty-four countries to reply to the following assertion: "Success in life is pretty much determined by forces outside our control." Not surprisingly, the majority of Americans disagreed with this statement. More so than people from other countries, respondents from the United States believe their economic fate rests in their own hands.[4] Americans continue to affirm the promise of upward social mobility as well. "Is it possible to start out poor, work hard, and become rich?" In 2005, 80 percent of respondents said yes to this question, up from 60 percent in 1983.[5] On the eve of the 2007 financial collapse, most Americans considered the United States, uniquely, to be a society of equals, a "land of opportunity" where individual effort pays off, where "everyone who works hard can get ahead," and where anyone can become rich.[6]

Even in the midst of the Great Recession, the vast majority of Americans cited hard work, ambition, and education as the most important factors promoting economic mobility, more important even that the state of the economy. Most Americans, 55 percent, also disagreed with the following statement: "In the United States, a child's chances of achieving financial success is tied to the income of his or her parents." The authors of this study conclude that despite tough economic times the "notion that America is a meritocracy where individuals can apply themselves and move ahead continues to endure."[7] By 2014, the public, according to some measures, was more pessimistic about the validity of the American Dream, but even then 60 percent of Americans agreed that "most people who want to get ahead can make it if they're willing to work hard."[8]

According to the individualistic ideology, opportunities in the United States are available for anyone motivated to succeed, economic outcomes are a function of ability and effort, and existing inequalities are fair and inevitable.[9] The logic of this ideology encourages its adherents to attribute poverty to the deficiencies of the poor and to favor individualistic solutions to problems of economic hardship. Policy advocates, regardless of political affiliation, thus typically target the poor for reform. Conservatives recommend improving poor people through tough love and moral uplift, while liberals call for more training and education. In the U.S. political culture, structural reforms—government job creation, public investment in poor communities, or redistribution of income and wealth, for example—rarely receive serious consideration. Measures such as these, besides facing strong opposition from powerful business groups, are a hard sell to a public schooled in the virtues of self-reliance and small government.

The set of beliefs associated with the principle of individualism is often said to have the status of a "dominant ideology" in the United States.[10] Even if not altogether dominant, the cultural power of the individualistic perspective outweighs that of the opposing structural perspective.[11] Americans are more frequently exposed to individualistic story lines, and like popular commercial jingles, such story lines are highly accessible to cognition, easy to recall and apply. The entertainment media, particularly television and movies, regularly disseminates morality tales promoting and reinforcing the individualistic ideology. Hollywood films routinely tell familiar stories about how determined and hardworking individuals overcome adversity to achieve success and realize their dreams. As Robert Bulman shows, the popular genre of urban high school films, from *Blackboard Jungle* to *Dangerous Minds*, conveys just this message, confirming what many audience members already take for granted: individual effort and a positive, can-do attitude, with a little prodding from dedicated teachers, are all that is necessary for disadvantaged teens to lift themselves out of poverty. [12] Stories of impoverished individuals pulling themselves up by their own bootstraps, trading in their rags for riches, are psychologically and emotionally powerful as well. And, if only in our fantasies, such stories also resonate with our personal lives and experiences.

Individualism is a powerful ideology also because it is the preferred ideology of the powerful, legitimating an economic and political system that perpetuates their privileged status. [13] This ideology acquires further credibility because it is thoroughly institutionalized in American culture, regularly affirmed in the educational, political, and economic systems and in the process of family socialization. Americans' routine exposure to ideologies of poverty and inequality is consistently skewed toward a language accentuating the efficacy of individual striving rather than the constraint of limited opportunities. Finally, the ideology of individualism is influential not only because it proposes easily understandable and culturally sanctioned explanations for poverty, but also because it suggests straightforward and uncontroversial solutions to the problem: education, hard work, and family values.

In the following sections, I briefly review some of the research on what Americans think about poverty and then reconsider the relative strength of individualism and structuralism in American political culture.

## BELIEFS ABOUT POVERTY AND THE POOR

Social scientists exploring the beliefs of the American public have uncovered two distinct theories of poverty. [14] One camp attributes poverty primarily to individual or internal factors, such as lack of motivation, irresponsible behavior, or deviant values. The other camp attributes poverty primarily to structural or external factors, such as discrimination, low-quality schools, or lack of jobs. [15] The majority of the populace, most studies show, falls into the first camp. [16] James Kluegel and Eliot Smith, for example, find that Americans "strongly endorse individual reasons for economic position, particularly for poverty, and reject liberal and (especially) radical explanations emphasizing structural causes."[17] Judith Chafel, in an extensive review of the literature, draws a similar conclusion. The American public for the most part, she states, is predisposed to "blame the victim"; perceives poverty as being "inevitable, necessary, and just"; and appears generally "content with the status quo."[18]

The influence of the individualistic ideology is evident also from studies of attitudes toward the poor. If the public attributes poverty to the failings of the poor rather than to structural causes, then they are likely also to have disparaging views of poor people. This is precisely what Catherine Cozzarelli and her colleagues discover. Based on data gathered from a sample of college students, they show that judgments about the character traits and personality attributes of the poor are much more negative than corresponding opinions about the middle class. Poor people, for instance, are typically regarded as being significantly less hardworking, responsible, friendly, proud, family oriented, or intelligent than middle-class people.[19] The individualistic propensity to blame the poor for their poverty goes hand in hand with the tendency to regard poor people, in one respect or another, as inferior.

Welfare recipients bear the brunt of negative stereotypes about the poor. Americans commonly believe that women on welfare do not really want to work, prefer living off welfare, could get along without government assistance if they tried, and have babies out of wedlock to increase their monthly payments.[20] Even many welfare recipients (though usually citing structural factors in their own individual cases) concur with the popular view that most women on public assistance are lazy, unmotivated, and inclined to abuse the system.[21]

Despite the ubiquitous presence of individualistic story lines in the cultural system, not all Americans think alike about issues of poverty, welfare, and inequality, nor do they all repudiate structural explanations. Beliefs about the causes of poverty vary by income, education, race, gender, religion, and other socioeconomic and demographic characteristics. Women, low-income individuals, and people who are non-white, younger, more educated, and less religious are more likely to cite structural factors as causes of poverty.[22] Attitudes toward the poor differ also depending on the segment of the poverty population in question. For example, as compared to studies of "generic" poverty, research on public views of homelessness has found stronger support for the structural viewpoint.[23] The American public also tends to have more favorable attitudes toward the white poor compared to the black poor,[24] women compared to men,[25] children compared to single mothers,[26] the elderly compared to the working-age poor,[27] and poor people who appear to be trying to get ahead compared to those who seem content to live off welfare.[28]

Further complicating the story, recent survey data also suggest that Americans today, several years into a persistently weak economic recovery, have become more favorably inclined toward a structural viewpoint. A 2014 study conducted by the Center for American Progress found that more than 75 percent of the public agreed with the following statement: "The primary reason so many people are living in poverty today is that our economy is failing to produce enough jobs that pay decent wages."[29] This is a surprising finding, even more so because support for this statement is no less strong among conservatives than it is among liberals. Significant partisan differences are apparent in most other items in this survey, and in the responses to another 2014 survey as well.[30] Remarkably, however, the normal pattern of partisan divergence is completely absent on this particular "agree or disagree" question. One possible explanation is that when conservatives today attribute poverty to a malfunctioning economy, they are not so much making a general declaration about the causes of poverty as they are expressing their antipathy toward what they perceive to be the failed economic policies of the Obama administration. To the extent this is the case, the data presented overstate the level of support for a structural view of poverty. But even assuming this survey finding reveals a more or less genuine phenomenon, what also remains uncertain is whether this unusually strong agreement with a structural argument is indicative of an enduring shift in Americans' beliefs about poverty or a transitory by-product of the Great Recession and the current political climate. Confusing the picture even more, the same Center for American Progress study reports that nearly 80 percent of the public, including 66 percent of conservatives, agree that "most people living in poverty are decent people who are working hard to make ends meet." Yet a majority of the public, and 75 percent of conservatives, also agree that "too many poor people would rather live off of government programs and benefits than work to lift themselves out of poverty." This survey, as I discuss more fully in the next section, makes one thing clear: when Americans express support for a structural explanation, this does not necessarily imply that they see poor people in a positive light or categorically reject an individualistic perspective on poverty.[31]

## STRONG INDIVIDUALISM, WEAK STRUCTURALISM

Studies of public opinion on a variety of social policy issues reveal that Americans do not slavishly adhere to the principle of individualism.[32] They hold views that are often ambiguous, uncertain, and inconsistent; they endorse and shift easily between multiple and often contradictory theories; what they presume to be true in general or as a matter of abstract principle often conflicts with what they regard as true in the concrete case of particular individuals; and their beliefs about poverty are sensitive to the manner in which the issue is framed.[33] While the individualistic ideology certainly exerts a powerful cultural influence, Americans nevertheless remain divided in their understanding of the sources of poverty, with many acknowledging the importance of structural causes. Most Americans also resist the laissez-faire policy prescriptions that follow from the individualistic ideology. Their embrace of individualism is tempered by a countervailing commitment to egalitarian values. They believe government has a responsibility to guarantee equality of opportunity and ensure that the basic needs of all citizens are met.[34] Indeed, many Americans even favor increased government spending on programs to reduce poverty.[35]

Despite these findings, however, and the sometimes muddy picture that emerges from public opinion studies, there are a number of reasons to think that individualism remains a dominant ideology. Particularly in the arenas of mainstream public discourse and policy formation, the individualistic perspective prevails over the structural perspective.

First, most Americans believe there are many causes of poverty—some internal, some external. Individualism and structuralism are not necessarily perceived as being incompatible.[36] Individualists do not always deny the relevance of structural factors, and those affirming structural causes do not necessarily reject a baseline individualistic perspective.[37] African Americans and Latinos in particular, Matthew Hunt finds, strongly agree with *both* individualistic and structural explanations for poverty.[38] Structural views, he suggests, "may be combined with, or layered on to, an existing individualistic base."[39] Survey data collected over many years give evidence of such a bedrock individualism, showing that over 90 percent of Americans cite "lack of effort" as an important cause of poverty.[40] The general pattern, it would be fair to say, is one of widespread acceptance of individualism, with a sizable population *also* supporting structural explanations.[41] People often agree with structural explanations, but this by no means precludes them from having a more general and deeply rooted adherence to the dominant individualistic ideology.

Second, as compared to their individualistic counterparts, those who support structural arguments are more ambivalent about their beliefs, less firmly tied to their position, and less likely to draw policy recommendations consistent with their structural viewpoint. Proponents of individualism, no doubt due in part to its greater cultural currency, are less liable to alter their view over time. In contrast to the "stable effects of individualism," Hunt observes, "structuralist beliefs are more variable, more responsive to group memberships, personal experiences, and the prevailing social climate."[42] In the U.S. political tradition, the principle of individualism and the belief in limited government are stronger than competing humanitarian and egalitarian values that might inspire support for structural programs to combat poverty.[43] Thus, while many Americans "want the government to help the poor," they also "insist that the role be limited and not replace an individual's obligation to pursue self-reliance."[44] In contrast to individualism, which is firmly grounded in the political culture, the influence of structuralism is more uncertain and tenuous and less likely to engender a strong commitment to structural solutions.

Third, a strong structural perspective emphasizes increasing inequality in the distribution of wealth and power, the inability of the American political economy to generate enough decent-paying jobs, and the failure of American political institutions to live up to the democratic ideal. But many Americans who are perceived as falling into the structural camp endorse a weak structuralism only. What they usually have in mind when they say poverty is caused by external circumstances is that poor people cannot get ahead because of a deprived family background or inadequate schools—because of inequality of opportunity. Consistent with the liberal human capital approach, weak structuralists favor measures designed to help the poor help themselves, including initiatives to expand education and training programs. They show much less support, however, for the redistribution of income and wealth or for policies to fight poverty and inequality through direct government expenditures.[45] In its call for modest though certainly desirable reforms, this weak structuralism affirms a traditional conception of American society as a meritocracy in the making.[46] In contrast to a strong structuralism, the weak version does not contradict the individualistic perspective so much as it qualifies it.

Fourth, while many Americans recognize that "structural barriers" hinder poor people from escaping poverty, this is muted in its implications by being joined with the belief that "anyone who works hard enough can overcome such barriers."[47] A majority of Americans agree with this statement: "One of the big problems in this country is that we don't give everyone an equal chance." And yet an even larger majority believes that "most people who don't get ahead should not blame the system, they only have themselves to blame."[48] Even when respondents acknowledge, for example, that women and racial and ethnic minorities encounter discrimination, they refuse to accept this as an excuse for failure. As Nancy DiTomaso finds, furthermore, the obstacles to success people sometime face are commonly regarded, at least by white Americans, as being more often than not of their own making.[49] The American public believes in both the efficacy of individual effort and the existence of structural barriers to achievement. But the first belief trumps the second, leaving only a watered-down, weak version of structuralism.

Fifth, according to what Robinson and Bell call the "underdog principle," the poor are less likely than the rich to regard existing inequalities as just.[50] People who favor structural explanations, similarly, whether weak or strong, tend to be located on the lower and less influential end of the social hierarchy. Proponents of structuralism are not only less consistent in their adherence to this perspective; they also occupy the political margins. As Lawrence Bobo points out, people holding beliefs challenging the dominant ideology tend to be disengaged from politics, excluded from public debate, and lacking in "'effective' public opinion."[51] Even in the face of structuralist dissent, individualism remains a dominant ideology because it is the ideology promoted by the powerful.

The ideological battle for the hearts and minds of the American public is important. What Americans think about the causes of poverty and how they feel about welfare recipients and the poor have an effect on their political policy preferences. Individuals inclined toward the structural perspective favor a more generous welfare system and are more likely to support redistributive policies.[52] People's beliefs have political implications; at the very least, they establish boundaries for what at the moment is politically possible. In the United States, where individualism remains the dominant ideology, this is bad news for the poor. As long as the majority of Americans, and an even larger majority of powerful Americans, adhere to an individualistic viewpoint—as long as they believe poverty is the fault of the poor and that government programs cause more harm than good—advocates for structural reforms of the sort needed to effectively address the problem of poverty face a steep uphill battle.

## THE NEWS MEDIA

Americans acquire most of their information about the world and their understanding of social and political issues from the media, especially from television news programs. The media play a powerful role in shaping the perceptions and opinions of the American public and fashioning the imagery and discourse surrounding issues of poverty.[53] While journalists do a good job of covering some issues, reporting on poverty is not their strong suit. News stories provide, at best, only cursory analysis of the structural causes of poverty and generally give tacit support to the dominant individualistic ideology. Media coverage of poverty serves less to enlighten the public or provoke genuine debate than to pass along the conventional wisdom. In this respect, the media are a significant part of the poverty problem.

The purpose of the news media in an ideal democratic world is to supply people with the information they need to fulfill their citizenship responsibilities and to ensure that political and economic leaders are held publicly accountable.[54] Judged by this standard, the U.S. news media are doing a miserable job. One important reason for this is that news organizations are subordinate parts of an increasingly concentrated system of corporate conglomerates.[55] The ability of the press to serve faithfully as a watchdog in the interest of democracy is fatally compromised by the media's location within the corporate system and by their own highly undemocratic structure. The corporate entities that own and operate newspapers, news magazines, and television and radio news programs have their own particular economic and political interests. These intrude, directly or indirectly, on the practice of journalism and the content of the news. The political, economic, and corporate setting within which producers, publishers, editors, and reporters work creates strong resistance to news stories that might, for example, trace the causes of poverty back to the behavior of large corporations, the economic and political power of big business, or the nature of capitalism itself.

Mainstream news organizations are not just owned by large corporations; they are also commercial, profit-seeking enterprises themselves. News programs and publications in the United States, increasingly so in recent decades, have come under the sway of business imperatives. The news is a commercial product: it is manufactured, marketed, and sold just like any other commodity. Journalism is as much a business as it is a profession, and as with any other business, its purpose is to make money. News organizations are pressured to be profitable; to restrain production costs; to cut back, for example, on expensive investigative reporting and foreign news coverage. In the news media today, as in the rest of corporate America, the bottom line prevails.

The news media are subject to the conservative sensibilities of their chief customers as well. Advertisers are not eager to pay for news programming that courts controversy, gives voice to dissident viewpoints, casts a negative light on the culture of consumerism, or exposes the business of America to critical scrutiny. To keep advertising revenues flowing in, the media also need to be concerned about attracting an audience—readers for newspapers and magazines, listeners for radio, and viewers for television. Caught up in a continuous scramble to improve ratings and expand audience share, news programs nowadays more than ever bow down to the "supra-ideology" of entertainment.[56] This creates an incentive to downplay hard and probing news in favor of scandals, car chases, puff pieces, celebrity gossip, melodramatic human interest stories, and the spectacle of opinion mongering that has become the meat and potatoes of the cable news networks.[57]

The news media create both noise and silence, drawing attention to some issues and diverting attention from others. They set the agenda, telling the public, by implication, what is important and what is not. The first thing that should be said about mainstream news coverage of poverty is that there is just not very much of it.[58] A recent Fairness and Accuracy in Reporting (FAIR) study of the three major nightly news networks (CBS, NBC, and ABC) during the fourteen-month period from January 2013 through February 2014 found a total of only twenty-three segments on poverty, fewer than two a month, with many of these being "uselessly brief or even dismissive."[59] Though poverty receives little coverage, and even less in-depth coverage, inequality has attracted considerable media attention in the past few years. But as *New York Times* reporter Jason DeParle acknowledges, the dominant story line on the topic of inequality is the growing wealth of the super rich, not the continuing deprivation of the persistently poor.[60] News stories explicitly addressing the problem of poverty are sufficiently rare that, as one media critic reports, their publication "becomes a sort of 'very special episode' of journalism that we sort of roll out every so often."[61] This quality of poverty coverage—its novelty—is likely to make the issue less rather than more salient to the public. In such stories, furthermore, the poor tend to be distanced and objectified, appearing merely as "objects of reporting" not as deserving citizens in their own right.[62] In any case, no matter how thoroughly we might read our daily newspapers, and no matter how many hours we

might spend watching news programs on television, we are unlikely to conclude from our exposure that poverty is a serious problem in the United
States, much less a structural problem. While journalists offer an occasional
story about the poor, for the most part poverty is a neglected social issue. The
media "have 'disappeared' the needy from the news."[63]

The second thing that should be said about mainstream news coverage is
it consistently represents poverty as an individual problem rather than a
social problem, a "personal trouble" rather than a "public issue."[64] When
news programs shine a light on the poor, they rarely provide much illumina-
tion. They can, at their best, offer a glimpse into the daily lives of poor
people, and can even puncture stereotypes, rouse passion, and elicit sympathy. But the systemic nature of poverty falls outside the normal purview of
news reporting.[65] The "very nature of journalism," Peter Parisi observes,
"seems opposed to portrayals of the 'big picture.'"[66] The gaze of the news
media is drawn toward the micro as opposed to the macro: isolated cases
more than recurring social patterns, personal circumstances more than social
context, and the shortcomings of individuals more than the inequities of the
political economy. Journalists provide *depictions* of the poor—people down
on their luck, in need of social assistance, or victims of their own bad
choices. But in the news media's efforts to capture the human drama, the less
visible social forces ultimately responsible for the persistence of poverty
remain hidden.

How do the news media, when they do not simply ignore the problem,
manage so consistently to miss the forest for the trees? How do the constraints and conventions of news reporting lead journalists to overlook the
big picture and portray poverty primarily as an individual problem? Without
presuming to be comprehensive, in what follows I identify several factors
pertaining to the practice of journalism and the organization of news coverage that encourage the media to obscure or misconstrue the structural bases
of American poverty.

## Framing Poverty in News Stories

The news media fabricate reports, and the coherence and effect of these
reports derive from how they are "framed"—how they are packaged or put
together.[67] On the infrequent occasions when television addresses issues of
poverty, news programs typically frame their reports in a manner that unwittingly induces viewers to blame poverty on the poor. Shanto Iyengar's research shows that the majority of news stories about poverty employ an

"episodic" as opposed to a "thematic" frame: they focus on the personal experiences of the poor rather than broader policy issues.[68] When television programs describe poverty in thematic terms, viewers are more likely to attribute the problem to social conditions, but when the more popular episodic frame is used, they hold poor people themselves responsible. How television news coverage presents the issue to the public, Iyengar argues, influences "what people take to be the causes and cures of poverty." By employing "episodic" rather than "thematic" frames in their stories about the poor, the news media reinforce the ideology of individualism.[69]

## News Reporting as Storytelling

When the news media address issues of poverty or welfare, as in the case of "episodic" reports, they commonly employ a narrative structure. They tell stories, mostly stories about individuals. This way of conveying information has the advantage of being universally familiar. The story form also makes news reports easy to follow, brings out the human dimension of a topic, gives audiences a rooting or booing interest, and invites them to compare their own stories to those told in the media.

Though storytelling is an effective (and affective) means of communication, for some subject matters, including poverty, the habitual use of personal narrative produces a distorted picture. In the first place, news stories are selective: they inevitably make a long story short and a complex story simple. They also spotlight some cases rather than others. And the particular individuals featured in reports on poverty and welfare are typically chosen less because they are representative than because they are available, interesting, or conform to stereotypical notions of the poor. What makes a better story, an extreme though sensational example or an unremarkable but average case?

News reports employing a storytelling technique also place individuals at the center of attention. This puts the focus on people's personal qualities and unique circumstances, implicitly underlining the causal role these play in perpetuating poverty. If social forces are brought into the tale at all, these are typically mentioned only in passing, leaving unquestioned the tendency to interpret social problems as individual troubles. "Personalized story frames," Parisi concludes, typically subordinate social structure to individual choice, thus lending support to the "ideology of individualism."[70]

## The Welfare Poor, the Newly Poor, and the Already Poor

For several years both before and after the enactment of welfare reform in 1996, news reports on poverty focused disproportionately on the welfare system and welfare recipients. As Ange-Marie Hancock shows, moreover, they also conveyed a stock picture of the welfare recipient: a single, jobless, teenage African American mother. By promoting the image of the "welfare queen," the news media validated sexist and racist stereotypes while also diverting attention from the economic and political causes of poverty. [71] Since Americans respond more negatively to the issue of welfare than to the issue of poverty, furthermore, the media's skewed coverage also had the effect of diminishing sympathy for the poor. [72]

The news media's preoccupation with the issue of welfare during these years left the erroneous impression that the poverty population and the welfare population were coterminous and that the poverty population and the working population were mutually exclusive. Explicit stories about the poor were almost always about welfare recipients, who were presumed to be non-workers, and stories about the hardships endured by American workers seldom mentioned poverty. In the early 2000s, before the onset of the Great Recession, the *New York Times* published numerous revealing articles on globalization, outsourcing, downsizing, long-term unemployment, jobless growth, and stagnant wages. But rarely in these articles did reporters from the *Times* underline the connection between the economic developments they documented and the problem of persistent poverty. By segregating reports on the poor from news about the economy, the media obscured the structural nature of the poverty problem and fostered a false image of a divide between the "underclass" and the working class. [73]

Since the 2007 recession, the pattern of news coverage has changed. Welfare recipients, a diminishing fraction of the poverty population, rarely make the headlines anymore. Nor do those whose poverty preceded the financial collapse. Instead, the media's attention today is focused on formerly middle-class people who have fallen on hard times due to the continued weakness of the American economy. [74] Far less attention is paid to the large segment of the poverty population who were struggling before the recession—people who had it bad then and have it even worse now. Sympathetic reports on the "newly" poor, furthermore, have the effect, through invidious comparison, of stigmatizing the "already" poor. [75] By relying on this particular story line, Stephen Pimpare argues, the news media implicitly reinforce the distinction between the "deserving" poor, hardworking Americans who have blamelessly lost their jobs, and the "undeserving" poor, work-averse freeloaders looking to live off the government dole.[76] This might help to explain why people today express more support for a structural perspective on poverty without this necessarily causing them to abandon a firmly entrenched individualistic perspective.

## The Racialization of Poverty and Welfare

When white Americans think about the poor, they think about black people. The media bear most of the responsibility for this racialization of poverty. The percentage of African Americans appearing in the pictures and footage accompanying news stories about the poor far exceeds their percentage in the real poverty population.[77] In their visual depictions of the poor, the news media convey the impression that poverty is primarily a black problem. The faces of African Americans, as Martin Gilens shows, are even more prominently on display when news articles take a negative tone, as when they address issues of welfare abuse or welfare dependency. White faces are featured more frequently in news stories that shine a more positive light on the poor, for example articles disclosing the hardships of the working poor, the tragedy of the "newly poor," or the plight of the elderly.[78] Black people are overrepresented in the media's visual coverage of poverty and welfare, and particularly so in news stories painting an unsympathetic picture of the poor.

Because white Americans equate being poor with being black, their thinking about poverty is filtered through their racial attitudes. And since many white Americans, even more so since the election of Barack Obama, have negative views of black people, they have negative views of the poor as well.[79] African Americans are a segment of the poverty population whites perceive to be particularly blameworthy and undeserving, a legacy of the common stereotype that black people are lazy. The more the media associate poverty and race, the more they strengthen disparaging attitudes toward both poor people and African Americans. The media-induced racialization of poverty fosters a blame-the-victim mentality, dampens public enthusiasm for social programs, and makes it difficult to mobilize white support for political and economic reforms that might alleviate the hardships of the poor.

## Reliance on Official and Mainstream Sources

News organizations depend heavily on official sources of information and analysis, including corporate spokespersons, government bureaucrats, anointed experts associated with think tanks, and the representatives of public and private social service organizations. These sources are readily available and eager to offer their views; they have the appearance of being authoritative and objective; they are media savvy, capable of presenting their thoughts in a manner consistent with journalistic requirements; and their respectability helps ensure that news reports remain within the boundaries of acceptable opinion. Reporters return to these reliable sources again and again, enhancing their credibility.[80]

The news media's reliance on credentialed and mainstream sources diminishes the range of debate on social issues. Because they lack the official status that comes from having an "institutional seal of approval," more politically marginal groups, including poor people themselves, are denied a fair and equal hearing in the press.[81] According to the recent FAIR study mentioned previously, of the fifty-four sources included in the twenty-three segments of nightly news coverage about the poor from January 2013 through February 2014, only twenty-two "were people personally affected by poverty."[82] The general pattern, Charlotte Ryan explains, is for established sources to set forth the "main message" of a story, with poor people and their advocates—who are typically represented as "special interests" rather than "democratic voices"—brought in to supply the "color."[83] In her analysis of the welfare reform debate in the 1990s, for example, Ryan found that, as compared to welfare recipients and their political allies, official sources were more frequently cited, more prominently cited, cited at greater length, treated with more respect, and presumed to be more credible.

## Putting Out the News on a Daily Basis

The organizational imperatives of publishing a daily paper or producing a nightly news broadcast, along with the built-in predilection to define news as what is new that day, distracts attention from the underlying structural and historical forces. The news media are drawn by their very nature as organs of daily information to highlight today's news developments and news makers. Local television news stations, indeed, take great pride in announcing that they are first on the scene or first to report a breaking story. Depth of analysis takes second seat to getting there before anyone else, and the next day the news begins all over again.

With their day-to-day focus on newsworthy individuals and dramatic events, the media provide insufficient analysis of more enduring social processes.[84] The news media are limited by an attention span both narrow and short: they not only neglect social structure; they neglect history as well. As Robert Entman argues, in the absence of coverage explicitly portraying poverty "as a continuing multifaceted social problem," journalists inevitably give support to the individualistic ideology.[85] The daily orientation of the media and the conception of news as what is happening now, along with the infrequent coverage of the poor, are bound to create the impression that poverty is an incidental rather than a systemic problem. Audiences might be less tempted to reduce poverty to bad choices or bad luck if the news media were more oriented toward the longer run, if they focused not just on immediate events, but on developments. Michael Schudson suggests that if "the media operated monthly or annually rather than daily," the social and historical forces that existing formats overlook might be more visible features of news coverage.[86]

## The Sound Bite Bias

In broadcast media especially, and in the print media to a lesser extent, coverage of social problems is subject to severe time and space constraints. Only a small percentage of potential news stories can be fit into the pages of the daily newspaper, and even fewer can be squeezed into a half-hour news telecast. News stories are short and getting shorter, with nightly television broadcasts nowadays pared down to "nineteen minutes of News McNuggets."[87] Even the most newsworthy events receive only a few columns of print or a couple of minutes of airtime. The media have the capacity to deal with news topics in only the most cursory manner and is often reduced to relaying sound bites, snippets of information and opinion. There is little time for nuance, complexity, or context. Television can portray a problem, identify victims, and reveal symptoms, but it lacks the resources to explore the complex socioeconomic causes of issues like poverty and inequality. Time and space limitations preclude in-depth reporting.

The inevitably superficial nature of news coverage works to the advantage of the individualistic perspective. The structural perspective offers a complicated theory of poverty, not amenable to a twenty-second summary. It is also a dissenting view in American political culture—harder to understand, more controversial, and certain to provoke resistance. To build a persuasive case for the structural view requires time, and this is precisely what the news media have in short supply.[88]

## Focus on Technical Issues

Daniel Hallin argues that the media typically underline *technical* issues rather than *political* issues in their coverage of news stories.[89] Journalists approach the topic of poverty from a technical angle when, for example, they write stories about the measurement of poverty or when they investigate policy effectiveness. How many people are poor and by what criteria? Are public- and private-sector efforts successful in boosting the skills of low-income workers, in providing food and shelter to destitute families, in enabling single mothers to make the transition from welfare to work? By turning the spotlight on measurement issues and policy evaluation, reporters leave the comforting illusion that the powers that be are earnestly applying themselves to the resolution of pressing social problems. In pursuing such technical questions, furthermore, and skirting more controversial issues, reporters also make themselves less vulnerable to accusations of political bias.

Journalists suppress important political questions when their stories address technical issues. By ignoring "conflicts of interest" and "clashes over the ends and values of political life," they depoliticize the issue of poverty.[90] By concentrating on technical issues, in addition, the news media treat the audience not as citizens, but as passive consumers of expert knowledge. This technical mode of journalism, Hallin observes, does not present news stories in a manner likely to provoke dialogue about larger social issues or engender reflection about what kind of society we have or would like to have.[91]

\* \* \*

News organizations are constrained in how they cover social problems by corporate imperatives and commercial interests, by competition for ratings and audience share, by the routine conventions and practices of professional journalism, and by subtle and not-so-subtle influences emanating from the larger political and economic environment. Subject to these pressures, the news media, ultimately, are much better at producing entertainment than enlightenment, and they certainly fall well short of providing the information, analysis, and range of viewpoints Americans need to deliberate rationally about the poverty problem. The news media communicate images of the poor and conceptions of poverty, and these influence the beliefs and policy preferences of the American public. In this capacity, the institution of news in the United States, far from functioning simply as a neutral recorder, is a significant part of the problem. Though often unwittingly so, the mainstream media serve as an ally of the dominant ideology: they obscure the structural causes of poverty and bolster the prevailing individualistic view.

Media effects, of course, are not overwhelming or irresistible.[92] News consumers do not just passively accept the portrait of poverty presented in the news media; audiences come away from their exposure to the news with different interpretations of what they have seen, heard, or read; and Americans do manage to acquire information about the world from sources other than the mainstream media. In the end, however, while they do not in any simple manner *cause* Americans to adopt a blame-the-victim perspective on poverty, the news media do reinforce the ideology of individualism and make it difficult for people to conceive of or embrace a coherent structural alternative.

## THE RIGHT-WING IDEOLOGY MACHINE

In the early 1970s, against the backdrop of a deteriorating economy, business leaders and their intellectual allies surveyed a grim landscape. They had suffered costly economic and political setbacks in the previous decade, including the burden of a series of new regulatory measures. And in the war of ideas, too, pro-business conservatism, so it seemed, was on the ropes. The federal government was enthralled to the liberal agenda; the news media delivered a steady stream of unflattering reports about business and businessmen; colleges and universities had become left-wing outposts; civil rights, anti-war, feminist, consumer, and environmental movements threw up a succession of radical challenges to the establishment worldview; and public opinion held corporate America in low regard.[93] In this hostile climate, business executives found themselves on the defensive. As the chair of Westinghouse at the time lamented, "College professors don't love us. The news media don't trust us. The government doesn't help us. . . . It's so lonesome out here in business land."[94]

In 1971, Lewis F. Powell, who would subsequently be appointed by Richard Nixon to the Supreme Court, circulated a memo within the U.S. Chamber of Commerce warning the business community that the "free enterprise system" was under attack and in "deep trouble." He admonished business leaders to rise up on their own behalf, urging them to take a more aggressive political and ideological stance in support of American capitalism.[95] Irving Kristol, William Simon, and other conservative thinkers echoed Powell's message during the 1970s,[96] and many corporate managers, too, came to realize they faced an ideological crisis.[97] With their backs against the wall, business interests set out to win over public opinion, turn the culture around, and alter the terms of political discourse. They formed powerful lobby and advocacy organizations and launched a concerted drive to combat left-liberal inroads in the media and the universities, attack big government and organized labor, and mobilize popular support for pro-business policies. This political resurgence of business yielded, as one of its products, a right-wing ideology machine that would over the course of the next three decades evolve into an imposing network of corporate sponsors, business groups, think tanks, media watchdog organizations, radio and television talk shows, Internet sites, conservative intellectuals, and right-wing politicians.

In their campaign to check the spread of anti-business ideas, conservatives did precisely what they regularly condemned liberals for doing: they threw money at the problem. Since the early 1970s, wealthy donors have invested heavily to advance the conservative cause and push public opinion to the right. Most of this huge sum has come from corporate contributions and from conservative foundations tied to rich business families: the Bradley Foundation, the Smith Richardson Foundation, the Scaife Family Foundations, the Castle Rock Foundation (funded by the Coors family fortune), the Koch family foundations, and the John M. Olin Foundation.[98] These institutions, with deep roots in corporate America, constitute the economic substructure of the right-wing ideology machine.

Conservative think tanks, with extensive corporate and foundation support, are the heavy artillery in the right-wing arsenal.[99] The American Enterprise Institute (1943), the Hoover Foundation (1919), and the Hudson Institute (1961) grew significantly during the 1970s and after thanks to an infusion of corporate money. The Heritage Foundation (1973), initially established with funding from the Coors family; the libertarian Cato Institute (1978); and the Manhattan Institute (1978) are among the most important of the newer organizations in the conservative armory.[100] According to one estimate, during the decade of the 1990s alone, right-wing think tanks spent $1 billion spreading the conservative gospel.[101] In 2012, the Heritage Foundation, increasingly allied with the Tea Party, spent $82 million by itself to advance the Republican cause.[102] Conservative think tanks and corporate foundations—this combination of "brains and money"—gave the right in the 1980s and 1990s the institutional standing and financial wherewithal to dominate political debate in the United States.[103]

The right also carried the war of ideas into the very heart of the enemy stronghold: the media. Corporate leaders and conservative thinkers in the 1970s, perturbed by a public culture that seemed decidedly unfriendly to business, attributed the problem to politically biased news reporting. The unrelentingly negative coverage of a partisan media, as they saw it, tarnished the image of business and eroded public support for the free-enterprise system.[104] To combat the influence of what they perceived to be antagonistic news media, the right pursued a two-pronged approach: intimidate the media from without and seize control from within. On the one hand, activists on the right established a number of media watchdog groups, including Accuracy in Media, the Media Institute, and the Center for Media and Public Affairs.[105] These organizations, with funding provided by the same corporate sources and wealthy families that subsidized right-wing think tanks, began monitoring the media, publicizing instances of presumed political bias, and pressuring news organizations to make room for conservative viewpoints. This strategy, with right-wing politicians and pundits adding their voices to the choir, has been extraordinarily successful. The repeated charge of "liberal bias" has raised such a din in the political culture that voices on the left have little chance of being heard. Cowed by an unremitting barrage of criticism, the mainstream news media now bend over backward to appear neutral, even as strident ideologues on talk radio, Fox News, and elsewhere openly serve as conservative propagandists.[106]

The right also launched a campaign to transform the media from within, to give a louder voice to conservative and pro-business points of view in news coverage. This effort, too, met with great success. News commentary over the past several decades has veered in a distinctly rightward direction. This is due in no small part to the rise of a large and highly visible right-wing "punditocracy."[107] Conservative commentators, including George Will, Charles Krauthammer, Newt Gingrich, Mike Huckabee, Michelle Malkin, and Glenn Beck, to name just a few, have attained a ubiquitous presence within the mainstream news media. They are frequent guests on the Sunday-morning news programs; they make regular appearances on talk radio, a venue dominated by the right; they operate Internet sites, including the popular *Drudge Report*; they write syndicated columns for newspapers across the country; they publish articles in the *National Review*, the *Weekly Standard*, the *American Spectator*, and other right-wing political magazines; and— including such notables as Bill O'Reilly, Sean Hannity, and Rush Lim- baugh—they host their own television and radio programs. The public vis- ibility and cultural influence of right-wing pundits far exceed that of their liberal counterparts, while commentators on the left are almost entirely ex- cluded from the mainstream media.

Armed with corporate and foundation money, the right since the 1970s has attained an impressive foothold in the news industry and has gained the upper hand in the battle for the hearts and minds of the American public. Presiding over a conservative strategy session in 2003, Paul Weyrich, co- founder of the Heritage Foundation, exulted in the achievements of the movement he helped set in motion: "There are 1,500 conservative radio talk show hosts. . . . You have Fox News. You have the Internet, where all the successful sites are conservative. The ability to reach people with our point of view is like nothing we have ever seen before!"[108]

Business leaders since the 1970s, while simultaneously engaged in an aggressive struggle to shift the balance of power within the economic and political systems, have also joined in a campaign, in alliance with conserva- tive strategists and intellectuals, to alter the ideological balance of power. This effort gave rise to a well-financed right-wing ideology machine that disgorges a continuous outpouring of high-profile books, opinion periodicals, policy reports, editorial statements, Internet gossip, and television and radio commentary. This "Republican propaganda mill," as Lewis Lapham calls it, has become a powerful voice in the American culture system.[109]

## THE RIGHTWARD TURN IN POVERTY DISCOURSE

The success of the right-wing ideology machine is nowhere more apparent than in the rightward drift of poverty discourse over the past forty years. Through the tireless proselytizing of think tank intellectuals, political pun- dits, business spokespersons, and the Republican leadership, conservatives have gained control over the intellectual and political agenda, defining what counts as common sense on issues of poverty, welfare, and race.[110] Concerns about racism, segregation, and unemployment have been swept away by a fixation on the self-destructive behaviors of the poor, the decline of the work ethic, and the failings of the welfare state. What was once a war on poverty has mutated into a "war against the poor"[111] and a "war on welfare."[112] The cultural and intellectual influence of the right is evident in the prominent position occupied by four key concepts in the mainstream poverty discourse since the 1970s: the underclass, government dependency, illegitimacy, and the perversity of the welfare system. I will discuss these themes in turn, though briefly, just enough to underline the key point that in each case the rhetoric of the right functions to obscure the structural nature of poverty.

## The Underclass

In the 1970s, the term "underclass" entered the poverty lexicon.[113] This concept, much like the culture of poverty theory, underlined the moral failings and behavioral pathologies of the poor. The underclass label shifted the focus from the difficulties poor people *experienced*, such as discrimination, segregation, underfunded schools, and inadequate job opportunities, to the problems they allegedly *caused*, such as crime, violence, and drugs.[114] While the underclass concept is generally applied only to a minority of the poor, mainly the residents of urban ghettos, the widespread dissemination of this catchy label has had the effect of redefining the problem of poverty. This reframing reinforces the perception that poverty is primarily a black problem, and one with cultural rather than economic or political origins. Though the specific term "underclass" does not have the currency today it had in the 1980s and 1990s, Republican leader Paul Ryan evoked just this idea on a radio program in 2014. Referring to the "cultural problem" of "our inner cities," he spoke "of men not working and just generations of men not even thinking about working or learning the value and the culture of work."[115] Ignoring entirely the persistent jobs shortage in the American economy, exacerbated by the Great Recession, Ryan reduced the problem of poverty to one of bad values and bad behavior.

## Government Dependency

Since the 1980s, the issue of welfare dependency, nowadays reconfigured as government dependency more generally, has taken center stage, replacing poverty "as the main object of social policy."[116] In the rhetoric of the right, indeed, the greatest evil is not that people are poor, but that they are receiving a welfare check, or food stamps, or unemployment compensation, or medical attention through the Medicaid program. The safety net, from this perspective, as Paul Ryan puts it, has become an all-too-comfortable "hammock that lulls able-bodied people to lives of dependency and complacency, that drains them of their will and their incentive to make the most of their lives." The even greater danger, a point emphasized especially by proponents of the Tea Party, is that liberal government programs are turning much of the country— 47 percent according to Mitt Romney and as much as 60 percent according to Paul Ryan—into a bunch of "freeloaders," "moochers," and "takers"—people who get from government more than they give.[117] From this standpoint, the central problem is not that people are suffering from poverty, but that the poverty of the poor, thanks to big government, has become a drain on the resources of hardworking, taxpaying Americans. The concept of government dependency, as deployed by the right, encourages Americans to think that the most serious issue is not lack of opportunities for education and employment, but the moral impairment of the poor and the hazardous inducements of the welfare state.

## Illegitimacy

According to Charles Murray, probably the most influential conservative spokesperson on social policy, "illegitimacy is the single most important social problem of our time—more important than crime, drugs, poverty, illiteracy, welfare, or homelessness because it drives everything else."[118] Robert Rector, point man for the Heritage Foundation, concurs. Poverty, he says, along with many other social ills, is essentially a by-product of "illegitimacy" and "family collapse."[119] Besides ignoring the poverty of women who have not had children out of wedlock, this thesis transforms a complex issue into a simple equation: bad values, abetted by the welfare system, cause illegitimacy, and illegitimacy causes poverty. This message has the virtue of being easy to communicate (who has not heard the worrying expression "children having children"?); it plays into the American inclination to ascribe social problems to deviant behavior; and it implies a straightforward and inexpensive solution: abstinence. With its narrowly individualistic focus, this rhetoric deflects attention from the larger social, political, and economic forces affecting economic attainment and family formation.

## The Perversity of the Welfare System

The 1970s witnessed the launching of a powerful "conservative disinformation campaign," one that continues to win converts today.[120] The gist of this campaign is that government is the problem not the solution and that government efforts to combat poverty cause more harm than good. The welfare state, critics charge, undermines the work ethic, encourages idleness, promotes out-of-wedlock births, discourages family formation, and saps individual responsibility. Murray, indeed, has proposed that the poor would be better off if the entire federal welfare system for the working-age population were dismantled.[121] The incessant reference to "failed" government policies, certainly one of the central themes of the right-wing propaganda machine, pervades the mainstream poverty discourse. According to a 2014 survey, nearly half of Americans and two-thirds of Republicans believe that aid to the poor "does more harm than good by making people too dependent on government."[122] This "perversity thesis" has a twofold effect.[123] First, it shifts the blame for social problems from the market to government, from the capitalist economy to liberal social programs. Second, it fuels skepticism about the efficacy of public policy, creating a reserve of ready opposition to what is, in reality, the only means possible for conducting a renewed war on poverty: the intervention of the federal government.

* * *

The underclass, dependency, illegitimacy, failed welfare system—the rhetoric of the right, partly through sheer repetition, has carried the day.[124] Through this language, conservatives mobilize their constituencies by targeting the usual suspects: urban minorities, welfare recipients, unwed mothers, and misguided liberals. The right toggles back and forth between two somewhat different views: poor people are deficient in intelligence and motivation, and poor people are blameless victims of a counterproductive welfare state. In either case, whether the emphasis is on the defects of the poor or the perils of government assistance, the conservative rhetoric obscures the structural dimension of the poverty problem.

Conservative intellectuals, pundits, and politicians have promoted a thoroughly individualistic perspective on poverty. They have directed public scrutiny toward the alleged pathologies of the poor while diverting attention from the failings of the American political economy. And they have ceaselessly denigrated the welfare state and liberal social programs, so effectively indeed that even Democrats seldom rise up in their defense. The right-wing ideology machine has been successful in propagating a view of poverty that, astonishingly, makes no reference to weak job growth, low wages, or rising inequality. Instead it offers "a substitute language, of deviance and deprivation."[125] Conservatives have managed to shift the focus of the poverty debate and social policy, inciting the public to notice one thing but not the other: to see the breakdown of the family, but not the deteriorating condition of American workers; to see the aberrant behavior of the "underclass," but not institutional discrimination and residential segregation; to see unwed mothers on welfare, but not work–family conflicts; to see corporate "job creators," but not the struggles of the working poor; to see the costs of social spending, but not the harm caused by cutbacks in government programs; to see the non-mainstream lives of the poor, but not the irresponsible policies of economic and political elites.

## CONCLUSION

The political culture in the United States predisposes Americans toward individualistic explanations for poverty and inequality, the normal operation of the mainstream media reinforces this tendency, and the right-wing ideology machine over the past several decades has pushed people's thinking in precisely the same direction. Little wonder many Americans blame poverty on the poor and structural solutions to the problem are largely absent from the political agenda.

What Americans believe about the causes of poverty and what they think should be done to combat the problem are significant in their own right, but also because they influence government policy. It is too simple, of course, to think that the government simply does what the electorate wants—otherwise we would have national health care, a higher minimum wage, gun control, and a cleaner environment. Social policy in our imperfect democracy, as we saw in chapter 6, does not echo the desires of the public as much as it reflects the distribution of economic and political power.[126] But public opinion is a factor. It is difficult to imagine the advent of a real war on poverty without somehow encouraging more Americans to take poverty seriously and recognize the structural nature of the problem. Terry Maguire, a welfare rights activist based in Philadelphia, makes this point: "You can't end poverty without winning the hearts and minds of the people. It's a battle of ideas, a battle of images, and ultimately a battle of stories."[127]

*Chapter Eight*

# The Social System and Poverty

## WE ARE NOT ALONE

We have relatives, friends, peers, neighbors, and co-workers. We belong to an assortment of groups, some by virtue of our race, ethnicity, or gender, others on a more voluntary basis: food co-ops, street gangs, book clubs, and social movements. We attend schools, churches, community meetings, and political rallies. We join with others at parks, basketball courts, golf courses, and music concerts. We get together for marriages and funerals, anniversaries and birthdays, weekend parties and poker games. We interact with a variety of officials, functionaries, and service professionals: principals and teachers, cops and judges, priests and therapists, bankers and lawyers, real estate and insurance agents, welfare caseworkers and medical personnel. We are also tied to others through our location in social space. We reside in a particular state and region, in an urban or rural area, in the city or the suburbs. We live in a "good" neighborhood or a "bad" neighborhood. In all these ways and more, we are connected to other people, and not just through market mechanisms, not just as self-interested buyers and sellers. Yet these distinctly *social* connections have significant *economic* consequences.[1]

Individualistic theories imagine that we each chart our own course. Our economic destinies are conditioned only by our personal attributes: our choices and preferences, abilities and talents, knowledge and skills, attitudes and values. Proponents of this perspective seem to envision economic life as a series of competitive races, with all contestants beginning from the same starting point and subject to the same rules and regulations. Non-contestants in any particular event are observers only. While they might stand on the sidelines and cheer for their favorites, they do not intervene in the competition. And because such contests take place on a level playing field, how individuals fare is entirely a matter of their own prowess and determination.

In reality, however, the race of life is far from fair. Not everyone begins from the same place, the rules do not apply equally to all contestants, and merit is by no means the only determinant of success.[2] In real-life competition, furthermore, we do not arrive at the starting gate or make our way from the starting gate to the finish line on our own. We sometimes rely on the kindness of strangers, and we certainly get a little help from our friends. Other people are not just spectators; they make a big difference in how well or how poorly we perform. If we are fortunate, the people we know will keep us informed about where and when important races are run, see to it we get entered into the most prestigious competitions, introduce us to the race officials, make sure we get a favorable starting position, and supply us with the skills and equipment we need to compete successfully. And once the race commences, they provide assistance along the way: guiding us toward the inside track, giving us a helpful boost now and then, subverting the efforts of our competitors, and perhaps even sometimes carrying us along on their shoulders. If we are not so fortunate, on the other hand, if we are not surrounded by people who are in a position to shower us with assistance, the race of life can be arduous, just finishing can be difficult, and victory doubtful. In the real-world race, without the benefit of a strong supporting cast, even people who possess a natural gift for running may find themselves left behind.

An individual's place in the social structure exerts a powerful influence on his or her economic prospects. Some are advantaged and others disadvantaged by their location in the network of social statuses, social relations, and social institutions. People's ability to acquire valuable cultural and human capital and the availability of opportunities for them to convert that capital into a good job and a decent life are significantly affected by the characteristics and composition of their social relationships and group affiliations, their neighborhoods and communities, their social networks and institutional ties. The individualistic perspective fails to provide an adequate understanding of inequality and poverty precisely because it neglects this crucial relationship between social structure and economic mobility. As Glen Loury observes, "The merit notion that, in a free society, each individual will rise to the level justified by his or her competence conflicts with the observation that no one travels that road entirely alone." The social system has relevance for an analysis of poverty because people's economic outcomes are shaped by their social contexts, and these produce differences in "what otherwise equally competent individuals can achieve."[3]

The individualistic perspective, as we have seen, offers a faulty analysis because it fails to recognize adequately how economic, political, and cultural forces contribute to the persistence of poverty. This chapter examines a further limitation of individualistic theories. In explaining why some people are more vulnerable to poverty than others, these theories place too much emphasis on the deficiencies of individuals and too little on the constraints of their social environment. With its narrow focus on individual attributes, the individualistic perspective ignores the influence of people's social location on their life chances.

My objective in this chapter is to illustrate the importance of social system variables for understanding poverty. I pursue this by discussing three phenomena that have received much recent attention in the social sciences: group memberships, neighborhood effects, and social networks. In each case, my purpose is to demonstrate the inadequacy of individualistic explanations and to show, in support of a structural perspective, that people's economic outcomes are contingent on social factors outside their immediate control.

## GROUP MEMBERSHIPS

The characteristics of the groups to which we belong influence our economic prospects. Group memberships matter in two ways. First, they contribute to the formation of what we normally think of as individual traits—our interests, preferences, beliefs, and abilities. Second, they determine our access to tangible resources, including opportunities for education, training, and employment. Group affiliations shape our aspirations and the means available to realize those aspirations. They affect both who we are and how we live our lives.

Groups differ in how they are formed and in their characteristics and composition. Individuals become group members through some combination of choice and constraint. Some group affiliations, along with the social identities they confer, derive from ascribed statuses, as in the case of groupings based on gender, race, and ethnicity. Some groups, including those made up of friends, peers, and cohorts, are by-products of social processes that sort people into neighborhoods, schools, and jobs. And some memberships are more voluntary, as when a parent participates in the PTA, a student pledges a sorority, or a worker joins a labor union or professional organization.

However they originate, groups exert an independent effect on individuals' economic lives, helping some and hurting others. People's prospects for accumulating wealth or avoiding poverty depend on their group memberships, not just their native abilities, achievement motivations, or human capital endowments. The outcomes people attain thus depart from what would be expected if individual attributes were the primary determinants of economic achievement. Because of their group memberships, for example, workers with equivalent skills may differ significantly in their occupational status and earnings, as studies of race and gender consistently show. Because groups matter, life chances are not reducible to individual-level characteristics.

Steven Durlauf, acknowledging the significance of group affiliations to economic attainment, proposes a "memberships theory" of poverty and inequality.[4] This theory, which he explicitly conceives in opposition to individualistic theories, "shifts the emphasis in a causal explanation of poverty from individual characteristics . . . to memberships and group influences that constrain individual outcomes."[5] Durlauf identifies a number of avenues through which group memberships influence individual achievement, including peer group effects, adult role model effects, and labor market connections.[6] The influence of peers, for example, might explain why some adolescents are drawn toward sports while others are more academically oriented, why some are politically engaged while others are apathetic, or why some hew to the straight and narrow while others are drawn toward delinquency and crime. Young people may be influenced by the experiences and example of their elders as well. By observing adults in their circle of acquaintances, adolescents make inferences about the payoffs of education, the likelihood of getting a good job, and the viability of the American Dream. Adult role models, wittingly or not, affect adolescents' aspirations and their vision of how best to make a life for themselves. Group affiliations matter also because they provide members with connections of varying quality that might be exploited to aid educational advancement or find employment. In these ways and others, group differences result in individual inequalities. The characteristics of the groups to which a person belongs, independent of individual and family characteristics, "condition the range of the individual's life economic prospects."[7]

A recurring theme in the literature on poverty is the potentially detrimental impact that the group memberships of the poor have on their norms and behaviors. But whether or not this occurs, as Durlauf emphasizes, depends on the surrounding material conditions. The cultural theory of poverty overlooks this important point when it posits an autonomous "underclass" subculture. Peer groups and role models typically promote patterns of deviant behavior only when the social and economic foundations are already weak and when conventional avenues of achievement are closed off. A group norm usually emerges and induces conformity when it has a genuine reality quotient, when it appears reasonably appropriate given the availability of opportunities and the experiences of group co-members.[8] Adolescents are more likely to think education is a sham when schools are run down, teachers have low expectations, and graduates fail to move up the occupational ladder. They are more apt to be persuaded of the benefits of illicit employment when legitimate jobs are scarce, demeaning, or dead end. And they are more liable to fall into a pattern of risky behavior when they perceive a bleak or uncertain future.[9]

Group memberships affect economic outcomes not only because co-members influence one another's aspirations, norms, and behaviors, but also because groups vary in their status and prestige. Some groups occupy a more privileged position relative to others: men compared to women, whites compared to non-whites, natives compared to immigrants, professionals compared to hourly workers. As a result of normal psychological processes, furthermore, individuals exhibit a preference for and have a more positive view of group co-members. They are psychologically inclined to perceive people who look, talk, and live the way they do as more intelligent, competent, and worthy than people who are different. Individuals also tend to adopt stereotypical views of those outside of their group and exhibit bias in evaluating their behavior and performance. The predisposition to categorize people into in-groups and out-groups, a cognitive process often operating beneath the level of awareness, is an important cause of discrimination, one with particularly significant consequences in educational and occupational settings.[10] Group memberships, due to such social psychological mechanisms, can either facilitate or impede the economic attainment of the individual. They are relevant because the members of some groups are regarded more highly and treated more favorably than the members of other groups. The benefits of belonging to a privileged group, moreover, as in the case of white males, for example, often flow automatically and invisibly to members, regardless even of whether they explicitly identify with the group.[11] The members of less-privileged groups, on the other hand, because they are judged more negatively and subject to prejudice and discrimination, encounter substantial obstacles to achievement and are more vulnerable to poverty.

Group memberships are relevant to individual attainment also because groups, not just individuals, are key actors in the competitive struggle for access to resources and opportunities, because groups often act in a deliberate manner to promote their members' interests, and because groups vary in their capacity to secure desirable outcomes. The life chances of individuals are tied to the power of the groups to which they belong. As Kim Weeden shows, for example, some occupational groups, professional groups in particular—through such means as licensing, certification, and credentialing—are able to boost the earnings of their members by restricting the supply of labor. By contrast, members of occupational groups who lack the power to implement such "social closure" practices, including most low-end service workers, are fully subject to the leveling effect of market forces. Workers' earnings thus imperfectly reflect their human capital, as individuals' wages depend also on whether or not they belong to occupational groups able to set favorable rules governing the operation of the labor market. [12]

Groups differ also in broader dimensions of social power—in their ability to affect the distribution of income and wealth, influence the course of government policy, and shape the imagery and messages disseminated by the cultural apparatus. Dominant groups, as Charles Tilly argues in his theory of "durable inequality," are able to exploit subordinate groups and hoard opportunities. [13] Because social institutions tend to favor powerful groups and because groups tend to channel resources to co-members, individuals belonging to privileged groups enjoy undeserved advantages while those belonging to less-privileged groups suffer undeserved disadvantages. [14] People's economic fate is not simply a function of their personal traits; it depends decisively on the status and power of their group memberships.

## NEIGHBORHOOD EFFECTS

Some neighborhoods are better than others, and whether a neighborhood is "good" or "bad" has consequences for the lives of its residents. Neighborhoods differ most importantly in their class and racial composition. The rich and the poor increasingly reside in separate and unequal communities, largely a by-product of rising economic inequality. As a result, fewer families today, compared to the 1970s, live in middle-income neighborhoods. [15] And though black–white residential segregation has slowly declined since the

1970s, racial and ethnic minorities, particularly in metropolitan regions, continue to live apart from non-Hispanic whites.[16] High-poverty neighborhoods, reflecting the intersection of class and race, are also usually "ghettos" or "barrios," populated primarily by African Americans and Latinos.[17] As of circa 2006 to 2010, nearly 8 million, mostly minority, children lived in such areas of concentrated poverty, an increase of 1.6 million since 2000.[18]

This pattern of residential segregation is among the most profound and disturbing features of American society. The experiences and life outcomes of two otherwise identical individuals vary greatly depending on where they happen to live. Regardless of their ability and how hard they might try to get ahead, kids growing up in the South Bronx, one of the poorest communities in the country, do not have anything like the same life chances as kids raised in wealthy Connecticut suburbs.[19] The inhabitants of different neighborhoods encounter "fundamentally different opportunities."[20] This is especially true at the extremes, for those who live in either very impoverished or very affluent communities. The undeniably deep disparities between poor neighborhoods and rich neighborhoods have only grown larger with the Great Recession.[21] The effect of such geographical inequalities on the educational and economic outcomes of community residents undermines the principle of equality of opportunity, refuting a core premise of the individualistic perspective.

Neighborhood inequalities magnify individual inequalities, with particularly adverse consequences for the poor. The misfortune of living in a poor neighborhood compounds the misfortune of living in a poor family. Individuals lacking in family resources, if they reside in high-poverty neighborhoods, are likely to be deprived of community resources as well. Because of neighborhood inequalities, poor families are often stuck with inferior schools, inadequate public facilities, and an unhealthy and sometimes dangerous residential environment. The social and economic mechanisms channeling affluent families into affluent neighborhoods and poor families into poor neighborhoods yield cumulative advantages for the former and cumulative disadvantages for the latter. The dearth of social resources in poor communities penalizes poor families, making it harder for them to escape poverty; the abundance of social resources in rich communities rewards rich families, making it easier for them to pass along their advantages to their offspring. The geographical distribution of social resources renders poverty and inequality self-perpetuating and persistent.[22]

The concept of "neighborhood effects" refers to the influence of neighborhood conditions on life outcomes over and beyond the effects of individual and family characteristics.[23] Research has focused especially on how the attributes of neighborhoods affect the life chances of children, adolescents, and young adults. Among the issues most commonly addressed in this literature are social and cognitive development, physical and mental health, school readiness and performance, educational attainment, sexual behavior and fertility, family formation, delinquency and crime, and, for adults, employment and earnings. Compared to their middle-class counterparts, and to poor children in low-poverty neighborhoods as well, children who grow up in impoverished neighborhoods are significantly handicapped. They have higher rates of infant mortality, child abuse, and low birth weight.[24] They are less prepared when they begin school, perform less well in the classroom, score lower on educational achievement tests, are more likely to drop out, and are less likely to attend college.[25] They have a greater risk of teenage and nonmarital births.[26] Poor children in poor neighborhoods also have a higher incidence of social, behavioral, and emotional problems. They are more likely to engage in delinquent and criminal behavior, use drugs and drink alcohol, and experience psychological distress and depression.[27] Children raised in poor neighborhoods have hard lives and are deprived of opportunities for personal development, a decent education, and a secure economic future. And as Patrick Sharkey documents, drawing attention to the intergenerational inheritance of both place and poverty, the prospects for such children are even bleaker if their parents, too, as is the case for many African Americans, grew up in poor neighborhoods.[28]

Poor communities influence life outcomes because they shape residents' values, attitudes, and aspirations and determine their access to resources and opportunities. But how precisely do high-poverty areas yield neighborhood effects and through what specific processes, mechanisms, or pathways do neighborhood conditions limit the life chances of the poor? Several features of impoverished communities have been hypothesized to play a role in causing negative outcomes.[29] A brief overview of four leading candidates, not mutually exclusive, can serve to clarify how location matters, illuminate some of the fundamental differences between the living circumstances of the rich and the poor, and suggest why some poor communities are better off than others.[30]

## Institutional Resources

Neighborhoods vary in the quantity and quality of their institutional resources: schools, libraries, child-care providers, recreational centers, youth programs, parks and playgrounds, medical facilities, stores, transportation systems, and social service agencies.[31] Community resources are a vital element of a healthy neighborhood landscape. They play a significant role in the process of socialization; they afford opportunities for safe and enriching activities; they supply essential services; they contribute to the acquisition of psychological, cultural, and human capital; and they function to stimulate political awareness and promote political solidarity. Affluent communities, rich in institutional resources, provide their residents with a multitude of benefits and contribute to the ability of privileged families to transmit advantages to their children. Institutional resources in high-poverty neighborhoods, on the other hand, are typically unavailable, inaccessible, unaffordable, and low quality.[32] Poor parents are often forced to compensate by pursuing various "resource-seeking strategies," including costly searches outside their neighborhoods to supply their children with vital services.[33] The absence of community resources is an especially severe problem for poor families because they have a greater need for the support that such resources offer and because they are less able to purchase equivalent services in the private market. The weakness of institutional resources in poor neighborhoods makes it difficult for already hard-pressed parents to ensure that their children receive a healthy upbringing, are adequately prepared for school and work, and have a reasonable opportunity for upward mobility.

## Labor Market Conditions

The state of the labor market in poor communities is another potential cause of adverse neighborhood effects. In the 1970s and 1980s, William Julius Wilson argues, poor urban communities were racked by a series of "structural economic changes": "the shift from goods-producing to service-producing industries, the increasing polarization of the labor market into low-wage and high-wage sectors, technological innovations, and the relocation of manufacturing industries out of the central cities."[34] This economic restructuring worsened an already weak central-city labor market, giving rise to a "new urban poverty" characterized by high levels of joblessness.[35] Adolescents and young adults in high-poverty neighborhoods have few local opportunities to learn the ropes of the work world, gain experience and training, build up a record of stable employment, cultivate labor market contacts, or earn a decent living.[36] Jobs in the community, if available at all, are usually low paying, dead end, insecure, and rife with frustration and conflict—as Daniel Dohan says about barrio jobs, "more a source of ongoing difficulty than a source of manifest opportunity."[37] The characteristics of local labor markets severely constrain poor people's employment prospects and their later-life economic outcomes. Adolescents who grow up in high-poverty neighborhoods and people who reside there as adults pay a high price. They have lower wages, work fewer hours, and spend more time below the poverty line than otherwise equivalent workers.[38]

## Collective Socialization

Family members socialize children, but their upbringing is influenced by a variety of community forces as well, including adult neighbors, peer groups, role models, and social institutions. Neighborhoods differ in the prevalence of these bearers of "collective socialization" and in their effectiveness at promoting norms and behaviors conducive to educational and occupational achievement.[39] In neighborhoods characterized by concentrated poverty, residential segregation, and social isolation, processes of collective socialization may be inadequate or even detrimental. The influence of delinquent peers and the paucity of positive adult role models, some research suggests, leave poor adolescents alienated from mainstream norms. They are also propelled into illicit behaviors by hostile treatment at the hands of external authorities (e.g., the police), by the brute reality of limited opportunities, and by perceptions of relative deprivation—the recognition of how daunting the obstacles are that they face as compared to more affluent teenagers.[40] Adolescents growing up under these harsh circumstances are bound to find it difficult to envision a successful future or believe that "playing by the rules" is a surefire recipe for avoiding poverty.

## Social Disorganization

A community exhibits social organization when residents are bound together through frequent interactions, social ties, and shared norms.[41] Social organization, according to Robert Sampson and his colleagues, promotes "collective efficacy."[42] Residents trust one another, they monitor the behavior of children in the neighborhood, and they are willing and able to intervene to enforce community norms and pursue common goals. Because high-poverty neighborhoods, deprived of essential resources, are often lacking in collective efficacy, patterns of informal social control are weaker. Children who grow up in such communities, accordingly, are more likely to get caught up in socially undesirable behaviors and in turn experience poor educational and employment outcomes. Social disorganization at the neighborhood level adds to the difficulties people face in their efforts to cope with or escape from poverty. [43]

The scholarship on neighborhood effects introduces a more structural dimension to the study of poverty and inequality by shifting the focus from the individual to the community and also to the "wider spatial environment" within which particular communities themselves are located. [44] And in contrast to individualistic theories, focused only on reforming the poor, this literature suggests the need for community development strategies targeted to fixing the ecological and institutional conditions in and around poor neighborhoods. [45] The insight that residential location, certainly at the extremes, is a powerful determinant of life chances, presents a significant challenge to the view that getting ahead is simply a matter of individual ability and effort.

## SOCIAL NETWORKS AND SOCIAL CAPITAL

People are not only members of groups and residents of neighborhoods; they are also nodes in social networks. [46] The life of any particular individual intersects at various points with the lives of any number of other individuals. The term "social network" is commonly used to denote the pattern of these recurrent interpersonal relationships. An individual's social network consists of the people he or she is connected to in one capacity or another: family members, friends, acquaintances, co-workers, and diverse "institutional agents," including teachers, child-care providers, social service workers, and criminal justice personnel. [47] The sum of these networks, the structure of social life, is sociologically significant because the ties binding people together, and connecting individuals to organizations, perform a variety of important social functions. They channel information, convey cultural messages, create social solidarities, forge expectations and obligations, facilitate the enforcement of social norms, engender relations of mutual trust, serve as sources of social support, and operate as conduits of power and influence.

Social scientists have coined the term "social capital" to refer to the distinctly *social* resources embedded in social networks. Unlike financial capital and human capital, properties of individuals located respectively in their "bank accounts" and "inside their heads," social capital is a uniquely structural resource.[48] It "inheres in the structure of relations between actors and among actors."[49] Social capital consists of the benefits people derive from their personal interactions and social relations. If we have ties to others, we are not solely dependent on our own personal resources; we can draw on our connections to family members, friends, and acquaintances to help us achieve our goals. The concept of social capital, by drawing attention to the importance of *social* as distinct from *individual* resources, challenges the premise that individuals are the solitary authors of their own economic lives. People's economic fate is shaped in a multitude of ways by their connections to others and by an assortment of more or less helping or hindering hands.

Individuals sometimes even make investments in social capital, strategically cultivating contacts ("networking") with the expectation of reaping rewards down the road from knowing the "right" people. Most social connections, however, do not originate from economic motives or self-interested calculations, but arise routinely as by-products of ordinary social behavior or through people's involvement in organizations—day-care centers, for example.[50] However formed, these connections can be accessed and mobilized for instrumental purposes. Through their networks, for example, individuals might acquire knowledge about housing, job openings, business opportunities, or government programs; they might transmit information to prospective employers about their availability and qualifications; they might procure letters of introduction, referrals, recommendations, or even job offers; they might obtain loans, investment tips, or other forms of financial assistance; they might receive advice, counseling, or emotional and psychological support; and they might get help in dealing with problems of child care, transportation, or spousal abuse. The luckiest people in the world are not necessarily people who *need* people, as Barbra Streisand sings, but people who *know* people.

The social science literature on social networks and social capital is highly relevant to the study of poverty and inequality.[51] Individuals vary in the extent and composition of their social ties, and in their concomitant access to information and influence.[52] Some are implicated in "resource-rich" networks that consist of well-placed contacts and convey timely, reliable, and useful information, while others are implicated in "resource-poor" networks.[53] As a consequence, individuals differ in the quantity and quality of their social capital, in their stock of social resources. These differences have consequences for people's economic lives, particularly because social connections are so important in matching workers to jobs. Employers regularly use networks to recruit employees, and job seekers frequently rely on connections with friends and acquaintances to find employment. According to Katherine O'Regan and John Quigley's estimate, "about half of all jobs are obtained through contacts."[54] The quality of our social networks thus plays a significant, though often unacknowledged, role in determining whether we are employed or unemployed, have a good job or a bad job, rise to the top or remain stuck at the bottom. The distribution of social resources results in enhanced opportunities for some and diminished opportunities for others. Differences in social capital, even where individuals are otherwise comparable, generate unequal economic outcomes. This focus on social network and social capital inequalities underscores the relevance of yet another set of social system variables affecting the economic fate of individuals.

The empirical research on the relationship between economic status and social resources supports three broad conclusions. First, people who are weak in social networks and social capital are vulnerable to poverty. Second, people who are poor tend to be weak in social networks and social capital.[55] Third, poor families are not uniformly lacking in social connections, and their ability to rise out of poverty and provide a more secure future for their children is dependent on the configuration and quality of their social ties and the effectiveness of their strategies for tapping social resources.[56] The concept of social networks can thus be usefully employed to illuminate the causes of poverty, the consequences of poverty, and why some people escape poverty while others remain poor. Biogenetic, cultural, and human capital theories, because they narrowly focus on individuals in abstraction from their social relationships, fail to grasp how poverty is embedded in larger social contexts. Bringing social networks into the picture underlines important structural features of poverty neglected by the individualistic perspective.

The poor are not all alike in their social networks, nor are they all equally deficient in social resources. In general, however, the social networks typical of the poor differ from those of the affluent, and these differences help to explain why many poor people are trapped in poverty. In what follows, I discuss some of the key social network characteristics of the poor, though briefly and only for the purpose of illustrating a key point: we cannot understand adequately the circumstances, struggles, and prospects of the poor if we attend only to their individual traits and neglect their social network and social capital characteristics.

## Size of Social Networks

The social networks of the poor are typically less extensive than those of the affluent. The most impoverished among the poor, including the homeless, the long-term unemployed, residents of extremely high-poverty neighborhoods, and the elderly, often have few enduring ties to other people.[57] This is partly because the poor are deficient in individual resources, including financial, cultural, and political capital.[58] Since they have so little to share, they are not valued network partners. Their poverty makes it difficult for them to provide assistance to others or fulfill the obligations social networks entail. They do not have money to lend, contacts to get a friend a job, a car to help neighbors with their transportation problems, or political leverage to secure favors from elected officials. Poor people who are short of resources from which others might benefit are susceptible to being excluded from social networks. They might also disengage voluntarily, cutting themselves off from contact with others out of concern about becoming a burden, forfeiting their independence, disappointing personal contacts, or their inability to reciprocate.[59] Even those who do have a modicum of resources might choose to withdraw from demanding networks so as not to deplete their own limited stock, or they might perceive greater costs than rewards from their network relations.[60] In any case, the resource constraints of the poor often leave them with impoverished social connections.

## Social Isolation

The social world of a sizable segment of the poverty population, racial and ethnic minorities in particular, consists mainly of other poor people. As a result of economic restructuring, residential segregation, and housing discrimination, many of the poor, particularly African Americans in high-poverty urban ghettos, are geographically isolated and, with the notable exception of personnel in the criminal justice system, have limited contact with people outside their neighborhoods. While they may have close ties with each other, the "truly disadvantaged" among the poor have minimal interaction with "individuals and institutions that represent mainstream society."[61] This "social isolation," Wilson argues, amplifies the problem of poverty because it diminishes access to positive role models, mentors, job contacts, employment information, and connections into the labor market.[62] Unemployed workers in high-poverty neighborhoods are embedded in social networks consisting disproportionately of other jobless people. Such people are a poor source for tips about job openings and are likely themselves to be seeking employment. The socially isolated jobless are vulnerable to network "congestion"—their connections include too few people who can provide useful job information and too many people who are in need of such information.[63]

The poor also disproportionately belong to negatively stereotyped outgroups—African Americans, Latinos, immigrants, welfare recipients, and single mothers. Even if they are not geographically isolated because of residential segregation, poor people may still experience social segregation. Since people tend to confine their networks to others similar to themselves, and since privileged groups tend to hoard their privileges, the poor have limited access to the valuable social resources that in-groups possess. Thus, non-white job seekers are often disadvantaged in the labor market due to their exclusion from more resource-rich white networks.[64] Deirdre Royster shows, for example, how racially exclusive social networks, by enabling white graduates from a vocational school to monopolize desirable blue-collar jobs, left equally, if not more, qualified black workers unemployed or underemployed.[65]

## Difficulty in Mobilizing Social Networks

Even when they are not socially isolated, the poor cannot necessarily count on getting help from their connections in the labor market. Sandra Smith, drawing on interviews with 105 low-income African Americans, found they were often unwilling to assist job-seeking friends and acquaintances.[66] They were particularly wary about using their influence when they had doubts about a person's reliability or work ethic and when they were concerned about their own often-insecure employment status. "Overwhelmingly," Smith reports, "respondents were fearful of making bad referrals that might tarnish their own reputations and threaten their labor market stability." As one of her interviewees explained, "If they going to use my name, I don't want them messing around. I don't want nobody messing up under my name."[67] Poor job seekers are disadvantaged not only because they lack influential social ties, Smith's study suggests, but also because their labor market contacts, due to their own precarious status, are reluctant to offer assistance.

## Preponderance of Strong Ties

The poor participate in social networks composed more of "strong ties," ties to relatives and friends, than "weak ties," ties to acquaintances.[68] Strong ties have their strengths; close friends are available, motivated to provide assistance, and willing perhaps to go out on a limb.[69] But, as Mark Granovetter emphasizes, weak ties also have certain strengths. Unlike people we know well, who tend to be very much like ourselves, people we know casually often differ from us, move in separate circles, and know people we do not know. The unique strength of weak ties is that they establish connections to individuals located in groups and neighborhoods other than our own. Weak ties thus create dispersed networks, and these are more likely to provide participants with access to "novel" rather than "redundant" information, about job opportunities, for example.[70] While all ties put us in the loop, weak ties put us in a bigger loop, supplying us with a wider range of interpersonal resources. The poor are disadvantaged because their networks consist more of strong ties than resource-rich weak ties.[71]

## Reliance on Disposable Ties

Matthew Desmond's research shows that many of the urban poor are lacking even in the strong ties associated with kinship networks. They do not have close and lasting relations with people they can count on for either emotional or material support. Instead of relatives or longtime friends, they rely on acquaintances for assistance in helping them to secure food, shelter, and child care, for example. These ties, Desmond finds, tended to be "emotionally intense," "demanding," and "suffocating," contrary to what is normally the case for weak ties. But they are also typically short-lived, unstable, and characterized by low levels of trust. And while such "disposable" ties may provide services that enable poor people to survive on a day-to-day basis, they are not a source of lasting support, and they do not yield the sort of resources that might help the poor to escape their poverty.[72]

## Homogeneous Social Networks

Social networks, according to Patricia Kelly, are particularly valuable if they are "composed of persons with differing social status, linked in a variety of ways, who play multiple roles in several fields of activity."[73] Weak ties are strong, but they are even stronger if they are diverse—if they are composed of people from different social and cultural backgrounds and if they include well-placed connections.[74] People implicated in networks consisting of weak *and* varied ties, including links to high-status contacts, have a greater chance of securing useful information, obtaining valuable referrals and recommendations, and otherwise extracting benefits from their social connections. The poor are disadvantaged because their networks, even if they include weak ties, tend to be more homogeneous and horizontal, consisting of people of the same social status as themselves, rather than varied and vertical. Thus, even when the poor successfully exploit their connections to find employment, they typically end up being routed into low-wage, dead-end jobs.[75] Because poor people lack influential contacts, their social ties, whether weak or strong, exhibit weakness rather than strength.

## Lack of Productive Social Capital

Social capital, Pierre Bourdieu observes, "exerts a multiplier effect."[76] Social connections facilitate the acquisition of human, cultural, and political capital and increase the value of these as well. Poor families are susceptible to persistent poverty in part because their lack of social capital impedes their ability to accumulate other forms of capital. Whether in the form of close family ties or close ties between families and schools, strong social networks improve the educational performance of children.[77] Because of the quality of their ties to teachers and school administrators, middle-class parents are able to ensure their children have access to scarce educational resources, including the attention of teachers.[78] Other research illustrates how mentors augment the human capital of new entrants into the labor force. Silvia Dominguez and Celeste Watkins document how low-income mothers gained valuable training and experience through their connections to higher-status coworkers.[79] Poor people who lack social capital, on the other hand, who do not have helpful ties into schools and labor markets, are disadvantaged in their ability to acquire education, training, and skills.

Social connections facilitate the formation of cultural capital as well, at least when such connections cut across class and race boundaries.[80] Having ties to an assortment of individuals with diverse backgrounds and experiences and to a variety of social institutions enhances people's opportunities to acquire knowledge about the workings of organizations, to learn how to navigate their way in otherwise alien social environments, and to gain a feeling of comfort and confidence in mainstream social settings. Low-income mothers, according to one study, reported significant benefits from their ties to higher-status people. The latter not only opened access to jobs, but also imparted valuable cultural capital by exposing poor women to subtle rules of the game and by offering "lessons about how to get ahead and function successfully in the work world."[81] Poor people deprived of social capital are likely to be inadequately informed about how to apply for jobs, how to create a favorable impression at interviews, how to conduct themselves in the workplace, and how to negotiate their way in the labor market. Because they lack quality social capital, poor people are liable to be deficient in cultural capital as well.

The absence of social capital also matters in the political arena. Low-income people who have little contact with upwardly mobile individuals tend to be disconnected from the political system. The socially isolated poor, Yvette Alex-Assensoh's research reveals, are less interested in politics, are less likely to be involved in political organizations, and (much more so for blacks than whites) are less likely to participate in the electoral process. The lack of social capital, especially evident in the case of African Americans in high-poverty neighborhoods, has a negative effect on their political awareness, on their capacity for political mobilization, and on their ability to exert political leverage.[82] A low level of social capital translates into a low level of political capital.

## Preponderance of Social Support Ties

The social networks typical of the poor, particularly those located in high-poverty urban neighborhoods, are smaller and consist more of strong ties than weak ties; they are made up of people who mainly know each other, networks that are tight knit and insular rather than dispersed and diversified; and they are homogeneous, composed mostly of other poor people. These networks embody valuable social resources. For example, they facilitate the participation of low-income mothers in the low-wage labor market by providing them with access to child care and transportation assistance.[83] But as Xavier de Souza Briggs argues, such networks engender a form of social capital that better serves the purpose of "social support," enabling the poor to "get by," than "social leverage," enabling the poor to "get ahead."[84] The predominance of social support networks among the poor is due not only to the configuration of their social ties, but also to their limited personal resources and to the circumstance of poverty itself, where day-to-day demands by necessity take precedence. Of course, to "get ahead" one must first "get by," but there is also a certain trade-off involved, as the pressures of daily survival sap a limited supply of social resources. Dominguez and Watkins explore this conflict in the case of African American and Latin American low-income mothers. They show how pressures from supportive ties inhibit women from making effective use of social leverage networks.[85] According to Sharon Hicks-Bartlett, similarly, many poor black mothers are caught "between a rock and a hard place." Their social support obligations, including the stressful demands of parenting in impoverished and unsafe communities, leave them unable to make a full-time commitment to the paid labor force.[86] These studies reveal how difficult it is for poor women, especially due to burdensome caregiving responsibilities, to create a balance between efforts to "get by" and efforts to "get ahead."

## Negative Social Capital

The social capital of the poor leaves them doubly disadvantaged. Their networks are less likely to consist of resources conducive to upward mobility and more likely to impose costs on their members.[87] The affluent are hardly immune from the harmful consequences that can arise from human relationships, of course. But the circumstances of the poor increase the probability that their networks will generate "negative social capital."[88] For example, the social networks of the poor, because they are tight knit and because their members have such pressing needs, are likely to be particularly "greedy," eliciting "omnivorous" demands.[89] Such networks, and the obligations they create, can drain the time, energy, and resources of their members. They produce anxiety and stress for both "givers," who may become overloaded with responsibilities, and "receivers," who may worry about their ability to reciprocate. Such networks also engender tension and conflict as individuals struggle to balance the needs of their immediate family members and the needs of extended kin, friends, and neighbors.[90]

Social networks, Alejandro Portes and others argue, also generate negative social capital if the ties binding people together are so strong they produce an oppressive conformity. Social connections can impede individual mobility as well if the pressure to remain loyal to the group inhibits individuals from pursuing conventional avenues of educational and occupational advancement.[91] Young people in Harlem, for example, according to Katherine Newman, had to steel themselves from ridicule by their peers if they chose to work at low-status fast-food restaurants.[92] Social networks engender negative social capital also insofar as they promote norms and identities encouraging deviant or criminal behavior. For many of the non-white poor, partly because they lack social connections into the primary labor market, jobs are scarce. Individuals in such circumstances are vulnerable to the influence of social connections supporting illicit activities, particularly when opportunities in the legitimate economy are less viable than those in the illegitimate underground economy. It is not surprising, given their limited options, that some poor teens and young adults, in their endeavor to find a place for themselves, gain respect, enter adulthood, and earn a living, embrace the "dark side" of social capital and find themselves joining a street gang or selling drugs.[93]

* * *

The social network characteristics of the poor are by-products of their poverty and contribute to the persistence of poverty as well. The poor are deficient in social ties that might help them escape poverty, and in a self-perpetuating cycle, their poverty in turn gives rise to impoverished social ties. The social networks of the poor enable them to "get by" in one fashion or another but not to "get ahead." Their social capital facilitates survival but does not generate human, cultural, or political capital conducive to economic mobility. Because they lack weak and varied ties, in addition, the poor are at a competitive disadvantage in the labor market. They do not hear about job openings, and employers, many of whom rely on networks to recruit employees, do not include them in the applicant pool. Because they are exclusionary and because "who you know is constrained by disadvantage," social networks, as Charles Kadushin observes, are "essentially unfair."[94] The problem faced by the poor is not simply a lack of individual resources, not simply a merit deficiency, as individualistic theories would have us believe, but a lack of social resources. The poor are impeded in their ability to get ahead not only because they are starting from so far behind, but also because, in contrast to their more well-connected counterparts, they are hobbled by their membership in networks lacking in valuable social resources.

## CONCLUSION

We all occupy a location in the social system. We are, among other things, members of groups, residents of neighborhoods, and participants in social networks. People's place in society, whether they are "insiders" or "outsiders," to put it simply, over and above their individual characteristics, has consequences for their economic outcomes. One individual belongs to the "right" groups, lives in a "good" neighborhood, and is a member of a re-source-rich network. A second individual belongs to the "wrong" groups, lives in a "bad" neighborhood, and is a member of a resource-poor network. Blessed with a multitude of advantages, the first person, even if he is untal-ented and lazy, has a good chance of attaining a middle-class life. Burdened with a multitude of disadvantages, the second person, even if she is able and determined, has a good chance of falling into poverty. As a result of differ-ences in their social locations, these two individuals compete on a playing field that is anything but level. The first swims with the tide; the second swims against the tide.

The unequal distribution of social resources gives some individuals and groups a competitive edge over others. People who are rich in social re-sources—whether these originate from their groups, their neighborhoods, or their networks—have the inside track when it comes to getting into elite schools, landing good jobs, and securing career-making promotions. On the flip side of their good luck, however, is the bad luck of those who are poor in social resources.[95] The gains enjoyed by advantaged groups come at the expense of disadvantaged groups. In a context where desirable positions are scarce, as in the labor market, success for the former is a *cause* of failure for the latter. If people from favored groups exploit their social connections to get good jobs, this is not just a happy result for them; it is also an unhappy result for their less favored, less well-connected, but equally qualified com-petitors. We take note of the lucky people who rise to the top, and we sometimes even register the unlucky people who remained trapped at the bottom, but we rarely acknowledge the causal connection between the good fortune of the first and the bad fortune of the second.

People who are members of out-groups, who reside in high-poverty neighborhoods, and who participate in impoverished social networks are particularly vulnerable to poverty. Their poverty in turn exacerbates the ad-versities that arise from their disadvantaged social location. The social sys-tem variables discussed in this chapter provide a perspective, one superior to that put forward by individualistic theories, that adds to our understanding of why certain groups—African Americans and Latinos, women and single mothers, immigrants and people born into working-class families—have dis-proportionately high rates of poverty. But while social location certainly matters, it determines *who* is susceptible to poverty; it does not explain why there is poverty at all or why poverty exists to the extent it does. In the current system, if anyone is going to endure poverty, it is going to be those

people who are members of out-groups, who reside in impoverished neighborhoods, and who lack social connections. But why is anyone poor? This
question cannot be answered by reference to social system variables. To
understand why poverty exists in the first place and why there is so much of
it, we would have to return to a consideration of the economic and political
systems. Poverty, fundamentally, is a problem of the political economy, not
the social system. The rate and severity of poverty are primarily functions of
the quantity and quality of available jobs and the level and composition of
government spending. These political economy variables determine how
many people are going to suffer from poverty at any point in time; social
system variables determine who among the population will be doing the
suffering.

But while poverty cannot be effectively combated through social systems
reforms in themselves, changes in the rules governing access to neighborhoods, schools, and jobs, including, for example, anti-discrimination legislation and affirmative action programs, can create a less segregated and more
equitable society, one in which opportunities for avoiding poverty are more
fairly distributed and where group memberships, neighborhood conditions,
and social networks, along with race, gender, and class background, do not
play such a prominent role in shaping life chances. Policies designed to
achieve equality of opportunity hold out the promise of reducing the influence of group membership, residential location, and social connections on
people's prospects for educational and occupational advancement.[96] Such
policies would benefit persistently disadvantaged groups, making it possible
for them to compete on a more equal footing. This would certainly be a
desirable outcome, one well worth fighting for, but in the absence of more
far-reaching changes in the political and economic systems, such reforms,
though a step in the right direction, would not eradicate poverty. On the other
hand, it might be harder to ignore the problem of poverty if opportunities
were more equalized and if the composition of the poverty population—by
race, gender, and class background—more closely approximated the composition of the population as a whole. If poverty were more clearly a problem
for "us" as well as "them," then we might be more strongly motivated to do
something about it.

# Part III

# A Structural Perspective on Poverty — Ten Obstacles

*Chapter Nine*

# Structural Obstacles and the Persistence of Poverty (I)

The problem of poverty in the United States is rooted in diverse economic, political, cultural, and social forces beyond the immediate control of the individual. These forces have created a harsh environment for poorer Americans. There are not enough decent-paying jobs to accommodate the supply of potential workers. Government programs provide relatively little assistance to low-income households. The mainstream news media downplay the seriousness of the poverty problem and obscure its structural sources. And millions of people remain vulnerable to poverty because they belong to disadvantaged groups, reside in impoverished neighborhoods, and participate in resource-poor social networks. The rate of poverty remains high in the United States because the poor are socially excluded, culturally stigmatized, politically marginalized, and stuck in the low-wage labor market.

I continue to make the case for a structural perspective on American poverty in this part of the book, but I shift the focus from the more distant "systems" forces, often operating beyond the level of everyday awareness, to the more immediate and pressing day-to-day difficulties experienced by the poor. Specifically, I examine ten obstacles or institutional problems commonly encountered by low-income households as they struggle to eke out a living. These obstacles, indicative of the deep inequalities in access to essential goods and services, impose daily hardships on the poor and obstruct their efforts to cope with or escape from the condition of poverty. In this chapter I discuss racial and ethnic discrimination, residential segregation, housing, education, and transportation. In chapter 10 I consider sex discrimination, child care, health and health care, retirement insecurity, and legal deprivation. These obstacles, emanating ultimately from the failings of the American political economy, are consequences of poverty, and they contribute to the persistence of that poverty as well, increasing the likelihood of poor people getting trapped at the bottom of society and passing along their economic status to their children.

Proponents of individualistic theories, when they acknowledge such problems, ascribe them to people's own deviant values and bad choices. If the poor experience difficulties or suffer hardships, this is due mainly to their own irresponsible conduct—they refuse to take care of their homes and neighborhoods, they fail to socialize their children, they care little about education, they don't save for the future, they embrace an unhealthy lifestyle, they get in trouble with the law, and rather than working hard to get ahead, they complain about discrimination. From this standpoint, if poor people would only behave properly and take responsibility for their own lives, the problems commonly associated with poverty would disappear.

I argue, in contrast, that the most serious problems experienced by the poor, including the ten addressed here, are structural, not self-inflicted. These problems are not incidental "personal troubles" affecting a mere "scatter of individuals." They are systemic, rooted in the normal operation of dominant social institutions, and they create genuine adversities for millions of Americans, not just the poor. These are "public issues of social structure."[1] They originate from and are perpetuated by a highly skewed distribution of economic and political power, by the massively unequal allocation of resources and opportunities in society, and by government policy that has become increasingly unresponsive to the interests and needs of average working Americans.

## RACIAL AND ETHNIC DISCRIMINATION

Poverty is not an equal opportunity problem. In 2012, the rates of poverty for African Americans and Hispanics, the two largest minority groups, were 27.2 and 25.6 percent, respectively, substantially higher than the 9.7 percent for non-Hispanic whites. Though they make up about one-quarter of the total population, African Americans and Hispanics constitute somewhat more than half of the poor and well more than half of the very poor.[2] They have lower levels of education, homeownership, income, and wealth. They have higher rates of unemployment, incarceration, single parenthood, and poor health. And they are more likely to work in the low-wage sector of the economy, reside in high-poverty neighborhoods, and attend high-poverty schools.[3]

Despite the accomplishments of the civil rights movement, vast inequalities by race and ethnicity persist into the twenty-first century. This is partly the consequence of past discrimination. Since before the nation was founded and continuing throughout the twentieth century, the lion's share of the gains from economic expansion has gone to white people, with each new generation building on its ancestors' good fortune. Government policy has also rendered "cumulative advantages" to whites and "cumulative disadvantages" to minorities.[4] During the New Deal era of the 1930s, extending into the 1940s and 1950s—a period when "affirmative action was white"—a succession of landmark social policies subsidized the birth of today's suburban middle class.[5] These measures legislated retirement and unemployment insurance, established the minimum wage, affirmed the right to unionize, expanded access to higher education, and created federally guaranteed home mortgages. Powerful southern legislators, to ensure the continued subordination of the black population, demanded local control over the new programs, however, and they insisted that agricultural and domestic occupations, where most black people were employed, be excluded from many New Deal provisions. So while these policies set millions of white families along the path toward the American Dream, racial and ethnic minorities—still barred from good neighborhoods, good schools, and good jobs—shared little in the general prosperity. The passage of civil rights laws and the Great Society legislation of the 1960s helped turn things around, but people of color still struggle against an oppressive historical legacy.[6]

The blatant racism of the past has by no means disappeared, but present-day prejudice and discrimination are often of a more subtle and hidden kind, less overt than during the years of Jim Crow.[7] In today's post–civil rights era, partly because discrimination is less visible, most whites deny that it constitutes a significant barrier to achievement, believing instead that the high incidence of minority poverty is primarily a consequence of insufficient motivation.[8] While acknowledging past discrimination, whites tend to see the disadvantages associated with race and ethnicity as lying *entirely* in the past and as having little influence on the present. A growing body of research, however, offers persuasive evidence of continued discrimination, stemming from some combination of individual prejudice, institutional practices, and government policies. The consequences of discrimination are particularly costly in the areas of employment and housing.[9]

Evidence from field experiments (or audit studies) that test for employment discrimination using matched pairs of white and non-white job seekers discloses a clear pattern of employment discrimination.[10] Equally qualified minority applicants are less likely than their white competitors to advance to the interview stage or be offered a job, and if hired they are more likely to be steered into lower-paying, dead-end positions.[11] In one eye-opening study, Devah Pager finds that black men without criminal records stand no better chance of getting a callback after submitting a job application than do equally qualified white men *with* criminal records.[12] Being black is at least as much of a liability in the labor market as being an ex-offender, and employment opportunities for black ex-offenders are exceedingly scarce.[13] In another innovative field experiment, Marianne Bertrand and Sendhil Mullainathan submitted responses to hundreds of help-wanted ads placed in Boston and Chicago newspapers. Applications bearing conventionally white-sounding names (e.g., Emily or Greg) received 50 percent more interview offers than those bearing conventionally black-sounding names (e.g., Lakisha or Jamal). Having a strong resume, furthermore, did not help "black" applicants nearly as much as it did "white" applicants, suggesting that education and training alone cannot solve the racial employment gap.[14]

Employers discriminate, in part, because they harbor derogatory stereotypes about racial and ethnic minorities. They judge black men in a particularly negative light, regarding them as lazy, unreliable, disobedient, and criminally inclined.[15] While African American males may have the requisite skills, they are alleged to "create tensions in the workplace" and have bad attitudes and a poor work ethic.[16] Particularly in the low-wage sector of the economy, employers perceive black men as being insufficiently "manageable, obedient, and pliable," especially as compared to recent immigrants.[17] Minority job seekers, due to cultural and linguistic differences and the wariness of distrustful employers, are also highly susceptible to negative evaluations in pre-employment interviews.[18] Racial bias is even more likely to affect hiring decisions in today's service economy, where the emphasis is on "soft" people skills rather than more objectively measurable "hard" skills.[19] Subjective judgments inevitably come into play in assessing soft skills, leaving more room for employers' appraisal of job candidates to be influenced, if only unconsciously, by prejudice and stereotypes. Research showing that employment discrimination is more prevalent in the "social skills" sector of the economy than in the technical skills sector supports this conclusion. [20]

Black and Latino job seekers are also disadvantaged in the labor market because many businesses have moved to the suburbs where the labor force is predominantly white, and because employers frequently use recruitment strategies that, whether by design or default, exclude minorities from the applicant pool. They announce job openings in local newspapers with a primarily white readership, rather than in metropolitan newspapers; they solicit applicants from suburban and Catholic schools, bypassing inner-city public schools; and they rely on racially exclusive informal networks to fill job vacancies. [21] Employers discriminate when they refuse to hire qualified minority applicants, but they also discriminate when their methods of recruitment deny racial and ethnic minorities the opportunity to compete for a job. [22]

As a result of employment discrimination, along with other labor market disadvantages, African Americans and Hispanics have unequal access to jobs, longer periods of unemployment, less chance of reemployment after a job loss, and they are more likely to drop out of the labor force. [23] Within the workplace, they are sometimes subject to harassment, mistreatment by supervisors, and arbitrary firings. They also tend to be segregated into lower-status occupations where they receive less on-the-job training, fewer opportunities for advancement, and lower earnings. [24] Reflecting the accumulation of labor market disadvantages over time, the lifetime earnings of racial and ethnic minorities are substantially lower than those of white workers. [25]

The adversities experienced by racial and ethnic minorities in the labor market also affect their housing options. Black and Latino families have less money to invest in homeownership, and they are less likely than otherwise equivalent white families to have relatives who can afford to help out with the down payment. [26] But in addition to the financial constraints, racial and ethnic minorities encounter discriminatory barriers in the housing market. They are not free to live just anywhere they wish. One obstacle is hostility, harassment, and other forms of "move-in violence" by the residents of predominantly white communities. [27] In one Chicago neighborhood, William Julius Wilson and Richard P. Taub report, white residents "generally viewed the arrival of even a few minorities as a threat to their well-being." [28] And as Judith DeSena shows in her study of Greenpoint, New York, white property owners employ a variety of strategies to prevent minorities from moving into "their" neighborhoods. They circumvent the open market by filling housing vacancies through personal referrals and word of mouth; they apply pressure on neighbors to make sure they do not sell or rent to black and Latino families; and they use their local political influence to ward off threats to residential segregation.[29]

Audit studies similar to those used in testing for employment discrimination reveal that racial and ethnic minorities are also treated adversely by real estate agents, mortgage lenders, and home insurers. Though housing discrimination declined in the 1990s, sales and rental agents still sometimes withhold information about housing availability, do not permit minorities to inspect properties on the market, offer them less favorable terms and conditions, and routinely steer whites to predominantly white neighborhoods and non-whites to predominantly minority neighborhoods.[30] According to comprehensive nationwide studies from 2000, African Americans and Hispanics are subject to some form of discrimination in approximately 20 percent of their visits to real estate and rental agents.[31]

Discrimination by lenders and insurers also limits housing options. When they make inquiries to mortgage lending institutions about financing, African Americans and Hispanics receive less information, assistance, encouragement, and follow-up.[32] Compared to white customers with similar characteristics, they are less likely to be approved for housing loans or mortgage refinancing.[33] In addition, since the 1990s, they are more likely to be drawn into the subprime lending market, where they pay higher fees and interest rates, are vulnerable to predatory lending practices, and face a greater risk of foreclosure, bad credit records, and debilitating indebtedness.[34] And because of discrimination in the property insurance market, minorities are also forced to pay higher premiums or are denied the housing insurance required to qualify for a home loan.[35]

Housing discrimination is a key factor underlying racial and ethnic inequality and the high rates of poverty experienced by African Americans and Hispanics. Because neighborhoods shape opportunities, discrimination in the housing market restricts prospects for education, employment, social mobility, and a safe and healthy residential environment.[36] And because homeownership is the largest investment for most families, housing discrimination also limits wealth accumulation. Racial and ethnic minorities are more likely to be confined to the rental market, and if they do manage to purchase a home, they benefit less from appreciation in property values, receiving a lower return on their housing investment.[37] This partly explains the massive racial wealth gap, with white households possessing twenty times the wealth of black households and eighteen times the wealth of Hispanic households.[38]

The result, in turn, is that racial and ethnic minorities have fewer assets they can draw upon to stave off poverty during hard times, finance their retirement, provide their children with a good education, and otherwise achieve a secure standard of living for themselves and their families. Disparities in homeownership, housing appreciation, and wealth contribute to the reproduction of racial and ethnic inequality and to the intergenerational transmission of poverty.[39]

These are hard times for working Americans, and for racial and ethnic minorities, the hard times are even harder. The adverse effects of economic deprivation, and the difficulties of coping with or escaping from poverty, are compounded by the cumulative effects of racial and ethnic discrimination.

## RESIDENTIAL SEGREGATION

In the mainstream political discourse and news media, the striking phenomenon of rich and poor, whites and non-whites inhabiting geographically separate and vastly unequal worlds goes largely unnoticed, or at least unmentioned. With the United States now well into the new millennium, residential segregation endures as a skeleton in the closet.[40]

The spatial divide between the rich and the poor has widened since the 1970s, with the result that both poverty and affluence have become increasingly concentrated.[41] On the racial front, data from the 2010 census show a slow and modest decline in black–white segregation since 1980, with residential patterns changing least in the most heavily segregated cities.[42] Meanwhile, levels of segregation between whites and Asians and between whites and Latinos have remained about the same. African Americans, however, still experience much more segregation than other minority groups. Indeed, several million black poor live under conditions of extreme isolation, what Douglas Massey and Nancy Denton call "hypersegregation."[43] Racially integrated communities do exist in the United States.[44] But the overwhelming reality is that African Americans, and Latinos to a lesser extent, live in neighborhoods separate from those occupied by non-Hispanic whites. The "problem of the color-line" is a problem of the twenty-first century no less than the twentieth.[45]

Contrary to popular impression, residential segregation, with reference specifically to black–white segregation, is not the result of people being naturally inclined to live among "their own kind." Individual choice matters, but the pattern of racially segregated neighborhoods is the expression of white preferences more than black preferences, and it is the product of racial fears and stereotypes more than in-group favoritism.[46] White people, motivated by some combination of anti-black prejudice and calculations of self-interest, desire racially homogeneous communities; they are unwilling to enter neighborhoods with more than a token black presence; and, as suggested by the concept of "white flight," they are quick to leave when minorities start moving in.[47] African Americans are more strongly committed to racial integration, but they have grown wary of white neighborhoods. They have realistic concerns about being unwelcome and resented, and they are reluctant to make themselves targets of hostility and harassment.[48] White racial prejudice, as Camille Zubrinsky Charles observes, is thus a "double whammy." It undermines integration not only through its influence on white people's residential decisions, but on the residential choices of black people as well.[49] White housing preferences are all the more important because they are embodied in and reinforced by a long history of government housing policies promoting racial segregation and by the discriminatory behavior of landlords, neighborhood associations, realtors, mortgage lenders, and home insurers.[50]

Where people live determines their prospects for education, employment, and mobility; their health and safety; their exposure to crime, violence, and environmental hazards; their access to stores and services, libraries and parks; the characteristics of their friends, peers, and acquaintances; the quality of their social contacts and networks; and their level of prestige and political influence. Social processes that sort people into neighborhoods by class and race aggravate existing inequalities. Residential segregation confers benefits on the privileged, enabling them to monopolize valuable resources, to ensure, for example, that they enjoy superior public amenities and that their children receive the highest-quality education. But for minorities and the poor, residential segregation, and its pernicious offspring, the ghetto and the barrio, piles hardship on top of hardship. It multiplies and magnifies the disadvantages of poverty, such that poor families suffer not only from their own low income, but from the deprivation of their surrounding communities as well. Data for the 2006–2010 period reveal that an increasing number of mostly minority children, now nearly 8 million, live in census tracts where 30 percent or more of the population is poor, a circumstance of concentrated poverty that has harmful and lasting effects.[51]

For more than a decade now, due especially to the discontinuation of court-ordered desegregation efforts, American schools have undergone a process of "resegregation."[52] Most white children attend schools that are overwhelmingly white. Black and Latino children attend predominantly minority schools. According to a recent report from the Civil Rights Project, 84 percent of Latino students and 74 percent of African American students attend majority non-white schools, and more than a third of each of these minority groups attend "intensely segregated schools," with fewer than 10 percent white students.[53] They are also more likely to attend high-poverty schools where the educational needs and challenges are great and where resources are scarce, facilities run down, and teachers less qualified.[54] Because of residential segregation and the growing economic divide between cities and suburbs and between poor and affluent neighborhoods, American children are offered separate and greatly unequal educational experiences. The segregated school system in the United States, described by Sheryll Cashin as the "great inequalizer," aggravates the problem of poverty and adds to the disadvantages faced by poor and minority children.[55]

Residential segregation is a barrier to employment as well as education. First, the labor market for urban minorities since the 1970s has deteriorated as high-wage manufacturing jobs have disappeared and as business firms have relocated from northern cities to the suburbs and to non-union states in the South and Southwest.[56] The distance between where poor and minority workers live and where the available jobs are located has grown. Because of this "spatial mismatch," urban workers may not hear about job openings; they may not apply, figuring employers would be reluctant to hire them; and, in any case, they may be unable to get to suburban jobs, either because commuting costs are unaffordable or because job sites are not accessible via public transportation.[57]

Second, residential segregation limits employment opportunities by reinforcing "social network segregation."[58] Most inner-city poor, due to social isolation, are acquainted mainly with people like themselves, disadvantaged minorities. Their social circles seldom include experienced mentors, influential job contacts, or persons of power and prestige. Because they reside in segregated neighborhoods, poor African Americans and Latinos are cut off from potentially valuable sources of employment information, and they lack the connections, referrals, and references often needed to gain entrée to good jobs.[59]

Third, as a result of residential segregation, neighborhoods acquire reputations; whether a neighborhood is judged good or bad, safe or dangerous, depends heavily on its racial composition. Perceptions of neighborhood quality influence employers' decisions about business location and employee recruitment. They draw inferences about the competence and dependability of job candidates based on their residential location. Employers' inclination to use "space" as a "signal" of workers' reliability disadvantages inner-city job seekers, particularly if they reside in neighborhoods that are commonly thought of as "ghettos" or "barrios."[60] African Americans and Latinos are not only susceptible to *race* discrimination, but to *place* discrimination as well.[61]

Residential segregation also disadvantages racial minorities and the poor, African Americans in particular, through a twofold effect on the operation of the housing market. On the one hand, black people tend to be steered or driven away from white neighborhoods and are thus denied opportunities for quality housing, social mobility, and asset accumulation. They are not altogether free to "move on up" by purchasing homes in better neighborhoods with better schools. As a consequence, they are less able than whites to benefit from the appreciation of housing values, to build a reserve of wealth, and to secure a prosperous middle-class life for themselves and their children.[62] On the other hand, white people typically do not search for housing in predominantly black neighborhoods. Because reduced demand suppresses housing values, black homeowners pay a significant "segregation tax"; they are penalized by a lower return for their housing investment.[63] African Americans are thus less able than whites to accumulate wealth through homeownership and convert their human capital and hard work into the American Dream.

Residential segregation and housing discrimination, along with the tendency for minority families to benefit less from inheritance, contribute to a "racial wealth gap."[64] Racial wealth disparities far exceed racial income disparities. While median income for black and Hispanic families is about 60 percent of that received by white families, the median net worth of black and Hispanic households is only 5 percent and 1 percent, respectively, of the median net worth of white households. More than a third of both African American and Hispanic households, furthermore, have zero or negative net worth, nearly twice the figure for white households.[65] Many minority families, accordingly, are "asset poor."[66] They have little wealth to fall back on— to cushion the effects of unemployment, cover the costs of a medical emergency, or help their children pay for college. Even middle-class black and Hispanic families, because they have few assets, are just a paycheck or two away from poverty.[67] Residential segregation deters wealth accumulation, and racial minorities as a result have a weak personal safety net and are less able to protect their children from downward mobility.

Residential segregation contributes not only to the social and economic marginalization of the poor, but to their political marginalization as well. Because they are impoverished, they have little influence on government policy; because they are spatially isolated, they also have few shared interests on the basis of which they can forge coalitions with more politically power-ful white and suburban residents. The interests of cities and suburbs, in fact, are more likely to collide than coalesce, particularly during an era of govern-ment retrenchment and fiscal austerity. The urban poor are in desperate need of government assistance to improve the quality of local schools and ser-vices, provide job training, and expand employment opportunities. Suburba-nites, however, are resistant to both tax increases and redistributive policies, and they prefer, of course, that scarce public resources flow in their direction. The political isolation of the inner-city poor makes them vulnerable to racist scapegoating and convenient targets for government cutbacks.[68]

Residential segregation is not the inevitable product of human nature or market forces. It is the result of racial prejudice and individual and institu-tional discrimination. Residential segregation is harmful in its consequences as well. It not only frustrates the dream of an integrated and truly democratic society; it also undermines equality of opportunity, limits severely the life chances of people already burdened with multiple disadvantages, and thwarts the efforts of the poor to survive and escape their poverty.[69]

## HOUSING

Despite working two jobs, Alpha Manzuelta cannot afford her own apart-ment; for the past three years she has been living in a homeless shelter. "I feel stuck," she explains.[70] Low-wage workers like Manzuelta are caught in a vicious mismatch between what jobs pay and what housing costs.[71] It is nearly impossible for poorer Americans to find a decent place to live and harder still to find a place that is reasonably priced and conveniently located. The unfortunate result is that they often end up spending more than they can afford for substandard housing in undesirable neighborhoods with a long commute to work.[72] Housing for poor families is also often unsafe, infested by rodents and insects, too cold in the winter and too hot in the summer, and sometimes equipped with broken appliances and faulty plumbing.[73] Many low-income people face an even more serious housing problem. On any given night in January 2013, more than six hundred thousand people were homeless, including a rising number of young adults. One-third of this homeless population lives in cars, under bridges, on the streets, or in some other unsheltered location.[74]

Poor families are often forced into desperate trade-offs and undesirable sacrifices just to make ends meet. They subsist by going without health insurance, relying on relatives for child care, and doing without a car. Housing, however, is a necessary expenditure. It is not only the largest item in most household budgets; it is a priority item as well. People need shelter before just about anything else, so rental or mortgage payments come first, with families sometimes even skimping on food to cover their housing costs. Housing is also a key ingredient of people's quality of life.[75] We need adequate housing to be safe and secure, to be physically and psychologically healthy, and to achieve a sense of comfort and personal well-being. A place to call home serves as a private sanctuary and a setting for friendship and family relations. The quality of our housing also shapes our prospects for economic success and our access to resources and opportunities, including schools, jobs, neighborhood amenities, and public services. A family's ability to avoid poverty, accumulate household wealth, and ensure a stable and sound upbringing for their children is dependent on the availability of decent housing.[76]

Housing is essential, but also expensive. As a result, millions of Americans are stuck with excessive mortgage or rental payments. A typical household, according to policy experts, can afford to spend no more than 30 percent of its total income on housing. Households are classified as having a "moderate" cost burden if they pay more than 30 percent and a "severe" cost burden if they pay more than 50 percent. In 2011, 42.3 million households had at least a moderate cost burden, including 20.6 million households with a severe cost burden, an increase of 6.7 million since 2001. For low-income families this problem is the norm. Almost 70 percent of households with annual incomes less than $15,000 are severely burdened by their housing costs, and another 31 percent of households earning between $15,000 and $29,999 also pay more than half of their income for housing.[77] Families so overwhelmed by housing costs live stressful and perilous lives, only a paycheck or two away from eviction and homelessness.

With housing absorbing so much of their income, millions of households experience material deprivation. They do not have enough money to adequately cover the cost of other necessities, including food, clothing, child care, transportation, and health care. Michael Stone calls this circumstance "shelter poverty."[78] A household is "shelter-poor" "if it cannot meet its non-housing needs at some minimum level of adequacy after paying for housing."[79] In 2001, according to Stone's calculations, before the Great Recession made a bad situation worse, approximately 32 million households in the United States were shelter poor, up from 19 million in 1970. The incidence of shelter poverty is significantly worse for some types of households than others: renters; larger households; minority households; and female-headed families, which make up almost half of the shelter poor.[80]

Homeownership is the centerpiece of the American Dream, but many homeowners are poor and many poor homeowners have housing problems. A home is a costly investment.[81] Prior to the financial crash of 2007–2009, housing prices were on an upward trajectory, creating an unsustainable housing bubble. This occurred for a variety of reasons, including a shift in the pattern of new construction toward larger and more luxurious homes, intensified competition among middle-class families for housing in good neighborhoods with good schools, and speculation in a volatile housing market.[82] The trickle-down effect of these dynamics, in combination with low and stagnant wages, deepened the housing crisis for poorer households. With the onset of the Great Recession, numerous families, both poor and middle class, have abandoned or deferred the dream of homeownership. Many others are burdened by high mortgage payments and mortgage debt, or they are "underwater," saddled with negative equity. And since 2006, the number of foreclosures has increased by 400 percent, with the residents of poor and minority neighborhoods most likely to lose their homes.[83]

Most of the non-elderly poor and near poor, and many low-income elderly households as well, rent rather than own. The housing problem for this population is bad and getting worse. According to Shaun Donovan, secretary of housing and urban development, we are currently in the midst of "the worst rental affordability crisis that this country has ever known."[84] Rental costs are rising faster than earnings, particularly for households in the bottom income quintile, but also for many in the middle class.[85] In 2011, the number of cost-burdened renters, trending upward since 1970, was over 50 percent.[86] The number of "worst case housing needs"—low-income renters lacking housing assistance and being severely rent burdened or living in substandard housing (or both)—has skyrocketed since 2007, rising from 5.9 million to almost 8.5 million in 2011, including more than 3.2 million families with children.[87] Even many moderate-income workers have trouble paying the monthly rent. A full-time worker in 2014 would have to earn an hourly wage of $18.92, well more than twice the federal minimum, to afford a two-bedroom rental unit, and in not a single county in the country can a full-time worker at the minimum wage afford even a one-bedroom rental unit. [88]

The lack of affordable rental housing is partly due to increasing demand, as many people have been pushed out of the homeownership market, but the supply of reasonably priced rental units is also dwindling. Rental property at the low end of the price scale is old and "rapidly disappearing," a product of gentrification, abandonment, demolition, and the unwillingness of government policy makers to replenish the stock of affordable housing. [89] And construction of new rental units in recent years, as in the case of new home construction, has targeted more affluent consumers. The result is a "substantial undersupply of rental dwellings available for low-income households" and a growing rental affordability crisis. [90] Poor people face a difficult struggle just to find a place to live. In 2011, there were only thirty affordable, available, and physically adequate rental units for every one hundred low-income renters. [91]

Though poorer Americans, mostly renters, are the primary victims of the nation's housing problems, affluent homeowners are the primary beneficiaries of housing policy. More than one-half of the $270 billion spent by the federal government on housing assistance in 2012 went to households with incomes over $100,000, mainly in the form of tax deductions for mortgage interest payments and property taxes. The cost of these housing-related tax expenditures far exceeds housing assistance outlays for the poor, including "Section 8" housing vouchers. Indeed, the poorest 20 million households, with incomes of $20,000 or less, received a smaller share of total spending than did the 5 million households with incomes of $200,000 or more. [92] Low-income housing programs are not only less generous, but less widely available as well. Approximately 5 million poor families currently benefit from housing assistance, with households generally subsidized at a level that reduces their housing costs to no more than 30 percent of their total income. But unlike tax expenditures, which are distributed to every qualified household, housing assistance subsidies are allotted only until the money runs out. And there is nowhere near enough funding to provide subsidies for everyone who is eligible. Millions of low-income families are thus placed on lengthy waiting lists or left to fend for themselves in an inhospitable housing market. In 2011, only about 25 percent of needy households received assistance. [93] And with strong political resistance to spending increases, especially those targeted to less-powerful, low-income families, the housing problems faced by poorer Americans are likely only to get worse.

Millions of low-income households cannot afford decent housing, and the lack of adequate and affordable housing, as John Yinger argues, keeps poor families mired in poverty.[94] First, households burdened by high mortgage or rental costs have less money to devote to education, training, child care, health care, job searches, transportation, and other investments that might enable them and their children to escape poverty. Second, low-income families are forced into decrepit, dangerous, and overcrowded living circumstances. The poor quality of their housing exposes them to a range of health problems, including asthma, lead poisoning, stress, and injuries.[95] These health hazards impose immediate costs for medical expenses, and they take a long-run toll on the physical and psychological well-being of the poor, making it even more difficult for them to succeed in schools and in the labor market. Third, most poor households, because they cannot afford to own, do not benefit from the economic, social, and psychological rewards that come from homeownership. Many poor homeowners receive little or no return from their housing investment.[96] The workings of the housing market make it difficult for poor families to accumulate wealth and achieve upward mobility through homeownership. Fourth, market forces and housing discrimination leave many poor people, especially racial and ethnic minorities, confined to high-poverty neighborhoods. The residents of such neighborhoods are isolated from suburban employment opportunities and experience other deleterious consequences from living in an environment of concentrated poverty. In all these ways and more, the housing market "helps to push people into poverty and keep them there."[97]

Whether or not people have reasonable access to housing in the United States today is primarily dependent on market forces—meaning that people only get the housing they can pay for. This continued adherence to a market-driven housing policy is precisely the problem. In the absence of government measures explicitly designed to raise wages, lower costs, and increase the supply of affordable housing, low-income Americans are likely to suffer a "permanent housing crisis."[98]

## EDUCATION

All parents want their kids to get a good education. Because their futures are so uncertain, this may be especially true for the poor. They cannot assume their children will obtain adequate schooling, much less that they are destined for success. Of course, middle-class parents worry too, and they sacrifice and scrape to educate their children. But they also realistically anticipate that their struggles will be rewarded and their kids will indeed graduate from high school, get a college degree, and go on to enjoy the American Dream. For low-income families, however, the achievement of normal educational aspirations requires extraordinary effort and an abundance of good luck. They encounter a different and much harsher educational universe, where the odds are stacked against them. Poor parents do not have the financial assets, the political resources, the social networks, or the institutional support necessary to ensure that their sons and daughters receive the quality education expected of all American children.

Poverty begins at home, from the very moment of conception, and it has lasting effects on children's life outcomes, including their subsequent educational performance. First, poverty, because it is stressful and unhealthy, hinders learning. Children raised in poor families are susceptible to an assortment of physical and mental ailments, including low birth weight, malnutrition, and lead poisoning. These hit particularly hard during infancy and preschool years, impairing children's cognitive, behavioral, and emotional development.[99] Second, poverty is depriving. Poor families have limited resources to invest in their children's upbringing and early education. Compared to their more affluent counterparts, low-income parents spend less on clothing, toys, games, educational materials, and child-enrichment activities.[100] They rely on neighbors, friends, and relatives rather than more costly certified providers to meet their child-care needs. They cannot afford to enroll their kids in top-notch preschool programs, and the facilities within their means offer only substandard care and instruction.[101] Third, low-income children receive less cognitive stimulation in their homes. They are sometimes disadvantaged by the educational level and child-rearing practices of their parents; by a lack of "literacy-related activities"; by their more limited exposure to computers, books, reading, and intellectually enriching experiences; and by parents overburdened by the demands of work.[102] As a consequence of these and other factors, poor children, even before they begin kindergarten, are well behind their more affluent peers in math and verbal skills and overall school readiness. Children raised in low-income families suffer from a variety of "starting gate" inequalities, and partly because primary and secondary schools do so little to compensate for preschool disadvantages, these inequalities exert a powerful effect on later-life educational and socioeconomic outcomes.[103]

Poor children enter the educational system already handicapped by their home and neighborhood environments and by the stressful hardships of their preschool years. And then, in defiance of any sense of fair play, the neediest of the nation's children are crowded into the country's worst schools.[104] They are victimized by the enduring pattern of residential and educational segregation, by concentrated poverty, and by persistent disparities in per-pupil spending. Schools depend heavily on money from local property taxes, and since impoverished communities have a less substantial tax base, spending for poor and minority students, precisely those most in need of public resources, is lower than for middle-class students.[105] At the extremes, some schools spend two or three times more on their students than others. Inequalities within school districts and among states also leave many poorer children shortchanged.[106] The problem is even worse than it seems, however. To compensate for years of underinvestment in high-poverty schools and the cumulative disadvantages experienced by low-income children, poor schools need *more* resources than middle-class schools: equal funding is not adequate funding.[107]

School segregation and funding disparities yield highly unequal educational experiences and outcomes. Poor and minority students attend schools that are inferior in many respects: substandard physical structure, crowded classrooms, lower teacher expectations, and fewer supplies and facilities, including computers, Internet access, and science labs. Teachers in schools serving low-income students have a higher turnover rate, and they tend to have less training, experience, and subject knowledge and weaker math and verbal skills. Poorer schools are deficient also in the availability of gifted and advanced placement classes; in the size and expertise of the support staff, including guidance counselors and school psychologists; and in the overall level of student safety, comfort, and well-being.[108] Not all of these disparities, taken individually, are large, but they bunch together, with good schools good in many ways and bad schools bad in many ways. School inequalities also "add up," Meredith Phillips and Tiffani Chin observe, and they have a cumulative effect over time: "Some students experience a long string—maybe even twelve consecutive years—of 'bad' schools, while others may get a long string of 'good' schools."[109] Rather than equalizing opportunities, the existing educational system reinforces "the transmission of low socioeconomic status from parents to children."[110] In the United States, as a result, compared to many other countries, "socioeconomic disadvantage" is more likely to translate "directly into poor educational performance."[111]

Students in the United States encounter an educational system that is not only unequal but separate as well.[112] The vast majority of affluent white children attend schools that offer minimal opportunity for interaction with students of a different class or race. Low-income and minority children are packed into high-poverty schools or are slotted into low-achievement tracks in middle-class schools. Poor schools differ not only because they receive less money and are generally unequal in instructional quality, but also because the student body is disproportionately disadvantaged. This phenomenon—"the concentrations of poverty in American schools"—as Richard Kahlenberg argues, is a fundamental problem.[113] It creates an unfairly demanding educational setting for teachers who are already strapped for time and resources; it is liable to leave students with the impression they are being warehoused by an uncaring system; and it deprives children of a valuable educational asset, classmates who are academically well prepared and high achieving.[114] Segregated and high-poverty schools perpetuate a multitude of inequalities, undermining the educational achievement and life chances of low-income and minority students. As long as the school system remains divided by class and race, poor children will not have anything like an equal opportunity to realize their educational potential.

The earnings of workers with a college degree in today's economy exceed the earnings of workers with only a high school degree by somewhere between 40 and 50 percent, a disparity that has been trending upward since the 1980s.[115] And to no surprise, politicians and pundits can be found intoning the familiar higher education mantra whenever issues of poverty and inequality arise. American colleges and universities are not equal opportunity institutions, however, and their doors are not as wide open to the poor and the working class as they are to students from high-income families. While 82 percent of men and women from the top income quartile have a bachelor's degree by the age of twenty-four, only 8 percent of those from the bottom quartile are equally fortunate.[116] The system of higher education in the United States serves mainly to train the privileged, and the higher up one goes in the academic hierarchy, the more this is true. The class composition of the student body at more selective colleges and the top professional schools— "the pipelines to our principal corridors of power"—is particularly skewed.[117] Nearly three-quarters of the students at the country's elite institutions come from the top economic quartile, while only 3 percent come from the bottom quartile and only 10 percent from the bottom half.[118] Indeed, at the most prestigious schools, even middle-class applicants are being squeezed out by students from wealthy families.[119]

Less-affluent students enter the college market disadvantaged by their class background and by their less-than-equal primary and secondary schooling. On average, predictably, they have lower SAT scores and are less academically prepared than their more affluent competitors. But this tells only part of the story. As Anthony Carnevale finds, highly qualified kids from the bottom socioeconomic group are only about half as likely to attend a four-year college as comparable kids from the top socioeconomic group.[120] And when high-achieving low-income students do go to college, they are less likely than their more well-off counterparts to attend elite institutions. This pattern is partly the result of poor recruitment practices on the part of selective colleges.[121] But affluent students also possess numerous advantages in the application process. They have greater access to knowledgeable and well-connected high school guidance counselors; they can afford to enroll in expensive SAT prep courses; they receive valuable assistance, sometimes even from professional consultants, in writing resumes, preparing for interviews, and navigating complicated financial aid forms; they benefit from early admissions programs and in some cases from their status as "legacies" and children of wealthy donors; and they can more likely draw on the firsthand experience of parents, siblings, and friends.[122]

Money, too, remains a significant barrier to higher education for students from low-income families.[123] Working-class earnings have stagnated, state budgets have tightened, financial aid has failed to keep pace with the rising price of a college degree, and tuition costs have soared.[124] Between 1971 and 2011, according to Suzanne Mettler, the cost of attending a four-year public university increased from 6 to 9 percent of family income for those in the wealthiest quintile and from 42 to 114 percent for those in the poorest quintile.[125] A college education is becoming increasingly unaffordable for students from low-income families, and rather than remedying a troubling situation, lawmakers and college administrators are exacerbating the problem. Pell grants, the principal federal aid program for needy students, nowadays cover a significantly smaller share of college costs, 31 percent in 2012–2013 compared to nearly 80 percent in the 1970s.[126] The composition of government aid to higher education has also shifted, from scholarship grants, a crucial resource for working-class students, to guaranteed loans and tax credits targeted to more affluent families.[127] And with an eye on their national rankings, many colleges and universities, pressed into competition for high SAT applicants, have reshuffled their admissions priorities, replacing need-based aid with merit-based aid. [128] In general, the overall trend is that higher-income students are claiming a larger slice of a shrinking financial assistance pie. Less-affluent students, on the other hand, "are getting killed on the aid side, and they are getting killed on the tuition side." [129] Many able low-income and working-class students, as a consequence, forgo college, or they settle for a less expensive college, enroll in a two-year community college, work long hours to cover their tuition costs, or go deep into debt. [130] In any case, money has become an increasingly important determinant of who goes to college, what college they attend, whether or not they graduate, and how long it takes to complete a degree. [131]

People who lack a good education are vulnerable to poverty, and they would certainly benefit from a more equitable educational system. But as Richard Rothstein argues, even far-reaching educational reform is not enough to compensate for the larger societal effects of class disadvantage and racial discrimination. [132] Problems of poverty and inequality are fundamental; the problem of education is symptomatic. Creating more equal schools would be a step in the right direction. Ultimately, however, only by creating a more equal *society* can the educational achievement gap between the rich and the poor be narrowed.

## TRANSPORTATION

Not only are the jobs available to the poor lousy, but it is hard to get to them as well. Unable to find employment near her home, Intesar Museitef, a single mother with a six-year-old son, commutes four hours every workday to a seven-dollar-an-hour job as a home health-care aide. There is little else she can do. "If I leave this job," she explains, "I have nothing." [133] Atlanta resident Stacy Calvin also has a four-hour commute to work—two trains and a bus ride every day—spending nearly as much time on the road as she does at her part-time job. [134] Low-end workers like Museitef and Calvin are squeezed by scarce job prospects, stagnant wages, rising housing costs, and inadequate transportation. With limited residential choices, they are relegated to impoverished neighborhoods isolated from employment opportunities. Because they cannot always afford to live near work or are unwelcome in the community, they are stuck with long and costly daily commutes. The arduous trek from home to work and back consumes precious hours, at the expense of family, friends, leisure, and sleep. They also have little time to spend searching for higher-paying jobs or acquiring additional training and education. Low-income workers are caught up in a time trap that not only lessens the quality of their lives, but also restricts their opportunities for achieving a better future.[135]

The immediate problem for many of the poor is that they do not have the money to purchase, insure, and maintain a car. According to one study, approximately 20 percent of the poor and 12 percent of the near poor (those between 100 and 200 percent of the poverty line) live in households with no access to an automobile.[136] Without a car, they are reliant on public transportation, limited in the jobs they can search for and choose from, face longer commutes, and sometimes miss work or arrive late.[137] Access to an automobile is a key determinant of whether poor people are employed or unemployed and whether or not they manage to leave welfare for work.[138] Owning a car presents its own difficulties, however. "It's either your tires or extra gas or a part tearing up," laments one welfare recipient. "I can never really get ahead."[139] Even those who have a functioning vehicle confront some tough choices. To keep the gas tank filled for the drive to work, they limit family outings and visits to friends and cut back expenditures on other items, including food and leisure. One mother of three young children quit using her car, relying instead on a combination of trains and shuttles, but now it takes her more than twice as long to get to work. What she saves in money, she loses in time. "It's a nightmare," she says.[140]

Many poorer Americans, African Americans and Latinos in particular, are dependent on public transportation.[141] Buses and trains are much slower than cars, however. They do not always get passengers where they want to go, frequently leaving long distances to travel by foot or other means, and they do not always get passengers to their destinations when they need to be there. Katherine Boo, writing about the struggles of poor women in Oklahoma City, reports that bus drivers also sometimes refuse to stop for black customers.[142] Public transportation, furthermore, is just not designed for mothers running errands with children in tow, pushing strollers; carrying diapers, toys, juice boxes, and snacks; and laden with bags of groceries.[143] The fact that so many soccer moms drive SUVs is not entirely incomprehensible.

The public transit system in many cities does not mesh well with the needs of today's low-income workforce. Jobs in the growing service economy are geographically dispersed, sometimes located in out-of-the-way places not served by existing bus lines. Thousands of workers, including nannies, home health-care aides, and house cleaners, for example, are employed in people's homes, off the main thoroughfares.[144] Many low-wage workers in the expanding 24/7 economy have non-standard hours as well and are sometimes on the job in the middle of the night when public transportation is not readily accessible.[145] And because their work schedules often vary unpredictably from day to day and week to week, service workers cannot always plan in advance to meet their transportation requirements.

Workers reliant on public transportation, especially if they commute from inner-city neighborhoods, suffer the additional handicap that they are generally regarded as less desirable hires. Employers believe that bus and subway riders are prone to tardiness and absenteeism. They "have much more of a problem with consistency to getting to work," employers complain, and they always have a ready "excuse as far as being late."[146] Suburban employers sometimes even cite the unreliability of public transportation as an explanation for why they do not advertise jobs in metropolitan newspapers. "It seems prejudiced sometimes to say you don't want to hire them," a supervisor at an Atlanta construction firm remarked, but "we've got to have people that are flexible and can get to jobs everywhere and be there on time and not worry about set schedules for getting back and forth to work."[147]

Even if suburban employers were willing to hire city workers, many of the available jobs do not pay enough to compensate for the time and monetary costs of a long commute. Whether through choice or constraint, therefore, inner-city residents in the labor force are typically employed in or around the larger urban area.[148] They do not normally have great distances to travel, but they do have to venture outside their neighborhoods for employment. And because they are reliant on public transportation, their trips to work can still be long and inconvenient, even if they do not journey all the way out to the suburbs.[149] Some research suggests, indeed, that the real problem for the poor is less a "spatial mismatch" than an "automobile mismatch." Low-income workers spend more time getting to and from their jobs not because their commute *distance* is so great necessarily, but because their commute *mode*, public transportation, is so slow.[150] In either case, whether measured in miles or minutes, the distance between where workers live and where jobs are located creates transportation dilemmas for the poor and diminishes their employment opportunities.

Rural residents face particularly severe transportation problems. They often reside miles from employment sites, welfare offices, schools, medical facilities, day-care centers, and grocery stores. Many of the rural poor, like their urban counterparts, do not have the money to purchase a vehicle or keep it running; most of the jobs that are available, as one Iowa resident reported, "won't even pay for gas driving back and forth";[151] and more than a third of rural Americans live in areas where there is no public transportation at all.[152] For nine months, one woman in rural Oregon hitchhiked fifty-five miles each way to a job in Eugene.[153] Jennifer Mosher, a resident of rural Delaware County in New York, was fortunate enough to buy a cheap car—her "greatest blessing"—so she could get back and forth to work. But due to monthly loan payments, high gas costs, and the expense of constant repairs, car ownership also turned out to be her "biggest headache."[154] The transportation problems experienced by the suburban poor, a large and rapidly growing population, are similar. They too, often at the expense of their family lives, have to travel long distances to jobs that pay little more than the minimum wage.[155]

Transportation problems loom large in the lives of the poor. In their study of industrial restructuring in South Bend, Charles Craypo and David Cormier report that unreliable transportation was among the difficulties most frequently mentioned by the low-wage workers they interviewed.[156] April Kaplan cites research concluding that the lack of affordable transportation is an even more significant hurdle to successful participation in job training programs than is lack of child care.[157] Robert Bullard and his colleagues document how racial disparities in access to transportation deprive minorities of opportunities, rights, and quality of life.[158] Numerous studies show that transportation is an important barrier to employment for welfare recipients as well.[159]

Inadequate transportation, by limiting freedom of mobility, also causes low-income families a variety of non–work-related hardships. They are restricted to local restaurants and stores where goods and services are often expensive and of lesser quality. Parents are unable to travel outside their immediate neighborhoods to provide their children with enriching experiences and public services, including trips to museums, zoos, libraries, and parks. And they have a greater likelihood of missing appointments with medical personnel, welfare caseworkers, and other service professionals. Transportation is also a major expense for low-income families, more costly than anything other than housing; it eats up between one-quarter and one-third of total earnings, leaving poor families with little money left over to pay for other necessities.[160]

Spurred by political activists and the dictates of welfare reform, many local public and private agencies have implemented modest initiatives to alleviate the transportation problems of the poor.[161] But in recent years, transit policies around the country, especially in big cities like Los Angeles, have threatened to make the problem worse by reallocating transportation resources from the urban poor to the suburban middle class. Partly because of concerns about air pollution and traffic congestion, transit agencies, as Mark Garrett and Brian Taylor argue, have focused more on increasing the availability of public transportation for suburban commuters, who would otherwise drive to work, than on upgrading services for low-income city residents, many of whom are already "transit dependent."[162] Thus in many cities, funding priorities have shifted from the expansion and improvement of bus operations to the development of new rail projects.[163] This changing pattern of public investment promotes an increasingly unequal two-tiered transit system, with heavily subsidized facilities serving more higher-income riders and resource-starved bus lines serving mostly poor, minority riders.[164] Garrett and Taylor attribute this disparity to the political, economic, and racial divide that separates cities and suburbs and to the strong aversion to redistributive social programs on the part of policy makers and the middle-class public. Their analysis draws attention to the role played by politics and power in creating a mismatch between the disbursement of public funds and the transportation needs of the poor.[165]

Transportation inequity is a consequence of poverty and powerlessness, and it is an obstacle to surviving and overcoming poverty as well. This is not an isolated problem that can be solved on its own. It is nested in an assortment of other structural problems: low-wage work, residential segregation, racial discrimination, and unaffordable housing. The lack of access to reliable transportation for poorer Americans is a by-product of the larger phenomenon of rising economic and political inequality. Inadequate transportation is more than a social problem; it is "a social justice issue."[166]

# Chapter Ten

# Structural Obstacles and the Persistence of Poverty (II)

## SEX DISCRIMINATION

Women, especially when they are mothers, even more so when they are single mothers, are vulnerable to poverty.[1] The rate of poverty for working-age women (eighteen to sixty-four) is 15.4 percent, compared to 11.9 percent for working-age men. The rate of poverty for female-headed families (no husband present) is almost twice that of male-headed families (no wife present), 30.9 percent compared to 16.4 percent, and almost five times that of married-couple families, 30.9 percent compared to 6.3 percent. And more than one-third of all persons in female-headed families are poor, nearly 16 million women and children.[2] Women face a greater risk of poverty because their earnings lag behind those of men. This gender gap results from differences between women and men in how much they work, what jobs they have, and how much they are paid.

The female-to-male earnings ratio is significantly less today than it was in the 1960s. But since 2000, indicative of a stalled gender revolution, there has been little progress in closing the wage gap. For more than a decade now, full-time working women still bring home only about 77 percent of the yearly earnings of their male counterparts; and African American and Hispanic women fare even less well, making only 68 percent and 59 percent respectively of the earnings for white males.[3] If we consider all workers, however, and not just full-timers, and if we consider long-term earnings, and not just annual earnings, the gender disparity is much greater. First, a significant number of women, 26.5 percent compared to 13.4 percent for men, work part time, and the hourly pay for part-time jobs is typically less than for full-time jobs.[4] Women not only work fewer hours than men, but their wages are also lower for each hour they work. Second, Stephen Rose and Heidi Hartmann find that measured across a fifteen-year period, 1983 to 1998, women earned only 38 percent of what men earned, far less than the 77 percent figure when the pay gap is calculated on an annual basis.[5] The longer-term "career wage gap" is even greater. According to one estimate, as a result of the gender pay gap, full-time working women on average lose approximately $434,000 in earnings over a forty-year career.[6] Of course, as Rose and Hartmann note, married women are somewhat insulated from "the effects of their own low earnings" by the usually higher pay of their husbands.[7] Single women, however, and single mothers in particular, are exposed to the full brunt of low earnings and, predictably, they are at much greater risk of poverty.

Women have less earning power than men partly because the unequal division of family responsibilities and caregiving duties restricts their participation in the labor market and the kinds of jobs they can take. They are limited in how much money they can make because they do the bulk of society's unpaid labor. According to recent estimates, somewhere between two-thirds and three-quarters of all unpaid caregivers are female; and adult women devote on average 4.4 hours per day to care work, as compared to 2.7 for adult men.[8] When they are employed, women typically work a "second shift" at home in addition to their regular jobs.[9] They do most of the cooking, cleaning, and other household chores, and if they are mothers they also handle most of the child-care duties, a pattern that, according to Paula England, seems highly "resistant to change."[10] The costs arising from the conflicting demands of work and family are borne disproportionately by women. Many women work a "third shift" as well. They engage in a variety of caregiving activities outside the home—tending aging parents, sick friends and relatives, or needy neighbors.[11] Though greatly undervalued compared to other kinds of labor, care work is vital to the functioning of society. It is often psychologically and emotionally rewarding as well, a "labor of love."[12] But because it inevitably results in career interruptions, women's role as primary caretaker substantially reduces their potential lifetime earnings.[13]

If they are mothers, women in the workforce encounter an additional obstacle: they make significantly less money than comparable non-mothers, with low-wage working women, those who can least afford it, enduring the highest cost. Women with children pay a "motherhood penalty," and the more children they have, the more they are penalized.[14] The "price of motherhood," furthermore, shows no signs of abating.[15] At least part of this motherhood penalty is due to employment discrimination. Mothers are generally perceived as lacking in competence and work commitment, and their job applications are less likely to elicit callbacks from employers than those of otherwise equivalent non-mothers.[16] Employers are wary of hiring women with children on the assumption that being a mother is incompatible with being a good worker. For some employers, indeed, the status of motherhood is itself "a marker of unreliability."[17]

A major portion of the gender pay gap is due to job segregation and the devaluation of women's work.[18] Though occupational sex segregation has declined since the 1960s, at least up until the 1990s, women are still frequently consigned to lower-paying and less desirable "women's jobs," while men are channeled into more rewarding and prestigious "men's jobs." Even when occupations have similar education and skill requirements, jobs where women predominate pay less and have fewer opportunities for advancement than jobs where men predominate, and the higher the proportion of women in a particular occupation, the lower the pay.[19] Some women, of course, prefer "women's jobs," but in general, the pattern of workplace segregation is more a product of constraint than choice. As we have seen, women's employment options are circumscribed on the one hand by the demands of the caregiving role, forcing many women into lower-paying part-time work, and on the other hand by the preferences of employers who worry that mothers are more committed to their children than to their jobs.

Whether they are mothers or not, women's access to jobs is also constrained by deep-rooted stereotypes about their attributes and capabilities and by cultural conceptions of what constitutes gender-appropriate work.[20] Women are commonly believed to be less rational, competent, and authoritative than men and more emotional, expressive, and nurturing. They are thus presumed to be better suited for some jobs than others. Gender stereotypes such as these may enter into the self-evaluations and employment preferences of men and women themselves, and they certainly come into play when workplace gatekeepers make decisions about hiring, promotion, training, and work assignments.[21] Employers perpetuate job segregation when they show a preference for male workers, when their employment decisions are based on antiquated assumptions about men's and women's needs and abilities, and when they fill job vacancies through informal, sex-segregated social networks. Women who do cross over into predominantly male occupations, furthermore, are often met with not-so-welcome reminders of their outsider status: their femininity may be questioned; they may be subject to ridicule, harassment, or ostracism; and they may encounter other forms of hostility and resistance from male co-workers determined to protect their privileged domain.[22]

Though sex discrimination within the labor market is less pervasive and blatant than in the past, largely due to anti-discrimination legislation, it is still a significant cause of gender inequality.[23] In one notable audit study conducted by David Neumark and his colleagues, matched pairs of women and men applied for jobs as waiters and waitresses at dozens of Philadelphia restaurants. Despite equivalent qualifications, men were significantly favored over women in expensive restaurants, where wages and tips were substantially higher, while women had a slight advantage at lower-paying, low-price restaurants.[24] In another study, science faculty were asked to rate the application materials for fictitious "male" and "female" candidates for a laboratory management position. Regardless of whether evaluators themselves were men or women, applicants designated with a "male" name were judged significantly more competent than applicants designated with a "female" name.[25] A now-defunct class-action lawsuit against Wal-Mart also provides evidence of sex discrimination. According to the plaintiffs in the case, Wal-Mart women were paid less than men for doing essentially the same jobs; their requests for pay increases and management training were ignored or greeted with hostility; they were passed over for promotions in favor of male workers with less seniority and lower performance ratings; and they were excluded from opportunities for advancement by a sexist corporate culture, an old boys' network, and an informal and subjective recruitment process.[26] In a more recent case, twelve female employees have brought a gender discrimination suit against Sterling Jewelers, charging it not only with paying women lower hourly wages than less experienced men, but also accusing the company of tolerating sexual harassment.[27]

Because they are often barred from more lucrative "men's jobs," women are overrepresented in the typically non-unionized low-wage service sector. They work as child- and health-care providers, waitresses, cashiers, receptionists, and housecleaners.[28] About 32 percent of women work at poverty-level wages, compared to 24.3 percent for men; women are almost twice as likely as men to have hourly earnings at or below the federal minimum wage; and women make up more than 90 percent of long-term low earners.[29] The jobs held by low-wage working women also typically lack health insurance, retirement benefits, sick leave, vacation time, and standardized work schedules. The prospects for many of these women have deteriorated in recent decades, moreover, as a changing economy has put a downward pressure on the wages of less-privileged workers. Since the late 1970s, in the United States more so than in other industrialized countries, workers in the bottom half of the wage distribution have experienced a substantial decline in their earnings relative to higher-wage workers. And since women are overrepresented in the low-wage sector, they have endured a disproportionate share of the costs resulting from increasing inequality.[30]

The challenge of combining motherhood and paid work is hard enough for middle-class married women. For single mothers forced to manage on their own, solely responsible for both bringing home the bacon and taking care of the kids, the difficulties are compounded, especially if they are trapped in the low end of the labor market. Because many single women with children are African American or Latino, they are not only penalized for being women and mothers, but they are susceptible to discrimination on the basis of race and ethnicity as well.[31] Single motherhood also tends to be concentrated among less-educated women, those with no more than a high school diploma. They face a difficult struggle trying to support a family by themselves in an economic environment increasingly unfavorable to workers without a college education. And to make matters worse, single mothers, especially welfare recipients, are also denigrated and stigmatized in the larger culture.[32] The economic hardships and psychological strains associated with single motherhood are felt not only by the mothers, of course, but also by their children, with potentially adverse effects on their later-life outcomes. The 1996 overhaul of the welfare system, by imposing work requirements on thousands of single mothers, has intensified the problems arising from low-wage employment and work-family conflicts.[33]

The absence of sensible social policies is another reason working-age women in the United States have lower earnings than men and face a higher risk of poverty. Compared to other industrialized countries, government in the United States provides relatively little assistance to working families, and even less to poor female-headed families. Tax policies are less redistributive and welfare policies less generous. Labor unions are weaker, fewer workers are covered by collective bargaining agreements, and the minimum wage is lower. And while citizens in most other developed nations benefit from comprehensive child-care subsidies and paid parental-leave policies, families in the United States are expected to carry the burden of raising children on their own.[34] The expansion of the Social Security system in the 1960s and 1970s contributed greatly to the reduction of elderly poverty, but no comparable government program has targeted single mothers and their children—despite the economic vulnerability of this population and despite high-minded public pronouncements about children being the future of the nation.

## CHILD CARE

Among the many changes in American society since World War II, few have been more far reaching than the remarkable growth in the labor force participation of women, especially wives and mothers.[35] In 1947, only 18.6 percent of women with children under eighteen and only 12 percent with preschool-age children were in the labor force. As recently as the 1960s, the rate of employment for women with children under six was still only between 20 and 25 percent. By 2010, 71.3 percent of women with children under eighteen were in the labor force, including 64.2 percent of mothers with children under six and 61.1 percent with children under three.[36] Today, regardless of the age of their children, most mothers are also paid workers—68.3 percent of mothers in married-couple families and 75.2 percent of mothers in female-headed families. Even the majority of women with children less than a year old are in the labor force.[37] The model of the family celebrated in television sitcoms of the 1950s—a male breadwinner, a stay-at-home mother, and children reared solely by their parents—has become the exception. The norm today is a paying job for mom and child care for the kids.

In 2011, 61 percent of preschool children (12.5 million) were in some kind of child care on a regular basis, averaging thirty-three hours per week.[38] Young children of low-income mothers spend even more time in non-parental care, according to one study more than fifty hours per week on average.[39] Among the numerous different forms of child care for preschoolers, the three types currently most in use, ranked from most to least expensive, are (1) center-based care, including preschools, nurseries, and day-care centers; (2) family day care, consisting of independent providers offering child-care services out of their homes; and (3) relative or kin care, often supplied by grandmothers or aunts, either in their own or in parents' homes.[40] While affluent families are more reliant on center-based care, low-income families, single and minority mothers in particular, depend more heavily on relatives, primarily because of cost considerations, "out of necessity rather than choice," but also because kin care is relatively trustworthy, convenient, and flexible.[41]

Poor families are severely constrained in their options because child care, an inherently labor-intensive practice, is expensive, and high-quality care is very expensive. According to one recent report, the average annual cost of full-time care for a four-year-old in a child-care center ranges from a low of $4,312 in Mississippi to a high of $12,355 in New York. The annual cost of infant care in most states is considerably higher, more expensive than rental costs in twenty-one states and more expensive than tuition at a public university in thirty-one states.[42] For low-income families, child care is a major budget item, eating up a large share of total earnings. Child-care expenditures absorb 30.1 percent of the monthly income of poor families, compared to 7.6 percent for families above the poverty line.[43] In many states, a minimum-wage worker with two children in a day-care center would have nothing left after paying the child-care bill. For single mothers working low-wage jobs, in the absence of substantial government assistance, child care in a licensed center with a well-trained staff is well beyond their financial means.[44]

In their efforts to manage child care, poor families, including those headed by single mothers, face an assortment of daunting problems. They have to find a competent and responsible provider, and one who is available at the right place, the right time, and for the right price. They have to arrange for their children to be dropped off and picked back up again, no easy matter for parents often lacking access to a reliable car or dependent on public transportation. They have to worry about finding time to care for sick kids without getting fired. They have to live with the guilt they may feel for not always being available when their children need them, and they also have to live with the stigma of not always complying with middle-class ideals of a "good mother" and a "good worker." They have to figure out how to coordinate child-care provision, family life, and the demands of work—all the while hoping to avoid harmful trade-offs. And if they are single mothers, they have to struggle with all these everyday challenges on their own, typically with little help from government and little sympathy from employers.[45]

These problems are all the more difficult to resolve because many low-income parents have non-standard jobs in the 24/7 service economy.[46] They work evenings, graveyard shifts, and weekends; they are sometimes on call, like many Wal-Mart employees, expected to come in to work on a moment's notice; they have no control over their break time, and because their hours are unpredictable, with changing work schedules from week to week, they cannot plan child-care arrangements very far in advance. Their lives are unstable and stressful, tough on both parents and children. The child-care industry, furthermore, which typically operates on a daytime, Monday-through-Friday schedule, is not designed to serve the needs of non-standard workers. Low-income families have little choice but to fall back on informal and sometimes ad hoc arrangements. But these can be difficult to organize, particularly when parents have no control over their working hours; nor can they always count on relatives, friends, and neighbors' being readily available or willing to watch over their children. In a minority of cases, work demands force parents to leave their children at home unattended, occasionally with disastrous consequences.[47]

Because of their limited resources and irregular work schedules, poor parents are forced to cobble together multiple child-care arrangements, relying on one primary caretaker during most of the day or week and then one or two secondary caretakers to fill in the gaps.[48] These arrangements are often unstable—a day-care provider ceases operations, a relative becomes unavailable, a government subsidy is terminated, or the quality of care proves unsatisfactory. As a result, as Ajay Chaudry shows in her study of low-wage working mothers, parents make frequent changes in their primary caregivers over time. This periodic disruption in care, besides the considerable inconvenience it causes, creates a less secure and consistent early-life experience for young children.[49]

Perhaps the most important concern for parents in making choices about child care is quality.[50] Low-income parents cannot always afford the best care, of course, but they certainly expect a level of care that will ensure their children's health, safety, happiness, and development during the early formative years. The quality of child care in the United States is generally unsatisfactory, however. Caring for children is currently practiced as a low-wage job, not a professional career.[51] In 2011, the average hourly wage for "child care workers" varied from a high of $12.60 in Massachusetts to a low of $8.55 in West Virginia, not a level of earnings likely to attract the most qualified people.[52] Staff members in child-care centers are often poorly trained, and the rate of turnover is high, making it hard for children to establish a close relationship with caretakers. Many child-care centers are also understaffed, with a ratio of caregivers to children well below what is necessary to maintain quality treatment. In Florida, for example, as Sharon Lerner reports, "one childcare provider can legally look after as many as eleven 2-year-olds, fifteen 3-year-olds, or twenty 4-year-olds, and even these astounding ratios," she observes, "are routinely violated."[53] Family day care and relative care, both of which are unregulated and unlicensed in most states, also often fail the quality test. In neither arrangement are caretakers supervised or trained, and in both they serve mainly in a custodial or babysitting capacity, rarely providing children with the kind of learning environment and educational experiences they need in their early years.[54] In sum, according to Suzanne Helburn and Barbara Bergmann, there is "a distressing amount of poor care" in the United States and "a paucity of good care." Most child care is "mediocre," they argue, and a "substantial number" of infants "receive care that is unacceptable." Inferior child care is not just a problem for the poor by any means. But children from low-income families, precisely those most in need of a boost up, rarely receive good care, and, as Helburn and Bergmann conclude, they are "more likely than not to receive care that is less than even minimally adequate."[55]

Poor families face extraordinary difficulties managing child care, and the problems they experience, as Julie Press argues, decrease their likelihood of avoiding or escaping poverty.[56] Child-care demands perpetuate poverty by limiting the time parents can devote to work, training, and education, thus reducing their earnings in both the short and the long terms. As Press shows, poor parents with child-care problems, mothers more so than fathers, are less likely to be in the labor force, they work fewer hours when they are employed, and they are more susceptible to periodic bouts of unemployment. They are also more likely to work only part time, be tardy or absent, quit a job or be fired as a result of child-care issues, and refuse a promising opportunity for the sake of a job with an accommodating boss or family-friendly hours. For parents whose employment options are limited to the low-wage sector, furthermore, it simply may not pay to get a job. The costs of child care and other work-related expenses, including transportation, may exceed potential earnings. Poor parents lacking adequate and affordable child care, because of its effect on work effort, are trapped in poverty. Their continued poverty, in turn, means they cannot afford quality child care, with potentially adverse effects on their children's educational development and later-life economic prospects. In this manner, the poverty of the parents is passed along to the children.[57]

The 1996 welfare reform legislation, the Personal Responsibility and Work Opportunity Reconciliation Act (PRWORA), established time limits on the receipt of welfare and imposed work requirements on welfare recipients, resulting in a significant increase in the labor force participation of single mothers. Poor women today, even those with young children, are expected to work, and most have little choice in the matter. Despite their child-care responsibilities, and like most other Americans, they need a job to make ends meet. To assist the working poor in managing their child-care needs, Congress created, as part of PRWORA, the Child Care and Development Fund (CCDF), a block grant program administered by the states.[58] But because the level of federal funding, on the decline since 2009, is woefully insufficient, many low-income families are unable to benefit from this program, with only about one out of every six eligible children receiving a subsidy.[59] Thousands of needy children are placed on wait lists, over sixty thousand in Florida alone, or they are simply turned away, and even those lucky enough to receive a subsidy sometimes have to pay high co-payment costs. Many providers, furthermore, refuse service to low-income families because the reimbursement rate for subsidized care remains well below market value.[60] Life for poor children without a subsidy and no set child-care arrangement is a "kaleidoscope of caretakers." One mother on a wait list in Virginia was reduced to allowing her eleven-year-old daughter to spend her after-school hours riding around on a city bus driven by the girl's grandmother.[61] Ultimately, the supply of good child care accessible to poor families falls well short of the growing demand. While the CCDF offers some financial assistance, it fails to address adequately the key child-care problems faced by low-income parents: affordability, availability, and quality.

Poverty exacerbates the problem of child care, and child care exacerbates the problem of poverty. This vicious cycle is the product of a system in which individual families are expected to shoulder the bulk of the financial burden for the care of their children. Child care in the United States is a private commodity not a public good. Families get only what they can pay for, and low-income families cannot pay for very much. In the absence of a much more stringently regulated and extensively funded public child-care system of the sort available in most other industrialized nations, the children of the working poor in the United States are bound to receive inferior care.[62]

## HEALTH AND HEALTH CARE

Poverty is bad for your health. More than 25 percent of the poor report just "fair or poor health," compared to only 5 percent of those in the upper-income bracket.[63] Poorer Americans, racial and ethnic minorities in particular, have a higher incidence of asthma, heart disease, high blood pressure, diabetes, cancer, and low birth weight.[64] Poverty is also a "thief," as Michael Reisch observes. It "steals years from one's life." Those on the lower end of the class structure, men in particular, are susceptible to premature death. While the life expectancy of upper-income men at age sixty-five has increased by six years since the 1970s, that of lower-income men has increased by just a little more than a year.[65] Poverty and inequality are not just unhealthy; they are killers as well. For the United States in 2000, Sandro Galea and his collaborators estimate that more than one hundred thousand deaths can be attributed to each of the following "social factors": low education, racial segregation, low social support, and "individual-level poverty," with another thirty-nine thousand resulting from "area-level poverty."[66] Health disparities by socioeconomic status are a nearly universal phenomenon. They are especially severe in the United States because the rate of poverty is so high, because the gap between the rich and the poor is large and growing, and because many low-income African Americans and Latinos experience added health risks from the cumulative effects of racial discrimination and residential segregation.[67]

The United States spends considerably more on health care than any other industrialized nation. But on measures of quality, access, and efficiency, the performance of the American health-care system is significantly worse than our peer countries, and the health of Americans by some measures, including infant mortality, also ranks near the bottom.[68] This paradox is partly due to inequities in health-care provision. People who can pay the price or have good health insurance typically receive excellent medical attention. But millions of Americans, including those most likely to suffer from illness, disease, and injury, do not have adequate access to quality care. Money is one factor. The poor, and many of those above the poverty line as well—increasingly so since 2000—are often forced by cost considerations to refrain from or delay getting medical and dental care or purchasing prescription drugs.[69] Insurance is another factor. The current system, with health coverage tied to employment, is rapidly unraveling. The percentage of private-sector workers with employment-based health insurance has been on the decline for three decades, with low-wage workers least likely to be covered. In 2010, only 25.9 percent of workers in the bottom quintile had health insurance through their employers, compared to 78.9 percent for workers in the top quintile.[70] Even if they have insurance, low-income workers face escalating costs—higher premiums, co-payments, and deductibles. Many cannot get the care they need. Some are even forced into bankruptcy by their physical and mental ailments, with nearly two-thirds of all bankruptcies in 2007 resulting from medical problems.[71] The approximately 48 million Americans who lack health insurance have it even worse. Few receive preventive care, some endure debilitating though treatable medical problems, others resort to alleviating their symptoms with over-the-counter drugs, and many of the uninsured, when all else fails, rely on emergency rooms for medical treatment.[72] The Affordable Care Act is certain to increase access to health insurance coverage, but given its beleaguered status and the many questions still unanswered about its implementation, how much "Obamacare" will improve the health status of the poor remains to be seen.[73]

Poor people do not receive the medical attention they need, but this is not the main cause of their health problems. Even if they had unlimited access to medical care, the poor would still have higher rates of morbidity and mortality. The real culprit is poverty itself. As Helen Epstein says, poverty is "enough to make you sick."[74] Poor households encounter a multitude of health risks in their social environment, often accompanied by feelings of anxiety and hopelessness, and the effects accumulate over time. This wears down their resistance, inducing a "generalized susceptibility" to illness and disease.[75] The effects are lasting as well. A history of early childhood poverty has persistently detrimental health consequences, even for those who subsequently manage to escape the ranks of the poor. People who experience economic adversity and stress during their preschool years are vulnerable to health problems as adults.[76]

What is it precisely about poverty that is so unhealthy?[77] First, the condition of poverty is not conducive to healthy living.[78] Poor people face myriad day-to-day struggles and pressure-filled lives. They experience high levels of chronic and daily stress, with few coping resources, and compared to people above the poverty line, they report more cases of "serious psychological distress."[79] They also inhabit a social environment—their neighborhoods, homes, schools, and workplaces—where the pursuit of a healthy lifestyle is not an easy option. The poor, not surprisingly, are more likely to smoke cigarettes and drink heavily and are less likely to eat nutritious food, exercise daily, be well informed about health issues, or visit a doctor on a regular basis. Most simply cannot afford the basics of a healthy life: a wholesome diet, proper clothing, adequate shelter, enriching leisure activities, a safe and comfortable living environment, and quality child care. The health risks are especially severe for those mired in deep poverty, the more than 20 million people, disproportionately children, whose household income places them below half the poverty line.[80]

Second, millions of poor households not only contend with their own health issues, but they are forced also to reside in unsafe and unhealthy neighborhoods.[81] Poor and racially segregated communities tend to have higher levels of crime and violence. They are often lacking in police, fire, and sanitation services; health-care centers; and medical personnel. They rarely feature running tracks, bicycle paths, or health clubs. And while many poor neighborhoods are "health deserts"—"lacking ready access to fresh, healthy, and affordable food"—what they do have in abundance are fast food restaurants, convenience marts, and liquor stores.[82] They also have lower levels of social integration and cohesion, such that individuals have fewer resources for acquiring health information and social support, and they have correspondingly higher levels of social isolation, increasing the likelihood that vulnerable individuals will have to cope with their illnesses on their own.[83] Poor neighborhoods, particularly those with a predominantly minority population, also have higher exposures to pollution and toxic waste.[84] And because high-poverty neighborhoods are stressful places to live, residents are susceptible to depression, anxiety, and other mental disorders.[85]

Third, poverty is unhealthy because many poor people, 2.5 million according to one estimate, live in overcrowded and physically inferior housing that has inadequate ventilation, pest infestation, and faulty plumbing and heating.[86] Poor children are commonly exposed to mold and mildew, rats and mice, cockroaches and dust mites in their homes—all of which increase the risk of infectious disease and asthma. Children living in older housing are also in danger of lead poisoning, harmful especially because it can impair cognitive development. Substandard housing increases the likelihood of fire and other residential accidents as well, one of the leading causes of injury and death among children, and it is harmful to their emotional and behavioral well-being.[87] The high cost of housing affects the health of low-income families also, because they are left with less money to cover other necessities essential to healthy living, including regular medical care.[88]

Fourth, the working conditions of poorer Americans contribute to higher rates of sickness, injury, and early death.[89] In today's economy, where many low-end jobs are unfulfilling, if not downright perilous, the "social experience" of work "translates into poor health."[90] Low-wage jobs rarely offer health insurance or sick leave, they are poorly paying and insecure, and they are also often exploitative and demeaning, hard on the body and the mind.

Workers in the low-wage sector are more likely to be exposed to toxic substances on the job; they are at greater risk of workplace illnesses, accidents, and fatalities; and they are sometimes forced to work despite their health problems or risk getting fired.[91] Often treated unfairly and compensated unjustly, they endure a demoralizing disconnect between effort and reward. They have little control over their working conditions, and in many jobs the strain from being subject to continuous monitoring and harsh supervision takes a physical and psychological toll. Many low-wage workers experience health problems, sleeping disorders, for example, because they work night shifts and other irregular hours. Such non-standard work schedules exacerbate the tensions parents experience in trying to manage the conflicting demands of work and family life.[92]

Poverty causes poor health, and poor health increases people's vulnerability to poverty.[93] Children with chronic physical and mental health ailments experience learning problems, miss days of class, have difficulty focusing on their schoolwork, fall behind their peers, and are more likely to drop out of school. When children with health ailments grow old enough to enter the labor market, they are less likely to be educationally prepared.[94] Because poor health is a significant barrier to employment, adults with health problems are at risk of poverty too. They are more likely to have irregular work histories, be fired or forced to quit because of ill health, and move from one job to another or cycle in and out of the labor force depending on their health status. Health issues may also limit the kinds of work people can do and lower their level of productivity and the quality of their job performance.

Even healthy adults, particularly women, sometimes incur economic costs from health problems. To deal with sick children, parents, or spouses, they may be forced to reduce their commitment to the labor force, trade in a full-time job for a part-time job, or drop out of the labor market altogether.[95] Poor health contributes to poverty also because individuals with illnesses and injuries have medical expenses, diminishing the amount of income available to cover other costs of living. Especially if their health problems are chronic, they are likely to have a lower level of lifetime savings and lower pension and Social Security contributions, increasing their vulnerability to poverty in their elderly years. Finally, the health problems experienced by one generation contributes to the poverty of the next by diminishing the resources adults can pass along to their children or, even worse, by burdening heirs with unpaid medical bills.[96]

Poor health adversely affects people's economic outcomes, but the bigger part of the story is how poverty adversely affects people's health. Poor people are unhealthy because they are economically deprived. But poverty causes ill health also because it inhibits individuals from achieving "autonomy, empowerment, and human freedom."[97] These are no less crucial to personal well-being than are food, shelter, and clothing. People experience chronic stress and stress-related health problems when these basic human needs go unfilled: when they have little control over their own lives, whether in their homes, workplaces, or communities; when they are excluded from the social and economic mainstream, unable to participate as full-fledged members of society; when they are disengaged from social life and lacking in sources of social support; when they are subject to disparaging cultural stigmas; when they are treated unfairly and denied opportunities for living a decent life; and when they are on the bottom looking up, with those on the top continually receding from view. The poor, under normal conditions, are powerless and marginalized—this perhaps more than anything else is what makes poverty a health hazard. Only by attacking the fundamental economic and political inequalities at the root of poverty can we make significant progress in addressing the health problems of the disadvantaged.

## RETIREMENT INSECURITY

The rate of poverty for the elderly fell from over 35 percent in 1959 to 15 percent in 1975, and over the next two decades it continued to decline, though more slowly, reaching 9.1 percent in 2012.[98] This dramatic reduction in elderly poverty over the past half century has been one of the great success stories of the American welfare state. Even so, the picture for seniors is far from rosy. The number of elderly poor is still substantial, 3.9 million in 2012, with several million more living a precarious existence just above the official poverty line.[99] The rates of poverty for older African Americans and Latinos remain exceptionally high, 21.9 and 20.6 percent, respectively, close to three times the rate for non-Hispanic whites.[100] Women over sixty-five are also at great risk of poverty, with a rate almost twice that of older men, and nearly two-thirds of elderly women living alone are unable to meet their basic monthly expenses.[101] Despite the notable progress achieved during the 1960s and 1970s, moreover, the incidence of poverty among the aged in the United States is still much higher than elsewhere in the industrialized world, and several times higher than in many European countries.[102]

The economic status of the elderly is bound to a retirement system that fails to provide adequate income security for millions of older Americans. This system is often described as a stool composed of three legs—Social Security, personal savings, and employment-based retirement savings. For poorer Americans, even in the best of times, these three legs have never been all that sturdy. Workers with low lifetime earnings, disproportionately women and racial/ethnic minorities, receive commensurately smaller Social Security checks; few manage to accumulate significant assets or savings during their working years; and most do not have a private pension plan to augment their retirement income. Even when the system works reasonably well, approximately one out of every ten older Americans falls below the poverty line. This three-legged retirement stool has become increasingly wobbly since the 1980s, with dire implications for the millions of aging low-wage workers. And with the 2007 financial collapse, even many solidly middle-class families—hit by job loss, falling income, and declining housing values—face a looming threat of retirement insecurity.

Despite the alarmist talk about its future and the chorus of criticism from conservative proponents of "privatization," Social Security is the most durable component of the retirement system, and certainly the most essential. It is the single largest source of income for two-thirds of women and one-half of men sixty-five and over, and it is the *only* source of income for nearly 30 percent of elderly women and 20 percent of elderly men. Black and Hispanic men and women and people of all races over the age of seventy-five are even more reliant on Social Security.[103] A large and growing share of the elderly population, reduced to hobbling around on just one feeble retirement leg, is almost entirely dependent on monthly Social Security checks.[104]

Social Security is critical to the survival of all but the most affluent retirees. It is also the nation's most effective anti-poverty program. Compared to the public pension systems in other industrialized countries, Social Security benefit levels are relatively low, certainly not generous enough to lift all the elderly above the poverty line.[105] In the absence of Social Security, however, nearly 15 million people would be added to the poverty numbers, increasing the rate of poverty for the older population from the current level of 9.1 percent to nearly 50 percent.[106] Social Security is particularly vital to the economic well-being of elderly women, who both live longer and are less likely to have other sources of income. Without Social Security, two-thirds of all unmarried women over sixty-five would be poor.[107]

The elderly population is reliant on Social Security partly because the personal savings leg of the retirement system is woefully inadequate. Relatively few retirees have substantial savings or income from assets, and this is especially true for racial/ethnic minorities and for households in the bottom half of the income distribution. The elderly in recent years have become increasingly burdened by debt as well. According to one recent report, the fifty-plus population in 2012 had an average combined credit card balance of $8,278, $2,000 more than the under-fifty population, a reversal of the historic pattern. [108] The indebtedness of the elderly has worsened also as a result of the 2007–2009 collapse of housing values. The percentage of older families with mortgage debt has increased sharply since 1989, and the value of that debt has increased even more sharply, by more than 300 percent. Between 2007 and 2010, in addition, the percentage of people aged fifty and over with "seriously delinquent" mortgage loans more than quadrupled. In 2011, 16 percent of mortgage loans held by the fifty-plus population were underwater, and many of the elderly have lost their homes or are at risk of foreclosure. [109] With millions of working Americans enduring stagnant or declining earnings, with affordable housing in short supply, and with the rising cost of health care and higher education, it is highly unrealistic to imagine that future retirees will be any more able than current retirees to build up a retirement nest egg through personal savings. [110]

Older Americans can achieve a comfortable retirement only if they have a private pension to supplement their Social Security benefits. The employer-sponsored pension has become the wobbliest leg of the retirement system, however, and this leg is missing entirely for most low-end workers. In 2010, only 11 percent of workers in the bottom earnings quintile benefited from pension coverage, down from 25 percent in 1979, and only 42 percent of all private-sector workers had any kind of a retirement plan. [111] Where an optional retirement plan is available through their employer, poorer workers, mainly because their earnings are so low, often do not participate, and when they do, they contribute a smaller share of what is already a paltry paycheck. The existing employment-based retirement system leaves many future retirees, including most of the working poor, without a pension leg to stand on and likely to end up dependent entirely on Social Security.

The changing nature of the private pension system has greatly exacerbated the problem of retirement insecurity. During the "golden age" of the post–World War II era, employees were typically covered by a "defined-benefit" (DB) pension plan. Similar to Social Security, these traditional pensions guaranteed workers a fixed and lifelong monthly payment upon retirement. Since the 1980s, however, employers by the droves have ceased offering DB plans or frozen those already in existence and have replaced these, if replaced at all, with "defined-contribution" (DC) plans instead, mostly of the 401(k) type.[112] These plans offer employees the option of contributing pretax income to their own individual investment accounts, sometimes with matching funds from employers. Between 1990 and 2011, the share of private-sector workers participating in DB plans declined from 35 percent to 18 percent, leaving more than 80 percent of workers without a guaranteed pension.[113] DB plans are more common in the public sector, though increasingly vulnerable to political attack, but in the private sector the number of workers covered by a DB plan is expected to "drop to the vanishing point over the next ten years or so."[114]

This shift from DB plans to DC plans has increased the risk of retirement insecurity for most working Americans. Under the new system, workers' contributions are voluntary rather than mandatory; employees rather than employers have primary responsibility for funding and managing their retirement accounts; the payout for retirees is uncertain, dependent on the vicissitudes of the stock market; the investment risk is borne entirely by employees, with employers freed from any long-term financial obligations to their workers; and DC plans, unlike DB plans, are not insured by the federal government.[115] Because pension wealth in 401(k)s is highly concentrated among more affluent workers, the shift from DB plans to DC plans has also resulted in an upsurge of retirement inequality, widening the gap between the rich and the poor. Between 1990 and 2010, median retirement savings increased from $46,000 to $160,000 for households in the top income fifth and from $5,000 to $8,000 for households in the bottom income fifth. Many upper-tier workers, riding the wave of soaring stock prices in the 1990s, benefited from the introduction of DC plans. But for the vast majority of workers, particularly those lower down in the earnings distribution, the demise of DB plans has reduced their potential retirement income. Not surprisingly, the rate of poverty for elderly householders without a DB pension is about nine times greater than for those with a DB pension.[116] The rise of the defined-contribution system has diminished the likelihood of a secure retirement for millions of working Americans.

Experts in the field believe that households are "at risk" if they cannot be expected to maintain their pre-retirement standard of living once they enter their retirement years. According to one recent study, the number of at-risk households increased from 31 percent in 1983 to 44 percent in 2007, and then in the wake of the financial crisis jumped to 53 percent in 2010, including 61 percent of low-income households.[117] A different measure of "retirement readiness" projects that approximately 80 percent of workers in the bottom quartile "lack adequate retirement income for basic retirement expenses."[118] In another study, the National Institute on Retirement finds that savings for retirement are "dangerously low," with the typical working-age household having only $3,000 in retirement savings and the typical near-retirement household having only $12,000. According to the author of this report, Nari Rhee, approximately 80 percent of working-age households face a "huge shortfall" in what they will need for retirement. "The hope of retirement security," she concludes, "is out of reach for many Americans in the face of a crumbling retirement infrastructure."[119]

Many elderly Americans have discovered that they simply cannot afford to retire. Some seniors of course prefer to continue working during their golden years, but many others do so because they must, and often despite chronic pain and poor health. Holding down three part-time jobs, sixty-two-year-old Susan Zimmerman says, "I will probably be working until I'm 100." But with the combination of weak employment growth and age discrimination, getting a job, however necessary, is not easy for older workers, particularly if they are reentering the labor market after being laid off, and getting a decent job is even harder.[120] The retirement outlook for younger workers is even grimmer, especially for those trapped in the low-wage sector, but also for many middle-class young adults saddled with student debt and still trying to find a steady job. Andrew Stern, president of the Service Employees International Union, suggests that "today's retirement plan for young workers is: 'I'm going to work until I die.'"[121] For poorer workers especially, victimized by low wages and the constant pressure of immediate expenses, there is little they can do on their own to improve their retirement prospects. In the absence of significant reforms—to raise the earnings of low-end workers, to increase their income from Social Security, and to overhaul a private pension system that largely excludes low-wage workers—the poverty experienced by millions of adults during their working years is bound to be reproduced as they cross the threshold into old age.

## LEGAL DEPRIVATION

Equal justice for all—this is the bedrock principle of the American legal system. The reality falls well short of the ideal, however. The poor and the working class, racial and ethnic minorities in particular, are frequent victims of injustice. They suffer from employment and housing discrimination, predatory lending practices, inequitable treatment by the legal system, and exploitative behavior by employers. If they work at Wal-Mart, their right to unionize is routinely violated.[122] If they are employed in "unregulated" industries, or at McDonald's, for example, they are often paid less than the legal minimum wage, refused overtime pay, forced to work off the clock, and denied rest periods and meal breaks.[123] If they want to keep their job in many workplaces around the country, they are forced to relinquish their constitutional right to free speech.[124] If they have been convicted of a felony, they may be one of the more than 5 million Americans denied the right to vote.[125] Even if they do not have a criminal record, they may be prevented from participating in the electoral process by deceitful voter suppression efforts.[126] If they are foreign workers recruited through the Guest Worker Program, they are often "systematically exploited and abused"—held in virtual bondage, regularly cheated out of their wages, and forced to endure horrible living conditions.[127] If they are low-income single mothers, they no longer have a legal entitlement to welfare benefits, and if they do receive public assistance, they are subject to an onerous system of regulations and sanctions, obliged to sacrifice their privacy rights, and pushed into the labor market regardless of their personal circumstances.[128]

Millions of Americans do not receive adequate medical assistance because they cannot afford it, and for the same reason, millions of Americans do not receive adequate legal assistance. In civil law, unlike criminal law, Americans do not have a right to counsel. The fact of unequal "access to lawyers" undermines the principle of equal "access to justice." Indeed, as one law professor argues, by virtue of the billions of dollars large corporations spend every year in legal fees, they, not individuals, have "the greatest access to justice."[129] Low-income Americans, on the other hand, because they rarely have the money to pay for a good lawyer, have great difficulty defending their rights, protecting their interests, or receiving equal protection before the law. Because of this legal deprivation, the poor are disadvantaged in their dealings with employers, landlords, creditors, merchants, utility companies, social service agencies, and other private and public authorities.

The Economic Opportunity Act of 1964, which inaugurated the war on poverty, was amended in 1966 and 1967 to include federal funding for legal services for the poor. This signaled recognition of the government's responsibility for guaranteeing access to legal assistance and for redressing inequities in the justice system. The advent of the legal services program, by assembling a corps of lawyers prepared to defend the rights of the poor and advocate on their behalf before administrative agencies, legislative bodies, and the courts, significantly altered the American legal environment, anticipating the possibility that equal justice would become a reality. One sign of this program's effectiveness was the growing hostility it provoked on the part of conservatives, with then-governor Ronald Reagan at the forefront of the opposition. [130]

In 1974, Congress consolidated the patchwork of legal aid under the authority of the Legal Services Corporation (LSC), a private, non-profit, government-funded organization. [131] The LSC expanded throughout the 1970s, and by 1981 it had offices in all fifty states and had reached a modest "minimum access" goal of two lawyers for every ten thousand poor persons. [132] Over the next two decades, however, legal services, proving all too successful in serving the interests of the poor, became the target of a reinvigorated right-wing campaign, prompted first by Reagan's election to the presidency and then by Republican victories in the 1994 congressional elections. While failing to abolish the LSC, the conservative assault did result in a substantial reduction in funding. Legal services lawyers were also increasingly hamstrung by numerous restrictions limiting their ability to secure "access to justice for poor people." [133] They were prohibited from engaging in class-action suits, political and legal advocacy, grassroots lobbying, and a host of other activities. [134] Conservative opponents of the program under the second Bush administration continued to underfund legal services and rein in its potential as a political force on the side of the poor. [135]

Even in 1981, when the budget for the LSC reached its peak, legal services providers did not have nearly enough resources to adequately assist low-income people with their legal problems, including family conflicts, foreclosure and bankruptcy cases, landlord–tenant disputes, consumer issues and dealings with employers, government agencies, and the courts. Since that time, the level of funding has declined steadily, even as the number of people eligible for assistance has increased. Adjusted for inflation, the budget for the LSC in 2013, despite support from the Obama administration, was less than half the 1980 level, and with continued pressure to reduce government spending, funding for the LSC is likely to decline even further over the foreseeable future.[136] The predictable result is "a huge gap today between the legal needs of low-income people and the capacity of the civil legal assistance system to meet those needs."[137] At present, there is at most one legal aid attorney for every 6,415 low-income people, one out of every two applicants eligible for legal aid is turned away, and the legal aid system is currently able to fulfill less than 20 percent of poorer Americans' legal needs.[138] As a consequence of this "justice gap," many people, despite their lack of qualifications and knowledge of legal procedures, have no choice but to serve as their own representatives in court.[139] The problem has worsened since the financial crisis as state and local governments have cut back court operating hours and laid off court employees, leaving many civil cases delayed or in limbo, thus denying litigants their day in court.[140] The "justice gap" in this country by international standards is also unusually large. According to the most recent report from the World Justice Project, the United States ranks a meager twenty-seventh in its ability to deliver civil justice in an affordable, timely, and effective manner, a lower ranking than nearly every other developed country.[141] Spending on civil legal aid in the United States is also much less than in other industrialized nations.[142] "In this vital area of equal access to justice," as Justice Early Johnson Jr. states, "we are truly an 'underdeveloped country.'"[143]

The inequities within the criminal justice system are even more disturbing, with devastating consequences for racial and ethnic minorities. Low-income African Americans and Hispanics, especially young black men, encounter disparities at every stage in the criminal justice process: who falls under the suspicion of law enforcement agencies, who gets stopped and questioned by the police, who gets arrested and charged with a crime, who goes to trial, who gets convicted, who gets incarcerated and for how long, who gets paroled, and what happens to them once they are released from prison.[144] As criminal defendants, the poor do at least have a constitutional right to legal counsel, but this by no means guarantees equal justice.[145] In too many cases, the lawyers assigned to indigent defendants are unqualified, inexperienced, or indifferent; overburdened and underpaid; short of time, resources, and staff; and capable of providing only "assembly-line justice."[146] Budgetary cutbacks have overwhelmed the public defender system in many states, effectively denying low-income defendants their constitutional right to legal counsel.[147] Even when they get competent representation, as Debra Emmelman reveals, poor and minority defendants, because they fall automatically into the category of the "morally suspect," are still vulnerable to unequal treatment. They do not receive a fair or sympathetic hearing and are unlikely to get the benefit of the doubt because the circumstances of their lives depart from the normative standpoint and cultural sensibilities of the largely white middle-class lawyers, judges, and juries who decide their fate.[148] As law professor Paul Butler bluntly puts it, "poor people lose . . . in our criminal justice system" not only because they are poorly represented, but also because "prosecutors and lawmakers treat them like losers."[149]

As the 1960s wound down, a halfhearted war on poverty gave way to a full-blown war on crime, one fought mainly with the weapon of mass incarceration. The size of the prison population, which had been relatively stable throughout the twentieth century, began a steep upward climb in the mid-1970s, a trend only weakly related to actual crime rates.[150] By 2012, the number of adults in prison or jail exceeded 2.2 million, down slightly from the high of 2010, with another 4.85 million on probation or parole.[151] This upsurge in imprisonment—with the United States now having by far the highest incarceration rate in the developed world—was partly due to the enactment of "tough on crime" sentencing policies.[152] Beginning in the 1970s, state governments imposed mandatory minimum sentences, abolished or limited parole, and otherwise pursued a "lock 'em up and throw away the key" crime-fighting strategy.[153] In today's criminal justice system, as a result, persons convicted of crimes, disproportionately poor and minority, are more likely to be incarcerated, more likely to serve many years behind bars, and less likely to benefit from early release.[154]

The principal driving force behind the prison boom was the combination of punitive sentencing practices and the aggressive war on drugs declared by the Reagan administration in the early 1980s. Between 1980 and 2005, drug arrests more than tripled, and the number of drug offenders behind bars increased by over 1,000 percent, from 41,000 in 1980 to 493,800 in 2003, a substantial share of the total prison population.[155] In 2011, drug offenders constituted nearly half the inmate population in federal prisons.[156] And most of these were not violent criminals or drug kingpins but were convicted for possession only, for low-level drug dealing, or for "public-order crimes."[157]

Racial and ethnic minorities, African Americans in particular, have borne the brunt of the "law and order" regime that took hold beginning in the 1970s. Because the war on drugs targeted inner-city communities and not, for example, college campuses, it not only increased the size of the prison population, it skewed its racial composition as well, contributing significantly to the racialization of crime and imprisonment. The war on drugs, partly because of harsher penalties for the use of crack versus powdered cocaine, greatly magnified black–white disparities in the penal system.[158] African Americans are far more likely than whites to be imprisoned for a drug offense, even though, as Michael Tonry documents, black people are no more likely than white people to use or sell illegal drugs.[159]

The decline of urban employment opportunities due to deindustrialization, the legislation of stringent sentencing policies, and a "race-conscious" war on drugs have dramatically increased the rate of incarceration for poorer Americans over the past thirty years and have made imprisonment a common experience in the lives of young minority men.[160] In 2012, 551,154 African Americans were locked up in state and federal prisons, more than 35 percent of the incarcerated population, and 332,202 Hispanics were also behind bars, making up another 22 percent.[161] According to estimates from the Sentencing Project, if the current trend continues, one in three black males and one in six Hispanic males born today will spend some part of their lives in prison.[162] Increasing imprisonment contributed modestly to the decline in the rate of crime during the 1990s.[163] But the consequences of mass incarceration, particularly over the long run, are very costly.[164] The money that might be invested in crime prevention, poverty reduction, or education is spent building prisons and housing prisoners instead. Poor communities, while also being subject to constant police surveillance, creating a climate of fear and suspicion, are deprived of a potentially valuable resource, as are the families of the imprisoned, including the approximately 1.5 million children with incarcerated parents.[165] The high level of imprisonment among African Americans also reinforces the crime–race connection in the public mind, stirring feelings of racial fear and resentment.[166] And every year over six hundred thousand offenders are released from prison bearing "the mark of a criminal record" and facing the problem of how to become reintegrated into society. If they are black, they have two strikes against them, making it exceedingly difficult to find a good job, settle into a normal life, and avoid more wasted years behind bars.[167] The "poor get prison," as Jeffrey Reiman quips, but it is also true that the imprisonment of millions of young, mostly minority, men significantly exacerbates the problem of poverty.[168] Indeed, "the punitive trend in criminal justice policy," Bruce Western and Becky Pettit suggest, "may be even tougher on the poor than it is on crime," and it is tough on poor communities as well.[169]

Justice is neither cheap nor color blind, and racial minorities and the poor get the short end of the stick both coming and going. In the area of civil law, they are not helped by the legal system as much as they have a right to be, and in the area of criminal law, they are harmed by the legal system more than they deserve to be. Because people are poor, they are victims of injustice; and because people are victims of injustice, they remain poor.

## CONCLUSION

"Poverty or near poverty is not a problem," David Shipler observes; "it is an array of interlocking problems."[170] These problems are cumulative, reinforcing, and causally interrelated. Racial discrimination promotes residential segregation, and residential segregation, besides intensifying racial prejudice, gives rise to a dual housing market and a separate and unequal school system. Adverse neighborhood conditions and substandard housing cause health problems; health problems not only eat up money that might be spent on better housing, higher-quality child care, or a new car, but they also perpetuate poverty by limiting the work effort of adults and the educational attainment of children. Transportation problems make it difficult for poor families to manage child care, child-care problems reinforce sex discrimination, and the combination of sex discrimination, child-care problems, and transportation problems makes it nearly impossible for parents, especially single mothers, to find and keep a good job. These problems, in turn, cause high levels of stress and anxiety, with poor people as a result becoming inordinately susceptible to illness and disease. And the cycle goes on, with endless permutations and combinations.

Most poor people confront several of these and other obstacles simultaneously. To focus attention on just a single problem, housing, for example, or even a series of problems examined sequentially, as I have done here, is likely to leave a misleading picture of the lives of the poor and the obstacles they face. Low-income households experience problems in bunches, with one exacerbating another, and when they find a solution to one, this often comes at the expense of aggravating others or creating entirely new troubles. The poor are often accused of making bad choices, but the real problem is that their circumstances so often force them to choose between altogether undesirable alternatives. They typically encounter a series of harsh dilemmas: go to work or stay home with a sick child; repair the car or fix the plumbing and heating; choose between eye care, dental care, or prescription drugs; put food on the table or pay the rent on time; accumulate credit card debt or deny their kids a present, a new article of clothing, or a night out at the movies; take on a second job, attend to the educational needs of their children, or get involved in local politics; try to find a better house in a better neighborhood or save for retirement. These dilemmas are not unique to the poor, of course, but the needs of low-income households are more pressing, their resources more limited, and their trade-offs more severe.

The obstacles identified here, along with many others, constrain the life chances of the poor, limit their options, and make it difficult for them to cope with their poverty and ensure a decent future for their children. This country faces serious problems in the areas of health care, retirement security, education, child care, housing, and all the rest, and for the poor, these problems have reached an immediate crisis level. These are not isolated social problems, however, and they cannot be remedied as such. They originate from deeply rooted inequalities within the economic and political systems. We cannot hope to address effectively the many social problems endured by the poor without confronting the underlying inequalities in wealth and power that are ultimately responsible for the persistence of poverty.

*Chapter Eleven*

# Conclusion

## POVERTY AND POWER

We need to change how we think about poverty in the United States. We need to shift the focus from the characteristics of the poor to the dynamics of the larger political economy, from the deficiencies of individuals to the failings of social institutions. Instead of attributing poverty to the presumably self-defeating values and behaviors of the poor, I propose an alternative structural perspective. Today's poverty problem, I argue, originates from deep-rooted disparities in income, wealth, and power. No program for alleviating poverty can be successful, moreover, without confronting these underlying economic and political inequalities. Poverty is a structural problem and it demands a structural solution.

A structural perspective maintains that poverty is caused by circumstances external to the poor—by economic, political, cultural, and social forces beyond the immediate control of the individual. These forces determine whether the rate of poverty goes up or down, whether the conditions of the poor get better or worse, and who among the population is most at risk. They shape the options available to people, their access to resources, their quality of life, and their prospects for social mobility. At the same time, by allocating advantages and disadvantages, these forces generate inequalities, enriching some and impoverishing others. Whether we have more or less poverty and inequality, therefore, cannot be explained by reference to individual ability and effort. Larger structural forces are at play, including the state of the economy, the contours of government policy, the climate of public opinion, and the pattern of social relations.

The structural perspective proposed in this book, as suggested by the title, underlines the connection between poverty and power. Steven Lukes defines power as "the capacity to bring about outcomes."[1] This capacity plays a causally significant role in forming the system of social stratification, distributing resources and opportunities, and, more generally, making the world the way it is. The exercise of power shapes the economic, political, cultural, and social circumstances in which we find ourselves. This capacity is deployed, for example, when employers fire employees with pro-union sentiments, replace full-time workers with part-timers and temps, or relocate operations overseas; when corporate lobbyists prevail on legislators to rescind objectionable regulations, enact favorable tax policies, or refrain from raising the minimum wage; when the news media, wittingly or not, induce the public to believe that poverty results from personal misfortune, that education and hard work are the keys to success, or that government is incapable of solving social problems; and when privileged groups conspire to maintain the exclusivity of their neighborhoods, schools, or social networks.

Power is the servant of interests and ideologies, and the exercise of power typically engenders resistance from individuals and groups upholding competing interests and ideologies. Where there is power there is conflict, and where there is conflict there are winners and losers. Power is also unequally distributed. Because the wealthy possess vast resources and occupy society's "strategic command posts," they are far more able than others to overcome opposition and bring about desired outcomes, even more so in recent years.[2] Over the past three or four decades, as we have seen, there has been a significant upward redistribution of economic, political, and ideological power—to the benefit of employers over employees, business over labor, the right over the left. The persistent class, race, and gender inequalities we observe in society, along with the widening gap between the rich and the poor, do not result from neutral market forces or differences in merit. These inequalities are by-products of a growing imbalance of power between the haves and the have-nots. This "power shift," under way since the 1970s, helps to explain why there is so much poverty in a country with so much wealth.[3]

A structural perspective implies a unique conception of the poverty problem. Poor people lack money, of course, but they also lack power, and this is the more fundamental issue. Poverty persists in large part because the ability to call the shots—to make economic and political policy, to allocate costs and rewards, and to control the flow of information and ideas—has become increasingly concentrated at the upper end of the class system, leaving poorer Americans all the more marginalized and vulnerable. Under normal circumstances, today's poor do not have the resources or leverage to demand higher wages and better working conditions, influence political leaders and government policy, alter the cultural discourse and imagery, or eradicate barriers to mobility caused by discrimination, segregation, and social exclusion. Poverty is not just a matter of income; it is also a matter of power. And no theory of poverty and inequality can be taken seriously if it fails to bring power fully into the picture.[4]

## PROGRAMS AND POWER

There is no shortage of good ideas for fighting poverty. The annual *Half in Ten* report, the guiding document of a campaign to reduce the rate of poverty by half in ten years, includes a comprehensive analysis of present-day conditions and a lengthy list of proposals for change.[5] A special 2012 edition of *The American Prospect*, entitled "The Poverty Issue," offers another set of worthy recommendations, as do many other recent reports, including *Prosperity Economics* by Jacob Hacker and Nate Loewentheil.[6] Books on poverty and inequality by academics, activists, and journalists also often contain valuable overviews of programs and strategies for combating poverty.[7] These and other sources identify a number of promising policy prescriptions, and there is even a great deal of agreement among them about which specific remedies are most worth pursuing.

Given the wealth of material already available, there is no need for another in-depth analysis of policy ideas and objectives. No book on poverty would be complete, however, without some thoughts about how to fix the problem. So, borrowing mostly from the works referred to in the previous paragraph, I present below, more in the form of broad goals than specific programs, a list of essential anti-poverty policies. To bring some order to this outline, I sort these policies into four somewhat overlapping categories distinguished according to the particular aspect of the poverty problem they address. Following this, in the final segment of this chapter I return once again to the issue of power.

## Income Support Policies

The policy proposals included in this category reduce the incidence and severity of poverty by putting more money into the hands of the poor, directly or indirectly, lifting them above, or at least closer to, the poverty line.

- Commit to a true full-employment economy, including public-sector job creation to overcome the chronic shortage of employment opportunities in the private sector.
- Provide job training, in conjunction with job creation, to assist displaced, discouraged, and less-skilled workers.
- Raise the minimum wage and index it to the rate of inflation, the rate of productivity, or average earnings.
- Establish living wage mandates to require employers to pay workers enough to support their families at a reasonable standard of living.
- Increase the Earned Income Tax Credit for low-wage families and expand coverage to include younger and childless workers.
- Modernize the unemployment insurance system to provide coverage for the growing population of female, immigrant, low-wage, part-time, and contingent workers.
- Create a more dependable safety net by increasing access to and benefit levels for public assistance programs, including Temporary Assistance for Needy Families (TANF), and by establishing uniform eligibility standards across states.
- Strengthen the public and private pension systems to reduce income insecurity among the elderly.
- Assist low-income Americans in accumulating assets through government-financed trust funds for children and government matching contributions to savings accounts for low-income families.
- Enact progressive tax reform to make the wealthy shoulder more of the burden for raising government revenues.

## Public Goods Policies

The policy proposals in this category would not increase the income of the poor, but they would improve their quality of life. Low-income families would receive vital resources and services, including child care and health care, in the form of universally guaranteed public goods rather than private commodities. This would also leave poor families with more money to cover other expenses. Measures of this sort would not lower the official rate of poverty, but they would diminish the level of material hardship, make income poverty more bearable, and alleviate some of its more costly and harmful consequences.

- Put in place universal health insurance along with accessible and affordable medical care.
- Offer high-quality child-care assistance for low-income families.
- Increase the supply of safe and affordable housing and the availability of housing vouchers and subsidies.
- Improve the public transportation system.
- Increase funding for the legal aid system and eliminate restrictions on the provision of legal assistance to the poor.

## Equal Opportunity Policies

Some Americans are disproportionately vulnerable to poverty, including especially racial and ethnic minorities, single mothers, and children. The policy proposals in this category, though they would not necessarily reduce the aggregate level of poverty, would make poverty more of an equal opportunity affliction, less likely to fall so heavily on those already suffering multiple disadvantages.

- Strengthen anti-discrimination legislation and implement more rigorous enforcement mechanisms.
- Maintain and extend affirmative action and comparable-worth programs to combat race and sex discrimination.
- Employ measures to reduce residential and educational segregation, including stronger enforcement of fair housing laws.
- Institute early childhood education programs to ensure that all children achieve their developmental potential and are adequately prepared when they enter the school system.
- Improve the quality of public schools and eliminate disparities in funding so all children, regardless of class, race, and residence, have an equal opportunity to receive a good education.
- Reduce financial barriers to higher education.
- End the war on drugs and reduce reliance on incarceration as the principal means for dealing with non-violent offenders.

- Combat stereotypical portraits of welfare recipients, single mothers, and racial and ethnic minorities in the media.
- Create more family-friendly workplaces, including flexible scheduling, paid sick leave, paid parental leave, and more equitable treatment for part-time workers.

## Empowerment Policies

While some policies fight poverty by putting more money into the hands of the poor, the measures in this final category work on a deeper level. They put more power into the hands of the poor, giving them a stronger economic and political voice. Policies of this kind are particularly important because without increased empowerment and activism, particularly on the part of poorer Americans themselves, it is unlikely that any new war on poverty will get very far off the ground.

- Revise labor laws to allow workers to form unions through a simple majority-vote, card-check procedure.
- Impose harsher penalties on employers who use illegal tactics to prevent unionization and who otherwise violate workers' rights.
- Enact campaign finance reform, including fully funded public financing, to reduce the corrupting influence of money in politics.
- Abolish felon disenfranchisement laws.
- Simplify the voter registration process.
- Strengthen prohibitions against voter intimidation and suppression strategies.
- Loosen the grip of the moribund two-party system by reforming electoral arrangements to create alternative voting procedures, including proportional representation, and facilitate multiparty competition.
- Support educational efforts and cultural change to encourage higher levels of political awareness, participation, and activism.
- Reform the corporate-dominated mainstream media system and support alternative news media more fully committed to the goal of promoting informed citizenship and democratic deliberation.
- Craft immigration reform that guarantees that all workers, including undocumented immigrants, have sufficient civil and citizenship rights to protect themselves from exploitive treatment by employers.

Viewed from within the severely constricted universe of mainstream American politics, the policies listed above might seem to have a pie-in-the-sky quality. And no doubt they will be difficult to achieve, some more difficult than others. But they are certainly feasible. Most of these policies, after all, are already in place in other advanced countries. If Europe and Canada can do it, we can do it too. Many, perhaps even the majority of Americans, and not just the poor, would benefit from these policies as well, so there may even be a sizable constituency prepared to support such reforms. These measures have another selling point. They are necessary if we hope to realize long-standing American ideals: a just economic system where opportunities are available to everyone and where rewards are distributed equitably; a genuinely democratic political system where the preferences of ordinary Americans, not the dictates of big business, determine the course of government policy; an enlightened political culture where informed citizens actively participate in the public discourse; and a social system where access to opportunities for education, housing, and employment is not dependent on class, race, gender, or family status.

Good programs and lofty ideals are not enough, however. If they were, the problem of poverty would have been solved a long time ago. We have the know-how, but we lack the political will and the political means necessary to put that knowledge into effect. This point takes us back to the central theme of this book: the connection between poverty and power. Poverty is not so much an intellectual or technical problem as it is a political problem; policy experts are less crucial to the fight against poverty than are political activists. Poverty endures not because extraordinary ingenuity is required to invent solutions, but because the power to enact needed reforms is lacking. The problem of poverty cannot be effectively remedied without coming to grips with the problem of power—and this means organization, confrontation, and political conflict. As Joe Soss reminds us, only through a willingness to fight for it can a victory against poverty be won.[8]

## MOVEMENTS AND POWER

Poverty is a stubbornly persistent condition. We might even be tempted to throw up our hands in the face of this seemingly intractable problem: "That's just the way things are." But there is nothing inevitable about millions of Americans living below the poverty line, and the changes needed to reduce poverty, including those cited in the previous section, are certainly within our grasp. We only have to look at the example of other industrialized nations to see this. Human beings have assembled the structures that perpetuate poverty in this country, and through human intervention these structures can be disassembled, reassembled, or replaced.

It is true, however, that no single person can do much about low-wage work, inferior schools, residential segregation, inadequate health care, or the outsourcing of jobs. But as the civil rights movement, the women's movement, and other examples of collective action show, if people band together and take a stand, they can transform the basic norms and institutions of society. They may not have much influence through normal political channels, clogged up by money; they may not have much of a voice in the larger political culture, dominated by a commercialized media system; and they may be lacking in wealth, prestige, connections, and other power resources. But they are not altogether powerless. Ordinary Americans, including the poor, as Frances Fox Piven argues, have considerable "potential power." As workers, consumers, tenants, students, welfare recipients, and community residents, we are all enmeshed in a web of cooperative activities, arrangements, and interdependencies whose continued existence depends on our ongoing participation and implicit consent. By withholding our contributions, refusing to play our assigned roles, and strategically violating the rules of the game, we can obstruct the normal workings of social institutions. This "disruptive power," manifest in civil disobedience, strikes, boycotts, demonstrations, protests, sit-ins, walkouts, and other forms of contentious political behavior, gives otherwise powerless people real leverage.[9] By skillfully exploiting this power to threaten or create disorder, poorer Americans and their allies can extract concessions from business owners, government officials, and other decision-making authorities, and they can generate momentum for more far-reaching reforms.

Poverty is created and maintained through the exercise of power, and it can be eradicated only through a countervailing or oppositional mobilization of power. This can be accomplished only through an upsurge of "organized people power," a democratic resurgence played out not just in voting booths, but also in workplaces, public bureaucracies, communities, and the streets.[10] This might seem hopelessly idealistic, but in fact thousands of advocacy groups, community and student activists, labor organizers, progressive intellectuals, and working Americans—based in what Earl Wysong, Robert Perrucci, and David Wright call "alternative power networks"—have been or are currently engaged in battles on many fronts to create a more just and equal society.[11] Consider just a few examples.[12] The United Students against Sweatshops, with affiliates on more than 150 campuses, is a student-run organization that works in partnership with labor and community groups to promote the rights of workers and the cause of economic justice.[13] Family Values @ Work and MomsRising, along with numerous other women's groups, have been at the forefront in battles over sex discrimination, health care, child care, sick leave, parental leave, and more flexible, family-friendly workplaces.[14] Founded in 1968, the Center for Community Change is a grassroots activist group committed to the organization and empowerment of low-income people around issues of social and economic justice.[15] Immigrant organizations, including the Immigrant Solidarity Network, have helped revitalize the labor movement in Los Angeles and elsewhere, pressing not only for better wages, but also for immigration reform and citizenship rights.[16] Activists in the environmental justice movement have exposed the pattern of hazardous wastes and pollutants being disproportionately located near poor and minority communities, and they have organized opposition to racist environmental, transportation, and development policies.[17] The living wage movement and grassroots efforts in numerous states and cities around the country to raise the minimum wage are among the most visible and successful demonstrations of how the application of political pressure can improve the lives of poorer Americans. By framing the problem of working poverty as an economic justice issue, these movements have garnered widespread public support and have managed to forge energetic coalitions of workers, union activists, community organizations, sympathetic politicians, academic experts, and religious groups.[18] One final example is the Occupy Wall Street movement. Though its future remains uncertain, Occupy tapped a wellspring of moral outrage. Putting a spotlight on the growing divide between the 1 percent and the 99 percent, it creatively dramatized the corporate subversion of American democracy and the grotesque extremity of today's economic inequality.[19]

The fate of poorer Americans, most of whom, after all, are in the workforce, hinges on one variable more than any other: the fortunes of the labor movement. The strength of the labor movement, in turn, is dependent on its ability to mobilize and deploy the potential power of the rank-and-file working class. Though very much on the defensive since the 1970s, the labor movement, including both unionized and non-unionized workers, is still the most potent expression of "people power," and it is the only institutional force in the United States capable over the long haul of challenging the economic, political, and cultural dominance of business.[20]

Out of necessity, unions today, compared to those of the past, serve more directly as vehicles for fighting poverty. With the decline of jobs in the manufacturing sector, union organizing efforts are targeting low-wage service workers, including custodians, hotel and restaurant employees, workers in the health-care industry, and other segments of the working poor. The Justice for Janitors movement, composed largely of Hispanic immigrants, is a case in point. Under the stewardship of the Service Employees International Union, janitors in Denver, Los Angeles, Houston, and other cities have conducted highly effective organizing drives and have negotiated contracts for higher wages, job security, and health benefits. The janitors' movement has succeeded in part by turning out a large number of rank-and-file workers; nurturing connections with community groups; getting public opinion on its side; and putting pressure on cleaning companies and building owners through "in your face" protests, disruptive demonstrations, and other dramatic forms of direct action.[21]

The Justice for Janitors campaign epitomizes today's "new unionism," where unions, especially "poor workers' unions," composed disproportionately of women, immigrants, and racial and ethnic minorities, look more like social movements than bureaucratic organizations.[22] For proponents of this new unionism, the labor movement is a dynamic force for social change, but only when it taps the collective power of the larger working class and when it emphasizes not just bread-and-butter union issues, but more fundamental "demands for democracy and equality."[23] This social-movement unionism requires organized labor to establish closer ties between local unions and their communities, including the non-union population of low-wage workers, the unemployed, welfare recipients, and other disadvantaged groups.[24] It also requires the labor movement to reinvent itself, by pursuing a partnership or "fusion" with other progressive social movements, including those organized around issues of race, gender, sexuality, the environment, globalization, and peace.[25] These coalition-building strategies, besides creating a substantial oppositional power base, hold out the promise of a narrow workplace unionism being transformed into a broader movement for social and economic justice.

Union organizing today, due especially to the combination of weak labor laws and determined employer opposition, is a daunting challenge. In response, many low-wage workers, with little immediate prospect of unionization, have instead formed innovative grassroots movements separate from, though sometimes intersecting with, organized labor.[26] For example, workers in the restaurant industry, including employees at Taco Bell and McDonald's, have sought to build public support for higher wages and improved working conditions by staging highly visible one-day strikes.[27] Many of these workers have been aided in their efforts by "worker centers," more than 140 of which have appeared throughout the country since the early 1990s.[28] Worker centers, including the New York Taxi Workers Alliance, the National Domestic Workers Alliance, and the Coalition of Immokalee Workers, are community-based institutions that, among other services, advocate on behalf of low-wage workers, provide legal assistance, form local coalitions, and help organize rallies and demonstrations.[29] One good example is the Restaurant Opportunities Centers United (ROC). Through such non-union tactics as the "public shaming" of targeted restaurants, ROC has helped workers in the food industry achieve higher pay and a more humane workplace environment; in the process—one sign of success—it has also managed to antagonize the National Restaurant Association, one of the most powerful trade associations in the country.[30]

A reinvigorated labor movement, with a stronger economic and political presence, can win benefits for the working class and the poor—higher wages, better working conditions, a more generous welfare state, and worker-friendly government policies. Beyond this, however, and of greater long-run importance, labor activism is a democratizing force. It opens opportunities for political participation and self-determination on the part of otherwise marginalized people; it empowers poorer Americans, enhancing their capacity for collective action and equipping them for future struggles. Today's labor movement, reconfigured as a genuine social movement, in conjunction with other social justice movements, has the ability to oppose a structure of power that has become dangerously imbalanced. These movements will not be hanging up any "mission accomplished" banners soon, of course, and they have probably suffered more defeats than victories, but their example does offer up a vision of how poor and working-class Americans can mobilize their potential power to promote social change.

It is sometimes said that poor people should pull themselves up by their own bootstraps. This is good advice. But for such efforts to be successful they must be collective rather than individual undertakings, political rather than purely personal endeavors. As a recipe for fighting poverty, a self-improvement approach might help particular individuals, giving them an edge over competitors in the labor market, but only a broad-based mobilization of power can bring about the economic and political changes needed to alleviate poverty in the aggregate. A collective bootstraps strategy, with poorer Americans taking the lead, joined together through labor unions, community groups, and grassroots organizations, is the best hope for a successful war against poverty. While poverty and powerlessness normally go hand-in-hand, the social justice movements on the scene today testify to the potential power possessed by poorer Americans. Only by more fully realizing this potential is there any chance of achieving the ambitious goal enunciated by Martin Luther King Jr. almost fifty years ago: "the total, direct and immediate abolition of poverty."[31]

# Notes

## 1. POVERTY AS A SOCIAL PROBLEM

1. Jeff Shesol, "The 'P' Word: Why Presidents Stopped Talking about Poverty," *New Yorker*, January 9, 2014, http://www.newyorker.com/news/news-desk/the-p-word-why-presidents-stopped-talking-about-poverty (accessed August 7, 2014).

2. For a particularly illuminating history of the war on poverty from the Kennedy-Johnson years into the Bush II administration, see Frank Stricker, *Why America Lost the War on Poverty—And How to Win It* (Chapel Hill: University of North Carolina Press, 2007); for a comprehensive assessment of the war on poverty on its fiftieth-year anniversary, see Martha J. Bailey and Sheldon Danziger, eds., *Legacies of the War on Poverty* (New York: Russell Sage, 2013); and on the invisibility of the poor in the immediate post-war years and their discovery in the 1960s, see Barbara Ehrenreich, *Fear of Falling: The Inner Life of the Middle Class* (New York: Pantheon, 1989), 17–56.

3. Martin Luther King Jr., *Where Do We Go from Here: Chaos or Community?* (New York: Harper & Row, 1967), 166.

4. Melissa Boteach and Donna Cooper, *What You Need When You're Poor: Heritage Foundation Hasn't a Clue* (Washington, DC: Center for American Progress, August 2011), http://www.americanprogress.org/issues/poverty/news/2011/08/05/10063/what-you-need-when-youre-poor (accessed August 7, 2014).

5. Michelle Goldberg, "Poverty Denialism," *The Nation*, November 25, 2013, 6–8.

6. For a scathing critique of this view, see Peter Van Buren, "Why Don't the Unemployed Get Off Their Couches? And Eight Other Critical Questions for Americans," *The UNZ Review: An Alternative Media Selection*, June 3, 2014, http://www.unz.com/article/why-dont-the-unemployed-get-off-their-couches (accessed August 7, 2014).

7. See, for example, Gregory Squires and Chester Hartman, eds., *There Is No Such Thing as a Natural Disaster: Race, Class, and Hurricane Katrina* (New York: Routledge, 2006).

8. The reference to "bold action" comes from a statement delivered by George W. Bush in New Orleans on September 12, 2005, about two weeks after Katrina swept through the Gulf Coast. Cited in Robert C. Lieberman, "'The Storm Didn't Discriminate': Katrina and the Politics of Color Blindness," *Du Bois Review* 3, no. 1 (Spring 2006): 10.

9. Neil deMause, "Katrina's Vanishing Victims," *Extra!*, July–August 2006, 17–23.

10. Michael Hout, Asaf Levanon, and Erin Cumberworth, "Job Loss and Unemployment," in *The Great Recession*, ed. David B. Grusky, Bruce Western, and Christopher Wimer (New York: Russell Sage, 2011), 63–69, 77–78.

11. Alan S. Blinder, *After the Music Stopped: The Financial Crisis, the Response, and the Work Ahead* (New York: Penguin, 2013), 12.

12. Blinder, *After the Music Stopped*, 210–36.

13. On the opposition to Obama's economic policies and the rise of the Tea Party, see Blinder, *After the Music Stopped*, 343–64; Theda Skocpol and Vanessa Williamson, *The Tea Party and the Remaking of Republican Conservatism* (New York: Oxford University Press, 2013).

14. See, for example, Ezra Klein, "Romney's Theory of the 'Taker Class,' and Why It Matters," *Washington Post*, September 17, 2012, http://www.washingtonpost.com/blogs/wonkblog/wp/2012/09/17/romneys-theory-of-the-taker-class-and-why-it-matters (accessed August 12, 2014), and Ben Craw and Zack Carter, "Paul Ryan: 60 Percent of Americans Are 'Takers,' Not 'Makers,'" *Huffington Post*, October 5, 2012, http://www.huffingtonpost.com/2012/10/05/paul-ryan-60-percent-of-a_n_1943073.html (accessed August 12, 2014); see also Skocpol and Williamson, *The Tea Party*, 64–68.

15. On the Occupy Wall Street movement, see Todd Gitlin, *Occupy Nation: The Roots, the Spirit, and the Promise of Occupy Wall Street* (New York: Itbooks, HarperCollins, 2012).

16. Barack Obama, *Remarks by the President on Economic Mobility* (Washington, DC: White House, Office of the Press Secretary, December 4, 2013), http://www.whitehouse.gov/the-press-office/2013/12/04/remarks-president-economic-mobility (accessed August 16, 2014); Jackie Calmes, "In Talk of Economy, Obama Turns to 'Opportunity' over 'Inequality,'" *New York Times*, February 3, 2014.

17. House Budget Committee Majority Staff, Chairman Paul Ryan, *Expanding Opportunity in America: A Discussion Draft from the House Budget Committee* (July 24, 2014), http://budget.house.gov/uploadedfiles/expanding_opportunity_in_america.pdf (accessed August 16, 2014); Paul Ryan, *Expanding Opportunity in America*, remarks as prepared for delivery at the American Enterprise Institute, July 24, 2014, http://budget.house.gov/uploadedfiles/expanding_opportunity_in_america.pdf (accessed August 16, 2014); for a critique of Ryan's proposal, see Stephanie Mencimer, "Paul Ryan's Anti-Poverty Plan Would Cost Billions to Implement. Will GOPers Go for That?," *Mother Jones*, July 25, 2014, http://www.motherjones.com/politics/2014/07/paul-ryan-anti-poverty-plan-would-cost-billions (accessed August 16, 2014).

18. For similar analyses, see Fred Block, Anna C. Korteweg, and Kerry Woodward, "The Compassion Gap in American Poverty Policy," *Contexts* 5, no. 2 (Spring 2006): 14–20, and Mark R. Rank, "Rethinking American Poverty," *Contexts* 10, no. 2 (Spring 2011): 16–21.

19. Alice O'Connor, *Poverty Knowledge: Social Science, Social Policy, and the Poor in Twentieth-Century U.S. History* (Princeton, NJ: Princeton University Press, 2001).

20. For a valuable overview of the data on poverty and the poor, see John Iceland, *Poverty in America: A Handbook*, 3rd ed. (Berkeley: University of California Press, 2013).

21. Carmen DeNavas-Walt, Bernadette D. Proctor, and Jessica C. Smith, *Income, Poverty, and Health Insurance Coverage in the United States: 2012*, U.S. Census Bureau, Current Population Reports, P60-245 (Washington, DC: Government Printing Office, 2013), 14, 17, 61, 63, tables 3, 4, B-2.

22. DeNavas-Walt, Proctor, and Smith, *Income, Poverty, and Health Insurance Coverage*, 18, table 5. On the insecure and uncertain lives of the near poor, see Katherine S. Newman and Victor Tan Chen, *The Missing Class: Portraits of the Near Poor in America* (Boston: Beacon

Press, 2007), and Jason DeParle, Robert Gebeloff, and Sabrina Tavernise, "Meet the Near Poor: Older, Married, Suburban and Struggling," *New York Times*, November 19, 2011.

23. DeNavas-Walt, Proctor, and Smith, *Income, Poverty, and Health Insurance Coverage*, 51.

24. John Halpin and Karl Agne, *50 Years after LBJ's War on Poverty: A Study of American Attitudes about Work, Economic Opportunity, and the Social Safety Net* (Washington, DC: Center for American Progress, January 2014), 8, http://www.americanprogress.org/wp-content/uploads/2014/01/WOP-PollReport2.pdf (accessed June 3, 2014).

25. On the public's view of the poverty line, with data through 1989, see Denton R. Vaughan, "Exploring the Use of the Public's Views to Set Income Poverty Thresholds and Adjust Them over Time," *Social Security Bulletin* 56, no. 2 (Summer 1993): 22–46; and for an update of Vaughan's findings, see Constance F. Citro and Robert T. Michael, *Measuring Poverty: A New Approach* (Washington, DC: National Academy Press, 1995), 34–35, 134–40, esp. 138–39, table 2-4.

26. There is a voluminous body of research on definitions and measures of poverty, including many detailed critiques of the official U.S. measure. See, for example, Citro and Michael, *Measuring Poverty*; Iceland, *Poverty in America*, 22–38; and Patricia Ruggles, *Drawing the Line: Alternative Poverty Measures and Their Implications for Public Policy* (Washington, DC: Urban Institute, 1990).

27. Elise Gould, Hilary Wething, Natalie Sabadish, and Nicholas Finio, *What Families Need to Get By: The 2013 Update of EPI's Family Budget Calculator* (Washington, DC: Economic Policy Institute, July 2013), 1–2, http://s4.epi.org/files/2013/ib368-basic-family-budgets.pdf (accessed June 3, 2014).

28. Timothy M. Smeeding, "Government Programs and Social Outcomes: Comparison of the United States with Other Rich Nations," in *Public Policy and Income Distribution*, ed. Alan J. Auerbach, David Card, and John M. Quigley (New York: Russell Sage, 2006), 162, table 4.2.

29. Lawrence Mishel, Josh Bivens, Elise Gould, and Heidi Shierholz, *The State of Working America*, 12th ed. (Ithaca, NY: Cornell University Press, 2012), 450, fig. 7W.

30. Timothy M. Smeeding and Lee Rainwater, "Comparing Living Standards across Nations: Real Incomes at the Top, the Bottom, and the Middle," Discussion Paper No. 120 (Social Policy Research Centre, December 2002), http://www.olin.wustl.edu/macarthur/papers/smeeding-livingstandards.pdf (accessed December 27, 2007).

31. On the rate of absolute poverty in the United States compared to other developed countries circa 2000, see Lyle Scruggs and James P. Allan, "The Material Consequences of Welfare States: Benefit Generosity and Absolute Poverty in 16 OECD Countries," *Comparative Political Studies* 39, no. 7 (September 2006): 880–904; see also Iceland, *Poverty in America*, 71–72.

32. Alberto Alesina and Edward L. Glaeser, *Fighting Poverty in the U.S. and Europe: A World of Difference* (Oxford: Oxford University Press, 2004), 47.

33. Mishel, Bivens, Gould, and Shierholz, *The State of Working America*, 450–52, figs. 7X and 7Y; see also Janet C. Gornick and Markus Jäntti, "Child Poverty in Cross-National Perspective: Lessons from the Luxembourg Income Study," *Children and Youth Services Review* 34 (2012): 558–68; UNICEF, *Child Well-Being in Rich Countries: A Comparative Overview*, Report Card No. 11 (Florence, Italy: UNICEF Office of Research, April 2013), 7–8.

34. UNICEF, *Child Well-Being in Rich Countries*, 2.

35. DeNavas-Walt, Proctor, and Smith, *Income, Poverty, and Health Insurance Coverage*, 13, fig. 4.

36. Mishel, Bivens, Gould, and Shierholz, *The State of Working America*, 437–40.

37. For a detailed look at the increasing severity of poverty in the 2000s, see Steven H. Woolf, Robert E. Johnson, and H. Jack Geiger, "The Rising Prevalence of Severe Poverty in America: A Growing Threat to Public Health," *American Journal of Preventive Medicine* 31, no. 4 (2006): 332–41.

38. Lawrence Mishel, Jared Bernstein, and Sylvia Allegretto, *The State of Working America 2006/2007* (Ithaca, NY: Cornell University Press, 2007), 288, table 6.5; DeNavas-Walt, Proctor, and Smith, *Income, Poverty, and Health Insurance Coverage*, 19, table 6.

39. Mishel, Bivens, Gould, and Shierholz, *The State of Working America*, 428; DeNavas-Walt, Proctor, and Smith, *Income, Poverty, and Health Insurance Coverage*, 18, table 5. On "deep poverty," see also Laudon Aron, Wendy Jacobson, and Margery Austin Turner, *Addressing Deep and Persistent Poverty: A Framework for Philanthropic Planning* (Washington, DC: Urban Institute, December 2013), http://www.urban.org/UploadedPDF/412983-addressing-deep-poverty.pdf (accessed June 4, 2014).

40. H. Luke Shaefer and Kathryn Edin, "The Rise of Extreme Poverty in the United States," *Pathways* (Summer 2014): 28–32; for their earlier analysis, see H. Luke Shaefer and Kathryn Edin, *Extreme Poverty in the United States, 1996 to 2011* (Ann Arbor, MI: National Poverty Center, February 2012), 2, http://www.npc.umich.edu/publications/policy_briefs/brief28/policybrief28.pdf (accessed June 3, 2014).

41. Gabriel Thompson, "Could You Survive on $2 a Day?," *Mother Jones*, December 13, 2012, http://www.motherjones.com/politics/2012/12/extreme-poverty-unemployment-recession-economy-fresno (accessed June 4, 2014).

42. Ruggles, *Drawing the Line*, 39–52.

43. Annie Lowrey, "Changed Life of the Poor: Squeak By, and Buy a Lot," *New York Times*, May 1, 2014; see also Lane Kenworthy, *Social Democratic America* (Oxford: Oxford University Press, 2014), 30–35, 47–48.

44. On the concept of "social exclusion" as it pertains to the problem of poverty, see Amartya Sen, "Social Exclusion: Concept, Application, and Scrutiny," Social Development Papers No. 1 (Manila, Philippines: Asian Development Bank, June 2000), http://www.adb.org/documents/books/social_exclusion/Social_exclusion.pdf (accessed December 30, 2007), and Brian Nolan and Ive Marx, "Economic Inequality, Poverty, and Social Exclusion," in *The Oxford Handbook of Economic Inequality*, ed. Wiemer Salverda, Brian Nolan, and Timothy M. Smeeding (Oxford: Oxford University Press, 2009), 315–41.

45. Iceland, *Poverty in America*, 47–49; Ann Huff Stevens, "Climbing Out of Poverty, Falling Back In: Measuring the Persistence of Poverty over Multiple Spells," *Journal of Human Resources* 34, no. 3 (Summer 1999): 557–88.

46. Mary Corcoran and Jordan Matsudaira, "Is It Getting Harder to Get Ahead? Economic Attainment for Two Cohorts," in *On the Frontier of Adulthood: Theory, Research, and Public Policy*, ed. Richard A. Settersten Jr., Frank F. Furstenberg Jr., and Ruben C. Rumbaut (Chicago: University of Chicago Press, 2005), 356–95.

47. Annette Bernhardt et al., *Divergent Paths: Economic Mobility in the New American Labor Market* (New York: Russell Sage, 2001), 111, 171, 166.

48. Roberta Rehner Iversen and Annie Laurie Armstrong, *Jobs Aren't Enough: Toward a New Economic Mobility for Low-Income Families* (Philadelphia: Temple University Press, 2006), 13–20; see also Paul Osterman and Beth Shulman, *Good Jobs America: Making Work Better for Everyone* (New York: Russell Sage, 2011), 24–25.

49. Mishel, Bivens, Gould, and Shierholz, *The State of Working America*, 143.

50. Daniel Aronson and Bhashkar Mazumder, "Intergenerational Economic Mobility in the U.S., 1940 to 2000," WP 2005–12 (Chicago: Federal Reserve Bank of Chicago, February

2007), http://www.chicagofed.org/publications/workingpapers/ wp2005_12.pdf (accessed December 30, 2007).

51. Tom Hertz, "Rags, Riches, and Race: The Intergenerational Economic Mobility of Black and White Families in the United States," in *Unequal Chances: Family Background and Economic Success*, ed. Samuel Bowles, Herbert Gintis, and Melissa Osborne Groves (New York: Russell Sage, 2005), 186, table 5.10. See also Tom Hertz, *Understanding Mobility in America* (Washington, DC: Center for American Progress, April 26, 2006), 6–20, and Bhashkar Mazumder, "Fortunate Sons: New Estimates of Intergenerational Mobility in the United States Using Social Security Earnings Data," *Review of Economics and Statistics* 87, no. 2 (May 2005): 235–55.

52. Miles Corack, *Chasing the Same Dream, Climbing Different Ladders: Economic Mobility in the United States and Canada* (Economic Mobility Project, Pew Charitable Trusts, January 2010), http://www.pewtrusts.org/uploadedFiles/wwwpewtrustsorg/Reports/Economic_Mobility/PEW_EMP_US-CANADA.pdf (accessed June 9, 2014); Miles Corack, "Income Inequality, Equality of Opportunity, and Intergenerational Mobility," *Journal of Economic Perspectives* 27, no. 3 (Summer 2013): 79–102.

53. Jo Blanden, "Cross-Country Rankings in Intergenerational Mobility: A Comparison of Approaches from Economics and Sociology," *Journal of Economic Surveys* 27, no. 1 (2013): 38–73; Mishel, Bivens, Gould, and Shierholz, *The State of Working America*, 151–54.

54. Jason DeParle, "Harder for Americans to Rise from Economy's Lower Rungs," *New York Times*, January 5, 2012; Markus Jäntti et al., "American Exceptionalism in a New Light: A Comparison of Intergenerational Earnings Mobility in the Nordic Countries, the United Kingdom, and the United States," Discussion Paper No. 1938 (Bonn, Germany: Institute for the Study of Labor, 2006), 2, http://doku.iab.de/externe/2006/k060124f13.pdf (accessed December 30, 2007).

55. Raj Chetty, Nathanial Hendren, Patrick Kline, and Emmanuel Saez, "Where Is the Land of Opportunity? The Geography of Intergenerational Mobility in the United States," Working Paper No. 19843 (Cambridge, MA: National Bureau of Economic Research, January 2014); see also David Leonhardt, "Geography Seen as Barrier to Climbing Class Ladder," *New York Times*, July 22, 2013.

56. Jäntti et al., "American Exceptionalism"; Miles Corack, "Do Poor Children Become Poor Adults? Lessons from a Cross-Country Comparison of Generational Earnings Mobility," *Research on Economic Inequality* 13, no. 1 (2006): 143–88.

57. Hertz, "Rags, Riches, and Race," 179–83; Mishel, Bivens, Gould, and Shierholz, *The State of Working America*, 154–56.

58. Center for Budget and Policy Priorities, *Policy Basics: An Introduction to TANF* (Washington, DC: Center for Budget and Policy Priorities, December 2012), 5–6, http://www.cbpp.org/files/7-22-10tanf2.pdf (accessed June 9, 2014).

59. Peter Edelman, "We Have Blown a Huge Hole in the Safety Net" (TalkPoverty.org, May 22, 2014), http://talkpoverty.org/2014/05/22/edelman (accessed June 9, 2014); Jason DeParle, "Welfare Limits Left Poor Adrift as Recession Hits," *New York Times*, April 8, 2012.

60. See, for example, Robert Reich, "The War on Poor and Middle-Class Families" (Video), http://www.huffingtonpost.com/robert-reich/war-on-the-poor_b_4746497.html (accessed June 9, 2014).

61. Mark Robert Rank, "As American as Apple Pie: Poverty and Welfare," *Contexts* 2, no. 3 (Summer 2003): 41–49; Mark Robert Rank and Thomas A. Hirschl, "Rags or Riches? Estimating the Probabilities of Poverty and Affluence across the Adult American Life Span," *Social Science Quarterly* 82, no. 4 (December 2001): 651–69; Mark Robert Rank, *One Nation, Under-*

*privileged: Why American Poverty Affects Us All* (New York: Oxford University Press, 2004), 88–101.

62. Rank, *One Nation, Underprivileged*, 92–95.

63. Jacob C. Hacker, *The Great Risk Shift: The Assault on American Jobs, Families, Health Care, and Retirement—And How You Can Fight Back* (Oxford: Oxford University Press, 2006), 33.

64. Mark Robert Rank, Thomas A. Hirschl, and Kirk A. Foster, *Chasing the American Dream: Understanding What Shapes Our Fortunes* (Oxford: Oxford University Press, 2014), 77.

65. Rank, *One Nation, Underprivileged*, 88, 107; Rank, "As American as Apple Pie."

66. Michael Sherraden, *Assets and the Poor: A New American Welfare Policy* (Armonk, NY: M. E. Sharpe, 1991); Melvin L. Oliver and Thomas M. Shapiro, *Black Wealth/White Wealth: A New Perspective on Racial Inequality* (New York: Routledge, 1995); Dalton Conley, *Being Black, Living in the Red: Race, Wealth, and Social Policy in America* (Berkeley: University of California Press, 1999).

67. See James B. Davies, "Wealth and Economic Inequality," in Salverda, Nolan, and Smeeding, *Oxford Handbook of Economic Inequality*, 127–49.

68. Mishel, Bivens, Gould, and Shierholz, *The State of Working America*, 379, 384.

69. On the concept and measurement of "asset poverty," see Asena Caner and Edward N. Wolff, "Asset Poverty in the United States, 1984–1999," *Challenge* 47, no. 1 (January–February 2004): 5–52; Robert H. Haveman and Edward N. Wolff, "The Concept and Measurement of Asset Poverty: Levels, Trends, and Composition for the U.S., 1983–2001," *Journal of Economic Inequality* 2 (2004): 145–69; Asena Caner and Edward N. Wolff, "Asset Poverty in the United States, 1984–99: Evidence from the Panel Study of Income Dynamics," *Review of Income and Wealth* 50, no. 4 (December 2004): 493–518.

70. Jennifer Brooks and Kasey Wiedrich, *Assets and Opportunity Scorecard. Living on the Edge: Financial Insecurity and Policies to Rebuild Prosperity in America* (Washington, DC: CFED, January 2013), 3–4, http://assetsandopportunity.org/assets/pdf/2013_Scorecard_Report.pdf (accessed June 6, 2014).

71. Haveman and Wolff, "The Concept and Measurement of Asset Poverty," 153; Jennifer Brooks, Kasey Wiedrich, Lebaron Sims Jr., and Jennifer Medina, *Treading Water in the Deep End: Findings from the 2014 Assets and Opportunity Scorecard* (Washington, DC: CFED, January 2014), 3, http://assetsandopportunity.org/assets/pdf/2014_Scorecard_Report.pdf (accessed June 6, 2014). For a comprehensive analysis of asset poverty among African Americans, see Lori Latrice Martin, *Black Asset Poverty and the Enduring Racial Divide* (Boulder, CO: FirstForum Press, 2013).

72. Haveman and Wolff, "The Concept and Measurement of Asset Poverty," 152, 157, 160–61, 167n17; Rank, Hirschl, and Foster, *Chasing the American Dream*, 40–41.

73. Josh Bivens, Elise Gould, Lawrence Mishel, and Heidi Shierholz, *Raising America's Pay: Why It's Our Central Economic Policy Challenge* (Washington, DC: Economic Policy Institute, June 2014), 43–44, http://s2.epi.org/files/2014/Raising-America%27s-Pay-2014-Report.pdf (accessed June 6, 2014).

74. Caner and Wolff, "Asset Poverty in the United States," 46.

75. For three widely discussed studies, see Jacob S. Hacker and Paul Pierson, *Winner-Take-All Politics: How Washington Made the Rich Richer—And Turned Its Back on the Middle Class* (New York: Simon & Schuster, 2010); Joseph E. Stiglitz, *The Price of Inequality* (New York: Norton, 2012); and Thomas Piketty, *Capital in the Twenty-First Century*, trans. Arthur Goldhammer (Cambridge, MA: Belknap Press of Harvard University Press, 2014). For a useful guide to date on increasing inequality, see Chad Stone, Danilo Trisi, Arloc Sherman, and

William Chen, *A Guide to Statistics on Historical Trends in Income Inequality* (Washington, DC: Center on Budget and Policy Priorities, April 17, 2014), http://www.cbpp.org/files/11-28-11pov.pdf (accessed August 7, 2014).

76. Bivens et al., *Raising America's Pay*, 11, 19.

77. See Osterman and Shulman, *Good Jobs America*, 26–28.

78. DeNavas-Walt, Proctor, and Smith, *Income, Poverty, and Health Insurance Coverage*, 33, 50, tables A-1 and A-4.

79. Fred Block, "Is the American Dream Dying?" (Longview Institute, 2006), http://www.longviewinstitute.org/research/block/amer-dream (accessed December 27, 2007).

80. Eduardo Porter, "America's Sinking Middle Class," *New York Times*, September 19, 2013; David Leonhardt and Kevin Quealy, "U.S. Middle Class No Longer World's Richest," *New York Times*, April 23, 2014.

81. On increasing economic insecurity, see Bruce Western, Deirdre Bloome, Benjamin Sosnaud, and Laura Tach, "Economic Insecurity and Social Stratification," *Annual Review of Sociology* 38 (2012): 341–59; Jacob S. Hacker, "Working Families at Risk: Understanding and Confronting the New Economic Insecurity," in *Old Assumptions, New Realities: Economic Security for Working Families in the 21st Century*, ed. Robert D. Plotnick, Marcia K. Meyers, Jennifer Romich, and Steven Rathgeb Smith (New York: Russell Sage, 2011), 31–69; Shawn McMahon and Jessica Horning, *Living Below the Line: Economic Insecurity and America's Families* (Washington, DC: Wider Opportunities for Women, Fall 2013), http://www.wowonline.org/wp-content/uploads/2013/09/Living-Below-the-Line-Economic-Insecurity-and-Americas-Families-Fall-2013.pdf (accessed June 5, 2014).

82. For the classic statement of this argument, see Herbert J. Gans, "The Positive Functions of Poverty," *American Journal of Sociology* 78, no. 2 (September 1972): 275–89.

83. Alisha Coleman-Jensen, Mark Nord, and Anita Singh, *Household Food Security in the United States, 2012*, U.S. Department of Agriculture, Economic Research Report No. 155 (Washington, DC: Government Printing Office, September 2013), 4–8.

84. Sam Dillon, "Line Grows Long for Free Meals," *New York Times*, November 30, 2011.

85. Tammy Ouellette et al., *Measures of Material Hardship: Final Report*, U.S. Department of Health and Human Services (Washington, DC: Government Printing Office, April 2004), 55–79.

86. Thomas Piketty and Emmanuel Saez, "Top Incomes and the Great Recession: Recent Evolutions and Policy Implications" (paper presented at the Thirteenth Jacques Polak Annual Research Conference, November 8–9, 2012), figs. 3 and 2A, http://www.imf.org/external/np/res/seminars/2012/arc/pdf/PS.pdf (accessed June 8, 2014).

87. Deborah Hagreaves, "Can We Close the Pay Gap?," *New York Times*, March 30, 2014; Dominic Rushe, "US CEOs Break Pay Record as Top 10 Earners Take Home at Least $100 Million Each," *The Guardian*, October 22, 2013, http://www.theguardian.com/business/2013/oct/22/top-earning-ceos-100m-paychecks-record (accessed June 6, 2014).

88. Alexandra Stevenson, "Hedge Fund Moguls' Pay Has the 1% Looking Up," *New York Times*, May 6, 2014.

89. Walter Hamilton, "Number of Millionaires Reaches a New High," *Los Angeles Times*, March 13, 2014; Kerry A. Dolan and Luisa Kroll, "Inside the 2014 Forbes Billionaires List: Facts and Figures," http://www.forbes.com/sites/luisakroll/2014/03/03/inside-the-2014-forbes-billionaires-list-facts-and-figures (accessed June 5, 2014).

90. Steven Rattner, "The Rich Get Even Richer," *New York Times*, March 26, 2012.

91. Daniel Schraad-Tischler, *Social Justice in the OECD: How Do the Member States Compare?* (Gütersloh, Germany: Bertelsmann Stiftung, 2011), http://www.sgi-network.org/pdf/SGI11_Social_Justice_OECD.pdf (accessed June 5, 2014).

92. For a similar distinction between views of poverty, see Stricker, *Why America Lost the War on Poverty*; Leonard Beeghley, "Individual and Structural Explanations of Poverty," *Population Research and Policy Review* 7, no. 3 (1988): 201–22, and D. Stanley Eitzen and Kelly Eitzen Smith, *Experiencing Poverty: Voices from the Bottom* (Belmont, CA: Wadsworth, 2003), 15–19. Other overviews of the literature often identify a wide variety of different theories of poverty; see, for example, Harrell R. Rodgers Jr., *American Poverty in a New Era of Reform* (Armonk, NY: M. E. Sharpe, 2000), 69–82; James Jennings, "Persistent Poverty in the United States: Review of Theories and Explanations," in *A New Introduction to Poverty: The Role of Race, Power, and Politics*, ed. Louis Kushnick and James Jennings (New York: New York University Press, 1999), 13–38; William A. Kelso, *Poverty and the Underclass: Changing Perceptions of the Poor in America* (New York: New York University Press, 1994); and David L. Harvey and Michael Reed, "Paradigms of Poverty: A Critical Assessment of Contemporary Perspectives," *International Journal of Politics, Culture and Society* 6, no. 2 (1992): 269–97.

93. Greg M. Shaw and Robert Y. Shapiro, "The Polls-Trends: Poverty and Public Assistance," *Public Opinion Quarterly* 66, no. 1 (Spring 2002): 121–22.

94. Schiller, *The Economics of Poverty*, 6–8.

95. Rank, *One Nation, Underprivileged*, 169–91.

96. See Randy Albelda, Robert Drago, and Steven Shulman, *Unlevel Playing Fields: Understanding Wage Inequality and Discrimination* (New York: McGraw-Hill, 1997), and Frank Ackerman et al., eds., *The Political Economy of Inequality* (Washington, DC: Island Press, 2000).

# 2. THE BIOGENETIC THEORY OF POVERTY AND INEQUALITY

1. I borrow the term "biogenetic" as a label for this theory from Peter Knapp et al., *The Assault on Equality* (Westport, CT: Praeger, 1996).

2. Richard J. Herrnstein and Charles Murray, *The Bell Curve: Intelligence and Class Structure in American Life* (New York: Free Press, 1994). See also Charles Murray and Richard J. Herrnstein, "Race, Genes, and I.Q.—An Apologia," *New Republic*, October 31, 1994, 27–37, and Charles Murray, "*The Bell Curve* and Its Critics," *Commentary*, May 1995, 23–30. For useful summaries of *The Bell Curve*, see Claude S. Fischer et al., *Inequality by Design: Cracking the Bell Curve Myth* (Princeton, NJ: Princeton University Press, 1996), 217–24, and Terry W. Belke, "A Synopsis of *The Bell Curve*," in *Intelligence, Genes, and Success: Scientists Respond to* The Bell Curve, ed. Bernie Devlin et al. (New York: Copernicus, Springer-Verlag, 1997), 19–40.

3. Two book-length studies of *The Bell Curve* deserve to be singled out: Fischer et al., *Inequality by Design*, and Knapp et al., *The Assault on Equality*. For valuable compilations, see Devlin et al., *Intelligence, Genes, and Success*; Steven Fraser, ed., *The Bell Curve Wars: Race, Intelligence, and the Future of America* (New York: Basic Books, 1995); Kenneth Arrow, Samuel Bowles, and Steven N. Durlauf, eds., *Meritocracy and Economic Inequality* (Princeton, NJ: Princeton University Press, 2000); Russell Jacoby and Naomi Glauberman, eds., *The Bell Curve Debate: History, Documents, Opinions* (New York: Times Books, 1995); and Joe L. Kincheloe, Shirley R. Steinberg, and Aaron D. Gresson III, eds., *Measured Lies: The Bell Curve Examined* (New York: St. Martin's, 1996).

4. Herrnstein and Murray, *Bell Curve*, 25.

5. Herrnstein and Murray devote three chapters in *The Bell Curve* to issues of race and ethnicity (chapters 13, 14, and 15), specifically claiming that black–white differences in IQ have a significant genetic basis. For a review of the evidence contradicting this assertion, see Richard E. Nisbett, "Race, Genetics, and IQ," in *The Black-White Test Score Gap*, ed. Christopher Jencks and Meredith Phillips (Washington, DC: Brookings Institution Press, 1998), 86–102. Herrnstein and Murray also devote two chapters (chapters 19 and 20), about 10 percent of the entire text (!), to affirmative action.

6. Herrnstein and Murray, *Bell Curve*, 25–27. For criticism of the concept of a "cognitive elite," see Nicholas Lemann, "Is There a Cognitive Elite in America?," in Devlin et al., *Intelligence, Genes, and Success*, 315–25, and Alan Wolfe, "Has There Been a Cognitive Revolution in America? The Flawed Sociology of *The Bell Curve*," in Fraser, *The Bell Curve Wars*, 109–23.

7. On the "democratization of higher education" and "cognitive partitioning by occupation," see Herrnstein and Murray, *Bell Curve*, chapters 1 and 2.

8. Herrnstein and Murray, *Bell Curve*, 91.

9. Herrnstein and Murray, *Bell Curve*, 117.

10. Herrnstein and Murray, *Bell Curve*, 386. On the problem of "high-IQ criminality," overlooked by Herrnstein and Murray, see Andrew Hacker, "Caste, Crime, and Precocity," in Fraser, *The Bell Curve Wars*, 102–3.

11. Herrnstein and Murray, *Bell Curve*, 3–4, 14.

12. Herrnstein and Murray, *Bell Curve*, 105.

13. On the multidimensional nature of intelligence, see Howard Gardner, *Frames of Mind: The Theory of Multiple Intelligences* (New York: Basic Books, 1983), and Robert J. Sternberg, *The Triarchic Mind: A New Theory of Human Intelligence* (New York: Penguin, 1988).

14. On the influence of the test situation on test performance, particularly as this relates to the black–white test score gap, see Claude M. Steele and Joshua Aronson, "Stereotype Threat and Test Performance of Academically Successful African Americans," in Jencks and Phillips, *The Black-White Test Score Gap*, 401–27.

15. Christopher Jencks, "Racial Bias in Testing," in Jencks and Phillips, *The Black-White Test Score Gap*, 55–85.

16. See Fischer et al., *Inequality by Design*, 42–43, and Melvin L. Kohn, "Two Visions of the Relationship between Individual and Society: The Bell Curve versus Social Structure and Personality," in *A Nation Divided: Diversity, Inequality, and Community in American Society*, ed. Phyllis Moen, Donna Dempster-McClain, and Henry A. Walker (Ithaca, NY: Cornell University Press, 1999), 34–51. For an illuminating exploration of practical intelligence in the workplace, see Mike Rose, *The Mind at Work: Valuing the Intelligence of the American Worker* (New York: Viking, 2004).

17. For a useful discussion of what IQ tests actually measure, see N. J. Block and Gerald Dworkin, "IQ, Heritability, and Inequality," in *The IQ Controversy: Critical Readings*, ed. N. J. Block and Gerald Dworkin (New York: Random House, 1976), 410–73.

18. See Michael Daniels, Bernie Devlin, and Kathryn Roeder, "Of Genes and IQ," in Devlin et al., *Intelligence, Genes, and Success*, 45–70; Marcus W. Feldman, Sarah P. Otto, and Freddy B. Christiansen, "Genes, Culture, and Inequality," in Arrow, Bowles, and Durlauf, *Meritocracy and Economic Inequality*, 61–85.

19. Feldman, Otto, and Christiansen, "Genes, Culture, and Inequality," 65; Bernie Devlin, Michael Daniels, and Kathryn Roeder, "The Heritability of IQ," *Nature* 388 (July 31, 1997): 468–71; Robert Plomin, "Genetics and General Cognitive Ability," *Nature* 402 (December 2, 1999): C25–C29.

20. Plomin, "Genetics and General Cognitive Ability," C26–C27; Eric Turkheimer et al., "Socioeconomic Status Modifies Heritability of IQ in Young Children," *Psychological Science* 14, no. 6 (November 2003): 623–28.

21. See Daniels, Devlin, and Roeder, "Of Genes and IQ," 64–65, and Daniel P. Resnick and Stephen E. Fienberg, "Science, Public Policy, and *The Bell Curve*," in Devlin et al., *Intelligence, Genes, and Success*, 329.

22. Herrnstein and Murray, *Bell Curve*, 389.

23. Herrnstein and Murray, *Bell Curve*, 416 (italics added).

24. James J. Heckman, "Lessons from the Bell Curve," *Journal of Political Economy* 103, no. 3 (October 1995): 1110–11.

25. Douglas Wahlsten, "The Malleability of Intelligence Is Not Constrained by Heritability," in Devlin et al., *Intelligence, Genes, and Success*, 71–87; see also Richard E. Nisbett, *Intelligence and How to Get It: Why Schools and Culture Count* (New York: Norton, 2009), 21–38.

26. On the efficacy of interventions to raise intelligence, see Fischer et al., *Inequality by Design*, chapter 7; Richard Nisbett, "Race, IQ, and Scientism," in Fraser, *The Bell Curve Wars*, 44–48; Christopher Winship and Sanders Korenman, "Does Staying in School Make You Smarter? The Effect of Education on IQ in *The Bell Curve*," in Devlin et al., *Intelligence, Genes, and Success*, 215–34.

27. Wahlsten, "The Malleability of Intelligence," 71.

28. Daniels, Devlin, and Roeder, "Of Genes and IQ," 66.

29. Nisbett, *Intelligence and How to Get It*, 119–52; James J. Heckman, "Lifelines for Poor Children," *New York Times*, September 15, 2013.

30. Orley Ashenfelter and Cecilia Rouse, "Schooling, Intelligence, and Income in America," in Arrow, Bowles, and Durlauf, *Meritocracy and Economic Inequality*, 111.

31. Herrnstein and Murray, *Bell Curve*, 127, 135.

32. For a detailed analysis of the AFQT, see Fischer et al., *Inequality by Design*, 40–42, 55–69; see also Heckman, "Lessons from the Bell Curve," 1109–10.

33. Janet Currie and Duncan Thomas, "The Intergenerational Transmission of 'Intelligence': Down the Slippery Slopes of *The Bell Curve*," *Industrial Relations* 38, no. 3 (July 1999): 297–330.

34. See Douglas S. Massey, "Review Essay," *American Journal of Sociology* 101, no. 3 (November 1995): 752, and Stephen Jay Gould, "Curveball," in Fraser, *The Bell Curve Wars*, 19.

35. Kohn, "Two Visions," 39. For overviews of the conceptual, measurement, and statistical problems with Herrnstein and Murray's index of SES, see Fischer et al., *Inequality by Design*, chapter 4, and Knapp et al., *The Assault on Equality*, appendix 1.

36. Herrnstein and Murray, *Bell Curve*, 386.

37. See Fischer et al., *Inequality by Design*, chapter 4.

38. Fischer et al., *Inequality by Design*; Knapp et al., *Assault on Equality*; Sanders Korenman and Christopher Winship, "A Reanalysis of *The Bell Curve*," Working Paper No. 5230 (Washington, DC: National Bureau of Economic Research, 1995).

39. Herrnstein and Murray, *Bell Curve*, appendix 4. On the weak correlations reported by Herrnstein and Murray, see Gould, "Curveball," 18–20, and Howard Gardner, "Cracking Open the IQ Box," in Fraser, *The Bell Curve Wars*, 26–27.

40. Herrnstein and Murray, *Bell Curve*, 101.

41. John Cawley et al., "Cognitive Ability, Wages, and Meritocracy," in Devlin et al., *Intelligence, Genes, and Success*, 180, 190. See also John Cawley, James Heckman, and Ed-

ward Vytlacil, "Meritocracy in America: Wages within and across Occupations," *Industrial Relations* 38, no. 3 (July 1999): 250–96.

42. Herrnstein and Murray, *Bell Curve*, 117; see Fischer et al., *Inequality by Design*, 242n12.

43. On the "individualistic bias" of *The Bell Curve*, see Knapp et al., *The Assault on Equality*, 15–16, 219–21. Kohn also criticizes Herrnstein and Murray's "reductionist" approach, which ignores social structure and proposes explanations "entirely at the level of the individual." Kohn, "Two Visions," 35–36.

44. Herrnstein and Murray, *Bell Curve*, 511–12; for a critique, see Knapp et al., *The Assault on Equality*, chapter 3.

45. For a sustained critique of the meritocracy thesis, see Stephen J. McNamee and Robert K. Miller Jr., *The Meritocracy Myth*, 3rd ed. (Lanham, MD: Rowman & Littlefield, 2014).

46. Valerie E. Lee and David T. Burkam, *Inequality at the Starting Gate: Social Background Differences in Achievement as Children Begin School* (Washington, DC: Economic Policy Institute, 2002); Marcia K. Meyers et al., "Inequality in Early Childhood Education and Care: What Do We Know?," in *Social Inequality*, ed. Kathryn M. Neckerman (New York: Russell Sage, 2004), 223–69; Betty Hart and Todd R. Risley, *Meaningful Differences in the Everyday Experience of Young American Children* (Baltimore, MD: Paul H. Brookes, 1995).

47. Jonathan Kozol, *Savage Inequalities: Children in America's Schools* (New York: Crown, 1991); Jonathan Kozol, *The Shame of the Nation: The Restoration of Apartheid Schooling in America* (New York: Crown, 2005). On class and race inequities, see Meredith Phillips and Tiffani Chin, "School Inequality: What Do We Know?," in Neckerman, *Social Inequality*, 467–519.

48. Peter Sacks, *Tearing Down the Gates: Confronting the Class Divide in American Education* (Berkeley: University of California Press, 2007), 115.

49. Cawley et al., "Cognitive Ability, Wages, and Meritocracy," 180. See also Cawley, Heckman, and Vytlacil, "Meritocracy in America," 250–96.

50. On issues of gender and race, see Fischer et al., *Inequality by Design*, 88–91, 171–203.

51. Charles Tilly, *Durable Inequality* (Berkeley: University of California Press, 1998).

52. Fischer et al., *Inequality by Design*, 180–81.

53. On the confusion between causation and correlation in Herrnstein and Murray's analysis of the relationship between IQ and poverty, see Knapp et al., *The Assault on Equality*, 213, 218–19; Leon J. Kamin, "Lies, Damned Lies, and Statistics," in Jacoby and Glauberman, *The Bell Curve Debate*, 81–105; and K. C. Cole, "Innumeracy," in Jacoby and Glauberman, *The Bell Curve Debate*, 73–80.

54. Kohn, "Two Visions," 46.

55. Knapp et al., *The Assault on Equality*, 225.

56. Fischer et al., *Inequality by Design*, 18.

57. Turkheimer et al., "Socioeconomic Status Modifies Heritability." For a useful discussion of this and other relevant research, see also David C. Berliner, "Our Impoverished View of Educational Research," *Teachers College Record* 108, no. 6 (June 2006): 949–95.

58. Herrnstein and Murray, *Bell Curve*, 52.

59. See Knapp et al., *The Assault on Equality*, 82–85, 219–20, and Kohn, "Two Visions," 36. For an especially valuable discussion of this problem in *The Bell Curve*, see Fischer et al., *Inequality by Design*, 7–10 and chapter 5.

60. See Mark Robert Rank, *One Nation, Underprivileged: Why American Poverty Affects Us All* (New York: Oxford University Press, 2004), 50. Rank underlines the important distinction between two separate questions: "Who loses out at the economic game?" and "Why does the game produce losers in the first place?"

61. The 10 percent estimate comes from Fischer et al., *Inequality by Design*, 14.

# 3. THE CULTURAL THEORY OF POVERTY AND INEQUALITY

1. See, for example, Thomas Sowell, *Ethnic America: A History* (New York: Basic Books, 1981); Thomas Sowell, *Race and Culture: A World View* (New York: Basic Books, 1994); Lawrence E. Harrison, *Who Prospers? How Cultural Values Shape Economic and Political Success* (New York: Basic Books, 1992); and, more recently, Amy Chua and Jed Rubenfeld, *The Triple Package: How Three Unlikely Traits Explain the Rise and Fall of Cultural Groups in America* (New York: Penguin, 2014).

2. For two excellent critiques of this cultural theory of ethnic inequality, see Stephen Steinberg, *The Ethnic Myth: Race, Ethnicity, and Class in America*, updated and expanded ed. (Boston: Beacon Press, 1989), and William Darity Jr., "What's Left of the Economic Theory of Discrimination?," in *The Question of Discrimination: Racial Inequality in the U.S. Labor Market*, ed. Steven Shulman and William Darity Jr. (Middletown, CT: Wesleyan University Press, 1989), 335–74.

3. On the origins and development of the culture of poverty theory, see Alice O'Connor, *Poverty Knowledge: Social Science, Social Policy, and the Poor in Twentieth-Century U.S. History* (Princeton, NJ: Princeton University Press, 2001), 99–123, 196–210; Michael Katz, *The Undeserving Poor: America's Enduring Confrontation with Poverty*, 2nd ed. (New York: Oxford University Press, 2013), 9–29, 50–68.

4. Michael Harrington, *The Other America: Poverty in the United States* (New York: Macmillan, 1993 [1962]). On the circumstances of the publication, reception, and influence of this book, see Maurice Isserman, *The Other American: The Life of Michael Harrington* (New York: PublicAffairs, 2000), 195–220. On the culture of poverty theory in Harrington and after, see Barbara Ehrenreich, "Rediscovering Poverty," *The Nation*, April 2, 2012, 4, 6. For an overview of Harrington's argument and how his perspective on poverty changed subsequent to the publication of *The Other America*, see Edward Royce, "Michael Harrington and the Discovery of Poverty," in *Critical Problems in Argumentation*, ed. Charles Arthur Willard (Middletown, CT: Wesleyan University Press, 1989), 771–78.

5. Lewis presented his version of the culture (or subculture) of poverty theory in a series of books and articles. See Oscar Lewis, "The Culture of Poverty," in *Explosive Forces in Latin America*, ed. John J. TePaske and Sydney Nettleton Fisher (Columbus: Ohio State University Press, 1964), 149–73; Oscar Lewis, "The Culture of Poverty," *Scientific American*, October 1966, 19–25; Oscar Lewis, *La Vida: A Puerto Rican Family in the Culture of Poverty—San Juan and New York* (New York: Vintage, 1966), xlii–lii; and Oscar Lewis, "The Culture of Poverty," in *On Understanding Poverty: Perspectives from the Social Sciences*, ed. Daniel Patrick Moynihan (New York: Basic Books, 1968), 187–200. For an illuminating reinterpretation of Lewis, see David L. Harvey and Michael H. Reed, "The Culture of Poverty: An Ideological Analysis," *Sociological Perspectives* 39, no. 4 (1996): 465–95.

6. William Ryan, *Blaming the Victim*, rev. and updated ed. (New York: Vintage, 1976).

7. On how the "vocabulary of poverty" has changed since the 1960s, see Michael Katz, *The Undeserving Poor: From the War on Poverty to the War on Welfare* (New York: Pantheon, 1989), 3–8.

8. Edward C. Banfield, *The Unheavenly City Revisited* (Boston: Little, Brown, 1974), 54.

9. Banfield, *The Unheavenly City Revisited*, 235.

10. Banfield, *The Unheavenly City Revisited*, 61, 72, 234–35.

11. Banfield, *The Unheavenly City Revisited*, 143.

12. Banfield, *The Unheavenly City Revisited*, 238, 269–70.

13. William A. Kelso, *Poverty and the Underclass: Changing Perceptions of the Poor in America* (New York: New York University Press, 1994), 170, 164.

14. Lawrence M. Mead, "A Biblical Response to Poverty," in *Lifting Up the Poor: A Dialogue on Religion, Poverty, and Welfare Reform*, ed. Mary Jo Bane and Lawrence M. Mead (Washington, DC: Brookings Institution Press, 2003), 70.

15. Mead, "A Biblical Response to Poverty," 67; Lawrence M. Mead, "A Reply to Bane," in Bane and Mead, *Lifting Up the Poor*, 121; see also Lawrence M. Mead, *The New Politics of Poverty: The Nonworking Poor in America* (New York: Basic Books, 1992), 143–45.

16. Mead, "A Reply to Bane," 121–22.

17. Mead, "A Biblical Response to Poverty," 62–66; Mead, *The New Politics of Poverty*, 110–32.

18. Charles Murray, "The Hallmark of the Underclass," *Wall Street Journal*, September 29, 2005.

19. Myron Magnet, *The Dream and the Nightmare: The Sixties' Legacy to the Underclass* (New York: Morrow, 1993), 38–39.

20. Magnet, *The Dream and the Nightmare*, 16.

21. Daniel Patrick Moynihan, *The Negro Family: The Case for National Action*, U.S. Department of Labor, Office of Policy Planning and Research (Washington, DC: Government Printing Office, March 1965), 29. The full text of this report, with the original pagination, is included in Lee Rainwater and William L. Yancey, eds., *The Moynihan Report and the Politics of Controversy* (Cambridge, MA: MIT Press, 1967).

22. Moynihan, *The Negro Family*, 5, 30.

23. Moynihan, *The Negro Family*, 47.

24. Mead, *The New Politics of Poverty*, 149; see also Harrison, *Who Prospers*, 207–11.

25. Dinesh D'Souza, *The End of Racism: Principles for a Multiracial Society* (New York: Free Press, 1995), 24, 100.

26. D'Souza, *The End of Racism*, 24, 477–524.

27. A recent exchange between Ta-Nehisi Coates and Jonathan Chait on black culture and the culture of poverty can be found at http://www.theatlantic.com/politics/archive/2014/03/other-peoples-pathologies/359841.

28. Magnet, *The Dream and the Nightmare*, offers the most fully developed rendition of this thesis; see also Kelso, *Poverty and the Underclass*, 154–56, and Joel Schwartz, *Fighting Poverty with Virtue: Moral Reform and America's Urban Poor, 1825–2000* (Bloomington: Indiana University Press, 2000), 145–49.

29. Magnet, *The Dream and the Nightmare*, 17.

30. Magnet, *The Dream and the Nightmare*, 19–20.

31. Kelso, *Poverty and the Underclass*, 34, 155–56.

32. The most influential example of this argument is Charles Murray, *Losing Ground: American Social Policy, 1950–1980* (New York: Basic Books, 1984).

33. George Gilder, *Wealth and Poverty* (New York: Basic Books, 1981), 69.

34. Harrison, *Who Prospers*, 211.

35. Cited in Charles M. Blow, "Poverty Is Not a State of Mind," *New York Times*, May 19, 2014.

36. Gilder, *Wealth and Poverty*, 68–70.

37. Schwartz, *Fighting Poverty with Virtue*.

38. Kelso, *Poverty and the Underclass*, 181.

39. Dick Armey, *The Freedom Revolution* (Washington, DC: Regnery Publishing, 1995), 228–33.

40. Marvin Olasky, *The Tragedy of American Compassion*, preface by Charles Murray (Washington, DC: Regnery Gateway, 1992); Marvin Olasky, *Renewing American Compassion*, foreword by Newt Gingrich (New York: Free Press, 1996); Marvin Olasky, *Compassionate Conservatism: What It Is, What It Does, and How It Can Transform America*, foreword by George W. Bush (New York: Free Press, 2000).

41. Newt Gingrich, "A Citizen's Guide for Helping the Poor," foreword to Olasky, *Renewing American Compassion*, ix–xiv.

42. Lawrence M. Mead, "The Rise of Paternalism," in *The New Paternalism: Supervisory Approaches to Poverty*, ed. Lawrence M. Mead (Washington, DC: Brookings Institution Press, 1997), 11, 20; see also Lawrence M. Mead, *Beyond Entitlement: The Social Obligations of Citizenship* (New York: Free Press, 1986).

43. For an excerpt from the text of PRWORA, see Gwendolyn Mink and Rickie Solinger, eds., *Welfare: A Documentary History of U.S. Policy and Politics* (New York: New York University Press, 2003), 642–47.

44. For an analysis of the "work first" philosophy, see Gordon Lafer, "Job Training for Welfare Recipients: A Hand Up or a Slap Down?," in *Work, Welfare, and Politics: Confronting Poverty in the Wake of Welfare Reform*, ed. Frances Fox Piven et al. (Eugene: University of Oregon Press, 2002), 175–95.

45. For a critique, based upon longitudinal data from the Panel Study of Income Dynamics, challenging all of these claims, see Mary Corcoran et al., "Myth and Reality: The Causes and Persistence of Poverty," *Journal of Policy Analysis and Management* 4, no. 4 (Summer 1985): 516–36.

46. Jens Ludwig and Susan Mayer, "'Culture' and the Intergenerational Transmission of Poverty: The Prevention Paradox," *The Future of Children* 16, no. 2 (Fall 2006): 175–96.

47. See Rebecca M. Blank, *It Takes a Nation: A New Agenda for Fighting Poverty* (New York: Russell Sage; Princeton, NJ: Princeton University Press, 1997), 13–23.

48. Indeed, contrary to popular imagery, the suburban poor substantially outnumber the urban poor; see Alan Berube and Elizabeth Kneebone, *Two Steps Back: City and Suburban Poverty Trends, 1995–2005* (Washington, DC: Brookings Institution, December 2006); Elizabeth Kneebone and Alan Berube, *Confronting Suburban Poverty in America* (Washington, DC: Brookings Institute Press, 2013).

49. On the dynamics of poverty, see John Iceland, *Poverty in America: A Handbook*, 2nd ed. (Berkeley: University of California Press, 2006), 48–49.

50. Mark Robert Rank, *One Nation, Underprivileged: Why American Poverty Affects Us All* (Oxford: Oxford University Press, 2004), 88–95.

51. Rank, *One Nation, Underprivileged*, 106–7.

52. For an excellent discussion of this point, see Michael Zweig, *The Working Class Majority: America's Best Kept Secret* (Ithaca, NY: Cornell University Press, 2000), 77–93.

53. Bradley R. Schiller, *The Economics of Poverty and Discrimination*, 9th ed. (Upper Saddle River, NJ: Pearson Prentice Hall, 2004), 65.

54. For critiques of the "underclass" label, see Herbert J. Gans, *The War against the Poor: The Underclass and Antipoverty Policy* (New York: Basic Books, 1995), and Leslie Inniss and Joe R. Feagin, "The Black 'Underclass' Ideology in Race Relations Analysis," *Social Justice* 16, no. 4 (Winter 1989): 13–34.

55. Mike Rose, "The Inner Life of the Poor," *Dissent* (Summer 2013): 71.

56. Magnet, *The Dream and the Nightmare*, 38–55.

57. For a good discussion of the questionable logic and methodology of the cultural theory, see Schiller, *The Economics of Poverty*, 141–44.

58. Mead, *New Politics of Poverty*, 148.

59. Banfield, *The Unheavenly City Revisited*, 235.

60. Magnet, *The Dream and the Nightmare*, 38–39.

61. Jacquelin W. Scarbrough, "Welfare Mothers' Reflections on Personal Responsibility," *Journal of Social Issues* 57, no. 2 (Summer 2001): 261–76.

62. William Julius Wilson, *When Work Disappears: The World of the New Urban Poor* (New York: Knopf, 1996), 180.

63. Jennifer L. Hochschild, *Facing Up to the American Dream: Race, Class, and the Soul of the Nation* (Princeton, NJ: Princeton University Press, 1995), 55–88; Alford A. Young Jr., *The Minds of Marginalized Black Men: Making Sense of Mobility, Opportunity, and Future Life Chances* (Princeton, NJ: Princeton University Press, 2004), 107–55.

64. Sandra L. Barnes, "Achievement or Ascription Ideology? An Analysis of Attitudes about Future Success for Residents in Poor Urban Neighborhoods," *Sociological Focus* 35, no. 2 (May 2002): 207–25.

65. Naomi Farber, "The Significance of Aspirations among Unmarried Adolescent Mothers," *Social Service Review* 63, no. 4 (December 1989): 523.

66. Rachel K. Jones and Ye Luo, "The Culture of Poverty and African-American Culture: An Empirical Assessment," *Sociological Perspectives* 42, no. 3 (1999): 454.

67. Joel E. Devine and James D. Wright, *The Greatest of Evils: Urban Poverty and the American Underclass* (New York: Aldine de Gruyter, 1993), 127.

68. Young, *The Minds of Marginalized Black Men*, 157.

69. On Ryan, see Charles M. Blow, "Paul Ryan, Culture and Poverty," *New York Times*, March 22, 2014.

70. See, for example, Wilson, *When Work Disappears*, 179–81, 251.

71. Roberta Rehner Iversen and Naomi Farber, "Transmission of Family Values, Work, and Welfare among Poor Urban Black Women," *Work and Occupations* 23, no. 4 (November 1996): 437–60.

72. Marta Tienda and Haya Stier, "Joblessness and Shiftlessness: Labor Force Activity in Chicago's Inner City," in *The Urban Underclass*, ed. Christopher Jencks and Paul E. Peterson (Washington, DC: Brookings Institution, 1991), 151.

73. Daniel Dohan, *The Price of Poverty: Money, Work, and Culture in the Mexican American Barrio* (Berkeley: University of California Press, 2003), 64.

74. See, for example, Haya Stier and Marta Tienda, *The Color of Opportunity: Pathways to Family, Welfare, and Work* (Chicago: University of Chicago Press, 2001), 157–62; Mark Robert Rank, *Living on the Edge: The Realities of Welfare in America* (New York: Columbia University Press, 1994), 111–27; and Alejandra Marchevsky and Jeanne Theoharis, *Not Working: Latina Immigrants, Low-Wage Jobs, and the Failure of Welfare Reform* (New York: New York University Press, 2006).

75. Iversen and Farber, "Transmission of Family Values," 446.

76. Stephen M. Petterson, "Are Young Black Men Really Less Willing to Work?," *American Sociological Review* 62, no. 4 (August 1997): 605–13; see also Stier and Tienda, *The Color of Opportunity*, 205–12.

77. John Schmitt, *Low-Wage Lessons* (Washington, DC: Center for Economic and Policy Research, January 2012), http://www.cepr.net/documents/publications/low-wage-2012-01.pdf (accessed May 10, 2012).

78. Bureau of Labor Statistics, *Economic News Release*, table A-8, http://www.bls.gov/news.release/empsit.t08.htm (accessed May 9, 2014). See also Steven Greenhouse, "A Part-

Time Life, as Hours Shrink and Shift," *New York Times*, October 28, 2012; Catherine Rampell, "For Millions, Part-Time Work Is Full-Time Wait for a Better Job," *New York Times*, April 20, 2013.

79. See Peter Van Buren, "Why Don't the Unemployed Get Off Their Couches? And Eight Other Critical Questions for Americans," *The UNZ Review: An Alternative Media Selection*, June 3, 2014, http://www.unz.com/article/why-dont-the-unemployed-get-off-their-couches (accessed August 7, 2014).

80. See, for example, Richard B. Freeman, "Employment and Earnings of Disadvantaged Young Men in a Labor Shortage Economy," in Jencks and Peterson, *The Urban Underclass*, 103–21, and Paul Osterman, "Gains from Growth? The Impact of Full Employment on Poverty in Boston," in Jencks and Peterson, *The Urban Underclass*, 122–34. For an overview of these and other studies, see David M. Gordon, *Fat and Mean: The Corporate Squeeze of Working Americans and the Myth of Managerial "Downsizing"* (New York: Free Press, 1996), 131–35.

81. Lawrence Mishel, Jared Bernstein, and Sylvia Allegretto, *The State of Working America, 2004/2005* (Ithaca, NY: Cornell University Press, 2005), 315.

82. See L. Randall Wray and Marc-Andre Pigeon, "Can a Rising Tide Raise All Boats? Evidence from the Clinton-Era Expansion," *Journal of Economic Issues* 34, no. 4 (December 2000): 811–45.

83. See Ronald B. Mincy, ed., *Black Males Left Behind* (Washington, DC: Urban Institute Press, 2006), and Peter Edelman, Harry J. Holzer, and Paul Offner, eds., *Reconnecting Disadvantaged Young Men* (Washington, DC: Urban Institute Press, 2006).

84. Alford A. Young Jr., "On the Outside Looking In: Low-Income Black Men's Conception of Work Opportunity and the Good Job," in *Coping with Poverty: The Social Contexts of Neighborhood, Work, and Family in the African-American Community*, ed. Sheldon H. Danziger and Ann Chic Lin (Ann Arbor: University of Michigan Press, 2000), 141–71; Andrew L. Reaves, "Black Male Employment and Self-Sufficiency," in Danziger and Lin, *Coping with Poverty*, 172–97.

85. See Devah Pager, "The Mark of a Criminal Record," *American Journal of Sociology* 108, no. 5 (March 2003): 937–75, and Bruce Western, Jeffrey R. Kling, and David F. Weiman, "The Labor Market Consequences of Incarceration," *Crime and Delinquency* 47, no. 3 (July 2001): 410–27.

86. See, for example, Scarbrough, "Welfare Mothers' Reflections on Personal Responsibility," 261–76; Kathryn Edin and Laura Lein, *Making Ends Meet: How Single Mothers Survive Welfare and Low-Wage Work* (New York: Russell Sage, 1997), 60–142; and Sandra Danziger et al., "Barriers to the Employment of Welfare Recipients," in *Prosperity for All? The Economic Boom and African Americans*, ed. Robert Cherry and William M. Rodgers III (New York: Russell Sage, 2000), 245–78.

87. Daniel T. Lichter, Christie D. Batson, and J. Brian Brown, "Welfare Reform and Marriage Promotion: The Marital Expectations and Desires of Single and Cohabiting Mothers," *Social Service Review* 78, no. 1 (March 2004): 21; see also Janice Wood, "Has the Battle over the Value of Marriage Been Won?," *PsychCentral*, July 2012, http://psychcentral.com/news/2012/07/22/has-the-battle-over-the-value-of-marriage-been-won/42062.html (accessed July 17, 2014).

88. Kathryn Edin and Maria Kefalas, *Promises I Can Keep: Why Poor Women Put Motherhood before Marriage* (Berkeley: University of California Press, 2005), 6.

89. Naomi Farber, "The Significance of Race and Class in Marital Decisions among Unmarried Adolescent Mothers," *Social Problems* 37, no. 1 (February 1990): 54.

90. Robin L. Jarrett, "Living Poor: Family Life among Single Parent, African American Women," *Social Problems* 41, no. 1 (February 1994): 36.

91. Edin and Kefalas, *Promises I Can Keep*; Elijah Anderson, *Code of the Street: Decency, Violence, and the Moral Life of the Inner City* (New York: Norton, 1999), 142–78; Kristen Luker, *Dubious Conceptions: The Politics of Teenage Pregnancy* (Cambridge, MA: Harvard University Press, 1996), 134–74.

92. William Julius Wilson, *The Truly Disadvantaged: The Inner City, the Underclass, and Public Policy* (Chicago: University of Chicago Press, 1987), 95–106.

93. Farber, "The Significance of Race and Class," 58.

94. Jarrett, "Living Poor," 38.

95. See Edin and Kefalas, *Promises I Can Keep*, 71–103, 111–19, 125–28; Luker, *Dubious Conceptions*, 158–60; and Wilson, *When Work Disappears*, 98–99, 102–5.

96. Edin and Kefalas, *Promises I Can Keep*, 47–49.

97. Edin and Kefalas, *Promises I Can Keep*, 106–7, 111–12, 119–24.

98. Edin and Kefalas, *Promises I Can Keep*, 130.

99. See Annie Lowry, "For Richer, For Poorer," *New York Times Magazine*, February 9, 2014; Kristi Williams, *Promoting Marriage among Single Mothers: An Ineffective Weapon in the War on Poverty* (Miami, FL: Council on American Families, June 2014), https://contemporaryfamilies.org/marriage-ineffective-in-war-on-poverty-report (accessed May 9, 2014).

100. Zweig, *The Working Class Majority*, 91.

101. Schwartz, *Fighting Poverty with Virtue*, 137.

102. Schwartz, *Fighting Poverty with Virtue*, xiv.

103. The concept of "higher immorality" comes from C. Wright Mills, *The Power Elite* (New York: Oxford University Press, 1956), 343–61.

104. Fred Block, "A Moral Economy," *The Nation*, March 20, 2006, 16–19.

# 4. THE HUMAN CAPITAL THEORY OF POVERTY AND INEQUALITY

1. Bradley R. Schiller, *The Economics of Poverty and Discrimination*, 9th ed. (Upper Saddle River, NJ: Prentice-Hall, 2004), 2.

2. The theory of human capital as presented in texts in labor economics and numerous technical books and articles addresses an assortment of issues. Poverty is only a minor concern in much of the literature, though the explanation for poverty implied by this theory is very influential, both in policy circles and in the public consciousness. My critique of human capital theory is narrowly focused on one central claim: that people are poor because they are deficient in education, skills, and work experience. For the classic statement of the theory of human capital, broadly conceived, see Gary S. Becker, *Human Capital: A Theoretical and Empirical Analysis, with Special Reference to Education*, 2nd ed. (Chicago: University of Chicago Press, 1975). For a more recent overview, see Jacob Mincer, "Human Capital: A Review," in *Labor Economics and Industrial Relations: Markets and Institutions*, ed. Clark Kerr and Paul D. Staudohar (Cambridge, MA: Harvard University Press, 1994), 109–41.

3. Alice H. Amsden, "Introduction," in *The Economics of Women and Work*, ed. Alice H. Amsden (New York: St. Martin's, 1980), 16.

4. E. Michael Foster, "Labor Economics and Public Policy: Dominance of Constraints or Preferences?," in *Labor Economics: Problems in Analyzing Labor Markets*, ed. William Darity Jr. (Boston: Kluwer, 1993), 269–94; Stephen A. Woodbury, "Culture and Human Capital:

Theory and Evidence or Theory versus Evidence," in *Labor Economics*, 239–67; Stephen Steinberg, "Human Capital: A Critique," *Review of Black Radical Political Economy* 14, no. 1 (Summer 1985): 67–74.

5. Randy Albelda, Robert Drago, and Steve Shulman, *Unlevel Playing Fields: Understanding Wage Inequality and Discrimination* (New York: McGraw-Hill, 1997), 125.

6. Jon Elster, *Sour Grapes: Studies in the Subversion of Rationality* (Cambridge: Cambridge University Press, 1983), 109–40.

7. See David M. Gordon, *Theories of Poverty and Underemployment* (Lexington, MA: D. C. Heath, 1972), 38; Eric A. Schutz, *Inequality and Power: The Economics of Class* (New York: Routledge, 2011), esp. 18–62.

8. Katherine Boo, "After Welfare," *New Yorker*, May 14, 2001, 98.

9. Milton Friedman and Rose Friedman, *Free to Choose: A Personal Statement* (New York: Avon, 1981).

10. See, for example, Richard D. Kahlenberg, *Left Behind: Unequal Opportunity in Higher Education* (New York: Century Foundation, 2004); Mamie Lynch, Jennifer Engle, and José L. Cruz, *Priced Out: How the Wrong Financial Aid Policies Hurt Low-Income Students* (Washington, DC: Education Trust, June 2011), 12, http://www.edtrust.org/sites/edtrust.org/files/PricedOutFINAL.pdf (accessed April 1, 2014).

11. Elizabeth Warren and Amelia Warren Tyagi, *The Two-Income Trap: Why Middle-Class Parents Are Going Broke* (New York: Basic Books, 2003), 32–46.

12. For an insightful historical study illuminating this point, see Jean Anyon, *Ghetto Schooling: A Political Economy of Urban Educational Reform* (New York: Teachers College, Columbia University, 1997).

13. See Richard Rothstein, *Class and Schools: Using Social, Economic, and Educational Reform to Close the Black-White Achievement Gap* (Washington, DC: Economic Policy Institute, 2004).

14. See, for example, Heidi Shierholz, Alyssa Davis, and Will Kimball, *The Class of 2014: The Weak Economy Is Idling Too Many Young Graduates* (Washington, DC: Economic Policy Institute, May 2014), http://s2.epi.org/files/2014/class-of-2014.pdf (accessed May 3, 2014).

15. Howard M. Wachtel, *Labor and the Economy*, 3rd ed. (Fort Worth, TX: Dryden Press, Harcourt Brace Jovanovich, 1992), 204n15.

16. On inequality among workers with equivalent human capital characteristics, see Lawrence Mishel, Josh Bivens, Elise Gould, and Heidi Shierholz, *The State of Working America*, 12th ed. (Ithaca, NY: Cornell University Press, 2012), 213–14, 228–32, and Richard B. Freeman, *America Works: The Exceptional U.S. Labor Market* (New York: Russell Sage, 2007), 46–47.

17. Edward N. Wolff, *Does Education Really Help? Skill, Work, and Inequality* (Oxford: Oxford University Press, 2006), 11–15.

18. See Barbara Ehrenreich, *Bait and Switch: The (Futile) Pursuit of the American Dream* (New York: Metropolitan Books, 2005); Louis Uchitelle, *The Disposable American: Layoffs and Their Consequences* (New York: Knopf, 2006).

19. Heidi Shierholz, "Long-Term Unemployment Is Elevated across All Education, Age, Occupation, Industry, Gender, and Racial and Ethnic Groups," *Economic Policy Institute Blog*, April 2014, http://s4.epi.org/files/2013/Class-of-2013-graduates-job-prospects.pdf (accessed April 30, 2014).

20. Dalton Conley, *The Pecking Order: A Bold New Look at How Family and Society Determine Who We Become* (New York: Vintage, 2004), 125; see also Damon Darlin, "More Pounds, Few Dollars," *New York Times*, December 2, 2006.

21. I will discuss the disadvantages associated with gender and race/ethnicity and the problem of discrimination more fully in chapters 9 and 10.

22. For an overview of some of the relevant data and competing explanations for gender and racial inequality, see Barbara F. Reskin and Irene Padavic, "Sex, Race, and Ethnic Inequality," in *Handbook of the Sociology of Gender*, ed. Janet Saltzman Chafetz (New York: Kluwer Academic/Plenum, 1999), 343–74.

23. See Vincent J. Roscigno, *The Face of Discrimination: How Race and Gender Impact Work and Home Lives* (Lanham, MD: Rowman & Littlefield, 2007).

24. Pierre Bourdieu, "The Forms of Capital," in *Handbook of Theory and Research for the Sociology of Education*, ed. John G. Richardson (New York: Greenwood, 1986), 241–58.

25. Bourdieu, "Forms of Capital," 243–45.

26. Stephen J. McNamee and Robert K. Miller Jr., *The Meritocracy Myth*, 3rd ed. (Lanham, MD: Rowman & Littlefield, 2014), 17, 77, 85–89.

27. Yasemin Besen-Cassino, "Cool Stores Bad Jobs," *Contexts* 12, no. 4 (Fall 2013): 42–47.

28. See Gordon Lafer, *The Job Training Charade* (Ithaca, NY: Cornell University Press, 2002), 67–77; George Farkas, "Cognitive Skills and Noncognitive Traits and Behaviors in Stratification Processes," *Annual Review of Sociology* 29 (2003): 541–62; James J. Heckman, "Hard Evidence on Soft Skills," *Focus* 29, no. 2 (Fall–Winter 2012–2013): 3–8.

29. Peter Cappelli, "Is the 'Skills Gap' Really about Attitudes?," *California Management Review* 37, no. 4 (Summer 1995): 108–24.

30. Richard C. Edwards, "Individual Traits and Organizational Incentives: What Makes a 'Good' Worker?," *Journal of Human Resources* 11, no. 1 (Winter 1976): 51–68.

31. Edwards, "Individual Traits and Organization Incentives," 58–59.

32. Roger Waldinger and Michael I. Lichter, *How the Other Half Works: Immigration and the Social Organization of Labor* (Berkeley: University of California Press, 2003), 15.

33. Barbara Ehrenreich, *Nickel and Dimed: On (Not) Getting By in America* (New York: Henry Holt, Metropolitan, 2001), 110–11.

34. The concept of "cheerful robot" comes from C. Wright Mills, *The Sociological Imagination* (New York: Oxford University Press, 1959), 175.

35. Ehrenreich, *Nickel and Dimed*, 210–11; see also Randy Hodson, *Dignity at Work* (New York: Cambridge University Press, 2001).

36. Samuel Bowles and Herbert Gintis, "Does Schooling Raise Earnings by Making People Smarter?," in *Meritocracy and Economic Inequality*, ed. Kenneth Arrow, Samuel Bowles, and Steven N. Durlauf (Princeton, NJ: Princeton University Press, 2000), 125; see also Samuel Bowles, Herbert Gintis, and Robert Szarka, "Escalating Differences and Elusive 'Skills': Cognitive Abilities and the Explanation of Inequality," in *Race, Poverty, and Domestic Policy*, ed. Michael Henry (New Haven, CT: Yale University Press, 2004), 431–48.

37. On the socialization function of schools, see Samuel Bowles and Herbert Gintis, "Schooling in Capitalist America Revisited," *Sociology of Education* 75, no. 1 (January 2002): 12–14.

38. I will discuss social networks and social capital more fully in chapter 7.

39. Nan Lin, "Inequality in Social Capital," *Contemporary Sociology* 29, no. 6 (November 2000): 787.

40. William Julius Wilson, *The Truly Disadvantaged: The Inner City, the Underclass, and Public Policy* (Chicago: University of Chicago Press, 1987), 60.

41. Katherine Newman, *No Shame in My Game: The Working Poor in the Inner City* (New York: Knopf, 1999), 77–85, 161–74.

42. Deirdre A. Royster, *Race and the Invisible Hand: How White Networks Exclude Black Men from Blue-Collar Jobs* (Berkeley: University of California Press, 2003), 115.

43. Andrew Weiss, *Efficiency Wages: Models of Unemployment, Layoffs, and Wage Dispersion* (Princeton, NJ: Princeton University Press, 1990).

44. On this point, and for an influential analysis of the implications challenging human capital theory's understanding of the labor market, see Lester C. Thurow, *Generating Inequality: Mechanism of Distribution in the U.S. Economy* (New York: Basic Books, 1975), 75–97.

45. William A. Darity Jr., "The Human Capital Approach to Black-White Earnings Inequality: Some Unsettled Questions," *Journal of Human Resources* 17, no. 1 (Winter 1982): 84.

46. I will address the shortage of jobs more fully in chapter 5.

47. Ruy A. Teixeira and Lawrence Mishel, "Whose Skills Shortage—Workers or Management?," *Issues in Science and Technology* 9, no. 4 (Summer 1993): 69.

48. D. W. Livingstone, *The Education-Jobs Gap: Underemployment or Economic Democracy* (Boulder, CO: Westview, 1998); see also D. W. Livingstone, ed., *Education and Jobs: Exploring the Gaps* (Toronto: University of Toronto Press, 2009).

49. Frederic L. Pryor and David L. Schaffer, *Who's Not Working and Why: Employment, Cognitive Skills, Wages, and the Changing U.S. Labor Market* (New York: Cambridge University Press, 1999), 74.

50. Stephen Vaisey, "Education and Its Discontents: Overqualification in America, 1972–2002," *Social Forces* 85, no. 2 (December 2006): 835–64. Vaisey's high estimate counts workers as overqualified if they have at least one year of education beyond that required for the job; his low estimate uses a three-year benchmark. On the problem of overqualification, see also Arne L. Kalleberg, *The Mismatched Worker* (New York: Norton, 2007), 69–98.

51. Richard Bedder, Christopher Denhart, and Jonathan Robe, *Why Are Recent College Graduates Underemployed? University Enrollments and Labor-Market Realities* (Washington, DC: Center for College Affordability and Productivity, January 2013), esp., 12–24, http://centerforcollegeaffordability.org/uploads/Underemployed%20Report%202.pdf (accessed May 3, 2014); see also Jaison R. Abel, Richard Deitz, and Yaqin Su, "Are Recent College Graduates Finding Good Jobs?," *Current Issues in Economics and Finance* 20, no. 1 (2014): 1–8, http://www.newyorkfed.org/research/current_issues/ci20-1.pdf (accessed May 3, 2014). On underemployment in the form of involuntary part-time work, see Arjun Jayadev and Michael Konczal, *The Stagnant Labor Market* (New York: Roosevelt Institute, September 2010), 5–10, http://www.rooseveltinstitute.org/sites/all/files/stagnant_labor_market.pdf (accessed May 3, 2014).

52. Pryor and Schaffer, *Who's Not Working and Why*, 4; Paul Beaudry, David A. Green, and Benjamin M. Sand, "The Great Reversal in the Demand for Skill and Cognitive Tasks," Working Paper 18901 (Cambridge, MA: National Bureau of Economic Research, March 2013).

53. See, for example, Beth Shulman, *The Betrayal of Work: How Low-Wage Jobs Fail 30 Million Americans* (New York: New Press, 2003).

54. Catherine Rampell, "It Takes a B.A. to Find a Job as a File Clerk," *New York Times*, February 20, 2013.

## 5. THE ECONOMIC SYSTEM AND POVERTY

1. Motoko Rich, "For the Unemployed Over 50, Fears of Never Working Again," *New York Times*, September 20, 2010; Alan Feuer, "Life on $7.25 an Hour," *New York Times*, December 1, 2013; Michael Powell, "Hauling Bags and Cleaning Planes for Little Pay and No Vacations of Their Own," *New York Times*, January 16, 2014; Steven Greenhouse, "On Register's Other Side, Little Money to Spend," *New York Times*, November 29, 2013; Robbie

Brown, "Mounting Bills and Pessimism," *New York Times*, December 4, 2010; Jennifer Medina, "Hardship Makes a New Home in the Suburbs," *New York Times*, May 10, 2014.

2. Binyamin Applebaum, "A Scarred U.S. Economy: Complete Recovery Looks Distant as Growth Lingers at Only 2%," *New York Times*, June 12, 2014; Paul Krugman, "A Permanent Slump?," *New York Times*, November 18, 2013.

3. Hilary W. Hoynes, Marianne E. Page, and Ann Huff Stevens, "Poverty in America: Trends and Explanations," *Journal of Economic Perspectives* 20, no. 1 (Winter 2006): 47–68.

4. Stephen A. Marglin and Juliet B. Schor, eds., *The Golden Age: Reinterpreting the Postwar Experience* (New York: Oxford University Press, 1990).

5. Harold Meyerson, "The Forty-Year Slump," *American Prospect* (September–October 2013): 20–33.

6. Edward N. Wolff, *Does Education Really Help? Skill, Work, and Inequality* (Oxford: Oxford University Press, 2006), 3–17.

7. Jacob C. Hacker, *The Great Risk Shift: The Assault on American Jobs, Families, Health Care, and Retirement—And How You Can Fight Back* (Oxford: Oxford University Press, 2006).

8. Sheldon H. Danziger and Robert H. Haveman, "The Evolution of Poverty and Antipoverty Policy," in *Understanding Poverty*, ed. Sheldon H. Danziger and Robert H. Haveman (New York: Russell Sage; Cambridge, MA: Harvard University Press, 2001), 13.

9. Josh Bivens, Elise Gould, Lawrence Mishel, and Heidi Shierholz, *Raising America's Pay: Why It's Our Central Economic Policy Challenge* (Washington, DC: Economic Policy Institute, June 2014), 11, 19, http://s2.epi.org/files/2014/Raising-America%27s-Pay-2014-Report.pdf (accessed June 6, 2014).

10. Thomas Piketty, *Capital in the Twenty-First Century*, trans. Arthur Goldhammer (Cambridge, MA: Belknap Press of Harvard University Press, 2014), 294–97.

11. Joseph Stiglitz, *The Price of Inequality* (New York: Norton, 2012), 3; see also Jacob S. Hacker and Paul Pierson, *Winner-Take-All Politics: How Washington Made the Rich Richer—And Turned Its Back on the Middle Class* (New York: Simon & Schuster, 2010), 12–25.

12. Richard B. Freeman, *America Works: The Exceptional U.S. Labor Market* (New York: Russell Sage, 2007), 32–40.

13. Bivens et al., *Raising America's Pay*, 6–7, 33.

14. Isabel V. Sawhill, "Poverty in the U.S.: Why Is It So Persistent?," *Journal of Economic Literature* 26, no. 3 (September 1988): 1092.

15. For a summary and detailed critique of the theory of skill-biased technological change, see Lawrence Mishel, Heidi Shierholz, and John Schmitt, *Don't Blame the Robots: Assessing the Job Polarization Explanation of Growing Wage Inequality* (Washington, DC: Economic Policy Institute, November 2013), http://s1.epi.org/files/2013/technology-inequality-dont-blame-the-robots.pdf (accessed June 17, 2014).

16. For devastating critiques of the education and training solution to problems of unemployment, inequality, and poverty, see Gordon Lafer, *The Job Training Charade* (Ithaca, NY: Cornell University Press, 2002), and Louis Uchitelle, *The Disposable American: Layoffs and Their Consequences* (New York: Knopf, 2006), 64–79.

17. Piketty, *Capital in the Twenty-First Century*, 304–8, 314; Paul Krugman, "Graduates versus Oligarchs," *New York Times*, February 27, 2006.

18. Michael J. Handel, *Implications of Information Technology for Employment, Skills, and Wages: A Review of Recent Research* (Arlington, VA: SRI International, July 2003), 25–26; Ian Dew-Becker and Robert J. Gordon, "Where Did the Productivity Growth Go? Inflation Dynamics and the Distribution of Income," *Brookings Papers on Economic Activity*, 2005, no. 2, 117–18.

19. Lawrence Mishel, Josh Bivens, Elise Gould, and Heidi Shierholz, *The State of Working America*, 12th ed. (Ithaca, NY: Cornell University Press, 2012), 286–91.

20. Arne L. Kalleberg, *The Mismatched Worker* (New York: Norton, 2007), 199–202.

21. Wolff, *Does Education Really Help?*, 12–14; Mishel, Bivens, Gould, and Shierholz, *The State of Working America*, 211–16.

22. Peter Gottschalk, "Inequality, Income Growth, and Mobility: The Basic Facts," *Journal of Economic Perspectives* 11, no. 2 (Spring 1997): 30.

23. Mishel, Bivens, Gould, and Shierholz, *The State of Working America*, 216, 178, fig. 4A, 302–5.

24. Jared Bernstein and Lawrence Mishel, "Seven Reasons for Skepticism about the Technology Story of U.S. Wage Inequality," in *Sourcebook of Labor Markets: Evolving Structures and Processes*, ed. Ivar Berg and Arne L. Kalleberg (New York: Kluwer, 2001), 414.

25. Lafer, *The Job Training Charade*, 61; see also Kim A. Weeden, "Why Do Some Occupations Pay More than Others? Social Closure and Earnings Inequality in the United States," *American Journal of Sociology* 108, no. 1 (July 2002): 55–101.

26. Mishel, Bivens, Gould, and Shierholz, *The State of Working America*, 299–301; Michael J. Handel, *Worker Skills and Job Requirements: Is There a Mismatch?* (New York: Economic Policy Institute, 2005).

27. Paul Beaudry, David A. Green, and Benjamin M. Sand, *The Great Reversal in the Demand for Skill and Cognitive Tasks*, Working Paper 18901 (Cambridge, MA: National Bureau of Economic Research, March 2013); Heidi Shierholz, *Is There Really a Shortage of Skilled Workers?* (Washington, DC: Economic Policy Institute, January 2014), http://www.epi.org/publication/shortage-skilled-workers (accessed June 13, 2014); see also Heidi Shierholz, Alyssa Davis, and Will Kimball, *The Class of 2014: The Weak Economy Is Idling Too Many Young Graduates* (Washington, DC: Economic Policy Institute, May, 2014), http://s2.epi.org/files/2014/Classof2014FINAL.pdf (accessed June 13, 2014).

28. U.S. Department of Labor, Bureau of Labor Statistics, *Employment Projections—2012–2022* (December 19, 2013), table 5, http://www.bls.gov/news.release/pdf/ecopro.pdf (accessed June 10, 2014); see also Mishel, Bivens, Gould, and Shierholz, *The State of Working America*, 305–9.

29. Phillip Moss, "Earnings Inequality and the Quality of Jobs: Current Research and a Research Agenda," in *Corporate Governance and Sustainable Prosperity*, ed. William Lazonick and Mary O'Sullivan (New York: Palgrave, 2002), 201; see also James S. Mosher, "U.S. Wage Inequality, Technological Change, and Decline in Union Power," *Politics & Society* 35, no. 2 (June 2007): 225–64.

30. For criticisms of this view, see Handel, *Implications of Information Technology*; Lafer, *The Job Training Charade*, 53–57; and Moss, "Earnings Inequality," 197–201, 205–11.

31. James K. Galbraith, *Created Unequal: The Crisis in American Pay* (New York: Free Press, 1998), 31.

32. Wolff, *Does Education Really Help?*, 65.

33. On the numerous timing problems associated with the thesis of skill-biased technological change, see Lawrence Mishel, Jared Bernstein, and Sylvia Allegretto, *The State of Working America, 2004/2005* (Ithaca, NY: Cornell University Press, 2005), 206–8; David Howell, "Skills and the Wage Collapse," *American Prospect* 11, no. 15 (June 19–July 3, 2000): 74–75; and David Card and John E. DiNardo, "Skill-Biased Technological Change and Rising Wage Inequality: Some Problems and Puzzles," *Journal of Labor Economics* 20, no. 4 (October 2002): 733–83.

34. Galbraith, *Created Unequal*, 34–35.

35. David R. Howell, "Increasing Earnings Inequality and Unemployment in Developed Countries: Markets, Institutions, and the 'Unified Theory,'" *Politics & Society* 30, no. 2 (June 2002): 198–203; Peter Gottschalk and Timothy M. Smeeding, "Cross-National Comparisons of Earnings and Income Inequality," *Journal of Economic Literature* 35, no. 2 (June 1997): 633–87.

36. See Piketty, *Capital in the Twenty-First Century*, 315–21; Thomas A. DiPrete, "What Has Sociology to Contribute to the Study of Inequality Trends? A Historical and Comparative Perspective," *American Behavioral Scientist* 50, no. 5 (January 2007): 603–18.

37. Frank Levy and Peter Temin, "Inequality and Institutions in 20th Century America," Working Paper 17-17 (Cambridge, MA: Massachusetts Institute of Technology, May 1, 2007), http://www.newamerica.net/files/Inequality%20May%201%20 External.pdf (accessed December 30, 2007).

38. For examples of the "power shift" argument, see Thomas I. Palley, *Plenty of Nothing: The Downsizing of the American Dream and the Case for Structural Keynesianism* (Princeton, NJ: Princeton University Press, 1998); David M. Gordon, *Fat and Mean: The Corporate Squeeze of Working Americans and the Myth of Managerial "Downsizing"* (New York: Martin Kessler Books, Free Press, 1996); Beth Shulman, *The Betrayal of Work: How Low-Wage Jobs Fail 30 Million Americans and Their Families* (New York: New Press, 2003); and Chuck Collins and Felice Yeskel, *Economic Apartheid in America: A Primer on Economic Inequality and Insecurity*, rev. and updated ed. (New York: New Press, 2005).

39. Freeman, *America Works*, 109–27.

40. On the "crisis of profitability" in the late 1960s and after, and the response of employers, see Robert Brenner, *The Economics of Global Turbulence: The Advanced Capitalist Economies from Long Boom to Long Downturn, 1945–2005* (London: Verso, 2006), 274–75; on corporate restructuring, see Bennett Harrison and Barry Bluestone, *The Great U-Turn: Corporate Restructuring and the Polarization of America* (New York: Basic Books, 1990), 11–13, 38–52.

41. This and the following paragraph draw mainly on Gordon, *Fat and Mean*, 5–8, 61–94; see also Arne Kalleberg, *Good Jobs, Bad Jobs: The Rise of Polarized and Precarious Employment Systems in the United States, 1970s to 2000s* (New York: Russell Sage, 2011), 36–40, 72–73, and, for a somewhat different perspective, see Paul Osterman and Beth Shulman, *Good Jobs America: Making Work Better for Everyone* (New York: Russell Sage, 2011), 48–69.

42. Neil Fligstein, "Politics, the Reorganization of the Economy, and Income Inequality, 1980–2009," *Politics & Society* 38, no. 2 (May 2010): 233–42; Steven Pearlson, "When Shareholder Capitalism Came to Town," *American Prospect* (March–April 2014): 40–48; Kalleberg, *Good Jobs, Bad Jobs*, 28.

43. Floyd Norris, "Corporate Profits Grow and Wages Slide," *New York Times*, April 15, 2014; see also Lawrence Mishel, *Economy Built for Profits Not Prosperity* (Washington, DC: Economic Policy Institute, March 2013), http://www.foreconomicjustice.org/7485/economy-built-for-profits-not-prosperity (accessed June 13, 2014).

44. Tali Kristal, "The Capitalist Machine: Computerization, Workers' Power, and the Decline in Labor's Share within U.S. Industries," *American Sociological Review* 78, no. 3 (June 2013): 361–89; see also Jared Bernstein, "Why Labor's Share of Income Is Falling," *Economix* (blog), September 9, 2013, http://economix.blogs.nytimes.com/2013/09/09/why-labors-share-of-income-is-falling (accessed June 13, 2014).

45. Mishel, Bivens, Gould, and Shierholz, *The State of Working America*, 236, fig. 4U; Bivens et al., *Raising America's Pay*, 10.

46. Dew-Becker and Gordon, "Where Did the Productivity Growth Go?," 67–127.

47. Gordon, *Fat and Mean*, 81–82.

48. Lawrence Mishel and Alyssa David, *CEO Pay Continues to Rise as Typical Workers Are Paid Less* (Washington, DC: Economic Policy Institute, June 2014), http://s1.epi.org/files/2014/ceo-pay-continues-to-rise.pdf (accessed June 13, 2014).

49. Steven Greenhouse, "As Factory Jobs Disappear, Ohio Town Has Few Options," *New York Times*, September 13, 2003.

50. Jefferson Cowie and Joseph Heathcott, "Introduction: The Meanings of Deindustrialization," in *Beyond the Ruins: The Meanings of Deindustrialization*, ed. Jefferson Cowie and Joseph Heathcott (Ithaca, NY: Cornell University Press, 2003), 2.

51. Barry Bluestone and Bennett Harrison, *The Deindustrialization of America: Plant Closings, Community Abandonment, and the Dismantling of Basic Industry* (New York: Basic Books, 1982).

52. Bluestone and Harrison, *The Deindustrialization of America*, 6.

53. Charles Craypo and David Cormier, "Job Restructuring as a Determinant of Wage Inequality and Working-Poor Households," *Journal of Economic Issues* 34, no. 1 (March 2000): 21–42. For a personal account of the process of deindustrialization in Southeast Chicago by the daughter of a worker at Wisconsin Steel Works, see Christine J. Walley, "Deindustrializing Chicago: A Daughter's Story," in *The Insecure American: How We Got Here and What We Should Do about It*, ed. Hugh Gusterson and Catherine Besteman (Berkeley: University of California Press, 2010), 113–39.

54. Craypo and Cormier, "Job Restructuring," 26, table 2.

55. Craypo and Cormier, "Job Restructuring," 36–37.

56. For an important contribution toward understanding how the process of deindustrialization varies by place and period, see Cowie and Heathcott, *Beyond the Ruins*.

57. *The Economic Report of the President* (Washington, DC: Government Printing Office, 2006), 336, table B-46.

58. *Economic Report of the President* (Washington, DC: Government Printing Office, 2014), 382, table 14.

59. The "goods-producing" sector includes natural resources and mining, construction, and manufacturing, both durable and non-durable. The "service-providing" sector includes trade, transportation, and utilities; information; financial activities; professional and business services; education and health services; leisure and hospitality; and other services. Agricultural employment and government employment are separate categories. These classifications come from *The Economic Report of the President* (2014), 382, table B14.

60. Bureau of Labor Statistics, *Employment Projections—2012–2022*, table 5.

61. Annette Bernhardt et al., *Divergent Paths: Economic Mobility in the New American Labor Market* (New York: Russell Sage, 2001), 53–57.

62. For a useful discussion of how deindustrialization produces growing inequality as a result of industry changes in the composition of the workforce, see François Nielsen and Arthur S. Alderson, "Trends in Income Inequality in the United States," in Berg and Kalleberg, *Sourcebook of Labor Markets*, 363, 371–72.

63. Joseph R. Meisenheimer II, "The Service Industry in the 'Good' versus 'Bad' Jobs Debate," *Monthly Labor Review* 121, no. 2 (February 1998): 45.

64. Ruth Milkman, *Farewell to the Factory: Auto Workers in the Late Twentieth Century* (Berkeley: University of California Press, 1997), 43.

65. Milkman, *Farewell to the Factory*, 22–50.

66. Steven Rattner, "The Myth of Industrial Rebound," *New York Times*, January 26, 2014.

67. See Meisenheimer, "The Service Industry."

68. Mishel, Bivens, Gould, and Shierholz, *The State of Working America*, 247–48.

69. Marc Levinson, *The Box: How the Shipping Container Made the World Smaller and the World Economy Bigger* (Princeton, NJ: Princeton University Press, 2006).

70. Palley, *Plenty of Nothing*, 30, 80–83.

71. Collins and Yeskel, *Economic Apartheid in America*, 88.

72. Anonymous, "This Time, Get Global Trade Right," *New York Times*, April 20, 2014.

73. Stiglitz, *The Price of Inequality*, 59.

74. Harrison and Bluestone, *The Great U-Turn*, 8–10.

75. Mishel, Bivens, Gould, and Shierholz, *The State of Working America*, 254–55; Richard B. Freeman, "Globalization and Inequality," in *The Oxford Handbook of Economic Inequality*, ed. Wiemer Salverda, Brian Nolan, and Timothy M. Smeeding (Oxford: Oxford University Press, 2009), 582.

76. Freeman, *America Works*, 128–29; Freeman, "Globalization and Inequality," 577–79. See also Dani Rodrik, *Has Globalization Gone Too Far?* (Washington, DC: Institute for International Economics, 1997), 11–27.

77. See Aaron Bernstein, "Shaking Up Trade Theory," *BusinessWeek*, December 6, 2004, 116–20.

78. The format of my analysis here and some of the specific arguments borrow from Mishel, Bivens, Gould, and Shierholz, *The State of Working America*, 253–54.

79. Louis Uchitelle, "Made in the U.S.A. (Except for the Parts)," *New York Times*, April 8, 2005.

80. Ralph Blumenthal, "As Levi's Work Is Exported, Stress Stays Home," *New York Times*, October 19, 2003.

81. Charles Duhigg and Keith Bradsher, "How the U.S. Lost Out on iPhone Work," *New York Times*, January 22, 2012.

82. See Freeman, "Globalization and Inequality," 579–80; Alan Blinder, "Offshoring: The Next Industrial Revolution?," *Foreign Affairs* 85, no. 2 (March–April 2006): 113–28; L. Josh Bivens, *Offshoring*, EPI Issue Guide (Washington, DC: Economic Policy Institute, May 2006), http://www.epinet.org/issueguides/offshoring/epi_issue_guide_on_offshoring.pdf (accessed January 1, 2008).

83. Adrian Wood, "How Trade Hurts Unskilled Workers," *Journal of Economic Perspectives* 9, no. 3 (Summer 1995): 67.

84. Eduardo Porter, "In U.S. Groves, Cheap Labor Means Machines," *New York Times*, March 22, 2004.

85. Aaron Bernstein, "The Global Economy," *BusinessWeek*, August 10, 1992, 48.

86. Mishel, Bivens, Gould, and Shierholz, *The State of Working America*, 254.

87. Kate Bronfenbrenner, *Uneasy Terrain: The Impact of Capital Mobility on Workers, Wages, and Union Organizing* (Washington, DC: U.S. Trade Deficit Review Commission, 2000), 18, 46–47, 53.

88. Greenspan cited in Jim Stanford, "Power, Employment, and Accumulation," introduction to *Power, Employment, and Accumulation: Social Structures in Economic Theory and Practice*, ed. Jim Stanford, Lance Taylor, and Ellen Houston (Armonk, NY: M. E. Sharpe, 2001), 5.

89. Steven Greenhouse, "Falling Fortunes of the Wage Earner," *New York Times*, April 12, 2005.

90. Steven Greenhouse, "Employers Take a United Stand in Insisting on Labor Concessions," *New York Times*, July 11, 2003.

91. Stiglitz, *The Price of Inequality*, 61–62, 80.

92. Charles E. Lindblom, *Politics and Markets: The World's Political-Economic Systems* (New York: Basic Books, 1977), 170–88.

93. James Crotty, "The Case for International Capital Controls," in *Unconventional Wisdom: Alternative Perspectives on the New Economy*, ed. Jeff Madrick (New York: Century Foundation Press, 2000), 279.

94. On the threat posed by globalization to the social welfare state, see Rodrik, *Has Globalization Gone Too Far?*, 6, 49–67.

95. On globalization and democracy, both in the United States and in the developing world, see Stiglitz, *The Price of Inequality*, 138–45.

96. On the concept of neoliberal globalization, see Collins and Yeskel, *Economic Apartheid in America*, 87–96, and Dan Clawson, *The Next Upsurge: Labor and the New Social Movements* (Ithaca, NY: Cornell University Press, 2003), 131–63.

97. See Shulman, *The Betrayal of Work*, 111–12, and Jay R. Mandle, *Democracy, America, and the Age of Globalization* (New York: Cambridge University Press, 2008).

98. Eduardo Porter, "At the Polls, Choose Your Capitalism," *New York Times*, October 31, 2012; see also Stiglitz, *The Price of Inequality*, 277–78.

99. Arne L. Kalleberg, "Nonstandard Employment Relations: Part-Time, Temporary, and Contract Work," *Annual Review of Sociology* 26 (2000): 342–65; Kalleberg, *Good Jobs, Bad Jobs*, 75, 75–77; see also Katherine V. W. Stone, *The Decline in the Standard Employment Contract: Evidence from Ten Advanced Industrial Countries* (Los Angeles, CA: UCLA Institute for Research on Labor and Employment, December 2012), http://law.ucla.edu/~/media/Files/UCLA/Law/Pages/Publications/CEN_ICLP_PUB%20Decline%20Standard%20Contract.ashx (accessed June 16, 2014).

100. Robert Kuttner, "The Task Rabbit Economy," *American Prospect* (September/October 2013): 47.

101. Lance Morrow, "The Temping of America," *Time*, March 29, 1993, 40–41.

102. Janice Castro, "Disposable Workers," *Time*, March 29, 1993, 43–47.

103. Arne L. Kalleberg, Barbara F. Reskin, and Ken Hudson, "Bad Jobs in America: Standard and Nonstandard Employment Relations and Job Quality in the United States," *American Sociological Review* 65, no. 2 (April 2000): 256–78; Ken Hudson, "The Disposable Worker," *Monthly Review* 52, no. 11 (April 2001): 43–55; and U.S. Department of Labor, Bureau of Labor Statistics, *Contingent and Alternative Employment Arrangements, February 2005* (Washington, DC: Government Printing Office, July 27, 2005).

104. Abel Valenzuela Jr. et al., *On the Corner: Day Labor in the United States* (National Day Labor Study, January 2006), http://www.sscnet.ucla.edu/issr/csup/uploaded_files/Natl_DayLabor-On_the_Corner1.pdf (accessed October 22, 2014); see also Abel Valenzuela Jr., "Day Labor Work," *Annual Review of Sociology* 29 (2003): 307–33.

105. Steven Greenhouse, "Front Line in Day Laborer Battle Runs Right Outside Home Depot," *New York Times*, October 10, 2005.

106. For more detailed information on the characteristics of day laborers, see Valenzuela et al., *On the Corner*, 17–21.

107. Valenzuela et al., *On the Corner*, 9, table 3.

108. Valenzuela et al., *On the Corner*, 10.

109. Kirk Semple, "Immigrant Day Laborers, Far From Home and Losing Hope," *New York Times*, October 20, 2008.

110. Fernanda Santos, "In the Shadows, Day Laborers Left Homeless as Work Vanishes," *New York Times*, January 2, 2010.

111. Valenzuela, "Day Labor Work," 309.

112. Rebecca Smith, "Legal Protections and Advocacy for Contingent or 'Casual' Workers in the United States: A Case Study in Day Labor," *Social Indicators Research*, 2008, 197–213.

113. Valenzuela et al., *On the Corner*, 12–16; Roben Farzad, "The Urban Migrants," *New York Times*, July 20, 2005; Eyal Press, "The New Suburban Poverty," *The Nation*, April 23, 2007, 20–22.

114. Kalleberg, "Nonstandard Employment Relations," 346–47. On the origins and expansion of the temp industry, see Erin Hatton, *The Temp Economy: From Kelly Girls to Perma-temps in Postwar America* (Philadelphia: Temple University Press, 2011).

115. Lawrence Mishel, Jared Bernstein, and Sylvia Allegretto, *The State of Working America, 2006/2007* (Ithaca, NY: Cornell University Press, 2007), 239; see also Tian Luo, Amar Mann, and Richard Holden, "The Expanding Role of Temporary Help Services from 1990 to 2008," *Monthly Labor Review* (August 2010): 3–16.

116. Motoko Rich, "Weighing Costs, Companies Favor Temporary Help," *New York Times*, December 20, 2010; Jeff Green, "Temporary Workers Near U.S. Record Makes Kelly a Winner," *Bloomberg News*, May 10, 2013, http://www.bloomberg.com/news/2013-05-10/temporary-workers-near-u-s-record-makes-kelly-a-winner.html (accessed June 14, 2014); Charles Wilbanks, "Temp Work Raises Long-Term Questions for Economy," *Moneywatch*, March 7, 2013, http://www.cbsnews.com/news/temp-work-raises-long-term-questions-for-economy (accessed June 14, 2014).

117. See Miranda Deitz, *Temporary Workers in California Are Twice as Likely as Non-Temps to Live in Poverty: Problems with Temporary and Subcontracted Work in California* (Berkeley, CA: UC Berkeley Labor Center, August 2012), http://laborcenter.berkeley.edu/jobquality/temp_workers.pdf (accessed June 14, 2014), and Michael Grabell, "The Expendables: How the Temps Who Power Corporate Giants Are Getting Crushed," *ProPublica*, June 27, 2013, http://www.propublica.org/article/the-expendables-how-the-temps-who-power-corporate-giants-are-getting-crushe (accessed June 15, 2014).

118. Rich, "Weighing Costs."

119. Hatton, *The Temp Economy*, 68–78.

120. Camille Colastosti, "A Job without a Future," *Dollars & Sense*, May 1992, 9–11, 21; Hatton, *The Temp Economy*, 84.

121. Kalleberg, *The Mismatched Worker*, 181.

122. Kalleberg, *The Mismatched Worker*, 178–81; Chris Tilly, *Half a Job: Bad and Good Part-Time Jobs in a Changing Labor Market* (Philadelphia: Temple University Press, 1996), 1–5, 20–23.

123. Bureau of Labor Statistics, *Table A-8. Employed Persons by Class of Worker and Part-Time Status*, Economic News Release, June 6, 2014, http://www.bls.gov/news.release/empsit.t08.htm (accessed June 16, 2014).

124. Steven Greenhouse, "A Part-Time Life, as Hours Shrink and Shift," *New York Times*, October 28, 2012; Catherine Rampell, "For Millions, Part-Time Work Is Full-Time Wait for a Better Job," *New York Times*, April 20, 2013.

125. National Employment Law Project, *The Low-Wage Recovery: Industry Employment and Wages Four Years into the Recovery* (New York: National Employment Law Project, April, 2014), http://www.nelp.org/page/-/Reports/Low-Wage-Recovery-Industry-Employment-Wages-2014-Report.pdf?nocdn=1 (accessed June 16, 2014); Catherine Rampell, "Majority of Jobs Added in the Recovery Pay Low Wages, Study Finds," *New York Times*, August 31, 2012; Annie Lowrey, "Recovery Has Created Far More Low-Wage Jobs than Better-Paid Ones," *New York Times*, April 28, 2014.

126. National Employment Law Project, *Going Nowhere Fast: Limited Occupational Mobility in the Fast Food Industry* (New York: National Employment Law Project, July 2013), http://nelp.3cdn.net/84a67b124db45841d4_o0m6bq42h.pdf (accessed June 16, 2014).

127. Tilly, *Half a Job*, 20–23, 82–83, 145–53, 160–61.

128. Bernstein, "The Wage Squeeze," 55.

129. On rising job instability and its negative effect on workers' prospects for long-term success, see Bernhardt et al., *Divergent Paths*, 64–87.

130. See, for example, Annie Lowrey, "Long Out of Work, and Running Out of Options," *New York Times*, April 4, 2014; Floyd Norris, "For Long-Term Jobless, a Stubborn Trend," *New York Times*, November 30, 2013; Annie Lowrey and Catherine Rampell, "Jobless, and Hopeless, in America: Lingering Unemployment Poses a Long-Term Economic Risk," *New York Times*, November 2, 2012.

131. Economic Policy Institute, *Missing Workers: The Missing Part of the Unemployment Story* (Washington, DC: Economic Policy Institute, June 2014), http://www.epi.org/publication/missing-workers/ (accessed June 16, 2014).

132. On the decline of job quality, see John Schmitt and Janelle Jones, *Where Have All the Good Jobs Gone?* (Washington, DC: Center for Economic and Policy Research, July 2012), http://www.cepr.net/documents/publications/good-jobs-2012-07.pdf (accessed June 17, 2014).

133. On this distinction, see Philip Harvey, "Understanding the Unemployment Experience of Low-Wage Workers: Implications for Ethnographic Research," in *Laboring Below the Line: The New Ethnography of Poverty, Low-Wage Work, and Survival in the Global Economy*, ed. Frank Munger (New York: Russell Sage, 2002), 97.

134. Timothy Bartik, "Poverty, Jobs, and Subsidized Employment," *Challenge* 45, no. 3 (May–June 2002): 100–11.

135. Kalleberg, *The Mismatched Worker*, 188–89.

136. L. Randall Wray and Marc-Andre Pigeon, "Can a Rising Tide Raise All Boats? Evidence from the Clinton-Era Expansion," *Journal of Economic Issues* 34, no. 4 (December 2000): 811–45.

137. Wray and Pigeon, "Can a Rising Tide Raise All Boats?," 812.

138. Philip Harvey, "Combating Joblessness: An Analysis of the Principal Strategies That Have Influenced the Development of American Employment and Social Welfare Law during the 20th Century," *Berkeley Journal of Employment and Labor Law* 21 (2000): 679n3, 682, 705–9.

139. Harvey, "Combating Joblessness," 682.

140. Marlene Kim, "Are the Working Poor Lazy?," *Challenge* 41, no. 3 (May–June 1998): 97; see also Marlene Kim, "The Working Poor: Lousy Jobs or Lazy Workers?," *Journal of Economic Issues* 32, no. 1 (March 1998): 65–78.

141. Bivens et al., *Raising America's Pay*, 38.

142. Bob Sheak and Melissa Morris, "The Limits of the Job Supply in U.S. Capitalism," *Critical Sociology* 28, no. 3 (2002): 390.

143. Sheak and Morris, "The Limits of the Job Supply," 393–402.

144. Sheak and Morris, "The Limits of the Job Supply," 406–9.

145. Lafer, *The Job Training Charade*, 19–44. On his definition of "decently paying" jobs and his measurement procedures, see 26–32, 225–31.

146. Lafer, *The Job Training Charade*, 36, table 3.1.

147. Lafer, *The Job Training Charade*, 3.

148. Binyamin Appelbaum, "In Tepid Wage Growth, a Potent Sign of a Far-from-Healthy Economy," *New York Times*, May 5, 2014.

149. See, for example, Arjun Jayadev and Mike Konczal, *The Stagnating Labor Market* (New York: Roosevelt Institute, 2010), http://www.rooseveltinstitute.org/sites/all/files/stagnant_labor_market.pdf (accessed June 17, 2014).

150. National Employment Law Project, *The Low-Wage Recovery*; John Schmitt, *Low-Wage Lessons* (Washington, DC: Center for Economy and Policy Research, January 2012), http://

www.cepr.net/documents/publications/low-wage-2012-01.pdf (accessed June 17, 2014); Nelson Schwartz, "Payroll Data Shows a Lag in Wages, Not Just Hiring," *New York Times*, February 8, 2014.

151. David Leonhardt, "In Wreckage of Lost Jobs, Lost Power," *New York Times*, January 19, 2011.

152. See Lafer, *The Job Training Charade*, 41–44. The false assumption that what works to enable particular individuals to escape poverty will also work to reduce the overall rate of poverty is a central theme in Mark Rank's excellent book, *One Nation, Underprivileged: Why American Poverty Affects Us All* (New York: Oxford University Press, 2004). For a good discussion of the fallacy of inferring from the individual to the aggregate (the "fallacy of composition"), see Harvey, "Understanding the Unemployment Experience of Low-Wage Workers," 96.

# 6. THE POLITICAL SYSTEM AND POVERTY

1. For an insightful critique of the individualistic perspective from a "strongly political" standpoint, see David Brady, *Rich Democracies, Poor People: How Politics Explain Poverty* (Oxford: Oxford University Press, 2009), 3–19.

2. Timothy M. Smeeding, "Public Policy, Economic Inequality, and Poverty: The United States in Comparative Perspective," *Social Science Quarterly* 86, supplement (2005): 955–83; Andrea Brandolini and Timothy M. Smeeding, "Income Inequality in Richer and OECD Countries," in *The Oxford Handbook of Economic Inequality*, ed. Wiemer Salverda, Brian Nolan, and Timothy M. Smeeding (Oxford: Oxford University Press, 2009), 71–99.

3. Timothy M. Smeeding, "Poor People in Rich Nations: The United States in Comparative Perspective," *Journal of Economic Perspectives* 20, no. 1 (Winter 2006): 69–90; Brady, *Rich Democracies, Poor People*, 45–69.

4. See Michael Hout, Asaf Levanon, and Erin Cumberworth, "Job Loss and Unemployment," in *The Great Recession*, ed. David B. Grusky, Bruce Western, and Christopher Wimer (New York: Russell Sage, 2011), 59–81; Timothy M. Smeeding, Jeffrey P. Thompson, Asaf Levanon, and Esra Burak, "Poverty and Income Inequality in the Early Stages of the Great Recession," in Grusky, Western, and Thompson, *The Great Recession*, 82–126.

5. Lawrence Mishel, Josh Bivens, Elise Gould, and Heidi Shierholz, *The State of Working America*, 12th ed. (Ithaca, NY: Cornell University Press, 2012), 450–51.

6. Timothy M. Smeeding, Lee Rainwater, and Gary Burtless, "U.S. Poverty in a Cross-National Context," in *Understanding Poverty*, ed. Sheldon H. Danziger and Robert H. Haveman (New York: Russell Sage; Cambridge, MA: Harvard University Press, 2001), 181; see also Smeeding, "Poor People in Rich Nations," 85–86.

7. Mishel, Bivens, Gould, and Shierholz, *The State of Working America*, 448–49; David Brady, Andrew S. Fullerton, and Jennifer Moren Cross, "More than Just Nickels and Dimes: A Cross-National Analysis of Working Poverty in Affluent Democracies," *Social Problems* 57, no. 4 (November 2010): 559–85.

8. OECD Library, *Government Social Spending* (2013), http://www.oecd-ilibrary.org/social-issues-migration-health/government-social-spending_20743904-table1 (accessed June 30, 2014); Jay R. Mandle, *Democracy, America, and the Age of Globalization* (New York: Cambridge University Press, 2008), 30–36; Richard B. Freeman, *America Works: The Exceptional U.S. Labor Market* (New York: Russell Sage, 2007), 11–13.

9. Alberto Alesina and Edward L. Glaeser, *Fighting Poverty in the U.S. and Europe: A World of Difference* (Oxford: Oxford University Press, 2004), 17–20; see also Mandle, *Democracy, America, and the Age of Globalization*, 33–36.

10. Timothy M. Smeeding, "Government Programs and Social Outcomes: Comparison of the United States with Other Rich Nations," in *Public Policy and Income Distribution*, ed. Alan J. Auerbach, David Card, and John M. Quigley (New York: Russell Sage, 2006), 158.

11. See Lane Kenworthy, *Social Democratic America* (Oxford: Oxford University Press, 2014), 63–68 and fig. 3.6.

12. Alesina and Glaeser, *Fighting Poverty in the U.S. and Europe*, 21–23; Dan Zuberi, *Differences That Matter: Social Policy and the Working Poor in the United States and Canada* (Ithaca, NY: Cornell University Press, 2006), 67–85.

13. Janet C. Gornick and Marcia K. Meyers, *Families That Work: Policies for Reconciling Parenthood and Employment* (New York: Russell Sage, 2005), 41, table 2.1.

14. Gornick and Meyers, *Families That Work*, 121–46, 185–235; Sheila B. Kamerman, "Europe Advanced While the United States Lagged," in *Unfinished Work: Building Equality and Democracy in an Era of Working Families*, ed. Jody Heymann and Christopher Beem (New York: New Press, 2005), 321–24, 327–39.

15. Kamerman, "Europe Advanced While the United States Lagged," 310–21; Alesina and Glaeser, *Fighting Poverty in the U.S. and Europe*, 21–22.

16. Freeman, *America Works*, 7–19; Alesina and Glaeser, *Fighting Poverty in the U.S. and Europe*, 37–44; Zuberi, *Differences That Matter*, 86–107.

17. The data presented in this paragraph are from Smeeding, "Government Programs and Social Outcomes," 164–76; the poverty line in this study is set at "50 percent of median adjusted disposable income." See also Smeeding, "Public Policy, Economic Inequality, and Poverty," 973–75; Smeeding, "Poor People in Rich Nations," 79, table 4; and Jacob S. Hacker, Suzanne Mettler, and Dianne Pinderhughes, "Inequality and Public Policy," in *Inequality and American Democracy: What We Know and What We Need to Learn*, ed. Lawrence R. Jacobs and Theda Skocpol (New York: Russell Sage, 2005), 159–64.

18. See Mishel, Bivens, Gould, and Shierholz, *The State of Working America*, 452–54; Brian Nolan and Ive Marx, "Economic Inequality, Poverty, and Social Exclusion," in Salverda, Nolan, and Smeeding, *The Oxford Handbook of Economic Inequality*, 316–41; Janet C. Gornick and Markus Jäntti, "Child Poverty in Cross-National Perspective: Lessons from the Luxembourg Income Study," *Children and Youth Services Review* 34 (2012): 558–68.

19. Charles Murray, *Losing Ground: American Social Policy, 1950–1980* (New York: Basic Books, 1984).

20. Lane Kenworthy, "Do Social-Welfare Policies Reduce Poverty? A Cross-National Assessment," *Social Forces* 77, no. 3 (March 1999): 1119–39.

21. Cited in Jason DeParle, "In Debate on U.S. Poverty, 2 Studies Fuel an Argument on Who Is to Blame," *New York Times*, October 29, 1991.

22. Robert A. Dahl, *How Democratic Is the American Constitution?* (New Haven, CT: Yale University Press, 2002), 3; see also Sanford Levinson, *Our Undemocratic Constitution: Where the Constitution Goes Wrong (And How We the People Can Correct It)* (New York: Oxford University Press, 2006); and for a brief overview of the contemporary debate surrounding the U.S. Constitution, see Jeffrey Toobin, "Our Broken Constitution," *New Yorker*, December 9, 2013, 64–73.

23. My analysis in this section draws especially on Alesina and Glaeser, *Fighting Poverty in the U.S. and Europe*; Jeff Manza, "Unequal Democracy in America: The Long View," in *The New Gilded Age: The Critical Inequality Debates of Our Time*, ed. David B. Grusky and Tamar Kricheli-Katz (Stanford, CA: Stanford University Press, 2012), 131–58; Charles Noble, *Wel-*

*fare As We Knew It: A Political History of the American Welfare State* (New York: Oxford University Press, 1997); and Charles Noble, *The Collapse of Liberalism: Why America Needs a New Left* (Lanham, MD: Rowman & Littlefield, 2004).

24. On the characteristics of proportional representation systems, see Douglas J. Amy, *Behind the Ballot Box: A Citizen's Guide to Voting Systems* (Westport, CT: Praeger, 2000), 65–106, and for a convincing argument in favor of this system, see Douglas J. Amy, *Real Choices/New Voices: How Proportional Representation Elections Could Revitalize American Democracy*, 2nd ed. (New York: Columbia University Press, 2002).

25. Amy, *Real Choices/New Voices*, 177–79.

26. Alesina and Glaeser, *Fighting Poverty in the U.S. and Europe*, 81–87.

27. On the characteristics and operation of single-member-district, winner-take-all systems, and on their strengths and weaknesses, see Amy, *Behind the Ballot Box*, 27–63. For a thoroughgoing critique of the winner-take-all system, see Steven Hill, *Fixing Elections: The Failure of America's Winner Take All Politics* (New York: Routledge, 2002).

28. Hill, *Fixing Elections*, 279.

29. Torben Iverson and David Soskice, *Electoral Institutions, Parties, and the Politics of Class: Why Some Democracies Redistribute More than Others* (Berkeley, CA: Institute of Government Studies, 2005), http://repositories.cdlib.org/cgi/viewcontent.cgi?article=1092&context=igs (accessed December 31, 2007).

30. On the importance for poverty reduction of a strong left-wing political presence, see Brady, *Rich Democracies, Poor People*; Stephanie Moller et al., "Determinants of Relative Poverty in Advanced Capitalist Democracies," *American Sociological Review* 68, no. 1 (February 2003): 22–51; David Bradley et al., "Distribution and Redistribution in Postindustrial Democracies," *World Politics* 55, no. 2 (January 2003): 193–228; and David Brady, "The Politics of Poverty: Left Political Institutions, the Welfare State, and Poverty," *Social Forces* 82, no. 2 (December 2003): 557–82.

31. See Jules Lobel, "The Political Tilt of Separation of Powers," in *The Politics of Law: A Progressive Critique*, ed. David Kairys, 3rd ed. (New York: Basic Books, 1998), 591–616.

32. Alesina and Glaeser, *Fighting Poverty in the U.S. and Europe*, 90–93; Noble, *The Collapse of Liberalism*, 27, 31–33.

33. For an illustration of this process showing how corporate lobbyists and industry insiders managed to dictate the course of health-care reform, ensuring the priority of their interests over those of the general public, see Kevin Young and Michael Schwartz, "Healthy, Wealthy, and Wise: How Corporate Power Shaped the Affordable Care Act," *New Labor Forum* 23, no. 2 (May 2014): 30–40.

34. See Howard Rosenthal, "Politics, Public Policy, and Inequality: A Look Back at the Twentieth Century," in *Social Inequality*, ed. Kathryn M. Neckerman (New York: Russell Sage, 2004), 864–65.

35. Jacob S. Hacker and Paul Pierson, *Winner-Take-All Politics: How Washington Made the Richer Richer—And Turned Its Back on the Middle Class* (New York: Simon & Schuster, 2010), 43, 53, 83–85.

36. Noble, *The Collapse of Liberalism*, 27.

37. Alesina and Glaeser, *Fighting Poverty in the U.S. and Europe*, 87–90; Noble, *Welfare As We Knew It*, 28–30.

38. On the concept of "business confidence," see Fred Block, *Revising State Theory: Essays in Politics and Postindustrialism* (Philadelphia: Temple University Press, 1987), 59–62.

39. Charles E. Lindblom, *Politics and Markets: The World's Political-Economic Systems* (New York: Basic Books, 1977), 170–88.

40. See, for example, Louis Uchitelle, "States Pay for Jobs, but It Doesn't Always Pay Off," *New York Times*, November 10, 2003; Timothy Egan, "Towns Hand Out Tax Breaks, Then Cry Foul as Jobs Leave," *New York Times*, October 20, 2004; A. G. Sulzberger, "In War between States for Jobs, Businesses Stand to Gain Most," *New York Times*, April 8, 2011; Louise Story, "The Empty Promise of Tax Incentives," *New York Times*, December 2, 2012; Louise Story, "Lines Blur as Texas Gives Industries a Bonanza," *New York Times*, December 3, 2012; Louise Story, "Michigan Town Woos Hollywood, but Ends Up with a Bit Part," *New York Times*, December 4, 2012; and Andrew Ross Sorkin, "Renouncing Corporate Citizenship," *New York Times*, July 1, 2014. For an exposé showing how corporations shake down job-starved communities, see Greg LeRoy, *The Great American Jobs Scam: Corporate Tax Dodging and the Myth of Job Creation* (San Francisco: Berrett-Koehler, 2005).

41. See Brady, "The Politics of Poverty," 573–77.

42. Frances Fox Piven and Richard A. Cloward, *Poor People's Movements: Why They Succeed, How They Fail* (New York: Random House, 1977); Frances Fox Piven, *Challenging Authority: How Ordinary People Change America* (Lanham, MD: Rowman & Littlefield, 2006).

43. On the power shift in the political system, see Hacker and Pierson, *Winner-Take-All Politics*; Chuck Collins and Felice Yeskel, *Economic Apartheid in America: A Primer on Economic Inequality and Insecurity*, rev. and updated ed. (New York: New Press, 2005); Mark A. Smith, *The Right Talk: How Conservatives Transformed the Great Society into the Economic Society* (Princeton, NJ: Princeton University Press, 2007); and Beth Shulman, *The Betrayal of Work: How Low-Wage Jobs Fail 30 Million Americans and Their Families* (New York: New Press, 2003).

44. On the predicament of U.S. business in the early 1970s, see Edsall, *The New Politics of Inequality*, 112–14; Hacker and Pierson, *Winner-Take-All Politics*, 116–18; and Dan Clawson and Mary Ann Clawson, "Reagan or Business? Foundations of the New Conservatism," in *The Structure of Power in America: The Corporate Elite as a Ruling Class*, ed. Michael Schwartz (New York: Holmes & Meier, 1987), 201–4.

45. Cited in Leonard Silk and David Vogel, *Ethics and Profits: The Crisis of Confidence in American Business* (New York: Simon & Schuster, 1976), 72.

46. On the political mobilization of business in the 1970s and after, see Edsall, *New Politics*, 107–40; Hacker and Pierson, *Winner-Take-All Politics*, 118–36; Dan Clawson, Alan Neustadtl, and Mark Weller, *Dollars and Votes: How Business Campaign Contributions Subvert Democracy* (Philadelphia: Temple University Press, 1998), 146–66; Jerome L. Himmelstein, *To the Right: The Transformation of American Conservatism* (Berkeley: University of California Press, 1990), 129–64.

47. Clawson and Clawson, "Reagan or Business?," 205–7; John Micklethwait and Adrian Wooldridge, *The Right Nation: Conservative Power in America* (New York: Penguin, 2004), 76–80.

48. Edsall, *New Politics*, 120–23; G. William Domhoff, *Who Rules America? Power, Politics, and Social Change*, 5th ed. (Boston: McGraw-Hill, 2006), 101–2.

49. Clawson, Neustadtl, and Weller, *Dollars and Votes*, 150–54.

50. Collins and Yeskel, *Economic Apartheid in America*, 78.

51. Kay Lehman Schlozman, Sidney Verba, and Henry E. Brady, *The Unheavenly Chorus: Unequal Political Voice and the Broken Promise of American Democracy* (Princeton, NJ: Princeton University Press, 2012), 5–6, 117–262; Richard B. Freeman, "What, Me Vote?," in Neckerman, *Social Inequality*, 703–28.

52. Robert D. Putnam, *Bowling Alone: The Collapse and Revival of American Community* (New York: Simon & Schuster, 2000), 31–64. For a particularly informative analysis of class-

based changes in political participation, see Joe Soss and Lawrence R. Jacobs, "The Place of Inequality: Non-Participation in the American Polity," *Political Science Quarterly* 14, no. 1 (2009): 95–125.

53. Putnam, *Bowling Alone*, 216–75.

54. Robert Dahl, *On Political Equality* (New Haven, CT: Yale University Press, 2006), 87–91.

55. Thomas E. Patterson, *The Vanishing Voter: Public Involvement in an Age of Uncertainty* (New York: Vintage, 2003), 63–98.

56. Eric M. Uslaner, *Income Inequality in the United States Fuels Pessimism and Threatens Social Cohesion* (Washington, DC: Center for American Progress, December 2012), http://cdn.americanprogress.org/wp-content/uploads/2012/12/Uslaner.pdf (accessed August 7, 2014). See also Soss and Jacobs, "The Place of Inequality"; Joseph Stiglitz, *The Price of Inequality* (New York: Norton, 2012), 118–29; Doug McAdam, "The Politics of Occupy: Now and Looking Ahead," in *Occupy the Future*, ed. David B. Grusky, Doug McAdam, Rob Reich, and Debra Satz (Cambridge: MIT Press, 2013), 173; Elizabeth A. Bennett et al., "Disavowing Politics: Civic Engagement in an Era of Political Skepticism," *American Journal of Sociology* 119, no. 2 (September 2013): 518–48.

57. Manza, "Unequal Democracy," 135–38; Jean Chung, *Felony Disenfranchisement: A Primer* (Washington, DC: Sentencing Project, April 2014), http://www.sentencingproject.org/doc/publications/fd_Felony%20Disenfranchisement%20Primer.pdf (accessed July 2, 2014); Scott Keyes, Ian Millhiser, Tobin Van Ostern, and Abraham White, *Voter Suppression 101: How Conservatives Are Conspiring to Disenfranchise Millions of Americans* (Washington, DC: Center for American Progress, April 2012), http://cdn.americanprogress.org/wp-content/uploads/issues/2012/04/pdf/voter_supression.pdf (accessed July 2, 2014).

58. U.S. Department of Labor, Bureau of Labor Statistics, *Union Members—2013* (January 24, 2014), http://www.bls.gov/news.release/pdf/union2.pdf (accessed July 1, 2014); John Schmitt and Alexandra Mitukiewicz, *Politics Matters: Changes in Unionization Rates in Rich Countries, 1960–2010* (Washington, DC: Center for Economic and Policy Research, November 2011), http://www.cepr.net/documents/publications/unions-oecd-2011-11.pdf (accessed July 3, 2014). For a comprehensive analysis of the decline of organized labor in the United States, see Jake Rosenfeld, *What Unions No Longer Do* (Cambridge, MA: Harvard University Press, 2014).

59. Bruce Western and Jake Rosenfeld, "Unions, Norms, and the Rise in U.S. Wage Inequality," *American Sociological Review* 76, no. 4 (August 2011): 513–37; David Brady, Regina S. Baker, and Ryan Finnigan, "When Unionization Disappears: State Level Unionization and Working Poverty in the United States," *American Sociological Review* 78, no. 5 (October 2013): 872–96; Colin Gordon, "The Union Difference: Labor and American Inequality," in *Growing Apart: A Political History of American Inequality* (June 1, 2014), http://scalar.usc.edu/works/growing-apart-a-political-history-of-american-inequality/what-unions-did-labor-policy-and-american-inequality (accessed July 3, 2014); Lawrence Mishel, *Unions, Inequality, and Faltering Middle-Class Wages* (Washington, DC: Economic Policy Institute, August 2012), http://s2.epi.org/files/2012/ib342-unions-inequality-middle-class-wages.pdf (accessed July 3, 2014).

60. Rick Fantasia and Kim Voss, *Hard Work: Remaking the American Labor Movement* (Berkeley: University of California Press, 2004), 23–25.

61. Gordon, "The Union Difference"; Jonas Pontusson, "Trade Unions and Redistributive Politics" (Geneva: University of Geneva, April 2013), http://www.march.es/ceacs/eNews/economy/pdf/Pontusson.pdf (accessed July 3, 2014); Bjorn Gustafsson and Mats Johansson,

"In Search of Smoking Guns: What Makes Income Inequality Vary over Time in Different Countries," *American Sociological Review* 64, no. 4 (August 1999): 585–605.

62. David Madland and Nick Bunker, *Unions Make Democracy Work* (Washington, DC: Center for American Progress, January 2012), http://cdn.americanprogress.org/wp-content/uploads/issues/2012/01/pdf/unions_middleclass.pdf (accessed July 3, 2014); Cheol-Sung Lee, "Labor Unions and Good Governance: A Cross-National Comparative Analysis," *American Sociological Review* 72, no. 4 (August 2007): 585–609.

63. Benjamin Radcliff and Patricia Davis, "Labor Organizations and Electoral Participation in Industrial Democracies," *American Journal of Political Science* 44, no. 1 (January 2000): 133.

64. On the political implications of the decline of organized labor and how this has facilitated the right turn in American politics, see Edsall, *New Politics*, 141–78, and Shulman, *The Betrayal of Work*, 117–47.

65. Nelson Lichtenstein, *State of the Union: A Century of American Labor* (Princeton, NJ: Princeton University Press, 2002), 234–35.

66. Jeffrey M. Berry, *The New Liberalism: The Rising Power of Citizen Groups* (Washington, DC: Brookings Institution Press, 1999), 57; see also Manza, "Unequal Democracy in America," 151–53.

67. Berry, *The New Liberalism*, 55–57, 59–60.

68. Theda Skocpol, "Civic Transformation and Inequality in the Contemporary United States," in Neckerman, *Social Inequality*, 729–67; Theda Skocpol, "Voice and Inequality: The Transformation of American Civic Democracy," *Perspectives on Politics* 2, no. 1 (March 2004): 3–20; Theda Skocpol, "Advocates without Members: The Recent Transformation of American Civic Life," in *Civic Engagement in American Democracy*, ed. Theda Skocpol and Morris P. Fiorina (Washington, DC: Brookings Institution, 1999), 461–509; Theda Skocpol, *Diminished Democracy: From Membership to Management in American Civil Life* (Norman: University of Oklahoma Press, 2003).

69. Skocpol, "Advocates without Members," 462, 471, 499–500; Skocpol, "Civic Transformation and Inequality," 741–46; see also Matthew A. Crenson and Benjamin Ginsberg, *Downsizing Democracy: How America Sidelined Its Citizens and Privatized Its Public* (Baltimore, MD: Johns Hopkins University Press, 2002).

70. Skocpol, "Civic Transformation and Inequality," 758–59.

71. Crunk Feminist Collective, "The Power of Words: Racially Coded Political Rhetoric" (January 9, 2012), http://www.crunkfeministcollective.com/2012/01/09/the-power-of-words-racially-coded-political-rhetoric (accessed July 3, 2014); Charles M. Blow, "The G.O.P.'s 'Black People' Platform," *New York Times*, January 7, 2012. For an informative analysis of what is variously called "modern," "laissez-faire," or "colorblind" racism, see Eduardo Bonilla-Silva, *Racism without Racists: Color-Blind Racism and the Persistence of Racial Inequality in the United States*, 4th ed. (Lanham, MD: Rowman & Littlefield, 2014).

72. Martin Gilens, *Why Americans Hate Welfare* (Chicago: University of Chicago Press, 1999); see also Hana E. Brown, "Racialized Conflict and Policy Spillover Effects: The Role of Race in the Contemporary U.S. Welfare State," *American Journal of Sociology* 119, no. 2 (September 2013): 394–443.

73. John Harwood, "Behind the Roar of Political Debate, Whispers of Race Persist," *New York Times*, October 31, 2013.

74. In the post–civil rights era, the emergence of the ideology of color blindness and the racial realignment of the political parties, along with other factors, has engendered a new racial politics. But all the way back to the founding of the nation, the racial divide has left a political mark. Perhaps nowhere has the politics of race exerted more influence than in the development

of the American welfare state, and the ongoing development of the welfare state, in turn, has reshaped the politics of race. See, for example, Robert C. Lieberman, *Shifting the Color Line: Race and the American Welfare State* (Cambridge, MA: Harvard University Press, 1998); Robert C. Lieberman, *Shaping Race Policy: The United States in Comparative Perspective* (Princeton, NJ: Princeton University Press, 2005); Michael K. Brown, *Race, Money, and the American Welfare State* (Ithaca, NY: Cornell University Press, 1999); and Jill Quadagno, *The Color of Welfare: How Racism Undermined the War on Poverty* (New York: Oxford University Press, 1994).

75. Alesina and Glaeser, *Fighting Poverty in the U.S. and Europe*, 136–54; see also Erzo F. P. Luttmer, "Group Loyalty and the Taste for Redistribution," *Journal of Political Economy* 109, no. 3 (June 2001): 500–528.

76. See Michael D. Shear, "After Push by Obama, Minimum-Wage Action Is Moving to the States," *New York Times*, April 3, 2014.

77. Dan Clawson, Alan Neustadtl, and Denise Scott, *Money Talks: Corporate PACs and Political Influence* (New York: Basic Books, 1992).

78. Collins and Yeskel, *Economic Apartheid in America*, 70.

79. Gary Burtless and Christopher Jencks, "American Inequality and Its Consequences," in *Agenda for the Nation*, ed. Henry J. Aaron, James M. Lindsay, and Pietro S. Nivola (Washington, DC: Brookings Institution Press, 2003), 98.

80. Benjamin I. Page, Larry M. Bartels, and Jason Seawright, "Democracy and the Policy Preferences of Wealthy Americans," *Perspectives on Politics* 11, no. 1 (March 2013): 51–73; see also Martin Gilens, "Preference Gaps and Inequality in Representation," *PS: Political Science and Politics* 42, no. 2 (April 2009): 335–41; Jeffrey A. Winters and Benjamin I. Page, "Oligarchy in the United States," *Perspectives on Politics* 7, no. 4 (December 2009): 731–51; David Callahan and J. Mijin Cha, *Stacked Deck: How the Dominance of Politics by the Affluent & Business Undermines Economic Mobility in America* (New York: Demos, 2013), 3–10, http://www.demos.org/stacked-deck-how-dominance-politics-affluent-business-undermines-economic-mobility-america (accessed October 22, 2014).

81. Schlozman, Verba, and Brady, *The Unheavenly Chorus*, 158–62; Mandle, *Democracy, America, and the Age of Globalization*, 52–58.

82. Center for Responsive Politics, *Business-Labor-Ideology Split in PAC & Individual Donations to Candidates, Parties Super PACs and Outside Spending Groups* (May 2014), https://www.opensecrets.org/overview/blio.php (accessed July 5, 2014).

83. Adam Bonica, Nolan McCarty, Keith T. Poole, and Howard Rosenthal, "Why Hasn't Democracy Slowed Rising Inequality?," *Journal of Economic Perspectives* 27, no. 3 (Summer 2013): 111–13.

84. For a valuable overview of recent legal decisions governing political contributions, see Earl Wysong, Robert Perrucci, and David Wright, *The New Class Society: Goodbye American Dream?*, 4th ed. (Lanham, MD: Rowman & Littlefield, 2014), 145–62.

85. See Center for Responsive Politics, *Super PACs* (July 4, 2014), https://www.opensecrets.org/pacs/superpacs.php (accessed July 4, 2014).

86. Adam Lioz and Blair Bowie, *Election Spending in 2012: Post-Election Analysis of Federal Election Commission Data* (New York: Demos, November 2012), http://www.demos.org/publication/election-spending-2012-post-election-analysis-federal-election-commission-data (accessed July 4, 2014); Callahan and Cha, *Stacked Deck*, 18.

87. John Nichols and Robert W. McChesney, *Dollarocracy: How the Money and Media Election Complex Is Destroying America* (New York: Nation Books, 2013).

88. Jay Mandle, "The Politics of Democracy," *Challenge* 47, no. 1 (January–February 2004): 53; see also Mandle, *Democracy, America, and the Age of Globalization*.

89. Center for Responsive Politics, "Lobbying Database" (April 2014), http://www.opensecrets.org/lobby/index.php (accessed July 5, 2014).

90. Schlozman, Verba, and Brady, *The Unheavenly Chorus*, 430–32, 442.

91. See Wysong, Perrucci, and Wright, *The New Class Society*, 163–87.

92. Task Force on Inequality and American Democracy, *American Democracy in an Age of Rising Inequality* (Washington, DC: American Political Science Association, 2004), 11, http://www.apsanet.org/imgtest/taskforcereport.pdf (accessed December 15, 2005).

93. Bartels et al., "Inequality and American Governance," in Jacobs and Skocpol, *Inequality and American Democracy*, 127.

94. Larry M. Bartels, *Unequal Democracy: The Political Economy of the New Gilded Age* (New York: Russell Sage; Princeton, NJ: Princeton University Press, 2008), 282.

95. Martin Gilens, "Inequality and Democratic Responsiveness," *Public Opinion Quarterly* 69, no. 5 (2005): 788; Martin Gilens, *Affluence and Influence: Economic Inequality and Political Power in America* (New York: Russell Sage; Princeton, NJ: Princeton University Press, 2012), 81–85, 234; Martin Gilens and Benjamin I. Page, "Testing Theory of American Politics: Elites, Interest Groups, and Average Citizens," 38–42, forthcoming Fall 2014 in *Perspectives on Politics*, https://www.princeton.edu/~mgilens/Gilens%20homepage%20materials/Gilens%20and%20Page/Gilens%20and%20Page%202014-Testing%20Theories%203-7-14.pdf (accessed July 5, 2014).

96. U.S. Department of Labor, Wage and Hour Division, *The Fair Labor Standards Act of 1938, as Amended* (revised May 2011), 1, http://www.dol.gov/whd/regs/statutes/FairLaborStandAct.pdf (accessed July 7, 2014).

97. David Cooper, *Raising the Minimum Wage to $10.10 Would Lift Wages for Millions and Provide a Modest Economic Boost* (Washington, DC: Economic Policy Institute, December 2013), 6, fig. C, http://s1.epi.org/files/2014/EPI-1010-minimum-wage.pdf (accessed July 7, 2014); Council of Economic Advisors, *The Economic Case for Raising the Minimum Wage* (February 12, 2014), http://www.whitehouse.gov/blog/2014/02/12/economic-case-raising-minimum-wage (accessed July 8, 2014); Mishel, Bivens, Gould, and Shierholz, *The State of Working America*, 279–86.

98. Sylvia A. Allegretto and David Cooper, *Twenty-Three Years and Still Waiting for Change: Why It's Time to Give Tipped Workers the Regular Minimum Wage* (Washington, DC: Economic Policy Institute, July 2014), http://s2.epi.org/files/2014/EPI-CWED-BP379.pdf (accessed July 11, 2014).

99. Cooper, *Raising the Federal Minimum Wage*, 5, fig. B.

100. Lawrence Mishel, Ross Eisenbrey, and Alyssa Davis, *Top Restaurant Industry CEOs Made 721 Times More than Minimum Wage Workers in 2013* (Washington, DC: Economic Policy Institute, July 2, 2014), http://www.epi.org/publication/top-restaurant-industry-ceos-721-times-minimum (accessed July 7, 2014).

101. Council of Economic Advisors, *The Economic Case for Raising the Minimum Wage*, 8.

102. Cooper, *Raising the Federal Minimum Wage*, 3.

103. John Alpin and Karl Agne, *50 Years after LBJ's War on Poverty: A Study of American Attitudes about Work, Economic Opportunity, and the Social Safety Net* (Washington, DC: Center for American Progress, January 2014), 28, 30, table 13, http://cdn.americanprogress.org/wp-content/uploads/2014/01/WOP-PollReport2.pdf (accessed June 19, 2014).

104. Steven Greenhouse, "Raising the Floor on Pay," *New York Times*, April 10, 2012; U.S. Department of Labor, Wage and Hour Division, *Minimum Wage Laws in the States—January 1, 2014*, http://www.dol.gov/whd/minwage/america.htm (accessed July 7, 2014).

105. For background and data on the unemployment insurance program, see U.S. House of Representatives, Committee on Ways and Means, *2012 Green Book: Background Material and*

*Data on the Programs within the Jurisdiction of the Committee on Ways and Means,* chap. 4, http://greenbook.waysandmeans.house.gov/2012-green-book/chapter-4-unemployment-insurance (accessed July 8, 2014); Chad Stone and William Chen, *Introduction to Unemployment Insurance* (Washington, DC: Center on Budget and Policy Priorities, February 2013), http://www.cbpp.org/files/12-19-02ui.pdf (accessed July 8, 2014).

106. U.S. House of Representatives, *Green Book,* "Unemployment Insurance Introduction and Overview."

107. Rebecca Dixon, *Federal Neglect Leaves State Unemployment Systems in a State of Disrepair* (New York: National Employment Law Project, November 2013), http://www.nelp.org/page/-/UI/2013/NELP-Report-State-of-Disrepair-Federal-Neglect-Unemployment-Systems.pdf?nocdn=1 (accessed July 8, 2014).

108. See Jeffrey B. Wenger, *Divided We Fall: Deserving Workers Slip through America's Patchwork Unemployment Insurance System* (Washington, DC: Economic Policy Institute, August 2001), http://www.epinet.org/briefingpapers/divided.pdf (accessed December 31, 2007).

109. Freeman, *America Works,* 15; Julie M. Whittaker and Katelin P. Isaacs, *Unemployment Insurance: Programs and Benefits* (Congressional Research Service, September 2012), 6–7, http://greenbook.waysandmeans.house.gov/sites/greenbook.waysandmeans.house.gov/files/2012/documents/RL33362_gb_0.pdf (accessed July 8, 2014).

110. Wenger, "Divided We Fall," 11–15; Mishel, Bivens, Gould, and Shierholz, *The State of Working America,* 343–44.

111. See the Council of Economic Advisors and the Department of Labor, *The Economic Benefits of Extending Unemployment Insurance* (December 2013), http://www.whitehouse.gov/sites/default/files/docs/uireport-2013-12-4.pdf (accessed July 8, 2014); National Employment Law Project, *Share of Unemployed Receiving Jobless Aid Will Hit Record Low If Congress Fails to Renew Federal Unemployment Insurance* (New York: National Employment Law Project, December 2013), http://www.nclp.org/page/-/UI/2013/Issue-Brief-Record-Low-Share-Unemployed-Receiving-Jobless-Aid-Renew-EUC.pdf?nocdn=1 (accessed July 8, 2014).

112. Mishel, Bernstein, and Allegretto, *The State of Working America, 2006/2007* (Ithaca, NY: Cornell University Press, 2007), 238–47; National Employment Law Project, *Part-Time Workers and Unemployment Insurance* (New York: National Employment Law Project, February 2002), http://www.nelp.org/docUploads/pub37.pdf (accessed September 15, 2006).

113. Rebecca Smith, Rich McHugh, and Andrew Stettner, "Unemployment Insurance and Voluntary Quits: How States' Policies Affect Today's Families," *Challenge* 46, no. 3 (May–June 2003): 89–107.

114. Rebecca Smith et al., *Between a Rock and a Hard Place: Confronting the Failure of State Unemployment Insurance Systems to Serve Women and Working Families* (New York: National Employment Law Project, July 2003), http://www.nelp.org/docU-ploads/Between%20a%20Rock%20and%20a%20Hard%20Place%20070103%5F071503%5F092511.pdf (accessed January 13, 2008).

115. Wenger, "Divided We Fall," 5–9.

116. U.S. Government Accountability Office, *Unemployment Insurance: Role as Safety Net for Low-Wage Workers Is Limited* (December 2000), 5, 13–17, http://www.gao.gov/assets/240/231036.pdf (accessed July 8, 2014).

117. U.S. Government Accountability Office, *Unemployment Insurance: Economic Circumstances of Individuals Who Exhausted Benefits* (February 2012), http://www.gao.gov/assets/590/588680.pdf (accessed July 8, 2014).

118. Cited in Annie Lowrey, "States Cutting Weeks of Aid to the Jobless," *New York Times,* January 22, 2014.

119. Maurice Emsellem et al., *Failing the Unemployed: A State by State Examination of Unemployment Insurance Systems* (Washington, DC: Economic Policy Institute, 2002), 4.

120. For an excellent overview of welfare reform and its implementation, see Sharon Hays, *Flat Broke with Children: Women in the Age of Welfare Reform* (Oxford: Oxford University Press, 2003).

121. Hays, *Flat Broke with Children*, 41–42; Ellen Reese, *Backlash against Welfare Mothers: Past and Present* (Berkeley: University of California Press, 2005), 6–12.

122. U.S. House of Representatives, *Green Book*, "Table 7–9. Trends in the Cash Assistance Caseload: 1961 to 2010."

123. Carmen DeNavas-Walt, Bernadette D. Proctor, and Jessica C. Smith, *Income, Poverty, and Health Insurance Coverage in the United States: 2012*, U.S. Census Bureau, Current Population Reports, P60-245 (Washington, DC: Government Printing Office, 2013), 58, table B-2, 52, table B-1, 18 table 5.

124. Ife Floyd and Liz Schott, *TANF Cash Benefits Continued to Lose Value in 2013* (Washington, DC: Center on Budget and Policy Priorities, October 2013), http://www.cbpp.org/cms/?fa=view&id=4034 (accessed July 9, 2014); Megan C. Martin and Koen Caminada, "Welfare Reform in the U.S.: A Policy Overview Analysis," *Poverty and Public Policy* 3, no. 1 (2011): 26–27.

125. Sharon Parrott and Arloc Sherman, *TANF at 10: Program Results Are More Mixed than Often Understood* (Washington, DC: Center on Budget and Policy Priorities, August 17, 2006), 2; Kay E. Brown, *Temporary Assistance for Needy Families: Implications of Changes in Participation Rates* (Government Accountability Office, March 11, 2010), 3, http://www.gao.gov/assets/130/124169.pdf (accessed July 8, 2014).

126. See Joe Soss, Richard C. Fording, and Sanford Schram, *Disciplining the Poor: Neoliberal Paternalism and the Persistent Power of Race* (Chicago: University of Chicago Press, 2011), 262–92; Jason DeParle, "Welfare Limits Left Poor Adrift as Recession Hit," *New York Times*, April 8, 2012.

127. Frances Fox Piven, "Welfare and Work," in *Whose Welfare?*, ed. Gwendolyn Mink (Ithaca, NY: Cornell University Press, 1999), 88; see also Reese, *Backlash against Welfare Mothers*, 166–68.

128. Mary Corcoran et al., "How Welfare Reform Is Affecting Women's Work," *Annual Review of Sociology* 26 (2000): 241–69, and Daniel T. Lichter and Rukamalie Jayakody, "Welfare Reform: How Do We Measure Success?," *Annual Review of Sociology* 28 (2002): 117–41.

129. See, for example, Jane L. Collins and Victoria Mayer, *Both Hands Tied: Welfare Reform and the Race to the Bottom of the Low-Wage Labor Market* (Chicago: University of Chicago Press, 2010); Sandra Morgen, Joan Acker, and Jill Weigt, *Stretched Thin: Poor Families, Welfare Work, and Welfare Reform* (Ithaca, NY: Cornell University Press, 2010); Laura Lein and Deanna T. Schexnayder, *Life after Welfare Reform and the Persistence of Poverty* (Austin: University of Texas Press, 2007).

130. AFL-CIO, "Public Supports Workers Forming Unions, New Laws," http://www.aflcio.org/joinaunion/voiceatwork/efca/upload/EFCA_Polling_Summary.pdf (accessed December 31, 2007); see also Freeman, *America Works*, 83–84.

131. See Shulman, *The Betrayal of Work*, 117–47.

132. Fantasia and Voss, *Hard Work*, 34–77; see also Rick Fantasia, "The Assault on American Labor," in *Social Problems*, ed. Craig Calhoun and George Ritzer (New York: McGraw-Hill, 1993), 663–79.

133. Chirag Mehta and Nik Theodore, *Undermining the Right to Organize: Employer Behavior during Union Representation Campaigns* (Chicago: Center for Urban Economic Develop-

ment, December 2005), http://www.americanrightsatwork.org/mdocuments/ARAWReports/UROCUEDcompressedfullreport.pdf (accessed January 6, 2007); Kate Bronfenbrenner, *No Holds Barred: The Intensification of Employer Opposition to Organizing* (Washington, DC: Economic Policy Institute, May 2009), http://s3.epi.org/files/page/-/pdf/bp235.pdf (accessed June 10, 2014).

134. See Steven Greenhouse, "Labor Law Is Broken, Economist Says," *New York Times*, October 28, 2010; Ellen Dannin, *No Rights without a Remedy: The Long Struggle for Effective National Labor Relations Act Remedies* (Washington, DC: American Constitution Society for Law and Policy, June 2011), https://www.acslaw.org/sites/default/files/Dannin_No_Rights_Without_Remedy_0.pdf (accessed July 10, 2014); Nancy Schiffer, *Rights without Remedies: The Failure of the National Labor Relations Act* (Denver, CO: 2nd Annual CLE Conference, September 2008), http://apps.americanbar.org/labor/lel-annualcle/08/materials/data/papers/153.pdf (accessed July 10, 2014).

135. See Craig Becker and Judith Scott, "Isolating America's Workers," *The Nation*, October 8, 2012, 27–29.

136. Lance Compa, *Human Rights and Workers' Rights in the United States* (Washington, DC: AFL-CIO, 2005), http://www.aflcio.org/joinaunion/upload/compa.pdf (accessed January 14, 2008); see also Larry Peterson, "A Lazy Man's Labor Policy," *Dollars & Sense*, September–October 2007, 12–15, 42–43.

137. Bronfenbrenner, *No Holds Barred*.

138. John Schmitt and Ben Zipperer, *Dropping the Ax: Illegal Firings during Union Election Campaigns, 1951–2007* (Washington, DC: Center for Economic and Policy Research, March 2009), http://www.cepr.net/documents/publications/dropping-the-ax-update-2009-03.pdf (accessed July 13, 2014).

139. Schmitt and Zipperer, *Dropping the Ax*, 15.

140. See Lance Compa, *Unfair Advantage: Workers' Freedom of Association in the United States under International Human Rights Standards* (Ithaca, NY: Cornell University Press, 2004), xix–xx, 29–30, 171–89.

141. "Kicked While Down," unsigned editorial, *New York Times*, October 7, 2006.

142. Jim Grossfeld and John D. Podesta, "A Temporary Fix," *American Prospect*, March 2005, 15–17.

143. Richard D. Kahlenberg, "Labor Organizing as a Civil Right" (New York: Century Foundation, March 2004), 4.

144. Fantasia and Voss, *Hard Work*, 51.

145. Fantasia and Voss, *Hard Work*, 52; Compa, *Unfair Advantage*, xvii–xix, 31–32, 60.

146. Gordon Lafer, *The Legislative Attack on American Wages and Labor Standards, 2011–2012* (Washington, DC: Economic Policy Institute, October 2013), 24–28, http://s4.epi.org/files/2013/EPI-Legislative-Attack-on-American-Wages-Labor-Standards-10-31-2013.pdf (accessed July 10, 2014).

147. Lafer, *The Legislative Attack on American Wages*, 28–31; Annette Bernhardt et al., *Broken Laws, Unprotected Workers: Violations of Employment and Labor Laws in American Cities* (Chicago: Center for Urban Economic Development; New York: National Law Employment Project; and Los Angeles: UCLA Institute for Research on Labor and Employment, 2009), http://www.nelp.org/page/-/brokenlaws/BrokenLawsReport2009.pdf?nocdn=1 (accessed July 10, 2014). For a guide to the large body of research on wage theft, see National Employment Law Project, *Winning Wage Justice: A Summary of Research on Wage and Hour Violations in the United States* (New York: National Employment Law Project, July 2013), http://nelp.3cdn.net/6eb6a53686715c5463_2wm6bno4u.pdf (accessed July 11, 2014).

148. See, for example, Collins and Yeskel, *Economic Apartheid in America*, 87–125.

149. Sharon Parrott, Isaac Shapiro, and John Springer, *Selected Research Findings on Accomplishments of the Safety Net* (Washington, DC: Center on Budget and Policy Priorities, July 27, 2005).

# 7. THE CULTURAL SYSTEM AND POVERTY

1. Alice O'Connor, *Poverty Knowledge: Social Science, Social Policy, and the Poor in Twentieth-Century U.S. History* (Princeton, NJ: Princeton University Press, 2001).

2. Ann Swidler, "Culture in Action: Symbols and Strategies," *American Sociological Review* 51, no. 2 (April 1986): 273–86.

3. Eduardo Bonilla-Silva, *White Supremacy and Racism in the Post–Civil Rights Era* (Boulder, CO: Lynne Rienner, 2001), 62.

4. John Leland, "Why America Sees the Silver Lining," *New York Times*, June 13, 2004; see also Isabel V. Sawhill and John E. Morton, *Economic Mobility: Is the American Dream Alive and Well?* (Washington, DC: Economic Mobility Project, Pew Charitable Trusts, 2007), 2, http://www.economicmobility.org/assets/pdfs/EMP%20American%20Dream%20Report.pdf (accessed January 6, 2008).

5. Janny Scott and David Leonhardt, "Class in America: Shadowy Lines That Still Divide," *New York Times*, May 15, 2005.

6. James R. Kluegel and Eliot R. Smith, *Beliefs about Inequality: Americans' Views of What Is and What Ought to Be* (New York: Aldine de Gruyter, 1986), 44; see also Nancy DiTomaso, *The American Non-Dilemma: Racial Inequality without Racism* (New York: Russell Sage, 2013), 101–36, and Sandra L. Hanson and John Zogby, "The Polls—Trends: Attitudes about the American Dream," *Public Opinion Quarterly* 74, no. 3 (Fall 2010): 570–84.

7. Economic Mobility Project, *Findings from a National Survey & Focus Groups on Economic Mobility* (March 12, 2009), 3, 21, http://www.pewtrusts.org/~/media/legacy/uploadedfiles/wwwpewtrustsorg/reports/economic_mobility/EMP20200920Survey20on20Economic20Mobility20FOR20PRINT2031209pdf.pdf (accessed June 19, 2014); for similar findings, see Lane Kenworthy and Lindsay A. Owens, *Political Attitudes, Public Opinion, and the Great Recession* (Russell Sage Foundation and Stanford Center on Poverty and Inequality, October 2012), http://www.stanford.edu/group/recessiontrends/cgi-bin/web/sites/all/themes/barron/pdf/PublicOpinion_fact_sheet.pdf (accessed June 19, 2014).

8. Pew Research Center, *Most See Inequality Growing, but Partisans Differ over Solutions* (January 23, 2014), 3, http://www.people-press.org/files/legacy-pdf/1-23-14%20Poverty_Inequality%20Release.pdf (accessed June 19, 2014). See also Mark Robert Rank, Thomas A. Hirschl, and Kirk A. Foster, *Chasing the American Dream: Understanding What Shapes Our Fortunes* (Oxford: Oxford University Press, 2014), 84–85; Kay Lehman Schlozman, Sidney Verba, and Henry E. Brady, *The Unheavenly Chorus: Unequal Political Voice and the Broken Promise of American Democracy* (Princeton, NJ: Princeton University Press, 2012), 60–68.

9. This formulation of the ideology of individualism is adapted from Kluegel and Smith, *Beliefs about Inequality*, 37; see also Joe R. Feagin, *Subordinating the Poor: Welfare and American Beliefs* (Englewood Cliffs, NJ: Prentice-Hall, 1975), 91–92; Edward Ladd, *The American Ideology: An Exploration of the Origins, Meaning, and Role of American Political Ideals* (Storrs, CT: Roper Center for Public Opinion Research, 1994), 34–43, 53–58.

10. On the concept of the "dominant ideology," see Kluegel and Smith, *Beliefs about Inequality*, 5; Joan Huber and William Form, *Income and Ideology: An Analysis of the American Political Formula* (New York: Free Press, 1973), 4.

11. Michael Schudson, "How Culture Works: Perspectives from Media Studies on the Efficacy of Symbols," *Theory and Society* 18, no. 2 (March 1989): 153–80. To explain why some cultural representations are more influential than others, Schudson identifies "five dimensions of cultural power": "retrievability," "rhetorical force," "resonance," "institutional retention," and "resolution." Though I do not use his terminology, my analysis of the cultural influence of the individualistic ideology is a loose application of Schudson's framework.

12. Robert C. Bulman, *Hollywood Goes to High School: Cinema, Schools, and American Culture* (New York: Worth, 2005), 43–59.

13. Kluegel and Smith, *Beliefs about Inequality*, 247–55. The idea that adherence to the dominant ideology is strongest among those who most profit from its propagation is a central theme in Huber and Form, *Income and Ideology*; see also Joan Huber Rytina, William H. Form, and John Pease, "Income and Stratification Ideology: Beliefs about the American Opportunity Structure," *American Journal of Sociology* 75, no. 4, part 2 (January 1970): 703–16.

14. The pioneering work of Joe Feagin set the pattern for subsequent studies; see Feagin, *Subordinating the Poor*, 95–97, and Joe R. Feagin, "Poverty: We Still Believe That God Helps Those Who Help Themselves," *Psychology Today* 6 (1972): 101–10, 129.

15. Besides individualism and structuralism, public opinion research has also found evidence, though less definitive, of other popular theories of poverty as well, including "fatalism" and "culturalism." For a summary of these different "metatheories" of poverty, see Kevin B. Smith and Lorene H. Stone, "Rags, Riches, and Bootstraps: Beliefs about the Causes of Wealth and Poverty," *Sociological Quarterly* 30, no. 1 (1989): 94–95.

16. On the prevalence of individualistic explanations, see Feagin, "God Helps Those"; Feagin, *Subordinating the Poor*, 95–102; Smith and Stone, "Rags, Riches, and Bootstraps," 93–107; Kevin B. Smith, "I Made It Because of Me: Beliefs about the Causes of Wealth and Poverty," *Sociological Spectrum* 5, no. 3 (1985): 255–67; Catherine Cozzarelli, Anna V. Wilkinson, and Michael J. Tagler, "Attitudes toward the Poor and Attributions for Poverty," *Journal of Social Issues* 57, no. 2 (Summer 2001): 207–27; Daniel T. Lichter and Martha L. Crowley, *American Attitudes about Poverty and the Poor* (Population Reference Bureau, May 2002), http://www.prb.org/Publications/Articles/2002/AmericanAttitudesAboutPovertyandthe Poor.aspx (accessed June 19, 2014).

17. Kluegel and Smith, *Beliefs about Inequality*, 100–101.

18. Judith A. Chafel, "Societal Images of Poverty: Child and Adult Beliefs," *Youth and Society* 28, no. 4 (June 1997): 432, 434, 461.

19. Cozzarelli, Wilkinson, and Tagler, "Attitudes toward the Poor," 215.

20. See, for example, Greg M. Shaw and Robert Y. Shapiro, "The Polls-Trends: Poverty and Public Assistance," *Public Opinion Quarterly* 66, no. 1 (Spring 2002): 115–21; Joe R. Feagin, "America's Welfare Stereotypes," *Social Science Quarterly* 52, no. 4 (March 1972): 921–33.

21. Karen Seccombe, Delores James, and Kimberly Battle Walters, "'They Think You Ain't Much of Nothing': The Social Construction of the Welfare Mother," *Journal of Marriage and the Family* 60, no. 4 (November 1998): 849–65; Liane V. Davis and Jan L. Hagen, "Stereotypes and Stigma: What's Changed for Welfare Mothers," *Affilia* 11, no. 3 (Fall 1996): 319–37; Mark Robert Rank, *Living on the Edge: The Realities of Welfare in America* (New York: Columbia University Press, 1994), 142–44.

22. On the variation among individuals in beliefs about the causes of poverty, see Cozzarelli, Wilkinson, and Tagler, "Attitudes toward the Poor"; Matthew O. Hunt, "The Individual, Society, or Both? A Comparison of Black, Latino, and White Beliefs about the Causes of

Poverty," *Social Forces* 75, no. 1 (September 1996): 293–322; Linda Burzotta Nilson, "Reconsidering Ideological Lines: Beliefs about Poverty in America," *Sociological Quarterly* 22 (Autumn 1981): 531–48; and Anup K. Singh, "Attribution Research on Poverty: A Review," *Psychologia* 32 (1989): 143–48.

23. Barrett A. Lee, Sue Hinze Jones, and David W. Lewis, "Public Beliefs about the Causes of Homelessness," *Social Forces* 69, no. 1 (September 1990): 253–65.

24. Martin Gilens, *Why Americans Hate Welfare: Race, Media, and the Politics of Antipoverty Policy* (Chicago: University of Chicago Press, 1999); Shanto Iyengar, "Framing Responsibility for Political Issues: The Case of Poverty," *Political Behavior* 12, no. 1 (March 1990): 27–28.

25. Catherine Cozzarelli, Michael J. Tagler, and Anna V. Wilkinson, "Do Middle-Class Students Perceive Poor Women and Poor Men Differently?," *Sex Roles* 47, nos. 1–12 (2002): 519–29.

26. Iyengar, "Framing Responsibility," 26–27, 36.

27. Martin Gilens, "The American News Media and Public Misperceptions of Race and Poverty," in *Race, Poverty, and Domestic Policy*, ed. C. Michael Henry (New Haven, CT: Yale University Press, 2004), 341–42.

28. Jeffry A. Will, "The Dimensions of Poverty: Public Perceptions of the Deserving Poor," *Social Science Research* 22, no. 3 (September 1993): 312–32; Jeffry A. Will, *The Deserving Poor* (New York: Garland, 1993).

29. John Alpin and Karl Agne, *50 Years after LBJ's War on Poverty: A Study of American Attitudes about Work, Economic Opportunity, and the Social Safety Net* (Washington, DC: Center for American Progress, January 2014), 13, http://cdn.americanprogress.org/wp-content/uploads/2014/01/WOP-PollReport2.pdf (accessed June 19, 2014).

30. Pew Research Center, *Most See Inequality Growing*.

31. Alpin and Agne, *50 Years after LBJ's War on Poverty*, 13, 16.

32. See Gilens, *Why Americans Hate Welfare*, 31–39. Gilens convincingly shows that Americans' commitment to individualism is "bounded" rather than absolute and does not preclude support for government assistance to the poor.

33. See, for example, Claudia Strauss, "Not-So-Rugged Individualists: Americans' Conflicting Ideas about Poverty," in *Work, Welfare, and Politics: Confronting Poverty in the Wake of Welfare Reform*, ed. Frances Fox Piven et al. (Eugene: University of Oregon Press, 2002), 55–69.

34. Lawrence Bobo, "Social Responsibility, Individualism, and Redistributive Policies," *Sociological Forum* 6, no. 1 (March 1991): 71–92.

35. Halpin and Agne, *50 Years after LBJs War on Poverty*, 28–32.

36. Kluegel and Smith, *Beliefs about Inequality*, 87–88.

37. Kluegel and Smith, *Beliefs about Inequality*, 17, 93.

38. Hunt, "The Individual, Society, or Both?," 293–322. In a more recent study of beliefs about black–white inequality, Hunt finds declining support for structural explanations among both African Americans and Hispanics; see Matthew O. Hunt, "African American, Hispanic, and White Beliefs about Black/White Inequality, 1977–2004," *American Sociological Review* 72, no. 3 (June 2007): 390–415.

39. Hunt, "The Individual, Society, or Both?," 295.

40. Lawrence D. Bobo and Ryan A. Smith, "Antipoverty Policy, Affirmative Action, and Racial Attitudes," in *Confronting Poverty: Prescriptions for Change*, ed. Sheldon H. Danziger, Gary D. Sandefur, and Daniel H. Weinberg (New York: Russell Sage; Cambridge, MA: Harvard University Press, 1994), 375.

41. See, for example, Elizabeth L. Beck, Deborah M. Whitley, and James L. Wolk, "Legislators' Perceptions about Poverty: Views from the Georgia General Assembly," *Journal of Sociology and Social Welfare* 26, no. 2 (June 1999): 87–104.

42. Hunt, "The Individual, Society, or Both?," 294–95; see also Kluegel and Smith, *Beliefs about Inequality*, 101.

43. Stanley Feldman and John Zaller, "The Political Culture of Ambivalence: Ideological Responses to the Welfare State," *American Journal of Political Science* 36, no. 1 (February 1992): 268–307; Matthew C. Nisbet, *Communicating about Poverty and Low-Wage Work: A New Agenda* (Washington, DC: Inclusion, The Mobility Agenda, 2007), http://www.inclusionist.org/files/USUKPaper.pdf (accessed January 12, 2008).

44. Bobo and Smith, "Antipoverty Policy, Affirmative Action, and Racial Attitudes," 372.

45. See Leslie McCall, *The Undeserving Rich: American Beliefs about Inequality, Opportunity, and Redistribution* (New York: Cambridge University Press, 2013).

46. Nilson, "Reconsidering Ideological Lines," 545.

47. Hunt, "The Individual, Society, or Both?," 295; see also Hunt, "African American, Hispanic, and White Beliefs," 394; and Kluegel and Smith, *Beliefs about Inequality*, 101.

48. Tamara Draut, *New Opportunities? Public Opinion on Poverty, Income Inequality, and Public Policy: 1996–2002* (New York: Demos, 2002), 6–7.

49. DiTomaso, *The American Non-Dilemma*, 110–11.

50. Robert V. Robinson and Wendell Bell, "Equality, Success, and Social Justice in England and the United States," *American Sociological Review* 43, no. 2 (April 1978): 125–43.

51. Bobo, "Social Responsibility, Individualism, and Redistributive Policies," 85–88.

52. Will, "The Dimensions of Poverty," 312–32; Christina Fong, "Social Preferences, Self-Interest, and the Demand for Redistribution," *Journal of Public Economics* 82, no. 2 (2001): 225–46.

53. On the media's influence on public perceptions of the poor, see the discussion in Gilens, "The American News Media," 347–49.

54. On the news media in a democratic society and the failure of the U.S. media to perform adequately their watchdog role, see Robert A. Hackett, "The News Media and Civic Equality: Watch Dogs, Mad Dogs, or Lap Dogs?," in *Democratic Equality: What Went Wrong?*, ed. Edward Broadbent (Toronto: University of Toronto Press, 2001), 197–212, and James Curran, "Rethinking Media and Democracy," in *Mass Media and Society*, ed. James Curran and Michael Gurevitch, 3rd ed. (London: Hodder, 2000), 120–54.

55. Earl Wysong, Robert Perrucci, and David Wright, *The New Class Society: Goodbye American Dream?*, 4th ed. (Lanham, MD: Rowman & Littlefield, 2014), 189–215; Ben H. Bagdikian, *The New Media Monopoly* (Boston: Beacon Press, 2004); David Croteau and William Hoynes, *The Business of Media: Corporate Media and the Public Interest*, 2nd ed. (Thousand Oaks, CA: Pine Forge Press, 2005).

56. Neil Postman, *Amusing Ourselves to Death: Public Discourse in the Age of Show Business* (New York: Penguin, 1985), 87; see also Thomas E. Patterson, *Informing the News: The Need for Knowledge-Based Journalism* (New York: Vintage, 2013), 20–30.

57. On the commercialization of the news media and the influence of advertising, see Robert W. McChesney, *The Problem of the Media: U.S. Communication Politics in the 21st Century* (New York: Monthly Review, 2004), 83–89, 138–74, and Herbert J. Gans, *Democracy and the News* (Oxford: Oxford University Press, 2003), 21–30.

58. Margaret Sullivan, "Too Little for So Many, Even in The Times," *New York Times*, June 2, 2013; Steve Rendall, "A Poverty of Coverage," *Extra!*, September–October 2007; Neil deMause and Steve Rendall, "The Poor Will Always Be with Us," *Extra!*, September–October

2007, 9–13; Heather E. Bullock, Karen Fraser Wyche, and Wendy R. Williams, "Media Images of the Poor," *Journal of Social Issues* 57, no. 2 (Summer 2001): 232–33.

59. Steven Rendall, Emily Kaufmann, and Sara Qureshi, "Even GOP Attention Can't Make Media Care about Poor," *Extra!*, June 1, 2014, http://fair.org/extra-online-articles/even-gop-attention-cant-make-media-care-about-poor (accessed June 27, 2014).

60. Cited in Dan Froomkin, "It Can't Happen Here: Why Is There So Little Coverage of Americans Who Are Struggling with Poverty," *Nieman Reports*, Winter 2013, 2, http://www.nieman.harvard.edu/reports/article/102832/It-Cant-Happen-Here.aspx (accessed, June 22, 2014).

61. Cited in Froomkin, "It Can't Happen Here," 1.

62. Andrew R. Cline, "Citizens or Objects: A Case Study in News Coverage of Poverty," *Poverty & Public Policy* 3, no. 4 (2011): 1–8.

63. Miranda Spencer, "'Making the Invisible Visible': Antipoverty Activists Working to Make Their Own Media," *Extra!*, January–February 2003, 21.

64. C. Wright Mills, *The Sociological Imagination* (New York: Oxford University Press, 1959), 8–9.

65. For a discussion of how media depictions of the poor conceal the systemic nature of poverty, see Gregory Mantsios, "Media Magic: Making Class Invisible," in *Race, Class, and Gender in the United States: An Integrated Study*, ed. Paula S. Rothenberg, 5th ed. (New York: Worth, 2001), 564–66.

66. Peter Parisi, "A Sort of Compassion: The Washington Post Explains the 'Crisis in Urban America,'" *Howard Journal of Communications* 9 (1998): 187.

67. On the concept of "framing," see Robert M. Entman, "Framing: Toward Clarification of a Fractured Paradigm," *Journal of Communication* 43, no. 4 (Autumn 1993): 51–58. For three studies of framing on topics directly relevant to the issue of poverty, see Mark A. Smith, *The Right Talk: How Conservatives Transformed the Great Society into the Economic Society* (Princeton, NJ: Princeton University Press, 2007), 47–72; Christopher R. Martin, *Framed! Labor and the Corporate Media* (Ithaca, NY: Cornell University Press, 2004); and Diana Kendall, *Framing Class: Media Representations of Wealth and Poverty in America* (Lanham, MD: Rowman & Littlefield, 2005).

68. Iyengar, "Framing Responsibility," 19–40. For a valuable application and elaboration of Iyengar's analysis, identifying different variants of the "episodic" frame, see Kendall, *Framing Class*, 106–28.

69. Iyengar, "Framing Responsibility," 28–29; see also Carmen L. Manning-Miller, "Media Discourse and the Feminization of Poverty," *Explorations in Ethnic Studies* 17, no. 1 (January 1994): 79–88.

70. Parisi, "A Sort of Compassion," 201; see also Nisbet, *Communicating about Poverty*, 6–8.

71. Ange-Marie Hancock, *The Politics of Disgust: The Public Identity of the Welfare Queen* (New York: New York University Press, 2004), 65–87.

72. Ladd, *The American Ideology*, 39–40; Tom W. Smith, "That Which We Call Welfare by Any Other Name Would Smell Sweeter: An Analysis of the Impact of Question Wording on Response Patterns," *Public Opinion Quarterly* 51, no. 1 (Spring 1987): 75–83.

73. Michael Zweig, *The Working Class Majority: America's Best Kept Secret* (Ithaca, NY: Cornell University Press, 2000), 77–93.

74. For examples, see the opening paragraph of chapter 5.

75. Barbara Ehrenreich, "Too Poor to Make the News," *New York Times*, June 14, 2009; Neil deMause, "The Recession and the 'Deserving Poor': Poverty Finally on the Media Ra-

dar—But Only When It Hits the Middle Class," *Extra!*, February 1, 2009, http://fair.org/extra-online-articles/the-recession-and-the-deserving-poor (accessed June 25, 2014).

76. Pimpare cited in deMause, "The Recession and the 'Deserving Poor.'"

77. Gilens, *Why Americans Hate Welfare*, 102–32; Gilens, "The American News Media," 336–63; Rosalee A. Clawson and Rakuya Trice, "Poverty as We Know It: Media Portrayals of the Poor," *Public Opinion Quarterly* 64, no. 1 (Spring 2000): 53–64.

78. Gilens, *Why Americans Hate Welfare*, 121–27.

79. Sonya Ross and Jennifer Agiesta, "AP Poll: A Slight Majority of Americans Are Now Expressing Negative View of Blacks," *Washington Post*, October 27, 2012; Bobo and Smith, "Antipoverty Policy, Affirmative Action, and Racial Attitudes," 365–95; Maria Krysan, "Prejudice, Politics, and Public Opinion: Understanding the Sources of Racial Policy Preferences," *Annual Review of Sociology* 26 (2000): 135–68.

80. Charlotte Ryan, *Prime Time Activism: Media Strategies for Grassroots Organizing* (Boston: South End Press, 1991), 189–212; Charlotte Ryan, "Battered in the Media: Mainstream News Coverage of Welfare Reform," *Radical America* 26, no. 1 (January–March 1996): 29–41; on the "source problem" in the news media, see also Patterson, *Informing the News*, 33–59.

81. Ryan, *Prime Time Activism*, 192–93.

82. Rendall, Kaufmann, and Qureshi, "Even GOP Attention Can't Make Media Care about Poor."

83. Ryan, "Battered in the Media," 34–38, 40.

84. Patterson, *Informing the News*, 81–83.

85. Robert M. Entman, "Television, Democratic Theory, and the Visual Construction of Poverty," *Research in Political Sociology* 7 (1995): 149.

86. Michael Schudson, "The Sociology of News Production," *Media, Culture, and Society* 11, no. 3 (July 1989): 278.

87. Nancy Franklin, "Seeing Stars," *New Yorker*, September 26, 2005, 156.

88. For a sustained analysis of how sound-bite media work to the advantage of the right, see Jeffrey Scheuer, *The Sound Bite Society: Television and the American Mind* (New York: Four Walls Eight Windows, 1999).

89. Daniel C. Hallin, "The American News Media: A Critical Theory Perspective," in *Critical Theory and Public Life*, ed. John Forester (Cambridge, MA: MIT Press, 1985), 130.

90. Hallin, "The American News Media," 130.

91. Hallin, "The American News Media," 135.

92. For discussions of media effects, see Gans, *Democracy and the News*, 69–89.

93. Leonard Silk and David Vogel, *Ethics and Profits: The Crisis of Confidence in American Business* (New York: Simon & Schuster, 1976), 21–23.

94. Cited in David Vogel, *Fluctuating Fortunes: The Political Power of Business in America* (New York: Basic Books, 1989), 213.

95. Lewis F. Powell, "Attack on American Free Enterprise System," U.S. Chamber of Commerce, August 23, 1971, http://www.aspenlawschool.com/books/plater_environmentallaw/updates/02.5.pdf (accessed December 30, 2007). On Powell's memo and the onset of the right-wing ideological offensive in the early 1970s, see David Brock, *The Republican Noise Machine: Right-Wing Media and How It Corrupts Democracy* (New York: Crown, 2004), 39–41, 74–75, and John Micklethwait and Adrian Wooldridge, *The Right Nation: Conservative Power in America* (New York: Penguin, 2004), 77–78.

96. Brock, *The Republican Noise Machine*, 41–42, 45–46; Vogel, *Fluctuating Fortunes*, 221–22.

97. Vogel, *Fluctuating Fortunes*, 145, 194–95, 213–14; Jerome L. Himmelstein, *To the Right: The Transformation of American Conservatism* (Berkeley: University of California Press, 1990), 137.

98. For details on these foundations, their assets, and the role they played in funding the conservative counterrevolution, see Micklethwait and Wooldridge, *The Right Nation*, 77–79; Smith, *The Right Talk*, 86–94; Alice O'Connor, "Financing the Counterrevolution," in *Rightward Bound: Making America Conservative in the 1970s*, ed. Bruce J. Schulman and Julian E. Zelizer (Cambridge, MA: Harvard University Press, 2008), 148–68; Douglas S. Massey, *Return of the "L" Word: A Liberal Vision for the New Century* (Princeton, NJ: Princeton University Press, 2005), 151; and Lewis H. Lapham, "Tentacles of Rage: The Republican Propaganda Mills, a Brief History," *Harper's Magazine*, September 2004, 32.

99. On the rapid increase in funding for conservative think tanks in the 1970s and after, see Dan Clawson and Mary Ann Clawson, "Reagan or Business? Foundations of the New Conservatism," in *The Structure of Power in America: The Corporate Elite as a Ruling Class*, ed. Michael Schwartz (New York: Holmes & Meier, 1987), 205–7, and Ellen Reese, *Backlash against Welfare Mothers: Past and Present* (Berkeley: University of California Press, 2005), 151–52.

100. For basic information about right-wing think tanks, see Lapham, "Tentacles of Rage," 35; Massey, *Return of the "L" Word*, 144–51; and People for the American Way, *Profiles of Right Wing Organizations*, http://www.pfaw.org/right-wing-organizations (accessed June 23, 2014).

101. Micklethwait and Wooldridge, *The Right Nation*, 113; Matt Bai, "Notion Building," *New York Times Magazine*, October 12, 2003, 85.

102. Jennifer Steinhauer and Jonathan Weisman, "In the DeMint Era at Heritage, a Shift from Policy to Politics," *New York Times*, February 24, 2014.

103. Jean Stefancic and Richard Delgado, *No Mercy: How Conservative Think Tanks and Foundations Changed America's Social Agenda* (Philadelphia: Temple University Press, 1996), 4.

104. Vogel, *Fluctuating Fortunes*, 214–16.

105. Brock, *The Republican Noise Machine*, 74–115; Joe Conason, *Big Lies: The Right-Wing Propaganda Machine and How It Distorts the Truth* (New York: Thomas Dunne Books, St. Martin's Griffin, 2003), 35–41.

106. On the bogus charge of liberal bias and how this has pushed news coverage to the right, see Eric Alterman, *What Liberal Media? The Truth about Bias and the News* (New York: Basic Books, 2003).

107. Alterman, *What Liberal Media?*, 28–103; Eric Alterman, *Sound and Fury: The Washington Punditocracy and the Collapse of American Politics* (New York: HarperCollins, 1992).

108. Cited in Bai, "Notion Building," 84–85.

109. Lapham, "Tentacles of Rage."

110. See Reese, *Backlash against Welfare Mothers*, 151–63.

111. Herbert J. Gans, *The War against the Poor: The Underclass and Antipoverty Policy* (New York: Basic Books, 1995).

112. Michael B. Katz, *The Undeserving Poor: From the War on Poverty to the War on Welfare* (New York: Pantheon, 1989).

113. On the origins and dissemination of the "underclass" label, see Gans, *The War against the Poor*, 27–57; Leslie Inniss and Joe R. Feagin, "The Black 'Underclass' Ideology in Race Relations Analysis," *Social Justice* 16, no. 4 (Winter 1989): 13–34.

114. For valuable critiques of the underclass concept, in addition to those cited in the previous note, see Adolph Reed Jr., "The Underclass as Myth and Symbol: The Poverty of Dis-

course about Poverty," *Radical America* 24, no. 1 (January–March 1990): 21–40; Stephen Steinberg, "The Underclass: A Case of Color Blindness," *New Politics* 2, no. 3 (Summer 1989): 42–60; and Carole Marks, "The Urban Underclass," *Annual Review of Sociology* 17 (1991): 445–66.

115. Cited in Charles M. Blow, "Paul Ryan, Culture and Poverty," *New York Times*, March 22, 2014.

116. Sanford D. Schram, *Words of Welfare: The Poverty of Social Science and the Social Science of Poverty* (Minneapolis: University of Minnesota Press, 1995), 101.

117. Ryan, cited in Paul Krugman, "The Hammock Fallacy," *New York Times*, March 7, 2014; David Corn, "Secret Video: Romney Tells Millionaire Donors What He Really Thinks of Obama Voters," *Mother Jones*, September 17, 2012, http://www.motherjones.com/politics/2012/09/secret-video-romney-private-fundraisersee (accessed June 26, 2014); Ben Craw and Zack Carter, "Paul Ryan: 60 Percent of Americans Are 'Takers,' Not 'Makers,'" *Huffington Post*, October 5, 2012, http://www.huffingtonpost.com/2012/10/05/paul-ryan-60-percent-of-a_n_1943073.html (accessed June 26, 2014); Paul Krugman, "Moochers against Welfare," *New York Times*, February 17, 2012.

118. Charles Murray, "The Coming White Underclass," *Wall Street Journal*, October 29, 1993.

119. Robert Rector, "In Welfare Reform, Governors Miss the Point," in *Welfare: A Documentary History of U.S. Policy and Politics*, ed. Gwendolyn Mink and Rickie Solinger (New York: New York University Press, 2003), 638–39.

120. Michael Harrington, *The New American Poverty* (New York: Penguin, 1984), 37.

121. Charles Murray, *Losing Ground: American Social Policy, 1950–1980* (New York: Basic Books, 1984), 227–28.

122. Pew Research Center, *Most See Inequality Growing*, 2.

123. Albert O. Hirschman, *The Rhetoric of Reaction: Perversity, Futility, Jeopardy* (Cambridge, MA: Belknap Press of Harvard University Press, 1991), 11–42. Hirschman singles out the "perversity thesis" as one of three key arguments commonly invoked by conservatives in opposing social reforms and welfare state policies in particular. On the centrality of the "perversity thesis" in the welfare reform debate, past and present, see Margaret R. Somers and Fred Block, "From Poverty to Perversity: Ideas, Markets, and Institutions over 200 Years of Welfare Debate," *American Sociological Review* 70, no. 2 (April 2005): 260–87.

124. See O'Connor, *Poverty Knowledge*, 242–83.

125. O'Connor, *Poverty Knowledge*, 15.

126. See David Miller, "Media Power and Class Power: Overplaying Ideology," in *Socialist Register 2002: A World of Contradictions*, ed. Leo Panitch and Colin Leys (London: Merlin Press, 2001), 245–64.

127. Cited in Spencer, "'Making the Invisible Visible,'" 24.

# 8. THE SOCIAL SYSTEM AND POVERTY

1. This is one premise of what has come to be called the "new economic sociology." For an overview, see Mauro F. Guillen et al., eds., *The New Economic Sociology: Developments in an Emerging Field* (New York: Russell Sage, 2002).

2. For a thoroughgoing critique of the meritocracy thesis, see Stephen J. McNamee and Robert K. Miller Jr., *The Meritocracy Myth*, 3rd ed. (Lanham, MD: Rowman & Littlefield, 2014).

3. Glen C. Loury, "A Dynamic Theory of Racial Income Differences," in *Women, Minorities, and Employment Discrimination*, ed. Phyllis A. Wallace and Annette M. LaMond (Lexington, MA: Lexington Books, 1977), 176.

4. Steven N. Durlauf, "The Memberships Theory of Inequality: Ideas and Implications," in *Elites, Minorities, and Economic Growth*, ed. Elise S. Brezis and Peter Temin (Amsterdam: Elsevier, 1999), 161–77; Steven N. Durlauf, "The Memberships Theory of Poverty: The Role of Group Affiliations in Determining Socioeconomic Outcomes," in *Understanding Poverty*, ed. Sheldon H. Danziger and Robert H. Haveman (New York: Russell Sage; Cambridge, MA: Harvard University Press, 2001), 392–416.

5. Durlauf, "The Memberships Theory of Poverty," 396.

6. Durlauf, "The Memberships Theory of Poverty," 393–94; Durlauf, "The Memberships Theory of Inequality," 162–64.

7. Durlauf, "The Memberships Theory of Inequality," 163.

8. Durlauf, "The Memberships Theory of Inequality," 168.

9. See Mark Gould, "Race and Theory: Culture, Poverty, and Adaptation to Discrimination in Wilson and Ogbu," *Sociological Theory* 17, no. 2 (July 1999): 171–200.

10. Barbara F. Reskin, "The Proximate Causes of Employment Discrimination," *Contemporary Sociology* 29, no. 2 (March 2000): 319–28.

11. For a classical analysis of invisible privilege, see Peggy McIntosh, "White Privilege: Unpacking the Invisible Knapsack," in *Race, Class, and Gender in the United States*, ed. Paula S. Rothenberg, 5th ed. (New York: Worth, 2001), 163–68.

12. Kim A. Weeden, "Why Do Some Occupations Pay More than Others? Social Closure and Earnings Inequality in the United States," *American Journal of Sociology* 108, no. 1 (July 2002): 55–101. See also David Leonhardt, "Political Clout in the Age of Outsourcing," *New York Times*, April 19, 2006.

13. Charles Tilly, *Durable Inequality* (Berkeley: University of California Press, 1998).

14. Iris Marion Young, "Equality of Whom? Social Groups and Judgments of Injustice," *Journal of Political Philosophy* 9, no. 1 (2001): 1–18.

15. Douglas S. Massey, "The Age of Extremes: Concentrated Affluence and Poverty in the Twenty-First Century," *Demography* 33, no. 4 (November 1996): 395–412; Kendra Bischoff and Sean F. Reardon, *Residential Segregation by Income, 1970–2009* (US2010, Discover America in a New Century, October 2013), http://www.s4.brown.edu/us2010/Data/Report/report10162013.pdf (accessed May 23, 2014); Paul Taylor and Richard Fry, *The Rise of Residential Segregation by Income* (Washington, DC: Pew Research Center, August 2012), http://www.pewsocialtrends.org/2012/08/01/the-rise-of-residential-segregation-by-income (accessed May 23, 2014); Sabrina Tavernise, "Middle-Class Areas Shrink as Income Gap Grows, New Report Finds," *New York Times*, November 16, 2011.

16. John R. Logan and Brian J. Stults, *The Persistence of Segregation in the Metropolis: New Findings from the 2010 Census* (Project USA2010, March 2011), http://www.s4.brown.edu/us2010/Data/Report/report2.pdf (accessed April 6, 2014); John Iceland and Gregory Sharp, "White Residential Segregation in U.S. Metropolitan Areas: Conceptual Issues, Patterns, and Trends from the U.S. Census, 1980 to 2010," *Population Research and Policy Review* 32 (2013): 663–86.

17. Paul A. Jargowsky, *Poverty and Place: Ghettos, Barrios, and the American City* (New York: Russell Sage, 1997); Douglas S. Massey and Nancy A. Denton, *American Apartheid:*

*Segregation and the Making of the Underclass* (Cambridge, MA: Harvard University Press, 1993).

18. Kids Count, *Data Snapshot on High-Poverty Communities* (Baltimore, MD: Anne E. Casey Foundation, 2012), http://www.aecf.org/~/media/Pubs/Initiatives/KIDS%20COUNT/D/DataSnapshotonHighPovertyCommunities/KIDSCOUNTDataSnapshot_HighPovertyCommunities.pdf (accessed May 24, 2014).

19. On life in the South Bronx, see Jonathan Kozol, *Amazing Grace: The Lives of Children and the Conscience of a Nation* (New York: Crown, 1995).

20. Durlauf, "The Memberships Theory of Inequality," 171.

21. Ann Owens and Robert J. Sampson, *Community Well-Being and the Great Recession* (Stanford, CA: Stanford Center on Poverty and Inequality, May 2013).

22. See Steven N. Durlauf, "A Theory of Persistent Income Inequality," *Journal of Economic Growth* 1 (1996): 75–93.

23. My discussion of neighborhood effects draws especially on several comprehensive overviews of the scholarly research. For an influential early analysis, see Christopher Jencks and Susan Mayer, "The Social Consequences of Growing Up in Poor Neighborhoods," in *Inner City Poverty in the United States*, ed. Laurence E. Lynn Jr. and Michael G. H. McGeary (Washington, DC: National Academy Press, 1990), 111–86. For more recent reviews, see Mario Luis Small and Katherine Newman, "Urban Poverty after *The Truly Disadvantaged*: The Rediscovery of the Family, the Neighborhood, and Culture," *Annual Review of Sociology* 27 (2001): 23–45; Robert Samson, Jeffrey D. Morenoff, and Thomas Gannon-Rowley, "Assessing 'Neighborhood Effects': Social Processes and New Directions in Research," *Annual Review of Sociology* 28 (2002): 443–78; Tama Leventhal and Jeanne Brooks-Gunn, "The Neighborhoods They Live In: The Effects of Neighborhood Residence on Child and Adolescent Outcomes," *Psychological Bulletin* 126, no. 2 (2000): 309–37; Anne R. Pebley and Narayan Sastry, "Neighborhoods, Poverty, and Children's Well-Being," in *Social Inequality*, ed. Kathryn M. Neckerman (New York: Russell Sage, 2004), 119–45; and Martha A. Gephart, "Neighborhoods and Communities as Contexts for Development," in *Neighborhood Poverty*, vol. 1, *Contexts and Consequences for Children*, ed. Jeanne Brooks-Gunn, Greg J. Duncan, and J. Lawrence Aber (New York: Russell Sage, 1997), 1–43.

24. Gephart, "Neighborhoods and Communities," 26–28.

25. Leventhal and Brooks-Gunn, "The Neighborhoods They Live In," 315–18.

26. Leventhal and Brooks-Gunn, "The Neighborhoods They Live In," 320–21; Scott J. South and Kyle D. Crowder, "Neighborhood Effects on Family Formation: Concentrated Poverty and Beyond," *American Sociological Review* 64, no. 1 (February 1999): 113–32.

27. Leventhal and Brooks-Gunn, "The Neighborhoods They Live In," 318–20.

28. Patrick Sharkey, *Stuck in Place: Urban Neighborhoods and the End of Progress toward Racial Equality* (Chicago: University of Chicago Press, 2013).

29. For typologies identifying potential causal mechanisms responsible for neighborhood effects, see Jencks and Mayer, "The Social Consequences of Growing Up in a Poor Neighborhood," 113–15; Sampson, Morenoff, and Gannon-Rowley, "Assessing 'Neighborhood Effects,'" 457–58; Small and Newman, "Urban Poverty," 32–35; and Leventhal and Brooks-Gunn, "The Neighborhoods They Live In," 322–28.

30. Poor neighborhoods are not all alike, of course, and they also vary in quality over time; see, for example, Mario Luis Small, *Villa Victoria: The Transformation of Social Capital in a Boston Barrio* (Chicago: University of Chicago Press, 2004), and Mario L. Small, "No Two Ghettos Are Alike," *Chronicle Review* (March 21, 2014): B10–B12.

31. See Pebley and Sastry, "Neighborhoods, Poverty, and Children's Well-Being," 120, and Sampson, Morenoff, and Gannon-Rowley, "Assessing 'Neighborhood Effects,'" 458.

32. My terminology here borrows from Leventhal and Brooks-Gunn, "The Neighborhoods They Live In," 322.

33. Robin L. Jarrett, "Bringing Families Back In: Neighborhood Effects on Child Development," in *Neighborhood Poverty*, vol. 2, *Policy Implications in Studying Neighborhoods*, ed. Jeanne Brooks-Gunn, Greg J. Duncan, and J. Lawrence Aber (New York: Russell Sage, 1997), 48–64.

34. William Julius Wilson, *The Truly Disadvantaged: The Inner City, the Underclass, and Public Policy* (Chicago: University of Chicago Press, 1987), 39; see also William Julius Wilson, *When Work Disappears: The World of the New Urban Poor* (New York: Knopf, 1996), 25–50.

35. Wilson, *When Work Disappears*, 19.

36. For qualitative studies documenting labor market conditions and employment problems in poor communities, see Katherine Newman, *No Shame in My Game: The Working Poor in the Inner City* (New York: Knopf, 1999); Mercer L. Sullivan, *"Getting Paid": Youth Crime and Work in the Inner City* (Ithaca, NY: Cornell University Press, 1989), 55–105; and Daniel Dohan, *The Price of Poverty: Money, Work, and Culture in the Mexican American Barrio* (Berkeley: University of California Press, 2003), 37–98.

37. Dohan, *The Price of Poverty*, 38.

38. Thomas P. Vartanian, "Adolescent Neighborhood Effects on Labor Market and Economic Outcomes," *Social Service Review* 73, no. 2 (June 1999): 142–67; Manuel Pastor Jr. and Ara Robinson Adams, "Keeping Down with the Joneses: Neighbors, Networks, and Wages," *Review of Regional Studies* 26, no. 2 (1996): 115–45; Gary P. Green, Leann M. Tigges, and Irene Browne, "Social Resources, Job Search, and Poverty in Atlanta," *Research in Community Sociology* 5 (1995): 161–82.

39. On the concept of "collective socialization," see Small and Newman, "Urban Poverty," 33.

40. Small and Newman, "Urban Poverty," 33.

41. Wilson, *When Work Disappears*, 20–21, 61–64.

42. See Robert J. Sampson, Jeffrey D. Morenoff, and Felton Earls, "Beyond Social Capital: Spatial Dynamics of Collective Efficacy for Children," *American Sociological Review* 64, no. 5 (October 1999): 633–60; Robert J. Sampson, Stephen W. Raudenbush, and Felton Earls, "Neighborhoods and Violent Crime: A Multilevel Study of Collective Efficacy," *Science* 277 (August 15, 1999): 918–24.

43. Robert J. Sampson, *Great American City: Chicago and the Enduring Neighborhood Effect* (Chicago: University of Chicago Press, 2012), 152–55, 367–72.

44. Sampson, *Great American City*, 250, 272.

45. Ronald F. Ferguson and William T. Dickens, eds., *Urban Problems and Community Development* (Washington, DC: Brookings Institution Press, 1999).

46. The key early work on social networks is Mark S. Granovetter, *Getting a Job: A Study of Contacts and Careers*, 2nd ed. (Chicago: University of Chicago Press, 1995); for an overview of the literature, see John Field, *Social Capital* (London: Routledge, 2003).

47. On the concept of "institutional agent" in network analysis, see Ricardo D. Stanton-Salazar and Sanford M. Dornbusch, "Social Capital and the Reproduction of Inequality: Information Networks among Mexican-Origin High School Students," *Sociology of Education* 68, no. 2 (April 1995): 116–35.

48. Alejandro Portes, "Social Capital: Its Origins and Applications in Modern Sociology," *Annual Review of Sociology* 24 (1998): 7.

49. James S. Coleman, "Social Capital in the Creation of Human Capital," *American Journal of Sociology* 94, supplement (1988): S98.

50. Mark S. Granovetter, "A Theoretical Agenda for Economic Sociology," in Guillen et al., *The New Economic Sociology*, 37–38; Mario Luis Small, *Unanticipated Gains: Origins of Network Inequality in Everyday Life* (Oxford: Oxford University Press, 2009).

51. See Nan Lin, "Social Networks and Status Attainment," *Annual Review of Sociology* 25 (1999): 467–87; Nan Lin, "Inequality in Social Capital," *Contemporary Sociology* 29, no. 6 (November 2000): 785–95; Paul DiMaggio and Filiz Garip, "Network Effects and Social Inequality," *Annual Review of Sociology* 38 (2012): 93–118.

52. On the importance of considering networks as a source of both information *and* influence, see Karen Campbell, Peter V. Marsden, and Jeanne S. Hurlbert, "Social Resources and Socioeconomic Status," *Social Networks* 8 (1986): 97–117.

53. Lin, "Inequality in Social Capital," 787, 793.

54. Katherine M. O'Regan and John M. Quigley, "Family Networks and Youth Access to Jobs," *Journal of Urban Economics* 34, no. 2 (September 1993): 231; on the increasing importance of social networks and "internal referrals" in the hiring process, see Nelson D. Schwartz, "In Hiring, a Friend in Need Is a Prospect, Indeed," *New York Times*, January 27, 2013.

55. See, for example, Julie E. Miller-Cribbs and Naomi B. Farber, "Kin Networks among African Americans: Past and Present," *Social Work* 53, no. 1 (January 2008): 43–51.

56. Frank F. Furstenberg Jr. and Mary Elizabeth Hughes, "Social Capital and Successful Development among At-Risk Youth," *Journal of Marriage and the Family* 57, no. 3 (August 1995): 580–92; Robin L. Jarrett, "Growing Up Poor: The Family Experiences of Socially Mobile Youth in Low-Income African American Neighborhoods," *Journal of Adolescent Research* 19, no. 1 (January 1995): 111–35.

57. Leann M. Tigges, Irene Browne, and Gary P. Green, "Social Isolation of the Urban Poor: Race, Class, and Neighborhood Effects on Social Resources," *Sociological Quarterly* 39, no. 1 (1998): 53–77; Loic J. D. Wacquant and William Julius Wilson, "The Cost of Racial and Class Exclusion in the Inner City," *Annals of the American Academy of Political and Social Science* 501 (January 1989): 22–24.

58. Lin, "Social Networks and Status Attainment," 470, refers to this as the "strength of position proposition."

59. On the hard work required of single mothers to maintain reciprocity in their social networks, see Margaret K. Nelson, "Single Mothers and Social Support: The Commitment to, and Retreat from, Reciprocity," *Qualitative Sociology* 23, no. 3 (Fall 2000): 291–317; see also, with reference to the concept of "defensive individualism," Sandra Susan Smith, *Lone Pursuit: Distrust and Individualism among the Black Poor* (New York: Russell Sage, 2007), 22, 97–137.

60. Deborah E. Belle, "The Impact of Poverty on Social Networks and Supports,"*Marriage and Family Review* 5, no. 4 (Winter 1982): 91, 94; Miller-Cribbs and Faber, "Kin Networks and Poverty," 48.

61. Wilson, *The Truly Disadvantaged*, 60. For an alternative view, see Melvin L. Oliver, "The Urban Black Community as Network: Toward a Social Network Perspective," *Sociological Quarterly* 29, no. 4 (1988): 623–45.

62. On the social isolation thesis and the disadvantages that accrue to the poor from their lack of contacts with mainstream society, see Massey and Denton, *American Apartheid*, 160–62; Wacquant and Wilson, "The Cost of Racial and Class Exclusion," 8–25; Tigges, Browne, and Green, "Social Isolation of the Urban Poor," 53–77; and Bruce H. Rankin and James M. Quane, "Neighborhood Poverty and the Social Isolation of Inner-City African American Families," *Social Forces* 79, no. 1 (September 2000): 139–64.

63. William T. Dickens, "Rebuilding Urban Labor Markets: What Community Development Can Accomplish," in *Urban Problems and Community Development*, 406–8.

64. James R. Elliott, "Social Isolation and Labor Market Insulation: Network and Neighborhood Effects on Less-Educated Urban Workers," *Sociological Quarterly* 40, no. 2 (Winter 1999): 199–216; Jomills Henry Braddock II and James M. McPartland, "How Minorities Continue to Be Excluded from Equal Employment Opportunities: Research on Labor Market and Institutional Barriers," *Journal of Social Issues* 43, no. 1 (Spring 1987): 5–39.

65. Deirdre A. Royster, *Race and the Invisible Hand: How White Networks Exclude Black Men from Blue-Collar Jobs* (Berkeley: University of California Press, 2003).

66. Smith, *Lone Pursuit*; Sandra Susan Smith, "'Don't Put My Name on It': Social Capital Activation and Job-Finding Assistance among the Black Urban Poor," *American Journal of Sociology* 111, no. 1 (July 2005): 1–57.

67. Smith, "'Don't Put My Name on It,'" 27; see also Smith, *Lone Pursuit*, 56–96.

68. Mark S. Granovetter, "The Strength of Weak Ties," *American Journal of Sociology* 78, no. 6 (May 1973): 1360–80; Mark S. Granovetter, "The Strength of Weak Ties: A Network Theory Revisited," *Sociological Theory* 1 (1983): 201–33.

69. Granovetter, "A Network Theory Revisited," 209.

70. Campbell, Marsden, and Hurlbert, "Social Resources and Socioeconomic Status," 98.

71. Granovetter, "A Network Theory Revisited," 212–13.

72. Matthew Desmond, "Disposable Ties and the Urban Poor," *American Journal of Sociology* 117, no. 5 (March 2012): 1328–29.

73. Patricia Fernandez Kelly, "Social and Cultural Capital in the Urban Ghetto: Implications for the Economic Sociology of Immigration," in *The Economic Sociology of Immigration: Essays on Networks, Ethnicity, and Entrepreneurship*, ed. Alejandro Portes (New York: Russell Sage, 1995), 220; on the importance of variety in social networks, see also Bonnie Erickson, "Social Networks: The Value of Variety," *Contexts* 2, no. 1 (Winter 2003): 25–31.

74. Campbell, Marsden, and Hurlbert, "Social Resources and Socioeconomic Status," 98–99. On the effect of network diversity on employment prospects for disadvantaged women, see Jennifer A. Stoloff, Jennifer L. Glanville, and Elisa Jayne Bienenstock, "Women's Participation in the Labor Force: The Role of Social Networks," *Social Networks* 21 (1999): 91–108.

75. Elliott, "Social Isolation and Labor Market Insulation"; Lin, "Social Networks and Status Attainment," 470–76; Newman, *No Shame in My Game*, 77–85, 161–74.

76. Pierre Bourdieu, "The Forms of Capital," in *Handbook of Theory and Research for the Sociology of Education*, ed. John G. Richardson (New York: Greenwood Press, 1986), 249.

77. On the relationship between social capital and human capital, see Coleman, "Social Capital in the Creation of Human Capital," S109–S116; Stanton-Salazar and Dornbusch, "Social Capital and the Reproduction of Inequality," 116–35; Field, *Social Capital*, 45–50; Jay D. Teachman, Kathleen Paasch, and Karen Carver, "Social Capital and the Generation of Human Capital," *Social Forces* 75, no. 4 (June 1997): 1343–59.

78. Annette Lareau, *Unequal Childhoods: Class, Race, and Family Life* (Berkeley: University of California Press, 2003).

79. Silvia Dominguez and Celeste Watkins, "Creating Networks for Survival and Mobility: Social Capital among African-American and Latin-American Low-Income Mothers," *Social Problems* 50, no. 1 (February 2003): 111–35.

80. On the relationship between social capital and cultural capital, see Bonnie H. Erickson, "Culture, Class, and Connections," *American Journal of Sociology* 102, no. 1 (July 1996): 217–51.

81. Dominguez and Watkins, "Creating Networks for Survival and Mobility," 125.

82. Yvette Alex-Assensoh, "Race, Concentrated Poverty, Social Isolation, and Political Behavior," *Urban Affairs Review* 33, no. 2 (November 1997): 209–27.

83. Julia R. Henly, "Informal Support Networks and the Maintenance of Low-Wage Jobs," in *Laboring Below the Line: The New Ethnography of Poverty, Low-Wage Work, and Survival in the Global Economy*, ed. Frank Munger (New York: Russell Sage, 2002), 179–203.

84. Xavier de Souza Briggs, "Brown Kids in White Suburbs: Housing Mobility and the Many Faces of Social Capital," *Housing Policy Debate* 9, no. 1 (1998): 177–221. For the classic study of social networks and the survival strategies of poor black families, see Carol B. Stack, *All Our Kin: Strategies for Survival in a Black Community* (New York: Harper and Row, 1974).

85. Dominguez and Watkins, "Creating Networks for Survival and Mobility," 124, 126–29.

86. Sharon Hicks-Bartlett, "Between a Rock and a Hard Place: The Labyrinth of Working and Parenting in a Poor Community," in *Coping with Poverty: The Social Contexts of Neighborhood, Work, and Family in the African-American Community*, ed. Sheldon H. Danziger and Ann Chih Lin (Ann Arbor: University of Michigan Press, 2000), 27–51.

87. On the "negative" effects of social capital, see Belle, "The Impact of Poverty on Social Networks," 91–94; Portes, "Social Capital," 15–18; Alejandro Portes and Julia Sensenbrenner, "Embeddedness and Immigration: Notes on the Social Determinants of Economic Action," *American Journal of Sociology* 98, no. 6 (May 1993): 1338–44.

88. Portes, "Social Capital," 14.

89. Lewis Coser, *Greedy Institutions: Patterns of Undivided Commitment* (New York: Free Press, 1974), 4, 6.

90. Dominguez and Watkins, "Creating Networks for Survival and Mobility"; Portes and Sensenbrenner, "Embeddedness and Immigration," 1338–40; Belle, "The Impact of Poverty on Social Networks," 91–92; Nelson, "Single Mothers and Social Support," 291–317; John J. La Gaipa, "The Negative Effects of Informal Support Systems," in *Personal Relationships and Social Support*, ed. Steve Duck (London: Sage, 1990), 122–39.

91. Portes and Sensenbrenner, "Embeddedness and Immigration," 1340–44.

92. Newman, *No Shame in My Game*, 92–104.

93. See, for example, Dohan, *The Price of Poverty*, 27–29, 103–53; Wilson, *When Work Disappears*, 57–59; Philippe Bourgois, *In Search of Respect: Selling Crack in El Barrio* (Cambridge: Cambridge University Press, 1996); and Elijah Anderson, *Streetwise: Race, Class, and Change in an Urban Community* (Chicago: University of Chicago Press, 1990), 57–58.

94. Charles Kadushin, *Understanding Social Networks: Theories, Concepts, and Findings* (Oxford: Oxford University Press, 2012), 168, 172.

95. That gains for some often result in losses for others has led some observers to refer to the "negative," "other," or "dark" side of social resources. See Portes, "Social Capital," 15–16; Field, *Social Capital*, 71–90; Roger Waldinger, "The 'Other Side' of Embeddedness: A Case-Study of the Interplay of Economy and Ethnicity," *Ethnic and Racial Studies* 18, no. 3 (July 1995): 555–80.

96. Steven N. Durlauf, "Associational Redistribution: A Defense," *Politics & Society* 24, no. 4 (December 1996): 391–410.

# 9. STRUCTURAL OBSTACLES AND THE PERSISTENCE OF POVERTY (I)

1. C. Wright Mills, *The Sociological Imagination* (Oxford: Oxford University Press, 1959), 8–9.

2. Carmen DeNavas-Walt, Bernadette D. Proctor, and Jessica C. Smith, *Income, Poverty, and Health Insurance Coverage in the United States: 2012*, U.S. Census Bureau, Current Population Reports, P60-245 (Washington, DC: Government Printing Office, September 2013), 14, 18, tables 3 and 5.

3. For a comprehensive overview, see Matthew Desmond and Mustafa Emirbayer, *Racial Domination, Racial Progress: The Sociology of Race in America* (New York: McGraw-Hill, 2010).

4. Melvin L. Oliver and Thomas M. Shapiro, *Black Wealth/White Wealth: A New Perspective on Racial Inequality* (New York: Routledge, 1995), 51.

5. Ira Katznelson, *When Affirmative Action Was White: An Untold History of Racial Inequality in Twentieth-Century America* (New York: Norton, 2005).

6. Katznelson, *When Affirmative Action Was White*; Michael K. Brown et al., *Whitewashing Race: The Myth of a Color-Blind Society* (Berkeley: University of California Press, 2003), 26–33, 76–80.

7. Lincoln Quillian, "New Approaches to Understanding Racial Prejudice and Discrimination," *Annual Review of Sociology* 32 (2006): 299–328; Fredrick C. Harris and Robert C. Lieberman, eds., *Beyond Discrimination: Racial Inequality in a Postracist Era* (New York: Russell Sage, 2013).

8. On white racial attitudes, beliefs, and discourse and on what is sometimes called "modern" or "color-blind" racism, see Eduardo Bonilla-Silva, *Racism without Racists: Color-Blind Racism and the Persistence of Racial Inequality in the United States*, 4th ed. (Lanham, MD: Rowman & Littlefield, 2013); John D. Foster, *White Race Discourse: Preserving Racial Privilege in a Post-Racial Society* (Lanham, MD: Lexington Books, 2013).

9. For a broader treatment of the costs of racism, see Joe R. Feagin and Karyn McKinney, *The Many Costs of Racism* (Lanham, MD: Rowman & Littlefield, 2003).

10. For a comprehensive overview of the use of audit studies in testing for employment discrimination, see Devah Pager, "The Use of Field Experiments for Studies of Employment Discrimination: Contributions, Critiques, and Directions for the Future," *Annals of the American Academy of Political and Social Science* 609 (January 2007): 104–33. It is especially noteworthy that audit studies, which measure employer *behavior*, reveal more job discrimination than do survey research studies, which measure employer *attitudes*; see Devah Pager and Lincoln Quillian, "Walking the Talk? What Employers Say versus What They Do," *American Sociological Review* 70, no. 3 (June 2005): 355–80.

11. For an exemplary study, see Devah Pager, Bruce Western, and Bart Bonikowski, "Discrimination in a Low-Wage Labor Market: A Field Experiment," *American Sociological Review* 74, no. 5 (October 2009): 777–99.

12. Devah Pager, "The Mark of a Criminal Record," *American Journal of Sociology* 108, no. 5 (March 2003): 937–75; Devah Pager, *Marked: Race, Crime and Finding Work in an Era of Mass Incarceration* (Chicago: University of Chicago Press, 2007); see also Devah Pager and Bruce Western, "Discrimination in Low-Wage Labor Markets: Evidence from an Experimental Audit Study in New York City," submission to the Population Association of America Annual Meeting, 2005, http://paa2005.princeton.edu/download.aspx?submissionId=50874 (accessed December 30, 2007).

13. Bruce Western, *Punishment and Inequality in America* (New York: Russell Sage, 2006), 85–130.

14. Marianne Bertrand and Sendhil Mullainathan, "Are Emily and Greg More Employable than Lakisha and Jamal? A Field Experiment on Labor Market Discrimination," *American Economic Review* 94, no. 4 (September 2004): 991–1013.

15. William Julius Wilson, *When Work Disappears: The World of the New Urban Poor* (New York: Knopf, 1996), 111–46.

16. Joleen Kirschenman and Kathryn M. Neckerman, "'We'd Love to Hire Them, But . . .': The Meaning of Race for Employers," in *The Urban Underclass*, ed. Christopher Jencks and Paul E. Peterson (Washington, DC: Brookings Institution, 1991), 213.

17. Johanna Shih, "'. . . Yeah, I Could Hire This One, But I Know It's Gonna Be a Problem': How Race, Nativity, and Gender Affect Employers' Perceptions of the Manageability of Job Seekers," *Ethnic and Racial Studies* 25, no. 1 (January 2002): 99–119.

18. Kathryn M. Neckerman and Joleen Kirschenman, "Hiring Strategies, Racial Bias, and Inner-City Workers," *Social Problems* 38, no. 4 (November 1991): 441–42.

19. Philip Moss and Chris Tilly, "'Soft' Skills and Race: An Investigation of Black Men's Employment Problems," *Work and Occupations* 23, no. 3 (August 1996): 260–61.

20. Changhwan Kim and Christopher R. Tamborini, "The Continuing Significance of Race in the Occupational Attainment of Whites and Blacks: A Segmented Labor Market Analysis," *Sociological Inquiry* 76, no. 1 (February 2006): 23–51.

21. Wilson, *When Work Disappears*, 133–34; Neckerman and Kirschenman, "Hiring Strategies, Racial Bias, and Inner-City Workers," 437–41.

22. On how black workers are shut out of employment opportunities by racially exclusive social networks, see Deirdre A. Royster, *Race and the Invisible Hand: How White Networks Exclude Black Men from Blue-Collar Jobs* (Berkeley: University of California Press, 2003).

23. Peter Edelman, Harry J. Holzer, and Paul Offner, *Reconnecting Disadvantaged Young Men* (Washington, DC: Urban Institute Press, 2006), 11–36; Thomas S. Moore, "The Locus of Racial Discrimination in the Labor Market," *American Journal of Sociology* 116, no. 3 (November 2010): 909–42.

24. Vincent J. Roscigno, Lisette M. Garcia, and Donna Bobbitt-Zeher, "Social Closure and Processes of Race/Sex Employment Discrimination," *Annals of the American Academy of Political and Social Science* 609 (January 2007): 28–34; Vincent J. Roscigno, *The Face of Discrimination: How Race and Gender Impact Work and Home Lives* (Lanham, MD: Rowman & Littlefield, 2007); Lawrence D. Bobo and Susan A. Suh, "Surveying Racial Discrimination: Analyses from a Multiethnic Labor Market," in *Prismatic Metropolis: Inequality in Los Angeles*, ed. Lawrence D. Bobo et al. (New York: Russell Sage, 2000), 523–60.

25. Donald Tomaskovic-Devey, Melvin Thomas, and Kecia Johnson, "Race and the Accumulation of Human Capital across the Career: A Theoretical Model and Fixed-Effects Application," *American Journal of Sociology* 111, no. 1 (July 2005): 58–89.

26. Thomas Shapiro, *The Hidden Cost of Being African American: How Wealth Perpetuates Inequality* (Oxford: Oxford University Press, 2004); Kerwin Kofi Charles and Erik Hurst, "The Transition to Homeownership and the Black-White Wealth Gap," *Review of Economics and Statistics* 84, no. 2 (May 2002): 281–97.

27. Jeannine Bell, *Hate Thy Neighbor: Move-In Violence and the Persistence of Racial Segregation in American Housing* (New York: New York University Press, 2013); Roscigno, *The Face of Discrimination*, 162–67.

28. William Julius Wilson and Richard P. Taub, *There Goes the Neighborhood: Racial, Ethnic, and Class Tension in Four Chicago Neighborhoods and Their Meaning for America* (New York: Knopf, 2006), 20.

29. Judith N. DeSena, "Local Gatekeeping Practices and Residential Segregation," *Sociological Inquiry* 64, no. 3 (August 1994): 307–21.

30. John Yinger, "Housing Discrimination Is Still Worth Worrying About," *Housing Policy Debate* 9, no. 4 (1998): 893–927; Margery Austin Turner and Stephen L. Ross, "How Racial Discrimination Affects the Search for Housing," in *The Geography of Opportunity: Race and*

*Housing Choice in Metropolitan America,* ed. Xavier de Souza Briggs (Washington, DC: Brookings Institution, 2005), 81–100; Stephen L. Ross and Margery Austin Turner, "Housing Discrimination in Metropolitan America: Explaining Changes between 1989 and 2000," *Social Problems* 52, no. 2 (May 2005): 152–80; George Galster and Erin Godfrey, "By Words and Deeds: Racial Steering by Real Estate Agents in the U.S. in 2000," *Journal of the American Planning Association* 71, no. 3 (Summer 2005): 251–68.

31. Margery Austin Turner et al., *Discrimination in Metropolitan Housing Markets: National Results from Phase 1 HDS 2000* (Washington, DC: Urban Institute, November 2002); Shanna L. Smith and Cathy Cloud, "Welcome to the Neighborhood?: The Persistence of Discrimination and Segregation," in *The Integration Debate: Competing Futures for American Cities,* ed. Chester Hartman and Gregory D. Squires (New York: Routledge, 2010), 9–21.

32. Margery Austin Turner et al., *Other Things Being Equal: A Paired Testing Study of Mortgage Lending Institutions, Final Report,* U.S. Department of Housing and Urban Development, Office of Fair Housing and Equal Opportunity (Washington, DC: Government Printing Office, April 2002).

33. Oliver and Shapiro, *Black Wealth/White Wealth,* 136–41; Michael E. Hodge, Mark C. Dawkins, and Jack H. Reeves, "A Case Study of Mortgage Refinancing Discrimination: African American Intergenerational Wealth," *Sociological Inquiry* 77, no. 1 (February 2007): 23–43.

34. William Apgar and Allegra Calder, "The Dual Mortgage Market: The Persistence of Discrimination in Mortgage Lending," in Briggs, *The Geography of Opportunity,* 101–23; Richard Williams, Reynold Nesiba, and Eileen Diaz McConnell, "The Changing Face of Inequality in Home Mortgage Lending," *Social Problems* 52, no. 2 (May 2005): 181–208; Gregory D. Squires and Charis E. Kubrin, *Privileged Places: Race, Residence, and the Structure of Opportunity* (Boulder, CO: Lynne Rienner, 2006), 55–67.

35. Squires and Kubrin, *Privileged Places,* 69–93; Yinger, "Housing Discrimination Is Still Worth Worrying About," 901–2.

36. Squires and Kubrin, *Privileged Places,* 4–17.

37. Shapiro, *The Hidden Cost of Being African American,* 119–22; Chenoa Flippen, "Unequal Returns to Housing Investments? A Study of Real Housing Appreciation among Black, White, and Hispanic Households," *Social Forces* 82, no. 4 (June 2004): 1523–51.

38. Rakesh Kochhar, Richard Fry, and Paul Taylor, *Wealth Gaps Rise to Record Highs between Whites, Blacks and Hispanics* (Washington, DC: Pew Research Center, July 2011), http://www.pewsocialtrends.org/files/2011/07/SDT-Wealth-Report_7-26-11_FINAL.pdf (accessed April 20, 2014); see also Lawrence Mishel, Josh Bivens, Elise Gould, and Heidi Shierholz, *The State of Working America,* 12th ed. (Ithaca, NY: Cornell University Press, 2012), 385.

39. Darrick Hamilton and William Darity Jr., "Race, Wealth, and Intergenerational Poverty," *American Prospect,* September 2009, A10–A12.

40. For book-length studies of residential segregation specifically addressing its implications for the life chances of racial minorities and the poor, see Douglas S. Massey and Nancy A. Denton, *American Apartheid: Segregation and the Making of the Underclass* (Cambridge, MA: Harvard University Press, 1993); Paul A. Jargowsky, *Poverty and Place: Ghettos, Barrios, and the American City* (New York: Russell Sage, 1997); and Sheryll Cashin, *The Failures of Integration: How Race and Class Are Undermining the American Dream* (New York: Public-Affairs, 2004).

41. Douglas S. Massey, "The Age of Extremes: Concentrated Affluence and Poverty in the Twenty-First Century," *Demography* 33, no. 4 (November 1996): 395–412; Sean F. Reardon and Kendra Bischoff, "Income Inequality and Income Segregation," *American Journal of Soci-*

*ology* 116, no. 4 (January 2011): 1092–153; Paul Taylor and Richard Fry, *The Rise of Residential Segregation by Income* (Washington, DC: Pew Research Center, August 2012), http://www.pewsocialtrends.org/files/2012/08/Rise-of-Residential-Income-Segregation-2012.2.pdf (accessed April 6, 2014).

42. John R. Logan and Brian J. Stults, *The Persistence of Segregation in the Metropolis: New Findings from the 2010 Census* (Project USA2010, March 2011), http://www.s4.brown.edu/us2010/Data/Report/report2.pdf (accessed April 6, 2014); John Iceland and Gregory Sharp, "White Residential Segregation in U.S. Metropolitan Areas: Conceptual Issues, Patterns, and Trends from the U.S. Census, 1980 to 2010," *Population Research and Policy Review* 32 (2013): 663–86.

43. Massey and Denton, *American Apartheid*, 74–78; Camille Zubrinsky Charles, "The Dynamics of Racial Residential Segregation," *Annual Review of Sociology* 29 (2003): 170–71.

44. Ingrid Gould Ellen, *Sharing America's Neighborhoods: The Prospects for Stable Racial Integration* (Cambridge, MA: Harvard University Press, 2000); Michael T. Maly, *Beyond Segregation: Multiracial and Multiethnic Neighborhoods in the United States* (Philadelphia: Temple University Press, 2005).

45. W. E. B. Du Bois, *The Souls of Black Folk* (New York: Vintage, Library of America, 1990), 16.

46. Camille Zubrinsky Charles, "Can We Live Together? Racial Preferences and Neighborhood Outcomes," in Briggs, *The Geography of Opportunity*, 45–80; Keith R. Ihlanfeldt and Benjamin Scafidi, "Whites' Neighborhood Racial Preferences and Neighborhood Racial Composition in the United States: Evidence from the Multi-City Study of Inequality," *Housing Studies* 19, no. 3 (2004): 325–59; Maria Krysan, Reynolds Farley, Mick P. Couper, and Tyrone A. Forman, "Does Race Matter in Neighborhood Preferences? Results from a Video Experiment," *American Journal of Sociology* 115, no. 2 (September 2009): 527–59.

47. On white flight and white avoidance of racially mixed neighborhoods, see Lincoln Quillian, "Why Is Black-White Residential Segregation So Persistent? Evidence on Three Theories from Migration Data," *Social Science Research* 31, no. 2 (June 2002): 197–229; Maria Krysan, "Whites Who Say They'd Flee: Who Are They, and Why Would They Leave," *Demography* 39, no. 4 (November 2002): 675–96.

48. Cashin, *The Failures of Integration*, 17–28; Bell, *Hate Thy Neighbor*, 53–85; Maria Krysan and Reynolds Farley, "The Residential Preferences of Blacks: Do They Explain Persistent Segregation?," *Social Forces* 80, no. 3 (March 2002): 937–80.

49. Charles, "The Dynamics of Residential Segregation," 191.

50. Massey and Denton, *American Apartheid*; Gregory D. Squires, "Demobilization of the Individualistic Bias: Housing Market Discrimination as a Contributor to Labor Market and Economic Inequality," *Annals of the American Academy of Political and Social Science* 609 (January 2007): 200–214.

51. Kids Count, *Data Snapshot on High Poverty Communities*, 1–2, http://www.aecf.org/~/media/Pubs/Initiatives/KIDS%20COUNT/D/DataSnapshotonHighPovertyCommunities/KIDSCOUNTDataSnapshot_HighPovertyCommunities.pdf (accessed April 6, 2014); see also Robert J. Sampson, "Division Street, U.S.A.," *New York Times*, October 26, 2013.

52. Peter Irons, *Jim Crow's Children: The Broken Promise of the Brown Decision* (New York: Penguin, 2004), 259–314; Gary Orfield, John Kucsera, and Genevieve Siegel-Hawly, *E Pluribus . . . Separation: Deepening Double Segregation for More Students* (Los Angeles, CA: Civil Rights Project, September 2012).

53. Orfield, Kucsera, and Siegel-Hawly, *E Pluribus*, 9.

54. Meredith Phillips and Tiffani Chin, "School Inequality: What Do We Know?," in *Social Inequality*, ed. Kathryn M. Neckerman (New York: Russell Sage, 2004), 467–519.

55. Cashin, *The Failures of Integration*, 206.

56. George Galster, Ronald Mincy, and Mitch Tobin, "The Disparate Racial Neighborhood Impacts of Metropolitan Economic Restructuring," in *Race, Poverty, and Domestic Policy*, ed. C. Michael Henry (New Haven, CT: Yale University Press, 2004), 188–218.

57. Elizabeth Anderson, *The Imperative of Integration* (Princeton, NJ: Princeton University Press, 2010), 27–28; Laurent Gobillon, Harris Selod, and Yves Zenou, "The Mechanisms of Spatial Mismatch," *Urban Studies* 44, no. 12 (November 2007): 2401–27; Roberto M. Fernandez and Celina Su, "Space in the Study of Labor Markets," *Annual Review of Sociology* 30 (2004): 545–69.

58. Jomills Henry Braddock II and James M. McPartland, "How Minorities Continue to Be Excluded from Equal Employment Opportunities: Research on Labor Market and Institutional Barriers," *Journal of Social Issues* 43, no. 1 (Spring 1987): 5–39.

59. Anderson, *The Imperative of Integration*, 33–34; William Julius Wilson, *The Truly Disadvantaged: The Inner City, the Underclass, and Public Policy* (Chicago: University of Chicago Press, 1987), 60; Katherine S. Newman, *No Shame in My Game: The Working Poor in the Inner City* (New York: Knopf, 1999), 77–84.

60. Chris Tilly et al., "Space as a Signal: How Employees Perceive Neighborhoods in Four Metropolitan Labor Markets," in *Urban Inequality: Evidence from Four Cities*, ed. Alice O'Connor, Chris Tilly, and Lawrence D. Bobo (New York: Russell Sage, 2001), 304–38.

61. Kirchenman and Neckerman, "'We'd Love to Hire Them,'" 215–17.

62. Massey and Denton, *American Apartheid*, 149–53.

63. Shapiro, *The Hidden Cost of Being African American*; Flippen, "Unequal Returns to Housing Investments?"

64. Shapiro, *The Hidden Cost of Being African American*, 47–48.

65. Mishel, Bivens, Gould, and Shierholz, *The State of Working America*, 68, 385; see also Thomas Shapiro, Tatjanna Meschede, and Sam Osoro, *The Roots of the Widening Racial Wealth Gap: Explaining the Black-White Economic Divide* (Waltham, MA: Institute on Assets & Social Policy, February 2013), http://iasp.brandeis.edu/pdfs/Author/shapiro-thomas-m/racialwealthgapbrief.pdf (accessed April 20, 2014); George Lipsitz and Melvin L. Oliver, "Integration, Segregation, and the Racial Wealth Gap," in Hartman and Squires, *The Integration Debate: Competing Futures for American Cities*, 153–67.

66. Shapiro, *The Hidden Cost of Being African American*, 36–41; Lori Latrice Martin, *Black Asset Poverty and the Enduring Racial Divide* (Boulder, CO: First Forum Press, 2013).

67. On the economic vulnerability of middle-class black families, see Mary Pattillo-McCoy, *Black Picket Fences: Privilege and Peril among the Black Middle Class* (Chicago: University of Chicago Press, 1999).

68. Massey and Denton, *American Apartheid*, 153–60; Karen M. Paget, "Can Cities Escape Political Isolation?," *American Prospect*, January–February 1998, 54–62.

69. On how residential segregation undermines the democratic ideal, see Anderson, *The Imperative of Integration*, 89–111.

70. Mireya Navarro, "In New York, Having a Job, or 2, Doesn't Mean Having a Home," *New York Times*, September 18, 2013; see also Jack Healy, "In Wyoming, Many Jobs But No Place to Call Home," *New York Times*, January 13, 2013.

71. For an analysis of the economic context of the problem of affordable housing, see Chris Tilly, "The Economic Environment of Housing: Income Inequality and Insecurity," in *A Right to Housing: Foundations for a New Social Agenda*, ed. Rachel G. Bratt, Michael E. Stone, and Chester Hartman (Philadelphia: Temple University Press, 2006), 20–37.

72. See, for example, Barbara Ehrenreich, *Nickel and Dimed: On (Not) Getting by in America* (New York: Metropolitan Books, 2001), 12, 25–27, 138–41, 170–75, 200–201.

73. Seongyeon Auh et al., "Children's Housing Environments: Welfare Families in Iowa," *Family and Consumer Sciences Research Journal* 35, no. 2 (December 2006): 96–117.

74. Meghan Henry, Dr. Alvaro Cortes, and Sean Morris, *The 2013 Annual Homeless Assessment Report (AHAR) to Congress* (Washington, DC: U.S. Department of Housing and Urban Development, 2013), 6, https://www.onecpd.info/resources/documents/ahar-2013-part1.pdf (accessed April 24, 2014); Susan Saulny, "After Recession, More Young Adults Are Living in the Street," *New York Times*, December 19, 2012.

75. On "why housing matters," see Millennial Housing Commission, *Meeting Our Nation's Housing Challenges*, report to U.S. Congress (Washington, DC: Government Printing Office, May 30, 2002), 7–11, http://govinfo.library.unt.edu/mhc/MHCReport.pdf (accessed December 30, 2007).

76. Rachel G. Bratt, Michael E. Stone, and Chester Hartman, "Why a Right to Housing Is Needed and Makes Sense: Editors' Introduction," in Bratt, Stone, and Hartman, *A Right to Housing*, 1–19.

77. Joint Center for Housing Studies of Harvard University, *The State of the Nation's Housing 2013* (Cambridge, MA: Joint Center for Housing Studies of Harvard University, 2013), 4–5, 27–28, http://www.jchs.harvard.edu/sites/jchs.harvard.edu/files/son2013.pdf (accessed April 24, 2014).

78. Michael E. Stone, *Shelter Poverty: New Ideas on Housing Affordability* (Philadelphia: Temple University Press, 1993); Michael E. Stone, "Housing Affordability: One-Third of a Nation Shelter-Poor," in Bratt, Stone, and Hartman, *A Right to Housing*, 38–60.

79. Stone, "Housing Affordability," 44.

80. Stone, "Housing Affordability," 47–57.

81. On the perils of homeownership for low-income families, see Dean Baker, *Who's Dreaming? Homeownership among Low Income Families* (Washington, DC: Center for Economic and Policy Research, January 11, 2005), http://www.uta.edu/faculty/grovenstein/investments/americandream.pdf (accessed December 30, 2007).

82. Michael E. Stone, "Pernicious Problems of Housing Finance," in Bratt, Stone, and Hartman, *A Right to Housing*, 93–94; Rachel E. Dwyer, "Expanding Homes and Increasing Inequalities: U.S. Housing Development and the Residential Segregation of the Affluent," *Social Problems* 54, no. 1 (February 2007): 23–46; Elizabeth Warren and Amelia Warren Tyagi, *The Two-Income Trap: Why Middle-Class Parents Are Going Broke* (New York: Basic Books, 2004), 20–37.

83. Stone, "Pernicious Problems of Housing Finance," 96–98; Edward N. Wolff, Lindsay A. Owens, and Esra Burak, "How Much Wealth Was Destroyed in the Great Recession?," in *The Great Recession*, ed. David B. Grusky, Bruce Western, and Christopher Wimer (New York: Russell Sage, 2011), 132–41; Ingrid Gould Ellen and Samuel Dastrup, *Housing and the Great Recession* (Russell Sage Foundation and the Stanford Center on Poverty, October 2012), http://furmancenter.org/files/publications/HousingandtheGreatRecession.pdf (accessed March 30, 2014).

84. Cited in Shaila Dewan, "In Many Cities, Rent Is Rising out of Reach of Middle Class," *New York Times*, April 15, 2014.

85. John M. Quigley and Steven Raphael, "Is Housing Unaffordable? Why Isn't It More Affordable?," *Journal of Economic Perspectives* 18, no. 1 (Winter 2004): 192–93, 197–200.

86. National Low Income Housing Coalition, "Introduction," *Out of Reach 2013* (Washington, DC: National Low Income Housing Coalition, 2013), 5, http://nlihc.org/sites/default/files/oor/2013_OOR.pdf (April 24, 2014); Joint Center Housing Studies of Harvard University, *America's Rental Housing: Evolving Markets and Needs* (Cambridge, MA: Joint Center for

Housing Studies of Harvard University, 2013), 5–6, 28–29, http://www.jchs.harvard.edu/sites/jchs.harvard.edu/files/jchs_americas_rental_housing_2013_1_0.pdf (accessed April 24, 2014).

87. Barry L. Steffen, *Worst Case Housing Needs 2011, Report to Congress* (Washington, DC: U.S. Department of Housing and Urban Development, August 2013), 1, 5–6, http://www.huduser.org/Publications/pdf/HUD-506_WorstCase2011_reportv3.pdf (accessed April 24, 2014).

88. National Low Income Housing Coalition, *Out of Reach 2014* (Washington, DC: National Low Income Housing Coalition, 2014), 4, http://nlihc.org/sites/default/files/oor/2014OOR.pdf (accessed April 24, 2014); National Low Income Housing Coalition, *Out of Reach 2013*, 5.

89. Joint Center Housing Studies of Harvard University, *America's Rental Housing: Evolving Markets and Needs*, 19–21; Joint Center for Housing Studies of Harvard University, *America's Rental Housing: Homes for a Diverse Nation* (Cambridge, MA: Joint Center for Housing Studies of Harvard University, 2006), 16.

90. Quigley and Raphael, "Is Housing Unaffordable?," 199–200.

91. National Low Income Housing Coalition, *Out of Reach 2013*, 3–5.

92. Will Fischer and Barbara Sard, *Chart Book: Federal Housing Spending Is Poorly Matched to Need* (Washington, DC: Center on Budget and Policy Priorities, December 2013), 1–4, http://www.cbpp.org/cms/?fa=view&id=4067 (accessed April 24, 2014); Dushaw Hockett et al., *The Crisis in America's Housing: Confronting Myths and Promoting Balanced Housing Policy* (January 2005), 9, http://www.cepr.net/documents/publications/housing_book_2005_01.pdf (accessed December 28, 2007).

93. Economic Policy Program, *Housing Commission, Housing America's Future: New Directions for National Policy* (Washington, DC: Bipartisan Policy Center, February 2013), 11–12, http://bipartisanpolicy.org/sites/default/files/BPC_Housing%20Report_web_0.pdf (accessed April 24, 2014); Will Fischer and Chye-Ching Huang, *Mortgage Interest Deduction Is Ripe for Reform* (Washington, DC: Center on Budget and Policy Priorities, June 2013), 12, http://www.cbpp.org/files/4-4-13hous.pdf (accessed April 24, 2014); see also Yonah Freemark and Lawrence J. Vale, "Illogical Housing Aid," *New York Times*, October 31, 2012.

94. John Yinger, "Housing Discrimination and Residential Segregation as Causes of Poverty," in *Understanding Poverty*, ed. Sheldon H. Danziger and Robert H. Haveman (New York: Russell Sage; Cambridge, MA: Harvard University Press, 2001), 359–91.

95. See the Doc4Kids Project, *Not Safe at Home: How America's Housing Crisis Threatens the Health of Its Children* (Boston: Boston Medical Center, February 1998); Rebecca Cohen, *The Impacts of Affordable Housing on Health: A Research Summary* (Washington, DC: Center for Housing Policy, May 2011), http://www.nhc.org/media/files/Insights_HousingAndHealth Brief.pdf (accessed April 24, 2014); Howard L. Campbell and Joan R. McFadden, "Healthy Living: Housing Affordability and Its Impact on Family Health," *Journal of Family and Consumer Sciences* 98, no. 4 (November 2006): 49–51.

96. See Baker, "Who's Dreaming?"

97. Yinger, "Housing Discrimination," 359.

98. Peter Marcuse and W. Dennis Keating, "The Permanent Housing Crisis: The Failures of Conservatism and the Limitations of Liberalism," in Bratt, Stone, and Hartman, *A Right to Housing*, 139–62.

99. Gary W. Evans, Jeanne Brooks-Gunn, and Pamela Kato Klebanov, "Stressing Out the Poor: Chronic Physiological Stress and the Income-Achievement Gap," *Pathways* (Winter 2011): 16–21; Greg J. Duncan and Katherine Magnuson, "The Long Reach of Early Childhood Poverty," *Pathways* (Winter 2011): 22–27; Richard Rothstein, *Class and Schools: Using Social, Economic, and Educational Reform to Close the Black-White Achievement Gap* (Washington, DC: Economic Policy Institute, 2004), 37–45; Jack P. Shonkoff and Deborah A. Phil-

lips, *From Neurons to Neighborhoods: The Science of Early Childhood Development* (Washington, DC: National Academy Press, 2000), 182–217.

100. Shonkoff and Phillips, *From Neurons to Neighborhoods*, 267–96, 288–93; Suzanne Bianchi et al., "Inequality in Parental Investment in Child-Rearing: Expenditures, Time, and Health," in Neckerman, *Social Inequality*, 189–219; Neeraj Kaushal, Katherine Magnuson, and Jane Waldfogel, "How Is Family Income Related to Investments in Children's Learning?," in *Whither Opportunity? Rising Inequality, Schools, and Children's Life Chances*, ed. Greg J. Duncan and Richard J. Murnane (New York: Russell Sage, 2011), 187–205.

101. Marcia K. Meyers et al., "Inequality in Early Childhood Education and Care: What Do We Know?," in Neckerman, *Social Inequality*, 223–69.

102. Meredith Phillips, "Parenting, Time Use, and Disparities in Academic Outcomes," in Duncan and Murnane, *Whither Opportunity?*, 208–28; Valerie E. Lee and David T. Burkam, *Inequality at the Starting Gate: Social Background Differences in Achievement as Children Begin School* (Washington, DC: Economic Policy Institute, 2002); Betty Hart and Todd R. Risley, *Meaningful Differences in the Everyday Experience of Young American Children* (Baltimore, MD: Paul H. Brookes, 1995).

103. Lee and Burkam, *Inequality at the Starting Gate*. For a study documenting the strong influence on subsequent educational attainment of the social circumstances, family background, and resources of children at the time they enter the first grade, see Doris R. Entwisle, Karl L. Alexander, and Linda Steffel Olson, "First Grade and Educational Attainment by Age 22: A New Story," *American Journal of Sociology* 110, no. 5 (March 2005): 1458–502.

104. Jonathan Kozol, *The Shame of the Nation: The Restoration of Apartheid Schooling in America* (New York: Crown, 2005), and Jonathan Kozol, *Savage Inequalities: Children in America's Schools* (New York: Crown, 1991).

105. Kozol, *The Shame of the Nation*, 321–25.

106. Eduardo Porter, "In Public Education, Edge Still Goes to Rich," *New York Times*, November 6, 2013; Ary Spatig-Amerikaner, *Unequal Education: Federal Loophole Enables Lower Spending on Students of Color* (Washington, DC: Center for American Progress, August 2012); Bruce D. Baker and Sean P. Corcoran, *The Stealth Inequities of School Funding: How State and Local School Finance Systems Perpetuate Inequitable Student Spending* (Washington, DC: Center for American Progress, September 2012).

107. See Peter Schrag, *Final Test: The Battle for Adequacy in America's Schools* (New York: New Press, 2005), 79, on the contrast between "equity" and "adequacy." See also Richard Rothstein, *Brown v. Board at 60: Why Have We Been So Disappointed? What Have We Learned?* (Washington, DC: Economic Policy Institute, April 2014), 3–4, http://s3.epi.org/files/2014/EPI-Brown-v-Board-04-17-2014.pdf (accessed May 22, 2014).

108. Lee and Burkam, *Inequality at the Starting Gate*, 63–77; Meredith Phillips and Tiffani Chin, "School Inequality: What Do We Know?," in Neckerman, *Social Inequality*, 467–519; Cecilia Elena Rouse and Lisa Barrow, "U.S. Elementary and Secondary Schools: Equalizing Opportunity or Replicating the Status Quo?," *The Future of Children* 16, no. 2 (Fall 2006): 99–123.

109. Phillips and Chin, "School Inequality," 510–11.

110. Rouse and Barrow, "U.S. Elementary and Secondary Schools," 116.

111. OECD, *Lessons from PISA for the United States: Strong Performers and Successful Reformers in Education* (Paris: OECD Publishing, 2011), cited in Eduardo Porter, "For Schools, Long Road to a Level Playing Field," *New York Times*, May 21, 2014.

112. On the persistence of educational segregation, see Orfield, Kucsera, and Siegel-Hawley, *E Pluribus*; Gary Orfield, Genevieve Siegel-Hawley, and John Kucsera, *Sorting Out Deepening Confusion on Segregation Trends* (Los Angeles, CA: Civil Rights Project, March 2014), http://

civilrightsproject.ucla.edu/research/k-12-education/integration-and-diversity/sorting-out-deepening-confusion-on-segregation-trends/Segregation-Trends-Dispute-CRP-Researchers.pdf (accessed April 7, 2014); Richard Rothstein, *For Public Schools, Segregation Then, Segregation Since: Education and the Unfinished March* (Washington, DC: Economic Policy Institute, August 2013), http://s2.epi.org/files/2013/Unfinished-March-School-Segregation.pdf (accessed April 24, 2014).

113. Richard D. Kahlenberg, *Can Separate Be Equal? The Overlooked Flaw at the Center of No Child Left Behind* (Washington, DC: Century Foundation, 2004), 2–3.

114. Cashin, *The Failures of Integration*, 222–25; Richard D. Kahlenberg, "The Return of 'Separate But Equal,'" in *Inequality Matters: The Growing Economic Divide in America and Its Poisonous Consequences*, ed. James Lardner and David A. Smith (New York: New Press, 2005), 57–58.

115. Paul Taylor et al., *The Rising Cost of Not Going to College* (Washington, DC: Pew Research Center, February 11, 2014), http://www.pewsocialtrends.org/files/2014/02/SDT-higher-ed-FINAL-02-11-2014.pdf (accessed April 3, 2014); Mishel, Bivens, Gould, and Shierholz, *The State of Working America*, 211–22.

116. Mamie Lynch, Jennifer Engle, and José L. Cruz, *Priced Out: How the Wrong Financial Aid Policies Hurt Low-Income Students* (Washington, DC: The Education Trust, June 2011), 12, http://www.edtrust.org/sites/edtrust.org/files/PricedOutFINAL.pdf (accessed April 1, 2014).

117. Gene Nichol, "Educating for Privilege," *The Nation*, October 13, 2003, 22; David Leonhardt, "Top Colleges, Largely for the Elite," *New York Times*, May 25, 2011.

118. Anthony P. Carnevale and Stephen J. Rose, "Socioeconomic Status, Race/Ethnicity, and Selective College Admissions," in *America's Untapped Resource: Low-Income Students in Higher Education*, ed. Richard D. Kahlenberg (New York: Century Foundation Press, 2004), 106.

119. David Leonhardt, "As Wealthy Fill Top Colleges, Concerns Grow over Fairness," *New York Times*, April 22, 2004.

120. Anthony P. Carnevale, "A Real Analysis of Real Education," *Liberal Education* 94, no. 4 (Fall 2008): 56–57.

121. David Leonhardt, "Better Colleges Failing to Lure Poorer Strivers," *New York Times*, March 17, 2013; Caroline Hoxby and Christopher Avery, "The Missing 'One-Offs': The Hidden Supply of High-Achieving Low-Income Students," *Brookings Papers on Economic Activity*, Spring 2013, 1–50.

122. Robert H. Haveman and Timothy M. Smeeding, "The Role of Higher Education in Social Mobility," *The Future of Children* 16, no. 2 (Fall 2006): 126–28; Tamara Draut, *Strapped: Why America's 20- and 30-Somethings Can't Get Ahead* (New York: Doubleday, 2005), 46–50; Daniel Golden, *The Price of Admission: How America's Ruling Class Buys Its Way into Elite Colleges—And Who Gets Left Outside* (New York: Crown, 2006).

123. Richard D. Kahlenberg, "Cost Remains a Key Obstacle to College Access," *Chronicle of Higher Education*, March 10, 2006, B51–B52.

124. See Phil Oliff, Vincent Palacios, Ingrid Johnson, and Michael Leachman, *Recent Deep State Higher Education Cuts May Harm Students and the Economy for Years to Come* (Washington, DC: Center on Budget and Policy Priorities, March 2013), http://www.cbpp.org/files/3-19-13sfp.pdf (accessed April 24, 2014); Robert Hiltonsmith and Tamara Draut, *The Great Cost Shift Continues: State Higher Education Funding after the Recession* (New York: Demos, 2014).

125. Suzanne Mettler, "College: The Great Unleveler," *New York Times*, March 2, 2014.

126. Mettler, "College: The Great Unleveler"; Suzanne Mettler, "Equalizers No More: Politics Thwart College's Role in Upward Mobility," *Chronicle Review*, March 17, 2014, B4–B10.

127. Lawrence E. Gladieux, "Low-Income Students and the Affordability of Higher Education," in Kahlenberg, *America's Untapped Resource*, 28–31.

128. Stephen Burd, *Undermining Pell: How Colleges Compete for Wealthy Students and Leave the Low-Income Behind* (Washington, DC: New American Foundation, May 2013), http://education.newamerica.net/sites/newamerica.net/files/policydocs/Merit_Aid%20Final.pdf (accessed April 24, 2014); Dan Clawson and Max Page, *The Future of Higher Education* (New York: Routledge, 2011), 33–34; Tamara Draut, "The Growing College Gap," in Lardner and Smith, *Inequality Matters*, 92–94.

129. Donald Heller, cited in Robert Tomsho, "As Tuition Soars, Federal Aid to College Students Falls," *Wall Street Journal*, October 25, 2006.

130. Draut, *Strapped*, 7–9, 34–35; Andrew Martin and Andrew W. Lehren, "A Generation Hobbled by College Debt," *New York Times*, May 13, 2012; The Project on Student Debt, *Student Debt and the Class of 2012* (Washington, DC: Institute for College Access and Success, December 2013), http://projectonstudentdebt.org/files/pub/classof2010.pdf (accessed April 7, 2014.

131. Gladieux, "Low-Income Students," 19–23.

132. Rothstein, *Class and Schools*, 1–5, 129–47.

133. Joseph Berger, "4-Hour Trek across New York for 4 Hours of Work, and $28," *New York Times*, May 6, 2004.

134. David Leonhardt, "Geography Seen as Barrier to Climbing Class Ladder," *New York Times*, July 22, 2013.

135. Elizabeth Roberto, *Commuting to Opportunity: The Working Poor and Commuting in the United States* (Washington, DC: Brookings, February 2008), http://www.stanford.edu/group/scspi/_media/pdf/key_issues/transportation_policy.pdf (accessed March 29, 2014).

136. Alan Berube and Steven Raphael, *Access to Cars in New Orleans* (Washington, DC: Brookings Institution, 2005), table 3, http://www.brookings.edu/metro/20050915_katrinacarstables.pdf (accessed December 28, 2007).

137. Paul M. Ong, "Work and Automobile Ownership among Welfare Recipients," *Social Work Research* 20, no. 4 (December 1996): 255–62.

138. Charles L. Baum, "The Effects of Vehicle Ownership on Employment," *Journal of Urban Economics* 66 (2009): 151–63.

139. Karen Seccombe, Delores James, and Kimberly Battle Walters, "'They Think You Ain't Much of Nothing': The Social Construction of the Welfare Mother," *Journal of Marriage and the Family* 60, no. 4 (November 1998): 858.

140. Robin Pogrebin, "Full Tanks and Empty Wallets Put Squeeze on Working Class," *New York Times*, May 13, 2006.

141. Robert D. Bullard, "Introduction," in *Highway Robbery: Transportation Racism and New Routes to Equity*, ed. Robert D. Bullard, Glenn S. Johnson, and Angel O. Torres (Cambridge, MA: South End Press, 2004), 3–4.

142. Katherine Boo, "The Marriage Cure: Is Wedlock Really a Way out of Poverty?," *New Yorker*, August 18 and 25, 2003, 110–13.

143. On the unique transportation needs of low-income women, see Evelyn Blumenberg, "En-gendering Effective Planning," *Journal of the American Planning Association* 70, no. 3 (Summer 2004): 269–81; Evelyn Blumenberg, "Moving Welfare Participants to Work: Women, Transportation, and Welfare Reform," *Affilia* 15, no. 2 (Summer 2000): 259–76.

144. Berger, "4-Hour Trek across New York."

145. Harriet B. Presser, *Working in a 24/7 Economy: Challenges for American Families* (New York: Russell Sage, 2003).

146. Philip Moss and Chris Tilly, *Stories Employers Tell: Race, Skill, and Hiring in America* (New York: Russell Sage, 2001), 195.

147. Moss and Tilly, *Stories Employers Tell*, 195–96.

148. See Mark Garrett and Brian Taylor, "Reconsidering Social Equity in Public Transit," *Berkeley Planning Journal* 13 (1999): 9–10.

149. See Harry J. Holzer, Keith R. Ihlanfeldt, and David L. Sjoquist, "Work, Search, and Travel among White and Black Youth," *Journal of Urban Economics* 35, no. 3 (May 1994): 320–45.

150. Ong, "Work and Automobile Ownership among Welfare Recipients"; Brian D. Taylor and Paul M. Ong, "Spatial Mismatch or Automobile Mismatch? An Examination of Race, Residence, and Commuting in U.S. Metropolitan Areas," *Urban Studies* 32, no. 9 (1995): 1453–73.

151. Cynthia Needles Fletcher et al., "Small Towns and Welfare Reform," *Poverty Research News* 4, no. 5 (September–October 2000).

152. April Kaplan, "Transportation and Welfare Reform," *Welfare Information Network: Issue Notes* 1, no. 4 (May 1997): 1.

153. Erik Eckholm, "In Rural Oregon, These Are the Times That Try Working People's Hopes," *New York Times*, August 20, 2006.

154. Somini Sengupta, "Living on Welfare: A Clock Is Ticking," *New York Times*, April 29, 2001.

155. Jennifer Medina, "Hardship Makes a New Home in the Suburbs," *New York Times*, May 10, 2014.

156. Charles Craypo and David Cormier, "Job Restructuring as a Determinant of Wage Inequality and Working Poor Households," *Journal of Economic Issues* 34, no. 1 (March 2000): 36.

157. Kaplan, "Transportation and Welfare Reform," 2.

158. Bullard, Johnson, and Torres, *Highway Robbery*.

159. See Kaplan, "Transportation and Welfare Reform"; Sandra Danziger et al., "Barriers to the Employment of Welfare Recipients," in *Prosperity for All? The Economic Boom and African Americans*, ed. Robert Cherry and William M. Rodgers III (New York: Russell Sage, 2000), 245–78; and Paul Ong and Evelyn Blumenberg, "Job Access, Commute, and Travel Burden among Welfare Recipients," *Urban Studies* 35, no. 1 (1998): 77–93; Laura Lein and Deanna T. Schexnayder, *Life after Welfare: Reform and the Persistence of Poverty* (Austin: University of Texas Press, 2007), 77–96.

160. Jean Anyon, *Radical Possibilities: Public Policy, Urban Education, and a New Social Movement* (New York: Routledge, 2005), 84.

161. Kaplan, "Transportation and Welfare Reform"; Rich Stolz, "Race, Poverty, and Transportation," *Poverty and Race* 9, no. 2 (March–April 2000): 1–2, 8–10.

162. Garrett and Taylor, "Reconsidering Social Equity."

163. On the "bus versus rail" battle in Los Angeles, see Eric Mann, "Los Angeles Bus Riders Derail the MTA," in Bullard, Johnson, and Torres, *Highway Robbery*, 33–47.

164. Garrett and Taylor, "Reconsidering Social Equity," 23.

165. Garrett and Taylor, "Reconsidering Social Equity," 7.

166. Garrett and Taylor, "Reconsidering Social Equity," 23.

# 10. STRUCTURAL OBSTACLES AND THE PERSISTENCE OF POVERTY (II)

1. Diana Pearce introduced the expression "feminization of poverty" to refer to the disproportionately high rate of poverty among women and their dependents; see Diana Pearce, "The Feminization of Poverty: Women, Work, and Welfare," *Urban and Social Change Review* 11, nos. 1–2 (February 1978): 28–36.

2. Carmen DeNavas-Walt, Bernadette D. Proctor, and Jessica C. Smith, *Income, Poverty, and Health Insurance Coverage in the United States: 2012*, U.S. Census Bureau, Current Population Reports, P60-245 (Washington, DC: Government Printing Office, 2013), 16, 52, 64, tables B-1, B-3.

3. DeNavas-Walt, Proctor, and Smith, *Income, Poverty, and Health Insurance Coverage*, 50, table A-4; Arianne Hegewisch, Claudia Williams, and Angela Edwards, *The Gender Wage Gap: 2012* (Washington, DC: Institute for Women's Policy Research, March 2013), table 1, http://www.iwpr.org/publications/pubs/the-gender-wage-gap-2012 (accessed April 17, 2014). On the persistence of gender inequality, see Paula England, "The Gender Revolution: Uneven and Stalled," *Gender & Society* 24, no. 2 (April 2010): 149–66, and Stephanie Coontz, "The Myth of Male Decline," *New York Times*, September 30, 2012.

4. U.S. Department of Labor, Bureau of Labor Statistics, *Women in the Labor Force: A Databook*, Report 1040 (Washington, DC: Government Printing Office, February 2013), 74–76, table 20, http://www.bls.gov/cps/wlf-databook-2012.pdf (accessed April 14, 2014); see also Paul Taylor et al., *On Pay Gap, Millennial Women Near Parity—For Now* (Washington, DC: Pew Research Center, December 2013), 20–22, http://www.pewsocialtrends.org/files/2013/12/gender-and-work_final.pdf (accessed July 19, 2014).

5. Stephen J. Rose and Heidi I. Hartmann, *Still a Man's Labor Market: The Long-Term Earnings Gap* (Washington, DC: Institute for Women's Policy Research, 2004); Heidi Hartmann, Stephen J. Rose, and Vicky Lovell, "How Much Progress in Closing the Long-Term Earnings Gap?," in *The Declining Significance of Gender?*, ed. Francine D. Blau, Mary C. Brinton, and David B. Grusky (New York: Russell Sage, 2006), 125–55.

6. Jessica Arons, *Lifetime Losses: The Career Wage Gap* (Washington, DC: Center for American Progress Action Fund, December 2008), 2–3.

7. Rose and Hartmann, *Still a Man's Labor Market*, 25.

8. Suzanne Bianchi, Nancy Folbre, and Douglas Wolf, "Unpaid Care Work," in *For Love and Money: Care Provision in the United States*, ed. Nancy Folbre (New York: Russell Sage, 2012), 47, 52; see also Taylor et al., *On Pay Gap*, 22–23.

9. Arlie Hochschild, *The Second Shift* (New York: Avon, 1990).

10. Paula England, "Toward Gender Equality: Progress and Bottlenecks," in Blau, Brinton, and Grusky, *The Declining Significance of Gender?*, 250–52.

11. Naomi Gerstel, "The Third Shift: Gender and Care Work Outside the Home," *Qualitative Sociology* 23, no. 4 (Winter 2000): 467–83; Jane Gross, "As Parents Age, Baby Boomers and Business Struggle to Cope," *New York Times*, March 25, 2006.

12. My reference to care work as a "labor of love" borrows from Gerstel, "The Third Shift."

13. Taylor, *On Pay Gap*, 56–62.

14. Jane Waldfogel, "The Effect of Children on Women's Wages," *American Sociological Review* 62, no. 2 (April 1997): 209–17; Jane Waldfogel, "Understanding the 'Family Gap' in Pay for Women with Children," *Journal of Economic Perspectives* 12, no. 1 (Winter 1998): 137–56; Michelle J. Budig and Paula England, "The Wage Penalty for Motherhood," *American*

*Sociological Review* 66, no. 2 (April 2001): 204–25; Michelle J. Budig and Melissa J. Hodges, "Differences in Disadvantage: Variations in the Motherhood Penalty across White Women's Earnings Distribution," *American Sociological Review* 75, no. 5 (October 2010): 705–28.

15. Sarah Avellar and Pamela J. Smock, "Has the Price of Motherhood Declined over Time? A Cross-Cohort Comparison of the Motherhood Wage Penalty," *Journal of Marriage and the Family* 65, no. 3 (August 2003): 597–607.

16. Shelley J. Correll, Stephen Benard, and In Paik, "Getting a Job: Is There a Motherhood Penalty?," *American Journal of Sociology* 112, no. 5 (March 2007): 1297–338.

17. Vincent J. Roscigno, Lisette M. Garcia, and Donna Bobbitt-Zeher, "Social Closure and Processes of Race/Sex Employment Discrimination," *Annals of the American Academy of Political and Social Science* 609 (January 2007): 38.

18. For 2011 data on the gender composition of occupations, see U.S. Department of Labor, *Women in the Labor Force*, 29–42, tables 10 and 11; see also Coontz, "The Myth of Male Decline."

19. Rose and Hartmann, *Still a Man's Labor Market*, 13–19; Hartmann, Rose, and Lovell, "How Much Progress in Closing the Long-Term Earnings Gap?," 133–39.

20. Irene Padavic and Barbara Reskin, *Women and Men at Work*, 2nd ed. (Thousand Oaks, CA: Pine Forge Press, 2002), 42–44; David Cotter, Joan M. Hermsen, and Reeve Vanneman, "The End of the Gender Revolution? Gender Role Attitudes from 1977 to 2008," *American Journal of Sociology* 117, no. 1 (July 2011): 259–89; Cecilia L. Ridgeway, *Framed by Gender: How Gender Inequality Persists in the Modern World* (Oxford: Oxford University Press, 2011), 56–91.

21. Ridgeway, *Framed by Gender*, 92–126.

22. Roscigno, Garcia, and Bobbitt-Zeher, "Social Closure," 34–40; Padavic and Reskin, *Women and Men at Work*, 44–47, 75–85, 91–93.

23. See Donna Bobbitt-Zeher, "Gender Discrimination at Work: Connecting Gender Stereotypes, Institutional Policies, and Gender Composition of Workplace," *Gender & Society* 25, no. 6 (December 2011): 764–86.

24. David Neumark, with Roy J. Bank and Kyle D. Van Nort, "Sex Discrimination in Restaurant Hiring: An Audit Study," *Quarterly Journal of Economics* 111, no. 3 (August 1996): 915–41.

25. Corinne A. Moss-Racusin et al., "Science Faculty's Subtle Gender Biases Favor Male Students," *Proceeding of the National Academy of Sciences* 109, no. 41 (October 9, 2012): 16474–79; see also Kenneth Chang, "Bias Persists for Women of Science, a Study Finds," *New York Times*, September 25, 2012.

26. Liza Featherstone, *Selling Women Short: The Landmark Battle for Workers' Rights at Wal-Mart* (New York: Basic Books, 2004); Brad Seligman, "Patriarchy at the Checkout Counter: The *Dukes v. Wal-Mart Stores, Inc.* Class-Action Suit," in *Walmart: The Face of Twenty-First Century Capitalism*, ed. Nelson Lichtenstein (New York: New Press, 2006), 231–42.

27. Susan Antilla, "Fighting the Old Boys' Club," *New York Times*, March 29, 2014.

28. Sarah Jane Glyn, *The Gender Wage Gap Double Whammy* (Washington, DC: Center for American Progress, April 2012), http://www.americanprogress.org/issues/women/news/2012/04/16/11428/the-gender-wage-gap-double-whammy (accessed April 20, 2014); see also Barbara Ehrenreich, *Nickel and Dimed: On (Not) Getting By in America* (New York: Metropolitan Books, 2001); Beth Shulman, *The Betrayal of Work: How Low-Wage Jobs Fail 30 Million Americans and Their Families* (New York: New Press, 2003).

29. Lawrence Mishel, Josh Bivens, Elise Gould, and Heidi Shierholz, *The State of Working America*, 12th ed. (Ithaca, NY: Cornell University Press, 2012), 192, fig. 4e; U.S. Department of Labor, Bureau of Labor Statistics, *Highlights of Women's Earnings in 2012*, Report 1045

(Washington, DC: Government Printing Office, September 2013), 52–53, table 11; Rose and Hartmann, *Still a Man's Labor Market*, 11.

30. Francine D. Blau and Lawrence M. Kahn, "Gender Difference in Pay," *Journal of Economic Perspectives* 14, no. 4 (Fall 2000): 94–95.

31. On the relationship between poverty, family structure, and race and ethnicity, see John Iceland, *Poverty in America: A Handbook*, 2nd ed. (Berkeley: University of California Press, 2006), 91–94.

32. Ange-Marie Hancock, *The Politics of Disgust: The Public Identity of the Welfare Queen* (New York: New York University Press, 2004); Susan J. Douglas and Meredith W. Michaels, *The Mommy Myth: The Idealization of Motherhood and How It Has Undermined Women* (New York: Free Press, 2004), 173–202.

33. Laura Lein and Deanna T. Schexnayder, *Live after Welfare: Reform and the Persistence of Poverty* (Austin: University of Texas Press, 2007); Sandra Morgen, Joan Acker, and Jill Weigt, *Stretched Thin: Poor Families, Welfare Work, and Welfare Reform* (Ithaca, NY: Cornell University Press, 2010); Jane L. Collins and Victoria Mayer, *Both Hands Tied: Welfare Reform and the Race to the Bottom in the Low-Wage Labor Market* (Chicago: University of Chicago Press, 2010).

34. Padavic and Reskin, *Women and Men at Work*, 167–74; Steven Pressman, "Feminist Explanations for the Feminization of Poverty," *Journal of Economic Issues* 37, no. 2 (June 2003): 353–61; Karen Christopher et al., "The Gender Gap in Poverty in Modern Nations: Single Motherhood, the Market, and the State," *Sociological Perspectives* 45, no. 3 (Fall 2002): 219–42.

35. Susan Thistle, *From Marriage to the Market: The Transformation of Women's Lives and Work* (Berkeley: University of California Press, 2006).

36. U.S. House of Representatives, Committee on Ways and Means, *2012 Green Book: Background Material and Data on the Programs within the Jurisdiction of the Committee on Ways and Means* (Washington, DC: Government Printing Office, 2013), table 9-6, http://greenbook.waysandmeans.house.gov/sites/greenbook.waysandmeans.house.gov/files/2012/documents/Child%20Care%20Table%209-6.pdf (accessed April 19, 2014).

37. U.S. Department of Labor, *Bureau of Labor Statistics, Employment Characteristics of Families—2012* (Washington, DC: Government Printing Office, April 26, 2013), 2, http://www.bls.gov/news.release/pdf/famee.pdf (accessed April 19, 2014).

38. Lynda Laughlin, *Who's Minding the Kids? Child Care Arrangements: Spring 2011*, U.S. Census Bureau, Current Population Reports, P70-135 (Washington, DC: Government Printing Office, April 2013), 2, 6, http://www.census.gov/prod/2013pubs/p70-135.pdf (accessed April 19, 2014).

39. Ajay Chaudry, *Putting Children First: How Low-Wage Working Mothers Manage Child Care* (New York: Russell Sage, 2006), 73–74.

40. For two comprehensive discussions of the varied assortment of existing child-care arrangements, with analysis of their pros and cons, see Chaudry, *Putting Children First*, 28–84, 224–29, and Suzanne W. Helburn and Barbara R. Bergmann, *America's Child Care Problem: The Way Out* (New York: Palgrave, 2002), 87–122.

41. Heather Boushey, "Who Cares? The Child Care Choices of Working Mothers," Data Brief No. 1 (Washington, DC: Center for Economic and Policy Research, May 6, 2003), http://www.cepr.net/documents/publications/child_care_2003.htm (accessed December 31, 2007); Laughlin, *Who's Minding the Kids?*, 3–4, table 2.

42. Child Care Aware of America, *Parents and the High Cost of Child Care: 2013 Report* (Arlington, VA: Child Care Aware of America, 2013), 40–41, 48–51, appendices 1, 5, and 6,

http://usa.childcareaware.org/sites/default/files/cost_of_care_2013_103113_0.pdf (accessed April 19, 2014).

43. Laughlin, *Who's Minding the Kids?*, 15, table 6; see also Child Care Aware of America, *Parents and the High Cost of Child Care*, 52–59, appendices 7–10.

44. See the calculations in Helburn and Bergmann, *America's Child Care Problem*, 25–27.

45. See Collins and Mayer, *Both Hands Tied*, 83–113; Lein and Schexnayder, *Life after Welfare*, 81–86; Morgen, Acker, and Weigt, *Stretched Thin*, 162–77; Valerie Polakov, *Who Cares for Our Children: The Child Care Crisis in the Other America* (New York: Teachers College Press, 2007).

46. Harriet B. Presser, *Working in a 24/7 Economy: Challenges for American Families* (New York: Russell Sage, 2003), 174–213; Lisa Dodson and Wendy Luttrell, "Families Facing Untenable Choice," *Contexts* 10, no. 1 (Winter 2011): 38–42; Liz Watson, Lauren Frohlich, and Elizabeth Johnston, *Collateral Damage: Scheduling Challenges for Workers in Low-Wage Jobs and Their Consequences* (Washington, DC: National Women's Law Center, April 2014), http://www.nwlc.org/sites/default/files/pdfs/collateral_damage_scheduling_fact_sheet.pdf (accessed April 19, 2014); Nancy K. Cauthen, *Scheduling Hourly Workers: How Last Minute, "Just-in-Time" Scheduling Practices Are Bad for Workers, Families and Business* (New York: Demos, March 2011), 8–9, https://www.google.com/search?q=cauthan%2C+scheduling+hourly+workers&ie=utf-8&oe=utf-8&aq=t&rls=org.mozilla:en-US:official&client=firefox-a&channel=sb (accessed April 20, 2014).

47. On the prevalence and characteristics of children in self-care, see Laughlin, *Who's Minding the Kids?*, 12–14; see also Nina Bernstein, "Daily Choice Turned Deadly: Children Left on Their Own," *New York Times*, October 19, 2003.

48. Chaudry, *Putting Children First*, 72–76; Presser, *Working in a 24/7 Economy*, 186–88, 191–94.

49. Chaudry, *Putting Children First*, 85–118, 143–45, 154.

50. For extended discussions of child-care quality, including reviews of prior research, see Helburn and Bergmann, *America's Child Care Problem*, 55–157; Jane Waldfogel, *What Children Need* (Cambridge, MA: Harvard University Press, 2006), 72–81, 91–106.

51. Joan Fitzgerald, "Caring for Children as a Career," *American Prospect*, Summer 2002, A28–A31.

52. U.S. House of Representatives, *Green Book*, table 9.9; see also Helburn and Bergmann, *America's Child Care Problem*, 189–91.

53. Sharon Lerner, "The Kids Aren't Alright," *The Nation*, November 12, 2007, 26.

54. Chaudry, *Putting Children First*, 43–46, 70; Juliet Bromer and Julia R. Henley, "Child Care as Family Support: Caregiving Practices across Child Care Providers," *Children and Youth Services Review* 26 (2004): 941–64.

55. Helburn and Bergmann, *America's Child Care Problem*, 89, 122.

56. Julie E. Press, "Child Care as Poverty Policy: The Effect of Child Care on Work and Family Poverty," in *Prismatic Metropolis: Inequality in Los Angeles*, ed. Lawrence D. Bobo et al. (New York: Russell Sage, 2000), 338–82.

57. Press, "Child Care as Poverty Policy," 341, 373.

58. For background and information on the CCDF, see U.S. House of Representatives, *Green Book*, chapter 9.

59. National Women's Law Center, *Gaps in Support for Early Care and Education* (Washington, DC: National Women's Law Center, April 2014), 1, http://www.nwlc.org/sites/default/files/pdfs/gaps_in_support_for_early_care_and_education_april_2014.pdf (accessed April 19, 2014).

60. Karen Schulman and Helen Blank, *Pivot Point: State Child Care Assistance Policies, 2013* (Washington, DC: National Women's Law Center, 2013), 1–2, 6, 9, 10–12, http://www. nwlc.org/sites/default/files/pdfs/final_nwlc_2013statechildcareassistancereport.pdf (accessed January 8, 2015); National Women's Law Center, *Gaps in Support for Early Care and Education*, 1.

61. Sabrina Tavernise, "Aid for Child Care Drops When It's Needed Most," *New York Times*, December 14, 2011.

62. For an analysis showing that child-care provision in the United States is generally inferior to that of other industrialized countries, see Janet C. Gornick and Marcia K. Meyers, *Families That Work: Policies for Reconciling Parenthood and Employment* (New York: Russell Sage, 2003), 185–235; on the United States compared to other industrial countries, see also Elizabeth Palley, "Who Cares for Children? Why Are We Where We Are with American Child Care Policy?," *Children and Youth Services* Review 32 (2010): 155–63; Maegan Lokteff and Kathleen W. Piercy, "Who Cares for the Children? Lessons from a Global Perspective of Child Care Policy," *Journal of Child and Family Studies* 21, no. 1 (February 2012): 120–30.

63. Sarah A. Burgard and Molly M. King, "Health Inequality," *Pathways*, special issue, "The Poverty and Inequality Report" (2014): 42.

64. For a useful overview, see Donald A. Barr, *Health Disparities in the United States: Social Class, Race, Ethnicity, and Health* (Baltimore, MD: Johns Hopkins University Press, 2008).

65. Annie Lowrey, "Income Gap, Meet the Longevity Gap," *New York Times*, March 16, 2014; Barry P. Bosworth and Kathleen Burke, "Differential Mortality and Retirement Benefits in the Health and Retirement Study," *Economic Studies at Brookings* (April 8, 2014), http://www.brookings.edu/~/media/research/files/papers/2014/04/differential%20mortality%20retirement%20benefits%20bosworth/differential_mortality_retirement_benefits_bosworth_version_2.pdf (accessed April 28, 2014).

66. Sandro Galea et al., "Estimated Deaths Attributable to Social Factors in the United States," *American Journal of Public Health* 101, no. 8 (August 2011): 1456–65.

67. On the relationship between socioeconomic status and health, see Nancy E. Adler and Judith Stewart, eds., *The Biology of Disadvantage: Socioeconomic Status and Health* (Boston: Blackwell, 2010), and William Evans, Barbara Wolfe, and Nancy Adler, "The SES and Health Gradient: A Brief Review of the Literature," in *The Biological Consequences of Socioeconomic Inequalities*, ed. Barbara Wolfe, William Evans, and Teresa E. Seeman (New York: Russell Sage, 2012), 1–37.

68. Karen Davis, Kristof Stremikis, David Squires, and Cathy Schoen, *Mirror, Mirror on the Wall: How the U.S. Health Care System Compares Internationally* (New York: Commonwealth Fund, June 2014), http://www.commonwealthfund.org/~/media/files/publications/fund-report/2014/jun/1755_davis_mirror_mirror_2014.pdf (accessed June 17, 2014); OECD, *Health at a Glance 2013: OECD Indicators* (Paris: OECD Publishing, 2013), 37, 155–57, http://www.oecd.org/els/health-systems/Health-at-a-Glance-2013.pdf (accessed April 10, 2014).

69. Burgard and King, "Health Inequality," 46–48; U.S. Department of Health and Human Services, Centers for Disease Control and Prevention, National Center for Health Statistics, *Health, United States, 2012: With Special Feature on Emergency Care* (Washington, DC: Government Printing Office, 2013), 235–37, table 73, http://www.cdc.gov/nchs/data/hus/hus12.pdf (accessed April 10, 2014); Cathy Schoen et al., *Health Care in the Two Americas: Findings from the Scorecard on State Health System Performance for Low-Income Populations, 2013* (Commonwealth Fund, September 2013), 16, exhibit 4, http://www.commonwealthfund.org/~/media/Files/Publications/Fund%20Report/2013/Sep/1700_Schoen_low_income_scorecard_EXEC_SUMM_FINAL_v2.pdf (accessed April 10, 2014).

70. John Schmitt, "Can the Affordable Care Act Reverse Three Decades of Declining Health Insurance Coverage for Low-Wage Workers," in *What Works For Workers?*, ed. Stephanie Luce, Jennifer Luff, Joseph A. McCartin, and Ruth Milkman (New York: Russell Sage, 2014), 276–81; see also Elise Gould, *Employer-Sponsored Health Insurance Coverage Continues to Decline in New Decade* (Washington, DC: Economic Policy Institute, December 2012), http://s4.epi.org/files/2012/bp353-employer-sponsored-health-insurance-coverage.pdf (accessed May 7, 2014).

71. David U. Himmelstein et al., "Medical Bankruptcy in the United States, 2007: Results of a National Study," *American Journal of Medicine* 122, no. 8 (August 2009): 742–46.

72. For a harrowing account of how the uninsured scrape by, see Susan Starr Sered and Rushika Fernandopulle, *Uninsured in America: Life and Death in the Land of Opportunity* (Berkeley: University of California Press, 2005).

73. Schmitt, "Can the Affordable Care Act Reverse Three Decades of Declining Health Insurance Coverage," 273–304; Barbara Wolfe, "Poverty and Poor Health: Can Health Care Reform Narrow the Rich-Poor Gap?," *Focus* 28, no. 2 (Fall–Winter 2011–2012): 25–30.

74. Helen Epstein, "Enough to Make You Sick?," *New York Times Magazine*, October 12, 2003, 74–81, 98, 102–7.

75. S. Leonard Syme and Lisa F. Berkman, "Social Class, Susceptibility, and Sickness," in *The Sociology of Health and Illness: Critical Perspectives*, 7th ed., ed. Peter Conrad (New York: Worth, 2005), 24–30; see also Robert Sapolsky, "Sick of Poverty," *Scientific American*, December 2005, 92–99.

76. Gary W. Evans, Jeanne Brooks-Gunn, and Pamela Kato Klebanov, "Stressing Out the Poor: Chronic Physiological Stress and the Income-Achievement Gap," *Pathways* (Winter 2011): 16–21; Greg J. Duncan and Katherine Magnuson, "The Long Reach of Early Childhood Poverty," *Pathways* (Winter 2011): 22–27; Paul Tough, "The Poverty Clinic," *New Yorker*, March 21, 2011, 25–32; Moises Velasquez-Manoff, "Status and Stress," *New York Times*, July 27, 2013.

77. For one effort to systematically identify the links between socioeconomic status and health, see Nancy E. Adler and Katherine Newman, "Socioeconomic Disparities in Health: Pathways and Policies," *Health Affairs* 21, no. 2 (March–April 2002): 60–76.

78. On the health behavior of the poor, see Karen M. Emmons, "Health Behaviors in a Social Context," in *Social Epidemiology*, ed. Lisa Berkman and Ichiro Kawachi (Oxford: Oxford University Press, 2000), 242–66; Fred C. Pampel, Patrick M. Krueger, and Justin T. Denney, "Socioeconomic Disparities in Health Behaviors," *Annual Review of Sociology* 36 (2010): 349–70; James D. Wright and Laurie M. Joyner, "Health Behavior among the Homeless and the Poor," in *Handbook of Health Behavior Research*, ed. David S. Gochman, vol. 3 (New York: Plenum, 1997), 199–227.

79. Burgard and King, "Health Inequality," 44–45.

80. DeNavas-Walt, Proctor, and Smith, *Income, Poverty, and Health Insurance Coverage in the United States: 2012*, 14, 18, table 5; Steven H. Woolf, Robert E. Johnson, and H. Jack Geiger, "The Rising Prevalence of Severe Poverty in America: A Growing Threat to Public Health," *American Journal of Preventive Medicine* 31, no. 4 (October 2006): 332–41.

81. Jens Ludwig et al., "Neighborhood Effects on the Long-Term Well-Being of Low-Income Adults," *Science* 337, no. 6101 (September 2012): 1505–10; Janet Currie, "Health and Residential Location," in *Neighborhood and Life Chances: How Place Matters in Modern America*, ed. Harriet B. Newburger, Eugenie L. Birch, and Susan M. Wachter (Philadelphia: University of Pennsylvania Press, 2011), 3–17; Rucker C. Johnson, "The Place of Race in Health Disparities: How Family Background and Neighborhood Conditions in Childhood Im-

pact Later-Life Health," in Newburger, Birch, and Wachter, *Neighborhood and Life Chances*, 18–36.

82. United States Department of Agriculture, Agricultural Marketing Service, *Food Deserts*, http://apps.ams.usda.gov/fooddeserts/foodDeserts.aspx (accessed April 27, 2014); Kirsten A. Grimm, Latetia V. Moore, and Kelley S. Scanlon, "Access to Healthier Food Retailers—United States, 2011," in Centers for Disease Control and Prevention, *Morbidity and Mortality Weekly Reports, Supplement* 62, no. 3 (November 22, 2013): 20–26, http://www.cdc.gov/mmwr/pdf/other/su6203.pdf (accessed April 26, 2014); Latetia V. Moore and Ana V. Diez Roux, "Association of Neighborhood Characteristics with the Location and Type of Food Stores," *American Journal of Public Health* 96, no. 2 (February 2006): 325–31.

83. Lisa F. Berkman and Thomas Glass, "Social Integration, Social Networks, Social Support, and Health," in Berkman and Kawachi, *Social Epidemiology*, 137–73; Ichiro Kawachi and Lisa Berkman, "Social Cohesion, Social Capital, and Health," in Berkman and Kawachi, *Social Epidemiology*, 174–90; Debra Umberson, Robert Crosnoe, and Corinne Reczek, "Social Relationships and Health Behavior across the Life Course," *Annual Review of Sociology* 36 (2010): 139–57.

84. Robert J. Brulle and David N. Pellow, "Environmental Justice: Human Health and Environmental Inequalities," *Annual Review of Public Health* 27 (2006): 103–24.

85. Ingrid Gould Ellen, Tod Mijanovich, and Keri-Nicole Dillman, "Neighborhood Effects on Health: Exploring the Links and Assessing the Evidence," *Journal of Urban Affairs* 23, nos. 3–4 (2001): 397–98.

86. Howard L. Campbell and Joan R. McFadden, "Healthy Living: Housing Affordability and Its Impact on Family Health," *Journal of Family and Consumer Sciences* 98, no. 4 (November 2006): 49.

87. Campbell and McFadden, "Healthy Living," 49–51; Rebekah Levine Coley, Tama Leventhal, Alicia Doyle Lynch, and Melissa Kull, *Poor Quality Housing Is Tied to Children's Emotional and Behavioral Problems* (Chicago: MacArthur Foundation, September 2013), http://www.macfound.org/media/files/HHM_Policy_Research_Brief_-_Sept_2013.pdf (accessed April 28, 2014).

88. Rebecca Cohen, *The Impacts of Affordable Housing on Health: A Research Summary* (Washington, DC: Center for Housing Policy, May 2011), http://www.nhc.org/media/files/Insights_HousingAndHealthBrief.pdf (accessed April 26, 2014); Joseph Harkness and Sandra J. Newman, "Housing Affordability and Children's Well-Being: Evidence from the National Survey of America's Families," *Housing Policy Debate* 16, no. 2 (2005): 223–55.

89. On the relationship between working conditions and health status, see Tores Theorell, "Working Conditions and Health," in Berkman and Kawachi, *Social Epidemiology*, 95–117; Sarah Kuhn and John Wooding, "The Changing Structure of Work in the United States: Implications for Health and Welfare," in *Health and Social Justice: Politics, Ideology, and Inequity in the Distribution of Disease*, ed. Richard Hofrichter (San Francisco: Jossey-Bass, 2003), 251–61.

90. Lisa F. Berkman, "The Health Divide," *Contexts* 3, no. 4 (Fall 2004): 41.

91. Michael Powell, "For 2 Women in Queens and Many Others, a Sick Day Could Mean They're Fired," *New York Times*, October 23, 2012; Sherry L. Baron et al., "Nonfatal Work-Related Injuries and Illnesses—United States, 2010," in Centers for Disease Control and Prevention, *Morbidity and Mortality Weekly Reports, Supplement* 62, no. 3 (November 22, 2013): 35–40.

92. Presser, *Working in a 24/7 Economy*, 9.

93. See James P. Smith, "Healthy Bodies and Thick Wallets: The Dual Relation between Health and Economic Status," *Journal of Economic Perspectives* 13, no. 2 (Spring 1999): 145–66.

94. Anne Case and Christina Paxson, "Children's Health and Social Mobility," *The Future of Children* 16, no. 2 (Fall 2006): 151–96; Janet Currie, "Healthy, Wealthy, and Wise: Socioeconomic Status, Poor Health in Childhood, and Human Capital Development," *Journal of Economic Literature* 47, no 1 (2009): 87–122.

95. Taylor, *On Pay Gap*, 56–62.

96. Smith, "Healthy Bodies and Thick Wallets," 150–51.

97. Michael Marmot, "Harveian Oration: Health in an Unequal World," *Lancet* 368 (December 9–15, 2006): 2082.

98. DeNavas-Walt, Proctor, and Smith, *Income, Poverty, and Health Insurance Coverage*, 15, fig. 5. A supplemental poverty measure devised by the Census Bureau, correcting for some of the flaws of the official measure, finds that the rate of poverty for the elderly in 2012 is 14.8 percent rather than the officially reported 9.1 percent. See Kathleen Shorter, *The Research Supplemental Poverty Measure* (Washington, DC: U.S. Census Bureau, Current Population Reports, November 2013), 6, table 1, http://www.census.gov/prod/2013pubs/p60-247.pdf (accessed April 13, 2014).

99. DeNavas-Walt, Proctor, and Smith, *Income, Poverty, and Health Insurance Coverage*, 58, table B-2.

100. DeNavas-Walt, Proctor, and Smith, *Income, Poverty, and Health Insurance Coverage*, 59, 61, 63, table B-2; see also Wider Opportunities for Women (WOW), *Living below the Line: Economic Insecurity and Older Americans, No. 3: Race and Ethnicity* (Washington, DC: September 2013), http://www.wowonline.org/wp-content/uploads/2013/06/WOW-Living-Below-the-Line-Race-and-Ethnicity-2013.pdf (accessed April 12, 2014).

101. DeNavas-Walt, Proctor, and Smith, *Income, Poverty, and Health Insurance Coverage*, 16, fig. 6; Wider Opportunities for Women (WOW), *Living Below the Line: Economic Insecurity and Older Americans, No. 2: Women* (Washington, DC: September 2013), http://www.wowonline.org/wp-content/uploads/2013/09/Living-Below-the-Line-Economic-Insecurity-and-Older-Americans-Women-Sept-2013.pdf (accessed April 12, 2014); Stacy Torres, "Aging Women, Living Poorer," *Contexts* 13, no. 2 (Spring 2014): 72–74.

102. Timothy M. Smeeding, "Government Programs and Social Outcomes: Comparison of the United States with Other Rich Nations," in *Public Policy and Income Distribution*, ed. Alan J. Auerbach, David Card, and John M. Quigley (New York: Russell Sage, 2006), 162, table 4.2.

103. Jocelyn Fischer and Jeff Hayes, *The Importance of Social Security in the Incomes of Older Americans: Differences in Gender, Age, Race/Ethnicity, and Marital Status* (Washington, DC: Institute for Women's Policy Research, August 2013), 8–10, fig. 4, table 6, http://www.iwpr.org/initiatives/poverty (accessed April 12, 1014).

104. See Paul Sullivan, "The Tightwire Act of Living Only on Social Security," *New York Times*, September 12, 2012.

105. See Virginia P. Reno and Joni Lavery, "Social Security and Retirement Income Adequacy," Social Security Brief 25 (Washington, DC: National Academy of Social Insurance, May 2007): 3, fig. 2, http://www.nasi.org/usr_doc/SS_Brief_025.pdf (accessed December 31, 2007).

106. Fischer and Hayes, *The Importance of Social Security in the Incomes of Older Americans*, 12–14.

107. Fischer and Hayes, *The Importance of Social Security in the Incomes of Older Americans*, 14, fig. 6; for a comprehensive analysis of gender inequality in old age and a defense of family-friendly social welfare policies in opposition to those who favor market

solutions, see Madonna Harrington Meyer and Pamela Herd, *Market Friendly or Family Friendly? The State and Gender Inequality in Old Age* (New York: Russell Sage, 2007).

108. Amy Traub, *In the Red: Older Americans and Credit Card Debt* (Washington, DC: AARP Public Policy Institute, 2013), 5, http://www.demos.org/sites/default/files/publications/older-americans-and-credit-card-debt-AARP-ppi-sec.pdf (accessed April 2014).

109. Lori A. Trawinski, *Nightmare on Main Street: Older Americans and the Mortgage Market Crisis* (Washington, DC: AARP Public Policy Institute, 2012), http://www.aarp.org/content/dam/aarp/research/public_policy_institute/cons_prot/2012/nightmare-on-main-street-AARP-ppi-cons-prot.pdf (accessed April 14, 2014).

110. For one assessment, see Barbara A. Butrica and Mikki D. Ward, *What Are the Retirement Prospects of Middle-Class Americans?* (Washington, DC: AARP Public Policy Institute, 2013), http://www.aarp.org/content/dam/aarp/research/public_policy_institute/security/2013/retirement-prospects-middle-class-AARP-ppi-sec.pdf (accessed April 12, 2014).

111. Alicia H. Munnell, Rebecca Cannon Fraenkel, and Josh Hurwitz, *The Pension Coverage Problem in the Private Sector* (Boston: Center for Retirement Research, September 2012), 1–2, http://crr.bc.edu/wp-content/uploads/2012/09/IB_12-16-508.pdf (accessed April 14, 2014); Monique Morrissey and Natalie Sabadish, *Retirement Inequality Chartbook: How the 401k Revolution Created a Few Big Winners and Many Losers* (Washington, DC: Economic Policy Institute, September 2013), 10–11.

112. For a detailed assessment of this "great transformation" in the retirement system, see Edward N. Wolff, *The Transformation of the American Pension System* (Kalamazoo, MI: W. E. Upjohn Institute for Employment Research, 2011).

113. William J. Wiatrowski, "The Last Private Industry Pension Plans: A Visual Essay," *Monthly Labor Review*, December 2012, 4; see also Morrissey and Sabadish, *Retirement Inequality*, 12–13.

114. Charles R. Morris, *Apart at the Seams: The Collapse of Private Pension and Health Care Protections* (New York: Century Foundation Press, 2006), 22.

115. On the contrast between DB plans and DC plans and the consequences of the ongoing shift from the former to the latter, see Jacob Hacker, "Introduction: The Coming Age of Retirement Insecurity," in *Meeting California's Retirement Security Challenge*, ed. Nari Rhee (Berkeley, CA: UC Berkeley Center for Labor Research and Education, October 2011), 4–20, http://laborcenter.berkeley.edu/research/CAretirement_challenge_1011.pdf (accessed April 14, 2004).

116. Frank Porell and Diane Oakley, *The Pension Factor 2012: The Role of Defined Benefit Pensions in Reducing Elderly Economic Hardships* (Washington, DC: National Institute on Retirement Security, July 2012), 1, http://www.mnpera.org/vertical/Sites/%7BCB6D4845-437C-4F52-969E-51305385F40B%7D/uploads/pensionfactor2012_final.pdf (accessed April 14, 2014).

117. Alicia H. Munnell, Anthony Webb, and Francesca Golub-Sass, *The National Retirement Risk Index: An Update* (Boston: Center for Retirement Research, October 2012), 3, http://crr.bc.edu/wp-content/uploads/2012/11/IB_12-20-508.pdf (accessed April 14, 2014).

118. Jack Vanderhei, *Retirement Income Adequacy for Boomers and Gen Xers: Evidence from the 2012 EBRI Retirement Security Projection Model* (Washington, DC: Employee Benefit Research Institute, May 2012), 1, 4, http://www.ebri.org/pdf/notespdf/EBRI_Notes_05_May-12.RSPM-ER.Cvg1.pdf (accessed April 14, 2014).

119. Nari Rhee, *The Retirement Savings Crisis: Is It Worse than We Think?* (Washington, DC: National Institute on Retirement Savings, June 2013), 11–12, 20, http://www.nirsonline.org/storage/nirs/documents/Retirement%20Savings%20Crisis/retirementsavingscrisis_final.pdf (accessed April 14, 2014).

120. Catherine Rampell, "In Hard Economy for All Ages, Older Isn't Better . . . It's Brutal," *New York Times*, February 13, 2013; John Ireland, "Retiring Later Is Hard Road for Laborers," *New York Times*, September 13, 2010; Vincent J. Roscigno, "Ageism in the American Workplace," *Contexts* 9, no. 1 (Winter 2010): 16–21.

121. Cited in Bob Herbert, "Anxious about Tomorrow," *New York Times*, September 1, 2007.

122. Carol Pier, *Discounting Rights: Wal-Mart's Violations of U.S. Workers' Rights to Freedom of Association* (New York: Human Rights Watch, May 2007), http://www.hrw.org/reports/2007/us0507 (accessed December 15, 2007).

123. Annette Bernhardt, Siobhan McGrath, and James DeFilippis, *Unregulated Work in the Global City: Employment and Labor Law in New York City* (New York: Brennan Center for Justice, 2007); Steven Greenhouse, "McDonald's Workers File Wage Suits in 3 States," *New York Times*, March 13, 2014; Gordon Lafer, *The Legislative Attack on American Wages and Labor Standards, 2011–2012* (Washington, DC: Economic Policy Institute, October 2013), 24–35, 37.

124. Bruce Barry, *Speechless: The Erosion of Free Expression in the American Workplace* (San Francisco: Barrett-Koehler, 2007).

125. Jeff Manza and Christopher Uggen, *Locked Out: Felon Disenfranchisement and American Democracy* (Oxford: Oxford University Press, 2006); Keesha M. Middlemass, "Unfit to Vote: A Racial Analysis of Felon Disenfranchisement Laws," in *Racializing Justice, Disenfranchising Lives: The Racism, Criminal Justice, and Law Reader*, ed. Manning Marable, Ian Steinberg, and Keesha M. Middlemass (New York: Palgrave, 2007), 217–35.

126. Scott Keyes, Ian Millhiser, Tobin Van Ostern, and Abraham White, *Voter Suppression 101: How Conservatives Are Conspiring to Disenfranchise Millions of Americans* (Washington, DC: Center for American Progress, April 2012), http://www.americanprogress.org/wp-content/uploads/issues/2012/04/pdf/voter_supression.pdf (accessed April 15, 2014); Tova Andrea Wang, *The Politics of Voter Suppression: Defending and Expanding Americans' Right to Vote* (Ithaca, NY: Cornell University Press, 2012).

127. Mary Bauer, *Close to Slavery: Guestworker Programs in the United States* (Montgomery, AL: Southern Poverty Law Center, 2007), http://www.splcenter.org/legal/guestreport/index.jsp (accessed December 15, 2007); see also Felicia Mello, "Coming to America," *The Nation*, January 25, 2007, 14–24.

128. Collins and Mayer, *Both Hands Tied*; Sharon Hays, *Flat Broke with Children: Women in the Age of Welfare Reform* (Oxford: Oxford University Press, 2003); Adam Liptak, "Full Constitutional Protection for Some, But No Privacy for the Poor," *New York Times*, July 16, 2007.

129. Gary Blasi, "How Much Access? How Much Justice?," *Fordham Law Review* 73, no. 3 (December 2004): 879–80.

130. On the early development of the legal services program, see Alan W. Houseman and Linda E. Perle, *Securing Equal Justice for All: A Brief History of Civil Legal Assistance in the United States* (Washington, DC: Center for Law and Social Policy, January 2007), 7–17; National Legal Aid & Defender Association, *History of Civil Legal Aid* (Washington, DC: National Legal Aid & Defender Association, 2011), 2–4, http://www.nlada.org/About/About_HistoryCivil (accessed April 15, 2014).

131. On the history of the Legal Services Corporation, see Houseman and Perle, *Securing Equal Justice for All*, 19–48; National Legal Aid & Defender Association, *History of Civil Legal Aid*, 4–9; Michael B. Katz, *The Price of Citizenship: Redefining the American Welfare State* (New York: Metropolitan Books, 2001), 306–14.

132. Houseman and Perle, *Securing Equal Justice for All*, 24.

133. Houseman and Perle, *Securing Equal Justice for All*, 48.

134. Houseman and Perle, *Securing Equal Justice for All*, 30, 36–37; National Legal Aid & Defender Association, *History of Civil Legal Aid*, 5–7; Katz, *The Price of Citizenship*, 308–14.

135. Houseman and Perle, *Securing Equal Justice for All*, 45–47; "Legal Services under Attack," unsigned editorial, *New York Times*, December 20, 2002; Megan Tady, "Justice for Some," *In These Times*, web exclusive, October 25, 2007, http://www.inthesetimes.com/article/3386/justice_for_some (accessed December 15, 2007).

136. Alan W. Houseman, *Civil Legal Aid in the United States: An Update for 2013* (Washington, DC: Center for Law and Social Policy, November 2013), 11–12, http://www.clasp.org/resources-and-publications/publication-1/CIVIL-LEGAL-AID-IN-THE-UNITED-STATES-3.pdf (accessed April 15, 2014); Peter Edelman, ". . . And a Law for Poor People," *The Nation*, August 3–10, 2009, 23–24.

137. Alan Houseman, *The Justice Gap: Civil Legal Assistance Today and Tomorrow* (Washington, DC: Center for American Progress, June 2011), 3, http://www.americanprogress.org/wp-content/uploads/issues/2011/06/pdf/justice.pdf (accessed April 15, 2014).

138. Houseman, *The Justice Gap*, 3; Houseman, *Civil Legal Aid in the United States*, 8–10.

139. Neeta Pal, *Cut Off & Cut Out: Funding Shortfalls Force More Low-Income Families to Face Critical Legal Needs Alone* (New York: Brennan Center for Justice, 2011), https://www.brennancenter.org/sites/default/files/legacy/New%20needs%20update%20FINAL%20as%20of%205-19-11.pdf (accessed April 15, 2014); John T. Broderick Jr. and Ronald M. George, "A Nation of Do-It-Yourself Lawyers," *New York Times*, January 2, 2010; Ethan Bronner, "Right to Lawyer Can Be Empty Promise for Poor," *New York Times*, March 16, 2013.

140. John Schwartz, "Critics Say Budget Cuts for Courts Risk Rights," *New York Times*, November 27, 2011.

141. World Justice Project, *WJP Rule of Law Index 2014* (Washington, DC: World Justice Project, 2014), 30–31, http://worldjusticeproject.org/sites/default/files/files/wjp_rule_of_law_index_2014_report.pdf (accessed April 15, 2014).

142. Houseman, "Civil Legal Aid in the United States," 12–13; Earl Johnson, "Equal Access to Justice: Comparing Access to Justice in the United States and Other Industrial Democracies," *Fordham International Law Journal* 24 (2001): 83–110.

143. Johnson, "Equal Access to Justice," 98.

144. For overviews of the class and race bias in the criminal justice system, see Jeffrey Reiman and Paul Leighton, *The Rich Get Richer and the Poor Get Prison*, 10th ed. (Boston: Pearson, 2012); Mark Peffley and Jon Hurwitz, *Justice in America: The Separate Realities of Blacks and Whites* (Cambridge: Cambridge University Press, 2010).

145. David Cole, "Two Systems of Criminal Justice," in David Kairys, ed., *The Politics of Law*, 3rd ed. (New York: Basic Books, 1998), 410–33.

146. Adam Liptak, "County Says It's Too Poor to Defend the Poor," *New York Times*, April 15, 2003.

147. Erik Eckholm, "Citing Workload, Public Lawyers Reject New Cases," *New York Times*, November 9, 2008; Monica Davey, "Budget Woes Hit Defense Lawyers for the Indigent," *New York Times*, September 10, 2010.

148. Debra S. Emmelman, *Justice for the Poor: A Study of Criminal Defense Work* (Burlington, VT: Ashgate, 2003), 127.

149. Paul Butler, "Gideon's Muted Trumpet," *New York Times*, March 18, 2013.

150. Devah Pager, *Marked: Race, Crime, and Finding Work in an Era of Mass Incarceration* (Chicago: University of Chicago Press, 2007), 11–15.

151. Lauren E. Glaze and Erinn J. Herberman, *Correctional Populations in the United States, 2012* (U.S. Department of Justice, Office of Justice Programs, Bureau of Justice Statistics, December 2013), 3, http://www.bjs.gov/content/pub/pdf/cpus12.pdf (accessed April 15, 2014).

152. Eduardo Porter, "In the U.S., Punishment Comes before the Crimes," *New York Times*, April 30, 2014.

153. Bruce Western, *Punishment and Inequality in America* (New York: Russell Sage, 2006), 62–66; Michelle Alexander, *The New Jim Crow: Mass Incarceration in the Age of Colorblindness* (New York: New Press, 2012), 40–47.

154. On the racial dimension of arrest and imprisonment, see Alexander, *New Jim Crow*, 59–139; Michael Tonry, *Punishing Race: A Continuing American Dilemma* (Oxford: Oxford University Press, 2011), 26–52.

155. Marc Mauer and Ryan S. King, *A 25-Year Quagmire: The War on Drugs and Its Impact on American Society* (Washington, DC: The Sentencing Project, September 2007), 3, 10.

156. E. Ann Carson and William J. Sabol, *Prisoners in 2011* (U.S. Department of Justice, Office of Justice Programs, Bureau of Justice Statistics, December 2012), 1, http://bjs.gov/content/pub/pdf/p11.pdf (accessed April 15, 2014).

157. Mauer and King, *A 25-Year Quagmire*, 12–13; Carson and Sabol, *Prisoners in 2011*, 1.

158. Tonry, *Punishing Race*, 3–76; Alexander, *New Jim Crow*, 97–139.

159. Tonry, *Punishing Race*, 54–67; see also Jamie Fellner, *Decades of Disparity: Drug Arrests and Race in the United States* (New York: Human Rights Watch, 2009), http://www.hrw.org/sites/default/files/reports/us0309web_1.pdf (accessed April 15, 2014).

160. Manning Marable, "Introduction," in Marable, Steinberg, and Middlemass, *Racializing Justice*, 52–79.

161. The Sentencing Project, *Trends in U.S. Corrections* (Washington, DC: The Sentencing Project, April 2014), 5, http://sentencingproject.org/doc/publications/inc_Trends_in_Corrections_Fact_sheet.pdf (accessed April 16, 2014).

162. Marc Mauer and Ryan S. King, *Uneven Justice: State Rates of Incarceration by Race and Ethnicity* (Washington, DC: The Sentencing Project, July 2007), 1–2, http://www.sentencingproject.org/doc/publications/rd_stateratesofincbyraceandethnicity.pdf (accessed April 15, 2014).

163. Western, *Punishment and Inequality*, 168–88.

164. See Mary Pattillo, David Weiman, and Bruce Western, eds., *Imprisoning America: The Social Effects of Mass Incarceration* (New York: Russell Sage, 2004), and Todd R. Clear, *Imprisoning Communities: How Mass Incarceration Makes Disadvantaged Neighborhoods Worse* (New York: Oxford University Press, 2007).

165. Alice Goffman, *On the Run: Fugitive Life in an American City* (Chicago: University of Chicago Press, 2014); Bruce Western, Mary Pattillo, and David Weiman, "Introduction," in Pattillo, Weiman, and Western, *Imprisoning America*, 7–11.

166. See Loïc J. D. Wacquant, "Deadly Symbiosis: When Ghetto and Prison Meet and Mesh," *Punishment and Society* 3, no. 1 (2001): 95–134, esp.116–21.

167. Pager, *Marked*, 86–116; Western, *Punishment and Inequality*, 108–30.

168. Reiman and Leighton, *The Rich Get Richer and the Poor Get Prison*.

169. Bruce Western and Becky Pettit, "Beyond Crime and Punishment: Prisons and Inequality," *Contexts* 1, no. 3 (Fall 2002): 43; Todd R. Clear, *Imprisoning Communities: How Mass Incarceration Makes Disadvantaged Neighborhoods Worse* (Oxford: Oxford University Press, 2007).

170. David K. Shipler, *The Working Poor: Invisible in America* (New York: Knopf, 2004), 252.

## 11. CONCLUSION

1. Steven Lukes, "Power," *Contexts* 6, no. 3 (Summer 2007): 59.

2. C. Wright Mills, *The Power Elite* (New York: Oxford University Press, 1956), 4.

3. Chuck Collins and Felice Yeskel, with United for a Fair Economy, *Economic Apartheid in America: A Primer on Economic Inequality and Insecurity*, rev. and updated ed. (New York: New Press, 2005), 66.

4. On poverty as a "problem of power," see also Michael B. Katz, *The Undeserving Poor: America's Enduring Confrontation with Poverty*, 2nd ed. (Oxford: Oxford University Press, 2013), 273–77.

5. Melissa Boteach, Shawn Fremstad, Joy Moses, Erik R. Stegman, and Katie Wright, *Resetting the Poverty Debate: Renewing Our Commitment to Shared Prosperity* (Washington, DC: Half in 10, November 2013), http://ms.techprogress.org/ms-content/uploads/sites/12/2013/10/HalfInTen_2013_CAP-FINAL.pdf (accessed July 12, 2014).

6. "The Poverty Issue," *American Prospect* 23, no. 6 (July–August 2012); Jacob S. Hacker and Nate Loewentheil, *Prosperity Economics: Building an Economy for All* (Creative Commons, 2012), http://www.goiam.org/images/pdfs/Hacker%20-%20Prosperity%20Economics.pdf (accessed July 12, 2014); see also Robert B. Reich, "10 Practical Steps to Reverse Growing Inequality," *The Nation* (May 26, 2014): 12–17; Richard Kirsch, *10 Ways to Rebuild the Middle Class for Hard Working Americans: Making Work Pay in the 21st Century* (August 2012), http://www.nelp.org/page/-/Reports/10-Ways-Rebuild-Middle-Class-Economy-Good-Jobs.pdf?nocdn=1 (accessed July 12, 2004); Heather Boushey and Jane Ferrill, *A Women's Agenda for the 21st Century* (Washington, DC: Center for American Progress, May 2013), http://cdn.americanprogress.org/wp-content/uploads/2013/05/FarrellTopPolicyIdeasWomen-5.pdf (accessed July 17, 2014).

7. See, for example, Frank Stricker, *Why America Lost the War on Poverty—And How to Win It* (Chapel Hill: University of North Carolina Press, 2007), 235–43; Lane Kenworthy, *Social Democratic America* (Oxford: Oxford University Press, 2014); Sasha Abramsky, *The American Way of Poverty: How the Other Half Still Lives* (New York: Nation Books, 2013); Mark Robert Rank, *One Nation, Underprivileged: Why American Poverty Affects Us All* (New York: Oxford University Press, 2004), 193–241; and Beth Shulman, *The Betrayal of Work: How Low-Wage Jobs Fail 30 Million Americans and Their Families* (New York: New Press, 2003), 149–84.

8. Joe Soss, "The Poverty Fight," *Contexts* 11, no. 2 (Spring 2011): 84.

9. Frances Fox Piven, *Challenging Authority: How Ordinary People Change America* (Lanham, MD: Rowman & Littlefield, 2006), 20–21; Francis Fox Piven, "Movements Making Noise," *The Nation*, February 18, 2013, 12; Frances Fox Piven and Richard A. Cloward, "Rule Making, Rule Breaking, and Power," in *The Handbook of Political Sociology: States, Civil Societies, and Globalization*, ed. Thomas Janoski et al. (New York: Cambridge University Press, 2005), 33–53.

10. Collins and Yeskel, *Economic Apartheid*, 148. See also Charles Derber, *Hidden Power: What You Need to Know to Save Our Democracy* (San Francisco: Berrett-Koehler, 2005).

11. Earl Wysong, Robert Perrucci, and David Wright, *The New Class Society: Goodbye American Dream?*, 4th ed. (Lanham, MD: Rowman & Littlefield, 2014), 126–27, 270–71, 290–91. See also Collins and Yeskel, *Economic Apartheid*, 147–222, and Derber, *Hidden Power*, 197, 284–86, for lists of "progressive populist organizations."

12. See Greg Kaufmann, "How to Build an Anti-Poverty Movement," *The Nation*, February 3, 2014, 17–20.

13. For an assessment of the anti-sweatshop movement, see Dan Clawson, *The Next Up-surge: Labor and the New Social Movements* (Ithaca, NY: Cornell University Press, 2003), 173–93; information about United Students against Sweatshops is available online at http://usas.org (accessed July 3, 2014).

14. Information about Family Values @ Work is available online at http://familyvaluesatwork.org/about-us (accessed July 13, 2014); information about MomsRising is available online at http://www.momsrising.org (accessed July 13, 2014); see also Joan Blades and Kristin Rowe-Finkbeiner, *The Motherhood Manifesto: What America's Moms Want—And What to Do about It* (New York: Nation Books, 2006).

15. Information about the Center for Community Change is available online at http://www.communitychange.org (accessed July 13, 2014).

16. Information about the Immigrant Solidarity Network is available online at http://www.immigrantsolidarity.org (accessed July 13, 2014); see also Ruth Milkman, *L.A. Story: Immigrant Workers and the Future of the U.S. Labor Movement* (New York: Russell Sage, 2006).

17. For information on the environmental justice movement, see the Environmental Justice Resource Center, online at http://www.ejrc.cau.edu (accessed December 13, 2007).

18. For information on the living-wage movement, see, for example, Living Wage NYC, online at http://www.livingwagenyc.org/pagedetail.php?id=5 (accessed July 13, 2014) and the Los Angeles Alliance for a New Economy, online at http://www.laane.org (accessed July 13, 2014); for an assessment of the strengths and weaknesses of the living-wage movement, see Clawson, *The Next Upsurge*, 164–73, 187–93. For information on the minimum wage movement, see Raise the Minimum Wage, online at http://www.raisetheminimumwage.com (accessed July 13, 2014).

19. For one sympathetic report on the Occupy Wall Street movement, see Todd Gitlin, *Occupy Nation: The Roots, the Spirit, and the Promise of Occupy Wall Street* (New York: Itbooks, HarperCollins, 2012).

20. My discussion of the labor movement draws especially on Clawson, *The Next Upsurge*, and Rick Fantasia and Kim Voss, *Hard Work: Remaking the American Labor Movement* (Berkeley: University of California Press, 2004).

21. Roger Waldinger et al., "Helots No More: A Case Study of the Justice for Janitors Campaign in Los Angeles," in *Organizing to Win: New Research on Union Strategies*, ed. Kate Bronfenbrenner et al. (Ithaca, NY: Cornell University Press, 1998), 102–19, quote on 111; for a somewhat gloomier assessment of the Justice for Janitors campaign, see Jake Rosenfeld, *What Unions No Longer Do* (Cambridge, MA: Harvard University Press, 2014), 131–58.

22. On "new unionism" or "social movement unionism," see Fantasia and Voss, *Hard Work*, 120–59. On "poor workers' unions," see Vanessa Tait, *Poor Workers' Unions: Rebuilding Labor from Below* (Cambridge, MA: South End Press, 2005), and Robin D. G. Kelley, *Yo' Mama's Disfunktional! Fighting the Culture Wars in Urban America* (Boston: Beacon Press, 1997), 125–58.

23. Tait, *Poor Workers' Unions*, 5.

24. On the contribution of Jobs with Justice to this effort, see Steve Early and Larry Cohen, "Jobs with Justice: Mobilizing Labor-Community Coalitions," *WorkingUSA*, November–December 1997, 49–57; information about Jobs with Justice is available online at http://www.jwj.org (accessed July 16, 2014).

25. On the concept of "fusion," see Clawson, *The Next Upsurge*, 13–14, 194–99.

26. For a valuable survey of new forms of activism and "emerging institutions" within the labor movement, see Richard B. Freeman, "What Can Labor Organizations Do for U.S. Workers When Unions Can't Do What Unions Used to Do?," in *What Works for Workers: Public Policies and Innovative Strategies for Low-Wage Workers*, ed. Stephanie Luce et al. (New

York: Russell Sage, 2014), 50–78; see also Paul Osterman and Beth Shulman, *Good Jobs America: Making Work Better for Everyone* (New York: Russell Sage, 2011), 89–104.

27. See Steven Greenhouse, "With Day of Protests, Fast-Food Workers Call for Higher Pay," *New York Times*, November 30, 2012; Eduardo Porter, "Unionizing the Bottom of the Scale," *New York Times*, December 5, 2012; Steven Greenhouse, "Fighting Back against Wretched Wages," *New York Times*, July 28, 2013.

28. See Janice Fine, *Worker Centers: Organizing Communities at the Edge of the Dream* (Ithaca, NY: Cornell University Press, 2006), and Stefan J. Marculewicz and Jennifer Thomas, "Labor Organization by Another Name: The Worker Center Movement and Its Evolution into Coverage under the NLRA and LMRDA," *Engage* 13, no. 3 (October 2012): 79–91.

29. See Freeman, "What Can Labor Organizations Do," 63–66; Steven Greenhouse, "In Florida Tomato Fields, a Penny Buys Progress," *New York Times*, April 25, 2014.

30. Spencer Woodman, "ROC vs the NRA," *The Nation*, May 31, 2010, 21–24; Laura Flanders, "Serving Up Justice: The Movement for Restaurant Workers' Rights Heats Up," *The Nation*, September 2–9, 2013. For information on ROC, see ROCUNITED, online at http://rocunited.org (accessed July 16, 2014).

31. Martin Luther King Jr., *Where Do We Go from Here: Chaos or Community?* (New York: Harper & Row, 1967), 166.

# Selected Bibliography

Abramsky, Sasha. *The American Way of Poverty: How the Other Half Still Lives*. New York: Nation Books, 2013.

Ackerman, Frank, Neva R. Goodwin, Laurie Dougherty, and Kevin Gallagher, eds. *The Political Economy of Inequality*. Washington, DC: Island Press, 2000.

Adler, Nancy E., and Katherine Newman. "Socioeconomic Disparities in Health: Pathways and Policies." *Health Affairs* 21, no. 2 (March–April 2002): 60–76.

Albelda, Randy, Robert Drago, and Steven Shulman. *Unlevel Playing Fields: Understanding Wage Inequality and Discrimination*. New York: McGraw-Hill, 1997.

Alesina, Alberto, and Edward L. Glaeser. *Fighting Poverty in the U.S. and Europe: A World of Difference*. Oxford: Oxford University Press, 2004.

Alexander, Michelle. *The New Jim Crow: Mass Incarceration in the Age of Colorblindness*. New York: New Press, 2012.

Alex-Assensoh, Yvette. "Race, Concentrated Poverty, Social Isolation, and Political Behavior." *Urban Affairs Review* 33, no. 2 (November 1997): 209–27.

Amy, Douglas J. *Behind the Ballot Box: A Citizen's Guide to Voting Systems*. Westport, CT: Praeger, 2000.

———. *Real Choices/New Voices: How Proportional Representation Elections Could Revitalize American Democracy*. 2nd ed. New York: Columbia University Press, 2002.

Anderson, Elijah. *Streetwise: Race, Class, and Change in an Urban Community*. Chicago: University of Chicago Press, 1990.

———. *Code of the Street: Decency, Violence, and the Moral Life of the Inner City*. New York: Norton, 1999.

Anderson, Elizabeth. *The Imperative of Integration*. Princeton, NJ: Princeton University Press, 2010.

Arrow, Kenneth, Samuel Bowles, and Steven N. Durlauf, eds. *Meritocracy and Economic Inequality*. Princeton, NJ: Princeton University Press, 2000.

Bailey, Martha J., and Sheldon Danziger, eds. *Legacies of the War on Poverty*. New York: Russell Sage, 2013.

Bane, Mary Jo, and Lawrence M. Mead, eds. *Lifting Up the Poor: A Dialogue on Religion, Poverty, and Welfare Reform*. Washington, DC: Brookings Institution Press, 2003.

Banfield, Edward C. *The Unheavenly City Revisited*. Boston: Little, Brown, 1974.

Barnes, Sandra L. "Achievement or Ascription Ideology? An Analysis of Attitudes about Future Success for Residents in Poor Urban Neighborhoods." *Sociological Focus* 35, no. 2 (May 2002): 207–25.

Bartels, Larry M. *Unequal Democracy: The Political Economy of the New Gilded Age*. New York: Russell Sage; Princeton, NJ: Princeton University Press, 2008.

Bartik, Timothy. "Poverty, Jobs, and Subsidized Employment." *Challenge* 45, no. 3 (May–June 2002): 100–11.

Beeghley, Leonard. "Individual and Structural Explanations of Poverty." *Population Research and Policy Review* 7, no. 3 (1988): 201–22.

Bell, Jeannine. *Hate Thy Neighbor: Move-In Violence and the Persistence of Racial Segregation in American Housing*. New York: New York University Press, 2013.

Belle, Deborah E. "The Impact of Poverty on Social Networks and Supports." *Marriage and Family Review* 5, no. 4 (Winter 1982): 89–103.

Berg, Ivar, and Arne L. Kalleberg, eds. *Sourcebook of Labor Markets: Evolving Structures and Processes*. New York: Kluwer, 2001.

Berkman, Lisa F. "The Health Divide." *Contexts* 3, no. 4 (Fall 2004): 38–43.

Berkman, Lisa F., and Ichiro Kawachi, eds. *Social Epidemiology*. Oxford: Oxford University Press, 2000.

Bernhardt, Annette, Martina Morris, Mark S. Handcock, and Marc A. Scott. *Divergent Paths: Economic Mobility in the New American Labor Market*. New York: Russell Sage, 2001.

Bernstein, Jared, and Lawrence Mishel. "Seven Reasons for Skepticism about the Technology Story of U.S. Wage Inequality." In *Sourcebook of Labor Markets: Evolving Structures and Processes*, edited by Ivar Berg and Arne L. Kalleberg, 409–27. New York: Kluwer, 2001.

Berry, Jeffrey M. *The New Liberalism: The Rising Power of Citizen Groups*. Washington, DC: Brookings Institution Press, 1999.

Bivens, Josh, Elise Gould, Lawrence Mishel, and Heidi Shierholz. *Raising America's Pay: Why It's Our Central Economic Policy Challenge*. Washington, DC: Economic Policy Institute, 2014.

Blank, Rebecca M. *It Takes a Nation: A New Agenda for Fighting Poverty*. New York: Russell Sage; Princeton, NJ: Princeton University Press, 1997.

Blinder, Alan. "Offshoring: The Next Industrial Revolution?" *Foreign Affairs* 85, no. 2 (March–April 2006): 113–28.

Block, Fred, Anna C. Korteweg, and Kerry Woodward, with Zach Schiller and Imrul Mazid. "The Compassion Gap in American Poverty Policy." *Contexts* 5, no. 2 (Spring 2006): 14–20.

Bluestone, Barry, and Bennett Harrison. *The Deindustrialization of America: Plant Closings, Community Abandonment, and the Dismantling of Basic Industry*. New York: Basic Books, 1982.

Bobbott-Zeher, Donna. "Gender Discrimination at Work: Connecting Gender Stereotypes, Institutional Policies, and Gender Composition of Workplace." *Gender & Society* 25, no. 6 (December 2011): 764–86.

Bobo, Lawrence D. "Social Responsibility, Individualism, and Redistributive Policies." *Sociological Forum* 6, no. 1 (March 1991): 71–92.

Bobo, Lawrence D., and Ryan A. Smith. "Antipoverty Policy, Affirmative Action, and Racial Attitudes." In *Confronting Poverty: Prescriptions for Change*, edited by Sheldon H. Danziger, Gary D. Sandefur, and Daniel H. Weinberg, 365–95. New York: Russell Sage; Cambridge, MA: Harvard University Press, 1994.

Bonica, Adam, Nolan McCarty, Keith T. Poole, and Howard Rosenthal. "Why Hasn't Democracy Slowed Rising Inequality?" *Journal of Economic Perspectives* 27, no. 3 (Summer 2013): 103–24.

Bonilla-Silva, Eduardo. *White Supremacy and Racism in the Post–Civil Rights Era*. Boulder, CO: Lynne Rienner, 2001.

———. *Racism without Racists: Color-Blind Racism and the Persistence of Racial Inequality in the United States*. 4th ed. Lanham, MD: Rowman & Littlefield, 2014.

Bourdieu, Pierre. "The Forms of Capital." In *Handbook of Theory and Research for the Sociology of Education*, edited by John G. Richardson, 241–58. New York: Greenwood, 1986.

Bourgois, Philippe. *In Search of Respect: Selling Crack in El Barrio*. Cambridge: Cambridge University Press, 1996.

Boushey, Heather, Chauna Brocht, Bethney Gundersen, and Jared Bernstein. *Hardships in America: The Real Story of Working Families*. Washington, DC: Economic Policy Institute, 2001.

Braddock, Jomills Henry, II, and James M. McPartland. "How Minorities Continue to Be Excluded from Equal Employment Opportunities: Research on Labor Market and Institutional Barriers." *Journal of Social Issues* 43, no. 1 (Spring 1987): 5–39.

Bradley, David, Evelyne Huber, Stephanie Moller, François Nielsen, and John D. Stephens. "Distribution and Redistribution in Postindustrial Democracies." *World Politics* 55, no. 2 (January 2003): 193–228.

Brady, David. "The Politics of Poverty: Left Political Institutions, the Welfare State, and Poverty." *Social Forces* 82, no. 2 (December 2003): 557–82.

———. *Rich Democracies, Poor People: How Politics Explains Poverty*. Oxford: Oxford University Press, 2009.

Brady, David, Regina S. Baker, and Ryan Finnigan. "When Unionization Disappears: State-Level Unionization and Working Poverty in the United States." *American Sociological Review* 78, no. 5 (October 2013): 872–96.

Brady, David, Andrew S. Fullerton, and Jennifer Moren Cross. "More than Just Nickels and Dimes: A Cross-National Analysis of Working Poverty in Affluent Democracies." *Social Problems* 57, no. 4 (November 2010): 559–85.

Brandolini, Andrea, and Timothy M. Smeeding. "Income Inequality in Richer and OECD Countries." In *The Oxford Handbook of Economic Inequality*, edited by Wiemer Salverda, Brian Nolan, and Timothy M. Smeeding, 71–99. Oxford: Oxford University Press, 2009.

Bratt, Rachel G., Michael E. Stone, and Chester Hartman, eds. *A Right to Housing: Foundations for a New Social Agenda*. Philadelphia: Temple University Press, 2006.

Briggs, Xavier de Souza. "Moving Up Versus Moving Out: Neighborhood Effects in Housing Mobility Studies." *Housing Policy Debate* 8, no. 1 (1997): 195–234.

———. "Brown Kids in White Suburbs: Housing Mobility and the Many Faces of Social Capital." *Housing Policy Debate* 9, no. 1 (1998): 177–221.

———, ed. *The Geography of Opportunity: Race and Housing Choice in Metropolitan America*. Washington, DC: Brookings Institution, 2005.

Brock, David. *The Republican Noise Machine: Right-Wing Media and How It Corrupts Democracy*. New York: Crown, 2004.

Bronfenbrenner, Kate. *Uneasy Terrain: The Impact of Capital Mobility on Workers, Wages, and Union Organizing*. Washington, DC: U.S. Trade Deficit Review Commission, 2000.

Brown, Michael K., Martin Carnoy, Elliott Currie, Troy Duster, David B. Oppenheimer, Marjorie M. Shultz, and David Wellman. *Whitewashing Race: The Myth of a Color-Blind Society*. Berkeley: University of California Press, 2003.

Bullock, Heather E., Karen Fraser Wyche, and Wendy R. Williams. "Media Images of the Poor." *Journal of Social Issues* 57, no. 2 (Summer 2001): 229–46.

Bulman, Robert C. *Hollywood Goes to High School: Cinema, Schools, and American Culture*. New York: Worth, 2005.

Burtless, Gary. "Trends in the Level and Distribution of U.S. Living Standards: 1973–1993." *Eastern Economic Journal* 22, no. 3 (Summer 1996): 271–90.

Burtless, Gary, and Christopher Jencks. "American Inequality and Its Consequences." In *Agenda for the Nation*, edited by Henry J. Aaron, James M. Lindsay, and Pietro S. Nivola, 61–108. Washington, DC: Brookings Institution Press, 2003.

Callero, Peter L. *The Myth of Individualism: How Social Forces Shape Our Lives*. 2nd ed. Lanham, MD: Rowman & Littlefield, 2013.

Campbell, Karen, Peter V. Marsden, and Jeanne S. Hurlbert. "Social Resources and Socioeconomic Status." *Social Networks* 8 (1986): 97–117.

Caner, Asena, and Edward N. Wolff. "Asset Poverty in the United States, 1984–1999." *Challenge* 47, no. 1 (January–February 2004): 5–52.

———. "Asset Poverty in the United States, 1984–99: Evidence from the Panel Study of Income Dynamics." *Review of Income and Wealth* 50, no. 4 (December 2004): 493–518.

Cappelli, Peter. "Is the 'Skills Gap' Really about Attitudes?" *California Management Review* 37, no. 4 (Summer 1995): 108–24.

Card, David. "The Effect of Unions on Wage Inequality in the U.S. Labor Market." *Industrial and Labor Relations Review* 54, no. 2 (January 2001): 296–315.

Card, David, and John E. DiNardo. "Skill-Biased Technological Change and Rising Wage Inequality: Some Problems and Puzzles." *Journal of Labor Economics* 20, no. 4 (October 2002): 733–83.

Cashin, Sheryll. *The Failures of Integration: How Race and Class Are Undermining the American Dream*. New York: PublicAffairs, 2004.

Cawley, John, James Heckman, and Edward Vytlacil. "Meritocracy in America: Wages within and across Occupations." *Industrial Relations* 38, no. 3 (July 1999): 250–96.

Chafel, Judith A. "Societal Images of Poverty: Child and Adult Beliefs." *Youth and Society* 28, no. 4 (June 1997): 432–63.

Charles, Camille Zubrinsky. "The Dynamics of Racial Residential Segregation." *Annual Review of Sociology* 29 (2003): 167–207.

Chaudry, Ajay. *Putting Children First: How Low-Wage Working Mothers Manage Child Care*. New York: Russell Sage, 2006.

Cherry, Robert, and William M. Rodgers III, eds. *Prosperity for All? The Economic Boom and African Americans*. New York: Russell Sage, 2000.

Citro, Constance F., and Robert T. Michael. *Measuring Poverty: A New Approach*. Washington, DC: National Academy Press, 1995.

Clawson, Dan. *The Next Upsurge: Labor and the New Social Movements*. Ithaca, NY: Cornell University Press, 2003.

Clawson, Dan, and Mary Ann Clawson. "Reagan or Business? Foundations of the New Conservatism." In *The Structure of Power in America: The Corporate Elite as a Ruling Class*, edited by Michael Schwartz, 201–17. New York: Holmes & Meier, 1987.

Clawson, Dan, Alan Neustadtl, and Denise Scott. *Money Talks: Corporate PACs and Political Influence*. New York: Basic Books, 1992.

Clawson, Dan, Alan Neustadtl, and Mark Weller. *Dollars and Votes: How Business Campaign Contributions Subvert Democracy*. Philadelphia: Temple University Press, 1998.

Clawson, Rosalee A., and Rakuya Trice. "Poverty as We Know It: Media Portrayals of the Poor." *Public Opinion Quarterly* 64, no. 1 (Spring 2000): 53–64.

Clear, Todd R. *Imprisoning Communities: How Mass Incarceration Makes Disadvantaged Neighborhoods Worse.* New York: Oxford University Press, 2007.

Coleman, James S. "Social Capital in the Creation of Human Capital." *American Journal of Sociology* 94, supplement (1988): S95–S120.

Collins, Chuck, and Felice Yeskel, with United for a Fair Economy. *Economic Apartheid in America: A Primer on Economic Inequality and Insecurity.* Rev. and updated ed. New York: New Press, 2005.

Collins, Jane L., and Victoria Mayer. *Both Hands Tied: Welfare Reform and the Race to the Bottom in the Low-Wage Labor Market.* Chicago: University of Chicago Press, 2010.

Compa, Lance. *Unfair Advantage: Workers' Freedom of Association in the United States under International Human Rights Standards.* Ithaca, NY: Cornell University Press, 2004.

Conley, Dalton. *Being Black, Living in the Red: Race, Wealth, and Social Policy in America.* Berkeley: University of California Press, 1999.

———. *The Pecking Order: A Bold New Look at How Family and Society Determine Who We Become.* New York: Vintage, 2004.

Conrad, Peter, ed. *The Sociology of Health and Illness: Critical Perspectives.* 7th ed. New York: Worth, 2005.

Corak, Miles. "Do Poor Children Become Poor Adults? Lessons from a Cross-Country Comparison of Generational Earnings Mobility." *Research on Economic Inequality* 13, no. 1 (2006): 143–88.

———. "Income Inequality, Equality of Opportunity, and Intergenerational Mobility." *Journal of Economic Perspectives* 27, no. 3 (Summer 2013): 79–102.

Corcoran, Mary, Greg J. Duncan, Gerald Gurin, and Patricia Gurin. "Myth and Reality: The Causes and Persistence of Poverty." *Journal of Policy Analysis and Management* 4, no. 4 (Summer 1985): 516–36.

Corcoran, Mary, and Jordan Matsudaira. "Is It Getting Harder to Get Ahead? Economic Attainment for Two Cohorts." In *On the Frontier of Adulthood: Theory, Research, and Public Policy,* edited by Richard A. Settersten Jr., Frank F. Furstenberg Jr., and Ruben C. Rumbaut, 356–95. Chicago: University of Chicago Press, 2005.

Cowie, Jefferson, and Joseph Heathcott, eds. *Beyond the Ruins: The Meanings of Deindustrialization.* Ithaca, NY: Cornell University Press, 2003.

Cozzarelli, Catherine, Michael J. Tagler, and Anna V. Wilkinson. "Do Middle-Class Students Perceive Poor Women and Poor Men Differently?" *Sex Roles* 47, nos. 11–12 (2002): 519–29.

Cozzarelli, Catherine, Anna V. Wilkinson, and Michael J. Tagler. "Attitudes toward the Poor and Attributions for Poverty." *Journal of Social Issues* 57, no. 2 (Summer 2001): 207–27.

Craypo, Charles, and David Cormier. "Job Restructuring as a Determinant of Wage Inequality and Working-Poor Households." *Journal of Economic Issues* 34, no. 1 (March 2000): 21–42.

Croteau, David, and William Hoynes. *The Business of Media: Corporate Media and the Public Interest.* 2nd ed. Thousand Oaks, CA: Pine Forge Press, 2005.

Crotty, James. "The Case for International Capital Controls." In *Unconventional Wisdom: Alternative Perspectives on the New Economy,* edited by Jeff Madrick, 277–98. New York: Century Foundation Press, 2000.

Currie, Janet, and Duncan Thomas. "The Intergenerational Transmission of 'Intelligence': Down the Slippery Slope of *The Bell Curve.*" *Industrial Relations* 38, no. 3 (July 1999): 297–330.

Dahl, Robert. *On Political Equality.* New Haven, CT: Yale University Press, 2006.

Danziger, Sheldon H., and Peter Gottschalk. *America Unequal.* New York: Russell Sage, 1995.

Danziger, Sheldon H., and Ann Chic Lin, eds. *Coping with Poverty: The Social Contexts of Neighborhood, Work, and Family in the African-American Community.* Ann Arbor: University of Michigan Press, 2000.

Darity, William, Jr. "What's Left of the Economic Theory of Discrimination?" In *The Question of Discrimination: Racial Inequality in the U.S. Labor Market,* edited by Steven Shulman and William Darity Jr., 335–74. Middletown, CT: Wesleyan University Press, 1989.

Davis, Liane V., and Jan L. Hagen. "Stereotypes and Stigma: What's Changed for Welfare Mothers." *Affilia* 11, no. 3 (Fall 1996): 319–37.

DeNavas-Walt, Carmen, Bernadette D. Proctor, and Jessica C. Smith. *Income, Poverty, and Health Insurance Coverage in the United States: 2012.* U.S. Census Bureau, Current Population Reports, P60–245. Washington, DC: Government Printing Office, 2013.

Derber, Charles. *Hidden Power: What You Need to Know to Save Our Democracy.* San Francisco: Berrett-Koehler, 2005.

Desmond, Matthew. "Disposable Ties and the Urban Poor." *American Journal of Sociology* 117, no. 5 (March 2012): 1295–335.

Desmond, Matthew, and Mustafa Emirbayer. *Racial Domination, Racial Progress: The Sociology of Race in America.* New York: McGraw-Hill, 2010.

Devine, Joel E., and James D. Wright. *The Greatest of Evils: Urban Poverty and the American Underclass.* New York: Aldine de Gruyter, 1993.

Devlin, Bernie, Stephen E. Fienberg, Daniel P. Resnick, and Kathryn Roeder, eds. *Intelligence, Genes, and Success: Scientists Respond to* The Bell Curve. New York: Copernicus, Springer-Verlag, 1997.

Dew-Becker, Ian, and Robert J. Gordon. "Where Did the Productivity Growth Go? Inflation Dynamics and the Distribution of Income." *Brookings Papers on Economic Activity,* 2005, no. 2, 67–127.

DiPrete, Thomas A. "What Has Sociology to Contribute to the Study of Inequality Trends? A Historical and Comparative Perspective." *American Behavioral Scientist* 50, no. 5 (January 2007): 603–18.

DiTomaso, Nancy. *The American Non-Dilemma: Racial Inequality without Racism.* New York: Russell Sage, 2013.

Dodson, Lisa, and Wendy Luttrell. "Families Facing Untenable Choices." *Contexts* 10, no. 1 (Winter 2011): 38–42.

Dohan, Daniel. *The Price of Poverty: Money, Work, and Culture in the Mexican American Barrio.* Berkeley: University of California Press, 2003.

Dominguez, Silvia, and Celeste Watkins. "Creating Networks for Survival and Mobility: Social Capital among African-American and Latin-American Low-Income Mothers." *Social Problems* 50, no. 1 (February 2003): 111–35.

Draut, Tamara. *New Opportunities? Public Opinion on Poverty, Income Inequality, and Public Policy: 1996–2002.* New York: Demos, 2002.

D'Souza, Dinesh. *The End of Racism: Principles for a Multiracial Society.* New York: Free Press, 1995.

Duncan, Greg J., and Richard J. Murnane, eds. *Whither Opportunity? Rising Inequality, Schools, and Children's Life Chances.* New York: Russell Sage, 2011.

Durlauf, Steven N. "A Theory of Persistent Income Inequality." *Journal of Economic Growth* 1 (1996): 75–93.

———. "The Memberships Theory of Inequality: Ideas and Implications." In *Elites, Minorities, and Economic Growth,* edited by Elise S. Brezis and Peter Temin, 161–77. Amsterdam: Elsevier, 1999.

———. "The Memberships Theory of Poverty: The Role of Group Affiliations in Determining Socioeconomic Outcomes." In *Understanding Poverty*, edited by Sheldon H. Danziger and Robert H. Haveman, 392–416. New York: Russell Sage; Cambridge, MA: Harvard University Press, 2001.

Edelman, Peter. *So Rich, So Poor: Why It's So Hard to End Poverty in America*. New York: New Press, 2012.

Edelman, Peter, Harry J. Holzer, and Paul Offner. *Reconnecting Disadvantaged Young Men*. Washington, DC: Urban Institute Press, 2006.

Edin, Kathryn, and Maria Kefalas. *Promises I Can Keep: Why Poor Women Put Motherhood before Marriage*. Berkeley: University of California Press, 2005.

Edin, Kathryn, and Laura Lein. *Making Ends Meet: How Single Mothers Survive Welfare and Low-Wage Work*. New York: Russell Sage, 1997.

Edsall, Thomas Byrne. *The New Politics of Inequality*. New York: Norton, 1984.

Edwards, Richard C. "Individual Traits and Organizational Incentives: What Makes a 'Good' Worker?" *Journal of Human Resources* 11, no. 1 (Winter 1976): 51–68.

Ehrenreich, Barbara. *Fear of Falling: The Inner Life of the Middle Class*. New York: Pantheon, 1989.

———. *Nickel and Dimed: On (Not) Getting By in America*. New York: Henry Holt, Metropolitan, 2001.

———. *Bait and Switch: The (Futile) Pursuit of the American Dream*. New York: Metropolitan Books, 2005.

Eitzen, D. Stanley, and Kelly Eitzen Smith. *Experiencing Poverty: Voices from the Bottom*. Belmont, CA: Wadsworth, 2003.

Ellen, Ingrid Gould, Tod Mijanovich, and Keri-Nicole Dillman. "Neighborhood Effects on Health: Exploring the Links and Assessing the Evidence." *Journal of Urban Affairs* 23, nos. 3–4 (2001): 391–408.

Elliott, James R. "Social Isolation and Labor Market Insulation: Network and Neighborhood Effects on Less-Educated Urban Workers." *Sociological Quarterly* 40, no. 2 (Winter 1999): 199–216.

England, Paula. "The Gender Revolution: Uneven and Stalled." *Gender & Society* 24, no. 2 (April 2010): 149–66.

Entman, Robert M. "Television, Democratic Theory, and the Visual Construction of Poverty." *Research in Political Sociology* 7 (1995): 139–59.

Erickson, Bonnie. "Social Networks: The Value of Variety." *Contexts* 2, no. 1 (Winter 2003): 25–31.

Fantasia, Rick, and Kim Voss. *Hard Work: Remaking the American Labor Movement*. Berkeley: University of California Press, 2004.

Farber, Naomi. "The Significance of Aspirations among Unmarried Adolescent Mothers." *Social Service Review* 63, no. 4 (December 1989): 518–32.

———. "The Significance of Race and Class in Marital Decisions among Unmarried Adolescent Mothers." *Social Problems* 37, no. 1 (February 1990): 51–63.

Farkas, George. "Cognitive Skills and Noncognitive Traits and Behaviors in Stratification Processes." *Annual Review of Sociology* 29 (2003): 541–62.

Feagin, Joe R. "America's Welfare Stereotypes." *Social Science Quarterly* 52, no. 4 (March 1972): 921–33.

———. "Poverty: We Still Believe That God Helps Those Who Help Themselves." *Psychology Today* 6 (1972): 101–10, 129.

———. *Subordinating the Poor: Welfare and American Beliefs*. Englewood Cliffs, NJ: Prentice-Hall, 1975.

Fischer, Claude S., Michael Hout, Martin Sanchez Jankowski, Samuel R. Lucas, Ann Swidler, and Kim Voss. *Inequality by Design: Cracking the Bell Curve Myth.* Princeton, NJ: Princeton University Press, 1996.

Fligstein, Neil. "Politics, the Reorganization of the Economy, and Income Inequality, 1980–2009." *Politics & Society* 38, no. 2 (May 2010): 233–42.

Fortin, Nicole M., and Thomas Lemieux. "Institutional Changes and Rising Wage Inequality: Is There a Linkage?" *Journal of Economic Perspectives* 11, no. 2 (Spring 1997): 75–96.

Foster, John D. *White Racial Discourse: Preserving Racial Privilege in a Post-Racial Society.* Lanham, MD: Lexington Books, 2013.

Fraser, Steven, ed. *The Bell Curve Wars: Race, Intelligence, and the Future of America.* New York: Basic Books, 1995.

Freeman, Richard B. "Labor Market Institutions and Earnings Inequality." *New England Economic Review* (May–June 1996): 157–68.

———. "The Facts about Rising Economic Disparity." In *The Inequality Paradox: Growth of Income Disparity,* edited by James A. Auerbach and Richard S. Belous, 19–33. Washington, DC: National Policy Association, 1998.

———. *America Works: The Exceptional U.S. Labor Market.* New York: Russell Sage, 2007.

———. "Globalization and Inequality." In *The Oxford Handbook of Economic Inequality,* edited by Wiemer Salverda, Brian Nolan, and Timothy M. Smeeding, 575–99. Oxford: Oxford University Press, 2009.

Galbraith, James K. *Created Unequal: The Crisis in American Pay.* New York: Free Press, 1998.

Gans, Herbert J. "The Positive Functions of Poverty." *American Journal of Sociology* 78, no. 2 (September 1972): 275–89.

———. *The War against the Poor: The Underclass and Antipoverty Policy.* New York: Basic Books, 1995.

———. *Democracy and the News.* Oxford: Oxford University Press, 2003.

Gephart, Martha A. "Neighborhoods and Communities as Contexts for Development." In *Neighborhood Poverty,* vol. 1, *Contexts and Consequences for Children,* edited by Jeanne Brooks-Gunn, Greg J. Duncan, and J. Lawrence Aber, 1–43. New York: Russell Sage, 1997.

Gerstel, Naomi. "The Third Shift: Gender and Care Work Outside the Home." *Qualitative Sociology* 23, no. 4 (Winter 2000): 467–83.

Gilder, George. *Wealth and Poverty.* New York: Basic Books, 1981.

Gilens, Martin. *Why Americans Hate Welfare.* Chicago: University of Chicago Press, 1999.

———. "The American News Media and Public Misperceptions of Race and Poverty." In *Race, Poverty, and Domestic Policy,* edited by C. Michael Henry, 336–63. New Haven, CT: Yale University Press, 2004.

———. "Inequality and Democratic Responsiveness." *Public Opinion Quarterly* 69, no. 5 (2005): 778–96.

———. "Preference Gaps and Inequality in Representation." *PS: Political Science and Politics* 42, no. 2 (April 2009): 335–41.

———. *Affluence and Influence: Economic Inequality and Political Power in America.* New York: Russell Sage; Princeton, NJ: Princeton University Press, 2012.

Goffman, Alice. *On the Run: Fugitive Life in an American City.* Chicago: University of Chicago Press, 2014.

Gordon, David M. *Theories of Poverty and Underemployment.* Lexington, MA: D. C. Heath, 1972.

———. *Fat and Mean: The Corporate Squeeze of Working Americans and the Myth of Managerial "Downsizing."* New York: Free Press, 1996.

Gornick, Janet C., and Markus Jäntti. "Child Poverty in Cross-National Perspective: Lessons from the Luxembourg Income Study." *Children and Youth Services Review* 34 (2012): 558–68.

Gornick, Janet C., and Marcia K. Meyers. *Families That Work: Policies for Reconciling Parenthood and Employment.* New York: Russell Sage, 2005.

Gottschalk, Peter. "Inequality, Income Growth, and Mobility: The Basic Facts." *Journal of Economic Perspectives* 11, no. 2 (Spring 1997): 21–40.

Gottschalk, Peter, and Sheldon H. Danziger. "Family Income Mobility—How Much Is There, and Has It Changed?" In *The Inequality Paradox: Growth of Income Disparity,* edited by James A. Auerbach and Richard S. Belous, 92–111. Washington, DC: National Policy Association, 1998.

Gottschalk, Peter, and Timothy M. Smeeding. "Cross-National Comparisons of Earnings and Income Inequality." *Journal of Economic Literature* 35, no. 2 (June 1997): 633–87.

Gould, Mark. "Race and Theory: Culture, Poverty, and Adaptation to Discrimination in Wilson and Ogbu." *Sociological Theory* 17, no. 2 (July 1999): 171–200.

Granovetter, Mark S. "The Strength of Weak Ties." *American Journal of Sociology* 78, no. 6 (May 1973): 1360–80.

———. "The Strength of Weak Ties: A Network Theory Revisited." *Sociological Theory* 1 (1983): 201–33.

———. *Getting a Job: A Study of Contacts and Careers.* 2nd ed. Chicago: University of Chicago Press, 1995.

Green, Gary P., Leann M. Tigges, and Irene Browne. "Social Resources, Job Search, and Poverty in Atlanta." *Research in Community Sociology* 5 (1995): 161–82.

Grusky, David B., Doug McAdam, Bob Reich, and Debra Satz. *Occupy the Future.* Cambridge, MA: MIT Press, 2013.

Grusky, David B., Bruce Western, and Christopher Wimer, eds. *The Great Recession.* New York: Russell Sage, 2011.

Gustafsson, Bjorn, and Mats Johansson. "In Search of Smoking Guns: What Makes Income Inequality Vary over Time in Different Countries?" *American Sociological Review* 64, no. 4 (August 1999): 585–605.

Gusterson, Hugh, and Catherine Besteman, eds. *The Insecure American: How We Got Here and What We Should Do about It.* Berkeley: University of California Press, 2010.

Hacker, Jacob C. *The Great Risk Shift: The Assault on American Jobs, Families, Health Care, and Retirement—And How You Can Fight Back.* Oxford: Oxford University Press, 2006.

———. "Working Families at Risk: Understanding and Confronting the New Economic Insecurity." In *Old Assumptions, New Realities: Economic Security for Working Families in the 21st Century,* edited by Robert D. Plotnick, Marcia K. Meyers, Jennifer Romich, and Steven Rathgeb Smith, 31–69. New York: Russell Sage, 2011.

Hacker, Jacob C., and Paul Pierson. *Winner-Take-All Politics: How Washington Made the Rich Richer—And Turned Its Back on the Middle Class.* New York: Simon & Schuster, 2010.

Hallin, Daniel C. "The American News Media: A Critical Theory Perspective." In *Critical Theory and Public Life,* edited by John Forester, 121–46. Cambridge, MA: MIT Press, 1985.

Halpin, John, and Karl Agne. *50 Years after LBJ's War on Poverty: A Study of American Attitudes toward Work, Economic Opportunity, and the Social Safety Net.* Washington, DC: Center for American Progress, 2014.

Hancock, Ange-Marie. *The Politics of Disgust: The Public Identity of the Welfare Queen.* New York: New York University Press, 2004.

Handel, Michael J. *Worker Skills and Job Requirements: Is There a Mismatch?* New York: Economic Policy Institute, 2005.

Hanson, Sandra L., and John Zogby. "The Polls—Trends: Attitudes about the American Dream." *Public Opinion Quarterly* 74, no. 3 (Fall 2010): 570–84.

Harrington, Michael. *The New American Poverty*. New York: Penguin, 1984.

———. *The Other America: Poverty in the United States*. New York: Macmillan, 1993 [1962].

Harrison, Bennett, and Barry Bluestone, *The Great U-Turn: Corporate Restructuring and the Polarization of America*. New York: Basic Books, 1990.

Harrison, Lawrence E. *Who Prospers? How Cultural Values Shape Economic and Political Success*. New York: Basic Books, 1992.

Hart, Betty, and Todd R. Risley. *Meaningful Differences in the Everyday Experience of Young American Children*. Baltimore, MD: Paul H. Brookes, 1995.

Harvey, David L., and Michael Reed. "Paradigms of Poverty: A Critical Assessment of Contemporary Perspectives." *International Journal of Politics, Culture, and Society* 6, no. 2 (1992): 269–97.

———. "The Culture of Poverty: An Ideological Analysis." *Sociological Perspectives* 39, no. 4 (1996): 465–95.

Harvey, Philip. "Combating Joblessness: An Analysis of the Principal Strategies That Have Influenced the Development of American Employment and Social Welfare Law during the 20th Century." *Berkeley Journal of Employment and Labor Law* 21 (2000): 677–758.

Hatton, Erin. *The Temp Economy: From Kelly Girls to Permatemps in Postwar America*. Philadelphia, PA: Temple University Press, 2011.

Haveman, Robert H., and Edward N. Wolff. "The Concept and Measurement of Asset Poverty: Levels, Trends, and Composition for the U.S., 1983–2001." *Journal of Economic Inequality* 2 (2004): 145–69.

Hays, Sharon. *Flat Broke with Children: Women in the Age of Welfare Reform*. Oxford: Oxford University Press, 2003.

Helburn, Suzanne W., and Barbara R. Bergmann. *America's Child Care Problem: The Way Out*. New York: Palgrave, 2002.

Herrnstein, Richard J., and Charles Murray. *The Bell Curve: Intelligence and Class Structure in American Life*. New York: Free Press, 1994.

Hertz, Tom. "Rags, Riches, and Race: The Intergenerational Economic Mobility of Black and White Families in the United States." In *Unequal Chances: Family Background and Economic Success*, edited by Samuel Bowles, Herbert Gintis, and Melissa Osborne Groves, 165–91. New York: Russell Sage, 2005.

———. *Understanding Mobility in America*. Washington, DC: Center for American Progress, April 26, 2006.

Heyman, Jody. *The Widening Gap: Why America's Working Families Are in Jeopardy and What Can Be Done about It*. New York: Basic Books, 2000.

Hill, Steven. *Fixing Elections: The Failure of America's Winner Take All Politics*. New York: Routledge, 2002.

Himmelstein, Jerome L. *To the Right: The Transformation of American Conservatism*. Berkeley: University of California Press, 1990.

Hochschild, Jennifer L. *Facing Up to the American Dream: Race, Class, and the Soul of the Nation*. Princeton, NJ: Princeton University Press, 1995.

Hodgson, Godfrey. *More Equal than Others: America from Nixon to the New Century*. Princeton, NJ: Princeton University Press, 2004.

Howell, David R. "Theory-Driven Facts and the Growth in Earnings Inequality." *Review of Radical Political Economics* 31, no. 1 (Winter 1999): 54–86.

———. "Increasing Earnings Inequality and Unemployment in Developed Countries: Markets, Institutions, and the 'Unified Theory.'" *Politics & Society* 30, no. 2 (June 2002): 198–203.

Hoynes, Hilary W., Marianne E. Page, and Ann Huff Stevens. "Poverty in America: Trends and Explanations." *Journal of Economic Perspectives* 20, no. 1 (Winter 2006): 47–68.

Huber, Joan, and William Form. *Income and Ideology: An Analysis of the American Political Formula.* New York: Free Press, 1973.

Hudson, Ken. "The Disposable Worker." *Monthly Review* 52, no. 11 (April 2001): 43–55.

Huie, Stephanie A. Bond. "The Concept of Neighborhood in Health and Mortality Research." *Sociological Spectrum* 21 (2001): 341–58.

Hunt, Matthew O. "The Individual, Society, or Both? A Comparison of Black, Latino, and White Beliefs about the Causes of Poverty." *Social Forces* 75, no. 1 (September 1996): 293–322.

———. "African American, Hispanic, and White Beliefs about Black/White Inequality, 1977–2004." *American Sociological Review* 72, no. 3 (June 2007): 390–415.

Iceland, John. *Poverty in America: A Handbook.* 3rd ed. Berkeley: University of California Press, 2013.

Inniss, Leslie, and Joe R. Feagin. "The Black 'Underclass' Ideology in Race Relations Analysis." *Social Justice* 16, no. 4 (Winter 1989): 13–34.

Iversen, Roberta Rehner, and Annie Laurie Armstrong. *Jobs Aren't Enough: Toward a New Economic Mobility for Low-Income Families.* Philadelphia: Temple University Press, 2006.

Iversen, Roberta Rehner, and Naomi Farber. "Transmission of Family Values, Work, and Welfare among Poor Urban Black Women." *Work and Occupations* 23, no. 4 (November 1996): 437–60.

Iyengar, Shanto. "Framing Responsibility for Political Issues: The Case of Poverty." *Political Behavior* 12, no. 1 (March 1990): 19–40.

Jacobs, Lawrence R., and Theda Skocpol, eds. *Inequality and American Democracy: What We Know and What We Need to Learn.* New York: Russell Sage, 2005.

Jacoby, Russell, and Naomi Glauberman, eds. *The Bell Curve Debate: History, Documents, Opinions.* New York: Times Books, 1995.

Jargowsky, Paul A. *Poverty and Place: Ghettos, Barrios, and the American City.* New York: Russell Sage, 1997.

Jarrett, Robin L. "Living Poor: Family Life among Single Parent, African American Women." *Social Problems* 41, no. 1 (February 1994): 30–49.

Jencks, Christopher, and Susan Mayer. "The Social Consequences of Growing Up in Poor Neighborhoods." In *Inner City Poverty in the United States,* edited by Laurence E. Lynn Jr. and Michael G. H. McGeary, 111–86. Washington, DC: National Academy Press, 1990.

Jencks, Christopher, and Paul E. Peterson, eds. *The Urban Underclass.* Washington, DC: Brookings Institution, 1991.

Jencks, Christopher, and Meredith Phillips, eds. *The Black-White Test Score Gap.* Washington, DC: Brookings Institution Press, 1998.

Jencks, Christopher, Joe Swingle, and Scott Winship. "Welfare Redux." *American Prospect,* March 2006, 36–40.

Jennings, James. "Persistent Poverty in the United States: Review of Theories and Explanations." In *A New Introduction to Poverty: The Role of Race, Power, and Politics,* edited by Louis Kushnick and James Jennings, 13–38. New York: New York University Press, 1999.

Jones, Rachel K., and Ye Luo. "The Culture of Poverty and African-American Culture: An Empirical Assessment." *Sociological Perspectives* 42, no. 3 (1999): 439–58.

Kahlenberg, Richard D. *Left Behind: Unequal Opportunity in Higher Education.* New York: Century Foundation, 2004.

Kalleberg, Arne L. "Nonstandard Employment Relations: Part-Time, Temporary, and Contract Work." *Annual Review of Sociology* 26 (2000): 342–65.

————. *The Mismatched Worker.* New York: Norton, 2007.

————. *Good Jobs, Bad Jobs: The Rise of Polarized and Precarious Employment Systems in the United States, 1970s to 2000s.* New York: Russell Sage, 2011.

Kalleberg, Arne L., Barbara F. Reskin, and Ken Hudson. "Bad Jobs in America: Standard and Nonstandard Employment Relations and Job Quality in the United States." *American Sociological Review* 65, no. 2 (April 2000): 256–78.

Kamerman, Sheila B. "Europe Advanced While the United States Lagged." In *Unfinished Work: Building Equality and Democracy in an Era of Working Families,* edited by Jody Heymann and Christopher Beem, 309–47. New York: New Press, 2005.

Katz, Michael B. *The Undeserving Poor: From the War on Poverty to the War on Welfare.* New York: Pantheon, 1989.

————. *The Undeserving Poor: America's Enduring Confrontation with Poverty,* 2nd ed. New York: Oxford University Press, 2013.

Katznelson, Ira. *When Affirmative Action Was White: An Untold History of Racial Inequality in Twentieth-Century America.* New York: Norton, 2005.

Kelley, Robin D. G. *Yo' Mama's Disfunktional! Fighting the Culture Wars in Urban America.* Boston: Beacon Press, 1997.

Kelly, Patricia Fernandez. "Social and Cultural Capital in the Urban Ghetto: Implications for the Economic Sociology of Immigration." In *The Economic Sociology of Immigration: Essays on Networks, Ethnicity, and Entrepreneurship,* edited by Alejandro Portes, 213–47. New York: Russell Sage, 1995.

Kelso, William A. *Poverty and the Underclass: Changing Perceptions of the Poor in America.* New York: New York University Press, 1994.

Kendall, Diana. *Framing Class: Media Representations of Wealth and Poverty in America.* Lanham, MD: Rowman & Littlefield, 2005.

Kenworthy, Lane. *Jobs with Equality.* New York: Oxford University Press, 2008.

————. *Social Democratic America.* New York: Oxford University Press, 2014.

Kim, Marlene. "The Working Poor: Lousy Jobs or Lazy Workers?" *Journal of Economic Issues* 32, no. 1 (March 1998): 65–78.

————. "Are the Working Poor Lazy?" *Challenge* 41, no. 3 (May–June 1998): 85–99.

Kincheloe, Joe L., Shirley R. Steinberg, and Aaron D. Gresson III, eds. *Measured Lies: The Bell Curve Examined.* New York: St. Martin's, 1996.

King, Martin Luther, Jr. *Where Do We Go from Here: Chaos or Community?* New York: Harper & Row, 1967.

Kluegel, James R., and Eliot R. Smith. *Beliefs about Inequality: Americans' Views of What Is and What Ought to Be.* New York: Aldine De Gruyter, 1986.

Knapp, Peter, Jane C. Kronick, R. William Marks, and Miriam G. Vosburgh. *The Assault on Equality.* Westport, CT: Praeger, 1996.

Kohn, Melvin L. "Two Visions of the Relationship between Individual and Society: The Bell Curve versus Social Structure and Personality." In *A Nation Divided: Diversity, Inequality, and Community in American Society,* edited by Phyllis Moen, Donna Dempster-McClain, and Henry A. Walker, 34–51. Ithaca, NY: Cornell University Press, 1999.

Kozol, Jonathan. *Savage Inequalities: Children in America's Schools.* New York: Crown, 1991.

————. *Amazing Grace: The Lives of Children and the Conscience of a Nation.* New York: Crown, 1995.

————. *The Shame of the Nation: The Restoration of Apartheid Schooling in America.* New York: Crown, 2005.

Krysan, Maria, Reynolds Farley, Mick P. Couper, and Tyrone A. Forman. "Does Race Matter in Neighborhood Preferences? Results from a Video Experiment." *American Journal of Sociology* 115, no. 2 (September 2009): 527–59.

Krystal, Tali. "The Capitalist Machine: Computerization, Workers' Power, and the Decline in Labor's Share within U.S. Industries." *American Sociological Review* 78, no. 3 (June 2013): 361–89.

Ladd, Edward. *The American Ideology: An Exploration of the Origins, Meaning, and Role of American Political Ideals.* Storrs, CT: Roper Center for Public Opinion Research, 1994.

Ladd, Everett Carll, and Karlyn H. Bowman. *Attitudes toward Economic Inequality.* Washington, DC: American Enterprise Institute Press, 1998.

Lafer, Gordon. *The Job Training Charade.* Ithaca, NY: Cornell University Press, 2002.

———. "Job Training for Welfare Recipients: A Hand Up or a Slap Down?" In *Work, Welfare, and Politics: Confronting Poverty in the Wake of Welfare Reform,* edited by Frances Fox Piven, Joan Acker, Margaret Hallock, and Sandra Morgan, 175–95. Eugene: University of Oregon Press, 2002.

———. *The Legislative Attack on American Wages and Labor Standards, 2011–2012.* Washington, DC: Economic Policy Institute, 2013.

Lapham, Lewis H. "Tentacles of Rage: The Republican Propaganda Mills, a Brief History." *Harper's Magazine,* September 2004, 31–41.

Lee, Barrett A., Sue Hinze Jones, and David W. Lewis. "Public Beliefs about the Causes of Homelessness." *Social Forces* 69, no. 1 (September 1990): 253–65.

Lee, Cheol-Sung. "Labor Unions and Good Governance: A Cross-National Comparative Analysis." *American Sociological Review* 72, no. 4 (August 2007): 585–609.

Lee, Valerie E., and David T. Burkam. *Inequality at the Starting Gate: Social Background Differences in Achievement as Children Begin School.* Washington, DC: Economic Policy Institute, 2002.

Lein, Laura, and Deanna T. Schexnayder. *Life after Welfare: Reform and the Persistence of Poverty.* Austin: University of Texas Press, 2007.

Leventhal, Tama, and Jeanne Brooks-Gunn. "The Neighborhoods They Live In: The Effects of Neighborhood Residence on Child and Adolescent Outcomes." *Psychological Bulletin* 126, no. 2 (2000): 309–37.

Lewis, Oscar. "The Culture of Poverty." In *Explosive Forces in Latin America,* edited by John J. TePaske and Sydney Nettleton Fisher, 149–73. Columbus: Ohio State University Press, 1964.

———. "The Culture of Poverty." *Scientific American,* October 1966, 19–25.

———. "The Culture of Poverty." In *On Understanding Poverty: Perspectives from the Social Sciences,* edited by Daniel P. Moynihan, 187–200. New York: Basic Books, 1968.

Lichter, Daniel T., Christie D. Batson, and J. Brian Brown. "Welfare Reform and Marriage Promotion: The Marital Expectations and Desires of Single and Cohabiting Mothers." *Social Service Review* 78, no. 1 (March 2004): 2–25.

Lijphart, Arend. "Unequal Participation: Democracy's Unresolved Dilemma." *American Political Science Review* 91, no. 1 (March 1997): 1–14.

Lin, Nan. "Social Networks and Status Attainment." *Annual Review of Sociology* 25 (1999): 467–87.

———. "Inequality in Social Capital." *Contemporary Sociology* 29, no. 6 (November 2000): 785–95.

Livingstone, D. W. *The Education-Jobs Gap: Underemployment or Economic Democracy.* Boulder, CO: Westview, 1998.

Luce, Stephanie. *Fighting for a Living Wage.* Ithaca, NY: Cornell University Press, 2004.

Luce, Stephanie, Jennifer Luff, Joseph A. McCartin, and Ruth Milkman, eds. *What Works for Workers? Public Policies and Innovative Strategies for Low-Wage Workers.* New York: Russell Sage, 2014.

Ludwig, Jens, and Susan Mayer. "'Culture' and the Intergenerational Transmission of Poverty: The Prevention Paradox." *Future of Children* 16, no. 2 (Fall 2006): 175–96.

Luker, Kristen. *Dubious Conceptions: The Politics of Teenage Pregnancy.* Cambridge, MA: Harvard University Press, 1996.

Lukes, Steven. "Power." *Contexts* 6, no. 3 (Summer 2007): 59–61.

Magnet, Myron. *The Dream and the Nightmare: The Sixties' Legacy to the Underclass.* New York: Morrow, 1993.

Mandle, Jay. "The Politics of Democracy." *Challenge* 47, no. 1 (January–February 2004): 53–63.

———. *Democracy, America, and the Age of Globalization.* New York: Cambridge University Press, 2008.

Manning-Miller, Carmen L. "Media Discourse and the Feminization of Poverty." *Explorations in Ethnic Studies* 17, no. 1 (January 1994): 79–88.

Manza, Jeff. "Unequal Democracy in America: The Long View." In *The New Gilded Age: The Critical Inequality Debates of Our Time*, edited by David B. Grusky and Tamar Kricheli-Katz, 131–58. Stanford, CA: Stanford University Press, 2012.

Marable, Manning, Ian Steinberg, and Keesha M. Middlemass, eds. *Racializing Justice, Disenfranchising Lives: The Racism, Criminal Justice, and Law Reader.* New York: Palgrave, 2007.

Marchevsky, Alejandra, and Jeanne Theoharis. *Not Working: Latina Immigrants, Low Wage Jobs, and the Failure of Welfare Reform.* New York: New York University Press, 2006.

Martin, Lori Latrice. *Black Asset Poverty and the Enduring Racial Divide.* Boulder, CO: First Forum Press, 2013.

Massey, Douglas S. "The Age of Extremes: Concentrated Affluence and Poverty in the Twenty-First Century." *Demography* 33, no. 4 (November 1996): 395–412.

———. "The New Geography of Inequality in Urban America." In *Race, Poverty, and Domestic Policy*, edited by C. Michael Henry, 173–87. New Haven, CT: Yale University Press, 2004.

———. *Return of the "L" Word: A Liberal Vision for the New Century.* Princeton, NJ: Princeton University Press, 2005.

Massey, Douglas S., and Nancy A. Denton. *American Apartheid: Segregation and the Making of the Underclass.* Cambridge, MA: Harvard University Press, 1993.

Massey, Douglas S., and Mary J. Fischer. "The Geography of Inequality in the United States, 1950–2000." *Brookings-Wharton Papers on Urban Affairs*, 2003, 1–40.

Mazumder, Bhashkar. "Fortunate Sons: New Estimates of Intergenerational Mobility in the United States Using Social Security Earnings Data." *Review of Economics and Statistics* 87, no. 2 (May 2005): 235–55.

McCall, Leslie. *The Undeserving Rich: American Beliefs about Inequality, Opportunity, and Redistribution.* New York: Cambridge University Press, 2013.

McChesney, Robert W. *The Problem of the Media: U.S. Communication Politics in the 21st Century.* New York: Monthly Review, 2004.

McNamee, Stephen J., and Robert K. Miller Jr. *The Meritocracy Myth.* 3rd ed. Lanham, MD: Rowman & Littlefield, 2014.

Mead, Lawrence M. *Beyond Entitlement: The Social Obligations of Citizenship.* New York: Free Press, 1986.

———. *The New Politics of Poverty: The Nonworking Poor in America.* New York: Basic Books, 1992.

———, ed. *The New Paternalism: Supervisory Approaches to Poverty.* Washington, DC: Brookings Institution Press, 1997.

Meyers, Marcia K., Dan Rosenbaum, Christopher Ruhm, and Jane Waldfogel. "Inequality in Early Childhood Education and Care: What Do We Know?" In *Social Inequality,* edited by Kathryn M. Neckerman, 223–69. New York: Russell Sage, 2004.

Meyerson, Harold. "The Forty-Year Slump." *American Prospect* (September–October 2013): 20–33.

Micklethwait, John, and Adrian Wooldridge. *The Right Nation: Conservative Power in America.* New York: Penguin, 2004.

Milkman, Ruth. *Farewell to the Factory: Auto Workers in the Late Twentieth Century.* Berkeley: University of California Press, 1997.

———. *L.A. Story: Immigrant Workers and the Future of the U.S. Labor Movement.* New York: Russell Sage, 2006.

Mills, C. Wright. *The Sociological Imagination.* New York: Oxford University Press, 1959.

Mincy, Robert B., ed. *Black Males Left Behind.* Washington, DC: Urban Institute Press, 2006.

Mishel, Lawrence, Josh Bivens, Elise Gould, and Heidi Shierholz. *The State of Working America.* 12th ed. Ithaca, NY: Cornell University Press, 2012.

Mishel, Lawrence, Heidi Shierholz, and John Schmitt. *Don't Blame the Robots: Assessing the Job Polarization Explanation of Growing Wage Inequality.* Washington, DC: Economic Policy Institute, 2013.

Moller, Stephanie, Evelyne Huber, John D. Stephens, David Bradley, and François Neilsen. "Determinants of Relative Poverty in Advanced Capitalist Democracies." *American Sociological Review* 68, no. 1 (February 2003): 22–51.

Moore, Thomas S. "The Locus of Racial Discrimination in the Labor Market." *American Journal of Sociology* 116, no. 3 (November 2010): 909–42.

Morgen, Sandra, Joan Acker, and Jill Weight. *Stretched Thin: Poor Families, Welfare Work, and Welfare Reform.* Ithaca, NY: Cornell University Press, 2010.

Morone, James A., and Lawrence R. Jacobs, eds. *Healthy, Wealthy, and Fair: Health Care and the Good Society.* Oxford: Oxford University Press, 2005.

Mosher, James S. "U.S. Wage Inequality, Technological Change, and Decline in Union Power." *Politics & Society* 35, no. 2 (June 2007): 225–64.

Moss, Phillip. "Earnings Inequality and the Quality of Jobs: Current Research and a Research Agenda." In *Corporate Governance and Sustainable Prosperity,* edited by William Lazonick and Mary O'Sullivan, 183–225. New York: Palgrave, 2002.

Munger, Frank, ed. *Laboring Below the Line: The New Ethnography of Poverty, Low-Wage Work, and Survival in the Global Economy.* New York: Russell Sage, 2002.

Murray, Charles. *Losing Ground: American Social Policy, 1950–1980.* New York: Basic Books, 1984.

———. "*The Bell Curve* and Its Critics." *Commentary,* May 1995, 23–30.

Murray, Charles, and Richard J. Herrnstein. "Race, Genes, and I.Q.—An Apologia." *New Republic,* October 31, 1994, 27–37.

Newburger, Harriet B., Eugenie L. Birch, and Susan M. Wachter, eds. *Neighborhood and Life Chances: How Place Matters in Modern America.* Philadelphia: University of Pennsylvania Press, 2011.

Newman, Katherine S. *No Shame in My Game: The Working Poor in the Inner City.* New York: Knopf, 1999.

Newman, Katherine S., and Victor Tan Chen. *The Missing Class: Portraits of the Near Poor in America*. Boston: Beacon Press, 2007.

Nilson, Linda Burzotta. "Reconsidering Ideological Lines: Beliefs about Poverty in America." *Sociological Quarterly* 22 (Autumn 1981): 531–48.

Nisbett, Richard E. *Intelligence and How to Get It: Why Schools and Culture Matter*. New York: Norton, 2009.

Noble, Charles. *Welfare as We Knew It: A Political History of the American Welfare State*. New York: Oxford University Press, 1997.

———. *The Collapse of Liberalism: Why America Needs a New Left*. Lanham, MD: Rowman & Littlefield, 2004.

Nolan, Brian, and Ive Marx. "Economic Inequality, Poverty, and Social Exclusion." In *The Oxford Handbook of Economic Inequality*, edited by Wiemer Salverda, Brian Nolan, and Timothy M. Smeeding, 315–41. Oxford: Oxford University Press, 2009.

O'Connor, Alice. "Poverty Research and Policy for the Post-Welfare Era." *Annual Review of Sociology* 26 (2000): 547–62.

———. *Poverty Knowledge: Social Science, Social Policy, and the Poor in Twentieth-Century U.S. History*. Princeton, NJ: Princeton University Press, 2001.

———. "Financing the Counterrevolution." In *Rightward Bound: Making America Conservative in the 1970s*, edited by Bruce J. Schulman and Julian E. Zelizer, 148–68. Cambridge: Harvard University Press, 2008.

Oliver, Melvin L., and Thomas M. Shapiro. *Black Wealth/White Wealth: A New Perspective on Racial Inequality*. New York: Routledge, 1995.

Osterman, Paul, and Beth Shulman. *Good Jobs America: Making Work Better for Everyone*. New York: Russell Sage, 2011.

Padavic, Irene, and Barbara Reskin. *Women and Men at Work*. 2nd ed. Thousand Oaks, CA: Pine Forge Press, 2002.

Page, Benjamin I., Larry M. Bartels, and Jason Seawright. "Democracy and the Policy Preferences of Wealthy Americans." *Perspectives on Politics* 11, no. 1 (March 2013): 51–73.

Page, Benjamin I., and James R. Simmons. *What Government Can Do: Dealing with Poverty and Inequality*. Chicago: University of Chicago Press, 2000.

Pager, Devah. "The Mark of a Criminal Record." *American Journal of Sociology* 108, no. 5 (March 2003): 937–75.

———. *Marked: Race, Crime, and Finding Work in an Era of Mass Incarceration*. Chicago: University of Chicago Press, 2007.

Pager, Devah, Bruce Western, and Bart Bonikowski. "Discrimination in a Low-Wage Labor Market: A Field Experiment." *American Sociological Review* 74, no. 5 (October 2009): 777–99.

Palley, Thomas I. *Plenty of Nothing: The Downsizing of the American Dream and the Case for Structural Keynesianism*. Princeton, NJ: Princeton University Press, 1998.

Parisi, Peter. "A Sort of Compassion: The *Washington Post* Explains the 'Crisis in Urban America.'" *Howard Journal of Communications* 9 (1998): 187–203.

Patterson, Thomas E. *The Vanishing Voter: Public Involvement in an Age of Uncertainty*. New York: Vintage, 2003.

———. *Informing the News: The Need for Knowledge-Based Journalism*. New York: Vintage, 2013.

Pearce, Diana. "The Feminization of Poverty: Women, Work, and Welfare." *Urban and Social Change Review* 11, nos. 1–2 (February 1978): 28–36.

Pebley, Anne R., and Narayan Sastry. "Neighborhoods, Poverty, and Children's Well-Being." In *Social Inequality*, edited by Kathryn M. Neckerman, 833–47. New York: Russell Sage, 2004.

Petterson, Stephen M. "Are Young Black Men Really Less Willing to Work?," *American Sociological Review* 62, no. 4 (August 1997): 605–13.

Pettit, Becky. *Invisible Men: Mass Incarceration and the Myth of Black Progress.* New York: Russell Sage, 2012.

Pettit, Becky, and Jennifer L. Hook. *Gendered Tradeoffs: Family, Social Policy, and Economic Inequality in Twenty-One Countries.* New York: Russell Sage, 2009.

Phillips, Meredith, and Tiffani Chin. "School Inequality: What Do We Know?" In *Social Inequality*, edited by Kathryn M. Neckerman, 467–519. New York: Russell Sage, 2004.

Piketty, Thomas. *Capital in the Twenty-First Century.* Translated by Arthur Goldhammer. Cambridge, MA: Belknap Press of Harvard University Press, 2014.

Piketty, Thomas, and Emmanuel Saez. "Income Inequality in the United States, 1913–1998." *Quarterly Journal of Economics* 118, no. 1 (February 2003): 1–39.

Pimpare, Stephen. *A People's History of Poverty in America.* New York: New Press, 2008.

Piven, Frances Fox. "Welfare and Work." In *Whose Welfare?* edited by Gwendolyn Mink, 83–99. Ithaca, NY: Cornell University Press, 1999.

———. *Challenging Authority: How Ordinary People Change America.* Lanham, MD: Rowman & Littlefield, 2006.

Piven, Frances Fox, and Richard A. Cloward. *Poor People's Movements: Why They Succeed, How They Fail.* New York: Random House, 1977.

Polakov, Valerie. *Who Cares for Our Children: The Child Care Crisis in the Other America.* New York: Teachers College Press, 2007.

Pollin, Robert, and Stephanie Luce. *The Living Wage: Building a Fair Economy.* Rev. ed. New York: New Press, 2000.

Portes, Alejandro. "Social Capital: Its Origins and Applications in Modern Sociology." *Annual Review of Sociology* 24 (1998): 1–24.

Prasad, Monica. *The Land of Too Much: American Abundance and the Paradox of Poverty.* Cambridge, MA: Harvard University Press, 2012.

Press, Julie E. "Child Care as Poverty Policy: The Effect of Child Care on Work and Family Poverty." In *Prismatic Metropolis: Inequality in Los Angeles*, edited by Lawrence D. Bobo, Melvin L. Oliver, James H. Johnson Jr., and Abel Valenzuela Jr., 338–82. New York: Russell Sage, 2000.

Presser, Harriet B. *Working in a 24/7 Economy: Challenges for American Families.* New York: Russell Sage, 2003.

Pryor, Frederic L., and David L. Schaffer. *Who's Not Working and Why: Employment, Cognitive Skills, Wages, and the Changing U.S. Labor Market.* New York: Cambridge University Press, 1999.

Putnam, Robert D. *Bowling Alone: The Collapse and Revival of American Community.* New York: Simon & Schuster, 2000.

Quadagno, Jill. *The Color of Welfare: How Racism Undermined the War on Poverty.* New York: Oxford University Press, 1994.

Quillian, Lincoln. "New Approaches to Understanding Racial Prejudice and Discrimination." *Annual Review of Sociology* 32 (2006): 299–328.

Radcliff, Benjamin, and Patricia Davis. "Labor Organizations and Electoral Participation in Industrial Democracies." *American Journal of Political Science* 44, no. 1 (January 2000): 132–41.

Rainwater, Lee, and Timothy M. Smeeding. *Poor Kids in a Rich Country: America's Children in Comparative Perspective*. New York: Russell Sage, 2003.

Rainwater, Lee, and William L. Yancey, eds. *The Moynihan Report and the Politics of Controversy*. Cambridge, MA: MIT Press, 1967.

Rank, Mark Robert. *Living on the Edge: The Realities of Welfare in America*. New York: Columbia University Press, 1994.

———. "As American as Apple Pie: Poverty and Welfare." *Contexts* 2, no. 3 (Summer 2003): 41–49.

———. *One Nation, Underprivileged: Why American Poverty Affects Us All*. New York: Oxford University Press, 2004.

Rank, Mark Robert, and Thomas A. Hirschl. "Rags or Riches? Estimating the Probabilities of Poverty and Affluence across the Adult American Life Span." *Social Science Quarterly* 82, no. 4 (December 2001): 651–69.

Rank, Mark Robert, Thomas A. Hirschl, and Kirk A. Foster. *Chasing the American Dream: Understanding What Shapes Our Fortunes*. Oxford: Oxford University Press, 2014.

Rankin, Bruce H., and James M. Quane. "Neighborhood Poverty and the Social Isolation of Inner-City African American Families." *Social Forces* 79, no. 1 (September 2000): 139–64.

Reardon, Sean F., and Kendra Bischoff. "Income Inequality and Income Segregation." *American Journal of Sociology* 116, no. 4 (January 2011): 1092–153.

Reese, Ellen. *Backlash against Welfare Mothers: Past and Present*. Berkeley: University of California Press, 2005.

———. *They Say Cut Back, We Say Fight Back! Welfare Activism in an Era of Retrenchment*. New York: Russell Sage, 2011.

Reskin, Barbara F. "The Proximate Causes of Employment Discrimination." *Contemporary Sociology* 29, no. 2 (March 2000): 319–28.

Reskin, Barbara F., and Irene Padavic. "Sex, Race, and Ethnic Inequality." In *Handbook of the Sociology of Gender*, edited by Janet Saltzman Chafetz, 343–74. New York: Kluwer Academic/Plenum, 1999.

Ridgeway, Cecilia L. *Framed by Gender: How Gender Inequality Persists in the Modern World*. Oxford: Oxford University Press, 2011.

Robert, Stephanie A. "Socioeconomic Position and Health: The Independent Contribution of Community Socioeconomic Context." *Annual Review of Sociology* 25 (1999): 489–516.

Rodgers, Harrell R., Jr. *American Poverty in a New Era of Reform*. Armonk, NY: M. E. Sharpe, 2000.

Rodrik, Dani. *Has Globalization Gone Too Far?* Washington, DC: Institute for International Economics, 1997.

Roscigno, Vincent J. *The Face of Discrimination: How Race and Gender Impact Work and Home Lives*. Lanham, MD: Rowman & Littlefield, 2007.

Roscigno, Vincent J., Lisette M. Garcia, and Donna Bobbitt-Zeher. "Social Closure and Processes of Race/Sex Employment Discrimination." *Annals of the American Academy of Political and Social Science* 609 (January 2007): 17–48.

Rose, Stephen J., and Heidi I. Hartmann. *Still a Man's Labor Market: The Long-Term Earnings Gap*. Washington, DC: Institute for Women's Policy Research, 2004.

Rosenfeld, Jake. *What Unions No Longer Do*. Cambridge, MA: Harvard University Press, 2014.

Rosenthal, Howard. "Politics, Public Policy, and Inequality: A Look Back at the Twentieth Century." In *Social Inequality*, edited by Kathryn M. Neckerman, 861–92. New York: Russell Sage, 2004.

Rothstein, Richard. *Class and Schools: Using Social, Economic, and Educational Reform to Close the Black-White Achievement Gap*. Washington, DC: Economic Policy Institute, 2004.

Royster, Deirdre A. *Race and the Invisible Hand: How White Networks Exclude Black Men from Blue-Collar Jobs*. Berkeley: University of California Press, 2003.

Ruggles, Patricia. *Drawing the Line: Alternative Poverty Measures and Their Implications for Public Policy*. Washington, DC: Urban Institute, 1990.

Ryan, Charlotte. *Prime Time Activism: Media Strategies for Grassroots Organizing*. Boston: South End Press, 1991.

———. "Battered in the Media: Mainstream News Coverage of Welfare Reform." *Radical America* 26, no. 1 (January–March 1996): 29–41.

Ryan, William. *Blaming the Victim*. Rev. and updated ed. New York: Vintage, 1976.

Salverda, Wiemer, Brian Nolan, and Timothy M. Smeeding, eds. *The Oxford Handbook of Economic Inequality*. Oxford: Oxford University Press, 2009.

Sampson, Robert J. *Great American City: Chicago and the Enduring Neighborhood Effect*. Chicago: University of Chicago Press, 2012.

Sampson, Robert J., Jeffrey D. Morenoff, and Felton Earls. "Beyond Social Capital: Spatial Dynamics of Collective Efficacy for Children." *American Sociological Review* 64, no. 5 (October 1999): 633–60.

Sampson, Robert J., Jeffrey D. Morenoff, and Thomas Gannon-Rowley. "Assessing 'Neighborhood Effects': Social Processes and New Directions in Research." *Annual Review of Sociology* 28 (2002): 443–78.

Sawhill, Isabel V. "Poverty in the U.S.: Why Is It So Persistent?" *Journal of Economic Literature* 26, no. 3 (September 1988): 1073–119.

Sawhill, Isabel V., and John E. Morton. *Economic Mobility: Is the American Dream Alive and Well?* Washington, DC: Economic Mobility Project, Pew Charitable Trusts, 2007.

Scarbrough, Jacquelin W. "Welfare Mothers' Reflections on Personal Responsibility." *Journal of Social Issues* 57, no. 2 (Summer 2001): 261–76.

Scheuer, Jeffrey. *The Sound Bite Society: Television and the American Mind*. New York: Four Walls Eight Windows, 1999.

Schiller, Bradley R. *The Economics of Poverty and Discrimination*. 9th ed. Upper Saddle River, NJ: Pearson Prentice Hall, 2004.

Schlozman, Kay Lehman, Sidney Verba, and Henry E. Brady. *The Unheavenly Chorus: Unequal Political Voice and the Broken Promise of American Democracy*. Princeton, NJ: Princeton University Press, 2012.

Schram, Sanford D. *Words of Welfare: The Poverty of Social Science and the Social Science of Poverty*. Minneapolis: University of Minnesota Press, 1995.

Schudson, Michael. "How Culture Works: Perspectives from Media Studies on the Efficacy of Symbols." *Theory and Society* 18, no. 2 (March 1989): 153–80.

Schwartz, Joel. *Fighting Poverty with Virtue: Moral Reform and America's Urban Poor, 1825–2000*. Bloomington: Indiana University Press, 2000.

Scruggs, Lyle, and James P. Allan. "The Material Consequences of Welfare States: Benefit Generosity and Absolute Poverty in 16 OECD Countries." *Comparative Political Studies* 39, no. 7 (September 2006): 880–904.

Seccombe, Karen, and Kim A. Hoffman. *Just Don't Get Sick: Access to Health Care in the Aftermath of Welfare Reform*. New Brunswick, NJ: Rutgers University Press, 2007.

Seccombe, Karen, Delores James, and Kimberly Battle Walters. "'They Think You Ain't Much of Nothing': The Social Construction of the Welfare Mother." *Journal of Marriage and the Family* 60, no. 4 (November 1998): 849–65.

Sered, Susan Starr, and Rushika Fernandopulle. *Uninsured in America: Life and Death in the Land of Opportunity.* Berkeley: University of California Press, 2005.

Shapiro, Thomas M. *The Hidden Cost of Being African American: How Wealth Perpetuates Inequality.* Oxford: Oxford University Press, 2004.

Shapiro, Thomas M., and Edward N. Wolff, eds. *Assets for the Poor: The Benefit of Spreading Asset Ownership.* New York: Russell Sage, 2001.

Sharkey, Patrick. *Stuck in Place: Urban Neighborhoods and the End of Progress toward Racial Equality.* Chicago: University of Chicago Press, 2013.

Shaw, Greg M., and Robert Y. Shapiro. "The Polls-Trends: Poverty and Public Assistance." *Public Opinion Quarterly* 66, no. 1 (Spring 2002): 105–28.

Sheak, Bob, and Melissa Morris. "The Limits of the Job Supply in U.S. Capitalism." *Critical Sociology* 28, no. 3 (2002): 389–415.

Sherraden, Michael. *Assets and the Poor: A New American Welfare Policy.* Armonk, NY: M. E. Sharpe, 1991.

Shipler, David K. *The Working Poor: Invisible in America.* New York: Knopf, 2004.

Shulman, Beth. *The Betrayal of Work: How Low-Wage Jobs Fail 30 Million Americans and Their Families.* New York: New Press, 2003.

Skocpol, Theda. "Civic Transformation and Inequality in the Contemporary United States." In *Social Inequality,* edited by Kathryn M. Neckerman, 729–67. New York: Russell Sage, 2004.

———. "Voice and Inequality: The Transformation of American Civic Democracy." *Perspectives on Politics* 2, no. 1 (March 2004): 3–20.

Skocpol, Theda, and Morris P. Fiorina, eds. *Civic Engagement in American Democracy.* Washington, DC: Brookings Institution, 1999.

Skocpol, Theda, and Vanessa Williamson. *The Tea Party and the Remaking of Republican Conservatism.* Oxford: Oxford University Press, 2013.

Small, Mario Luis. *Villa Victoria: The Transformation of Social Capital in a Boston Barrio.* Chicago: University of Chicago Press, 2004.

———. *Unanticipated Gains: Origins of Network Inequality in Everyday Life.* Oxford: Oxford University Press, 2009.

Small, Mario Luis, and Katherine Newman. "Urban Poverty after *The Truly Disadvantaged*: The Rediscovery of the Family, the Neighborhood, and Culture." *Annual Review of Sociology* 27 (2001): 23–45.

Smeeding, Timothy M. "Public Policy, Economic Inequality, and Poverty: The United States in Comparative Perspective." *Social Science Quarterly* 86, supplement (2005): 955–83.

———. "Government Programs and Social Outcomes: Comparison of the United States with Other Rich Nations." In *Public Policy and Income Distribution,* edited by Alan J. Auerbach, David Card, and John M. Quigley, 149–218. New York: Russell Sage, 2006.

———. "Poor People in Rich Nations: The United States in Comparative Perspective." *Journal of Economic Perspectives* 20, no. 1 (Winter 2006): 69–90.

Smeeding, Timothy M., Robert Erikson, and Markus Jäntti, eds. *Persistence, Privilege, and Parenting: The Comparative Study of Intergenerational Mobility.* New York: Russell Sage, 2011.

Smeeding, Timothy M., Lee Rainwater, and Gary Burtless. "U.S. Poverty in a Cross-National Context." In *Understanding Poverty,* edited by Sheldon H. Danziger and Robert H. Haveman, 162–89. New York: Russell Sage; Cambridge, MA: Harvard University Press, 2001.

Smith, James P. "Healthy Bodies and Thick Wallets: The Dual Relation between Health and Economic Status." *Journal of Economic Perspectives* 13, no. 2 (Spring 1999): 145–66.

Smith, Kevin B., and Lorene H. Stone. "Rags, Riches, and Bootstraps: Beliefs about the Causes of Wealth and Poverty." *Sociological Quarterly* 30, no. 1 (1989): 93–107.

Smith, Mark A. *The Right Talk: How Conservatives Transformed the Great Society into the Economic Society.* Princeton, NJ: Princeton University Press, 2007.

Smith, Sandra Susan. "'Don't Put My Name on It': Social Capital Activation and Job-Finding Assistance among the Black Urban Poor." *American Journal of Sociology* 111, no. 1 (July 2005): 1–57.

———. *Lone Pursuit: Distrust and Defensive Individualism among the Black Poor.* New York: Russell Sage, 2007.

Somers, Margaret R., and Fred Block. "From Poverty to Perversity: Ideas, Markets, and Institutions over 200 Years of Welfare Debate." *American Sociological Review* 70, no. 2 (April 2005): 260–87.

Soss, Joe, Richard C. Fording, and Sanford Schram. *Disciplining the Poor: Neoliberal Paternalism and the Persistent Power of Race.* Chicago: University of Chicago Press, 2011.

Soss, Joe, and Lawrence R. Jacobs. "The Place of Inequality: Non-Participation in the American Polity." *Political Science Quarterly* 124, no. 1 (Spring 2009): 95–125.

Sowell, Thomas. *Ethnic America: A History.* New York: Basic Books, 1981.

———. *Race and Culture: A World View.* New York: Basic Books, 1994.

Squires, Gregory D., and Charis E. Kubrin. *Privileged Places: Race, Residence, and the Structure of Opportunity.* Boulder, CO: Lynne Rienner, 2006.

Stanton-Salazar, Ricardo D., and Sanford M. Dornbusch. "Social Capital and the Reproduction of Inequality: Information Networks among Mexican-Origin High School Students." *Sociology of Education* 68, no. 2 (April 1995): 116–35.

Steinberg, Stephen. *The Ethnic Myth: Race, Ethnicity, and Class in America.* Updated and expanded ed. Boston: Beacon Press, 1989.

Stevens, Ann Huff. "Climbing Out of Poverty, Falling Back In: Measuring the Persistence of Poverty over Multiple Spells." *Journal of Human Resources* 34, no. 3 (Summer 1999): 557–88.

Stier, Haya, and Marta Tienda. *The Color of Opportunity: Pathways to Family, Welfare, and Work.* Chicago: University of Chicago Press, 2001.

Stiglitz, Joseph E. *The Price of Inequality: How Today's Divided Society Endangers Our Future.* New York: Norton, 2012.

Strauss, Claudia. "Not-So-Rugged Individualists: Americans' Conflicting Ideas about Poverty." In *Work, Welfare, and Politics: Confronting Poverty in the Wake of Welfare Reform,* edited by Frances Fox Piven, Joan Acker, Margaret Hallock, and Sandra Morgen, 55–69. Eugene: University of Oregon Press, 2002.

Stricker, Frank. *Why America Lost the War on Poverty—And How to Win It.* Chapel Hill: University of North Carolina Press, 2007.

Sullivan, Mercer L. *"Getting Paid": Youth Crime and Work in the Inner City.* Ithaca, NY: Cornell University Press, 1989.

Tait, Vanessa. *Poor Workers' Unions: Rebuilding Labor from Below.* Cambridge, MA: South End Press, 2005.

Teixeira, Ruy A., and Lawrence Mishel. "Whose Skills Shortage—Workers or Management?" *Issues in Science and Technology* 9, no. 4 (Summer 1993): 69–74.

Tigges, Leann M., Irene Browne, and Gary P. Green. "Social Isolation of the Urban Poor: Race, Class, and Neighborhood Effects on Social Resources." *Sociological Quarterly* 39, no. 1 (1998): 53–77.

Tilly, Charles. *Durable Inequality.* Berkeley: University of California Press, 1998.

Tilly, Chris. *Half a Job: Bad and Good Part-Time Jobs in a Changing Labor Market.* Philadelphia: Temple University Press, 1996.

Tonry, Michael. *Punishing Race: A Continuing American Dilemma.* Oxford: Oxford University Press, 2011.

Uchitelle, Louis. *The Disposable American: Layoffs and Their Consequences.* New York: Knopf, 2006.

Vaisey, Stephen. "Education and Its Discontents: Overqualification in America, 1972–2002." *Social Forces* 85, no. 2 (December 2006): 835–64.

Valenzuela, Abel, Jr. "Day Labor Work." *Annual Review of Sociology* 29 (2003): 307–33.

Valenzuela, Abel, Jr., Nik Theodore, Edwin Melendez, and Ana Luz Gonzalez. *On the Corner: Day Labor in the United States.* National Day Labor Study, January 2006. www.uic.edu/cuppa/uicued/Publications/RECENT/onthecorner.pdf (accessed December 28, 2007).

Verba, Sidney, Kay Lehman Schlozman, and Henry E. Brady. "Political Equality: What Do We Know about It?" In *Social Inequality*, edited by Kathryn M. Neckerman, 635–66. New York: Russell Sage, 2004.

Vogel, David. *Fluctuating Fortunes: The Political Power of Business in America.* New York: Basic Books, 1989.

Wacquant, Loic J. D. "Three Pernicious Premises in the Study of the Ghetto." *International Journal of Urban and Regional Research* 21, no. 2 (June 1997): 341–53.

Wacquant, Loic J. D., and William Julius Wilson. "The Cost of Racial and Class Exclusion in the Inner City." *Annals of the American Academy of Political and Social Science* 501 (January 1989): 8–25.

Waldfogel, Jane. *What Children Need.* Cambridge, MA: Harvard University Press, 2006.

Waldinger, Roger, and Michael I. Lichter. *How the Other Half Works: Immigration and the Social Organization of Labor.* Berkeley: University of California Press, 2003.

Warren, Elizabeth, and Amelia Warren Tyagi. *The Two-Income Trap: Why Middle-Class Parents Are Going Broke.* New York: Basic Books, 2003.

Wasow, Bernard. *The New American Economy: A Rising Tide That Lifts Only Yachts.* New York: Century Foundation, 2004.

———. *Rags to Riches? The American Dream Is Less Common in the United States than Elsewhere.* New York: Century Foundation, 2004.

Weeden, Kim A. "Why Do Some Occupations Pay More than Others? Social Closure and Earnings Inequality in the United States." *American Journal of Sociology* 108, no. 1 (July 2002): 55–101.

Western, Bruce. *Punishment and Inequality in America.* New York: Russell Sage, 2006.

Western, Bruce, Deirdre Bloome, Benjamin Sosnaud, and Laura Tach. "Economic Insecurity and Social Stratification." *Annual Review of Sociology* 38 (2012): 341–59.

Western, Bruce, and Jake Rosenfeld, "Unions, Norms, and the Rise in U.S. Wage Inequality." *American Sociological Review* 76, no. 4 (August 2011): 513–37.

Will, Jeffry A. *The Deserving Poor.* New York: Garland, 1993.

Wilson, William Julius. *The Truly Disadvantaged: The Inner City, the Underclass, and Public Policy.* Chicago: University of Chicago Press, 1987.

———. *When Work Disappears: The World of the New Urban Poor.* New York: Knopf, 1996.

Wilson, William Julius, and Richard P. Taub. *There Goes the Neighborhood: Racial, Ethnic, and Class Tension in Four Chicago Neighborhoods and Their Meaning for America.* New York: Knopf, 2006.

Winters, Jeffrey A., and Benjamin I. Page. "Oligarchy in the United States." *Perspectives on Politics* 7, no. 4 (December 2009): 731–51.

Wolfe, Barbara, William Evans, and Teresa E. Seeman, eds. *The Biological Consequences of Socioeconomic Inequalities*. New York: Russell Sage, 2012.

Wolff, Edward N. *Does Education Really Help? Skill, Work, and Inequality*. Oxford: Oxford University Press, 2006.

Wood, Adrian. "How Trade Hurts Unskilled Workers." *Journal of Economic Perspectives* 9, no. 3 (Summer 1995): 57–80.

Woolf, Steven H., Robert E. Johnson, and H. Jack Geiger. "The Rising Prevalence of Severe Poverty in America: A Growing Threat to Public Health." *American Journal of Preventive Medicine* 31, no. 4 (2006): 332–41.

Wray, L. Randall, and Marc-Andre Pigeon. "Can a Rising Tide Raise All Boats? Evidence from the Clinton-Era Expansion." *Journal of Economic Issues* 34, no. 4 (December 2000): 811–45.

Earl Wysong, Robert Perrucci, and David Wright. *The New Class Society: Goodbye American Dream?* 4th ed. (Lanham, MD: Rowman & Littlefield, 2014).

Yinger, John. "Housing Discrimination and Residential Segregation as Causes of Poverty." In *Understanding Poverty*, edited by Sheldon H. Danziger and Robert H. Haveman, 359–91. New York: Russell Sage; Cambridge, MA: Harvard University Press, 2001.

Young, Alford A., Jr. *The Minds of Marginalized Black Men: Making Sense of Mobility, Opportunity, and Future Life Chances*. Princeton, NJ: Princeton University Press, 2004.

Zuberi, Dan. *Differences That Matter: Social Policy and the Working Poor in the United States and Canada*. Ithaca, NY: Cornell University Press, 2006.

Zweig, Michael. *The Working Class Majority: America's Best Kept Secret*. Ithaca, NY: Cornell University Press, 2000.

# Index

# About the Author

**Edward Royce** is professor emeritus of sociology at Rollins College. In addition to *Poverty and Power*, he is also the author of *The Origins of Southern Sharecropping* (1993) and *Classical Social Theory and Modern Society: Marx, Durkheim, Weber* (2015). He currently lives in Northampton, Massachusetts.

CPSIA information can be obtained at www.ICGtesting.com
Printed in the USA
BVOW07s2102160115

383725BV00001B/1/P

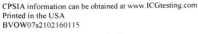